Moral Theory

ELEMENTS OF PHILOSOPHY

The Elements of Philosophy series aims to produce core introductory texts in the major areas of philosophy, among them metaphysics, epistemology, ethics and moral theory, philosophy of religion, philosophy of mind, aesthetics and the philosophy of art, feminist philosophy, and social and political philosophy. Books in the series are written for an undergraduate audience of second- through fourth-year students and serve as the perfect cornerstone for understanding the various elements of philosophy.

Moral Theory: An Introduction, Second Edition, by Mark Timmons

An Introduction to Social and Political Philosophy: A Question-Based Approach by Richard Schmitt

Epistemology: Classic Problems and Contemporary Responses, Second Edition, by Laurence BonJour

Aesthetics and the Philosophy of Art: An Introduction, Second Edition, by Robert Stecker

Aesthetics Today: A Reader edited by Robert Stecker and Ted Gracyk

Introduction to Ethics: A Reader edited by Andrew J. Dell'Olio and Caroline J. Simon

The Ethics of Business: A Concise Introduction by Al Gini and Alexei Marcoux

Introduction to the Philosophy of Sport by Heather Reid

Moral Theory

An Introduction

Second Edition

Mark Timmons

ROWMAN & LITTLEFIELD PUBLISHERS, INC.
Lanham • Boulder • New York • Toronto • Plymouth, UK

Published by Rowman & Littlefield Publishers, Inc.
A wholly owned subsidiary of The Rowman & Littlefield Publishing Group, Inc.
4501 Forbes Boulevard, Suite 200, Lanham, Maryland 20706
www.rowman.com

10 Thornbury Road, Plymouth PL6 7PP, United Kingdom

British Library Cataloguing in Publication Information Available

Library of Congress Cataloging-in-Publication Data
Timmons, Mark, 1951-
  Moral theory : an introduction / Mark Timmons.—2nd ed.
     p. cm. — (Elements of philosophy)
  Includes bibliographical references (p.   ) and index.
   ISBN 978-0-7425-6491-6 (cloth : alk. paper)—ISBN 978-0-7425-6492-3 (pbk. : alk.
paper)—ISBN 978-0-7425-6493-0 (electronic)
  1. Ethics. I. Title.
  BJ1012.T56 2013
  171—dc23

                                                                    2012029760

⊗™ The paper used in this publication meets the minimum requirements of
American National Standard for Information Sciences—Permanence of Paper
for Printed Library Materials, ANSI/NISO Z39.48-1992.

Printed in the United States of America

In loving memory of Marilyn Timmons

1930–2012

Contents

Contents

Preface

This book is a survey of various moral theories including divine command theory, moral relativism, natural law theory, consequentialism (including classical utilitarianism), ethical egoism, Kant's moral theory, moral pluralism, virtue ethics, and moral particularism (though particularism is often considered to be anti-theory). The ten chapters that discuss these theories are preceded by an introduction whose purpose is to expose readers to some basic concepts and ideas common to all or most of the theories featured in the rest of the book. The conclusion ties together certain general themes that emerge from the study of the various theories.

My main goal in writing this book is to provide an intermediate-level introduction to moral theory. I have tried to go beyond many introductory ethics texts by delving into some of the complexity involved in debates within and about moral theories. But I have also tried to refrain from too much complexity, as is evident from the many places throughout the text where I cut off discussion of some issue by leaving it for readers to ponder on their own. This text, then, is written for those individuals who are ready for something more challenging than an elementary treatment of the questions and issues that come up in moral theory but who are not yet ready to tackle advanced research in ethics.

Here is what's new in the second edition:

- In the decade since the first edition was published, there has been a flourish of work in moral psychology. So I have tried to bring some of this work, as well as work from the sciences generally, to bear on the moral theories discussed in this book. Relatedly, in the "Further Readings" recommendations following the chapters on the various types of moral theory (chapters 2–11), I have divided the recommendations into philosophical literature and empirical literature.

- I have added a chapter on ethical egoism, which includes a discussion of psychological egoism and some of the experimental work that addresses this type of egoism.
- The chapters on divine command theory and moral relativism have been expanded to include some discussion of what I call "restricted" versions of these theories. These versions are more plausible than their unrestricted counterparts, and so this second edition provides a more balanced discussion of these types of moral theory.
- The previous edition included two chapters on utilitarianism, a species of a much broader category of moral theory, consequentialism. In revising the first edition chapters I have tried to broaden my presentation somewhat to indicate more clearly the breadth of consequentialist approaches in normative moral theory. To reflect this change, I have re-titled the chapters as: *Consequentialism 1: Classical Utilitarianism* and *Consequentialism 2: Contemporary Developments*.
- I have made very substantial changes to the chapter on moral particularism in light of work in the past decade. It is probably closer to the truth to say that I wrote a new chapter on this topic.
- Throughout the text I have made various revisions for purposes of greater clarity, based partly on my experiences in using the previous edition in courses.

Acknowledgments

I wish to thank my editor, Jonathan Sisk, for his encouragement and patience. I benefited from comments (sometimes written, sometimes verbal) by Michael Gill, Michael Gorr, Terry Horgan, Elinor Mason, Christian Miller, Cole Mitchell, Susana Nuccetelli, Sarah Raskoff, Dave Shoemaker, Houston Smit, and Betsy Timmons. Thanks to Michael Bukoski, who wrote an excellent set of comments on the penultimate version of the entire manuscript, prompting a number of improvements. I am especially grateful to Doug Portmore, who generously offered to comment on chapters in this new edition as they were being revised. I took advantage of Doug's offer in revising chapters 1–4 and in drafting the new chapter on ethical egoism. The comments and suggestions I received from Michael and Doug were extremely helpful in making this second edition of the book an improvement over the first, though I was not able to fully address all of their excellent comments and suggestions.

1

An Introduction to Moral Theory

> Moral theory is the study of substantive moral conceptions, that is, the study of how the basic notions of the right, the good, and moral worth may be arranged to form different moral structures.
>
> —John Rawls (1975)

What makes an act right or wrong? What makes an individual morally good or bad? How can we come to correct conclusions about what we morally ought to do and what sorts of persons we ought to be? Moral theory attempts to provide systematic answers to these very general moral questions about what to do and how to be. Because moral theorists have given different answers to these questions, we find a variety of competing moral theories. This book contains a survey of some of the most important moral theories—theories that are of both historical and contemporary interest.

But what is a moral theory? What does such a theory attempt to accomplish? What are the central concepts that such theories make use of? Furthermore, how is a moral theory to be evaluated?

This chapter is an introduction to moral theory; it will address these and related questions and thus prepare readers for the chapters that follow. The kinds of general moral questions that are of concern in moral theory, and the apparent need for such theory, are easily raised by reflecting on disputed moral questions including, for example, questions about the morality of suicide.

1. A SAMPLE MORAL CONTROVERSY: SUICIDE

In 1997, the state of Oregon's Death with Dignity Act took effect, allowing physicians to assist patients in ending their own lives. From 1997 to 2012, 596 people

1

made use of the act in choosing the manner and time of their deaths. This unprecedented statute permitting physician-assisted suicide provoked highly charged debates about the legality and morality of this practice. Despite an attempt in 2001 by the George W. Bush administration to make physician-assisted suicide illegal, in 2006 the U.S. Supreme Court upheld the Oregon act. As of 2011, Washington and Montana have joined Oregon in permitting such assisted suicides. There are many other interesting legal issues that these two acts raise, but our concern is with the moral controversy that the Oregon act stirred.[1]

The moral debate over physician-assisted suicide concerns the larger issue of the morality of suicide, and moral arguments both for and against the Death with Dignity Act often depend on moral claims about suicide. Those who think that there is nothing necessarily wrong with suicide often argue that deciding to end one's own life is consistent with the dignity that is inherent in every individual. Thus, according to this line of reasoning, choosing to end one's life when continued existence threatens one's dignity is morally permissible. Those opposed to suicide on moral grounds sometimes argue that God has dominion over our bodies and so the choice between life and death belongs to him.[2] Another commonly voiced argument against suicide is that this kind of act is wrong because allowing it would inevitably lead to bad consequences such as the killing of terminally ill patients against their wills.

The moral controversy over suicide generally, and physician-assisted suicide in particular, is but one of a number of moral controversies including abortion, treatment of animals, capital punishment, sexuality, privacy, gun control, drugs, and discrimination. Debate about these issues focuses on reasons for holding one or another moral viewpoint about them. As just noted, appeal to the idea of human dignity has sometimes been offered as a reason in support of the claim that suicide is not necessarily morally wrong, while we find that appeals to the will of God and to the alleged bad consequences of allowing suicide are sometimes used to argue that suicide is morally wrong. Giving reasons like this for some claim that one wants to establish is what philosophers call giving an argument for the claim. So, moral debates like the one over the morality of suicide feature arguments on both sides of the issue.

To understand and evaluate such arguments, three main tasks must be undertaken. First, there is the *conceptual* task of clarifying important concepts such as that of human dignity. What are we talking about when we make claims about human dignity? In what does one's dignity consist? Unless we have an answer to this question, we will not really understand moral arguments that make use of this concept.

A second main task in understanding moral arguments requires that we *evaluate various claims* being made in the sorts of arguments mentioned above. Is it true that suicide is against God's will? Is it true that allowing suicide would lead to bad social consequences? Is it true that suicide is consistent with human dignity? These claims are controversial and require examination.

A third main task concerning moral arguments involves *evaluating basic moral assumptions* that are often unstated in the giving of such arguments. For instance, when someone argues that suicide is wrong because it is contrary to God's will, the unstated assumption is that if an action is contrary to God's will, then it is wrong. Is this assumption correct? Again, the claim that suicide is wrong because it would have bad consequences assumes that if an action would have bad consequences, then it is wrong. Is this assumption correct?

Such moral assumptions often express ideas about what makes an action right or wrong, and hence about the nature of such actions. And questions about the nature of right and wrong, as well as about the nature of good and bad, are central in the study of moral theory. And in this way, reflection on ordinary moral debate and discussion, featuring moral arguments, leads us to the kinds of questions that a moral theory attempts to answer.

In order to explain more fully the project of moral theory, we need to consider (1) the main aims of moral theory, (2) the role of moral principles within a moral theory, (3) the main categories of moral evaluation, (4) the structure of such theories, and finally (5) questions about the evaluation of moral theories. These topics will occupy us in the remaining sections of this chapter.

2. THE AIMS OF MORAL THEORY

It will help in trying to understand what a moral theory is all about if we consider the main aims of moral theory—what such a theory is out to accomplish. There are two fundamental aims of moral theory: one practical, the other theoretical.

The practical aim of moral theory has to do with the desire to have some method to follow when, for example, we reason about what is right or wrong. Scientists employ scientific methodology in arriving at scientific conclusions about various phenomena under investigation. Similarly, we might hope to discover a proper moral methodology—a *decision procedure*, as it is often referred to by moral philosophers—whose use would provide a means of discovering answers to moral questions and in general guide moral deliberation and choice.

We can summarize the practical aim this way:

> *Practical aim.* The main practical aim of a moral theory is to provide a decision procedure whose use by suitably informed agents will reliably lead them to correct moral verdicts about matters of moral concern in contexts of moral deliberation and choice.

The theoretical aim of moral theory has to do with coming to understand the underlying nature of right and wrong, good and bad. When someone claims that an action is morally wrong, it makes sense to ask them *why* they think the action in question is wrong. We thus assume that when an action is morally right or wrong, there is something about the action that *makes* it right or wrong. (A similar point can be made in relation to claims about the goodness and badness of whatever has these properties. But for simplicity's sake, let us just focus for the moment on questions about the rightness and wrongness of actions.)

To explain further, consider an analogy. What makes some liquid water (as opposed to ammonia or some other liquid) is its chemical composition. Underlying all bodies of water—big and small—is the fact that the liquid in question has a certain chemical composition. The fact that some liquid is H_2O is what makes it water. Something analogous might well be true about morality. We assume that when an action is right or wrong, there is something about the action that makes it right or wrong. Moreover, it is natural to wonder whether there might be some fixed set of underlying features of actions that make them right or wrong. Perhaps there is one such underlying feature, but perhaps there is more than one. Then again, we may find that although the rightness or wrongness of actions depends on certain underlying features of actions, such features vary so much from case to case that there is no fixed set of underlying features to be discovered.

The theoretical aim of moral theory, then, is to explore the underlying nature of right and wrong action in order to be able to explain what it is about an action that makes it right or wrong. If we suppose that there is some fixed set of underlying features that make all right actions right and all wrong actions wrong, they will serve as *standards*, or *moral criteria*, of right and wrong action. Similar remarks apply to matters of good and bad: part of the theoretical aim of a moral theory is to discover what it is about persons and other items having value that makes them good or bad.

We can express the main theoretical aim this way:

> *Theoretical aim.* The main theoretical aim of a moral theory is to discover those underlying features of actions, persons, and other items of moral evaluation that make them right or wrong, good or bad.

The practical and theoretical aims of moral theory are commonly thought to be related to one another in that satisfying one is either required for, or at least the best way of, satisfying the other. To explain this point and to deepen our understanding of the main aims of moral theory, let us consider the role of moral principles in moral theory.

3. MORAL PRINCIPLES AND THEIR ROLE IN MORAL THEORY

In the field of ethics, *moral principles* are to be understood as very general moral statements that purport to set forth conditions under which an action is right or wrong or something is good or bad.[3]

Here is a sample moral principle:

> An action is right if and only if (and because) the action does not interfere with the well-being of those individuals who are likely to be affected by the action.

For present purposes, we need not worry about what counts as interfering with the well-being of individuals, or whether the principle is true. The thing to notice about this principle is that it asserts a connection between an action being right and it not interfering with the well-being of certain individuals. (The "and because" indicates that what follows it is supposed to provide a criterion of wrongness—a specification of what *makes* an action wrong.) We were just noting that a moral theory has both a practical and a theoretical aim. Moral principles have traditionally played a central role in attempts by moral philosophers to accomplish both of these aims. Let us see how.

In attempting to satisfy the practical aim of providing a decision procedure for correct moral reasoning, moral philosophers have often been guided by the idea that such reasoning must be based on moral principles. Here is a simple example.

Suppose Natasha claims that it would be wrong for her to lie about her job experience on a job application, even when she is reasonably certain that a lie about this matter would not be found out. Suppose further that she is asked to give her reasons for thinking this, and, being a reflective person, she responds by pointing out that her lying in these circumstances might well negatively affect the chances of other applicants' getting the job and thereby interfere with the well-being of others. And so we imagine her attempting to justify the claim that her lying would be wrong by appealing to the sample moral principle stated above. Natasha's line of reasoning could be set out as follows.

Moral principle: An action is right if and only if (and because) the action does not interfere with the well-being of those individuals who are likely to be affected by the action.

Factual claim: The act of lying on a job application would likely interfere with the well-being of at least some individuals who are applying for the job.

Conclusion: The act of lying on a job application is not right (and hence is wrong).

The point of this example is simply that the practical aim of providing a decision procedure for arriving at justified moral verdicts about actions (and other items of moral concern) has often been supposed to be a matter of reasoning from moral principles to conclusions about actions (and other items of moral concern). Understood as a decision procedure, then, a moral principle guides proper moral reasoning by indicating those features of actions whose recognition can guide one to well-reasoned verdicts about the morality of actions.

Of course, not any old moral principles will serve to satisfy this practical aim. In order to provide a decision procedure to guide correct moral reasoning, the moral principles used must themselves be correct. And this brings us to the theoretical aim of moral theory and the role of principles in achieving this aim.

In attempting to satisfy the theoretical aim of explaining what makes an action right or wrong or what makes something good or bad, moral philosophers have typically sought to formulate moral principles that express this information. In fulfilling this theoretical aim, then, a moral principle concerned with right and wrong action can be understood as indicating those most basic features of actions that make them right or wrong. According to our example principle, it is facts about how an action would affect the well-being of a certain group of individuals that are supposed to explain what makes an action right or wrong.

Moreover, moral principles that serve to explain what makes actions right or wrong will thus unify morality by revealing those basic features that determine in general an action's rightness or wrongness. (Similar remarks apply to principles of goodness and badness.) Finding the underlying unity behind the diversity of moral phenomena has thus been an aim of traditional moral theory—an aim that can supposedly be achieved by discovering moral principles that satisfy the main theoretical aim of moral theory.[4] Discovering an underlying unity that connects and explains right and wrong action would be a way of *systematizing* morality—bringing a kind of order or scheme to the multitude of actions that are properly classified as either right or wrong.

So, moral principles are often cast by moral theorists in a dual role. In light of the theoretical aim of moral theory, these principles purport to specify those underlying features in virtue of which an action, person, or other item of moral evaluation has the moral quality it has. In this way, moral principles aim to systematize morality—revealing to us the underlying nature of right and wrong, good and bad. In light of the practical aim of moral theory, such principles are also supposed to be something that suitably informed agents can in principle use to guide moral deliberation and choice.

Let us return for a moment to the issue of the morality of suicide. A correct set of moral principles functioning as moral criteria would enable us to understand what makes an action of suicide right or wrong, thus giving us insight into the moral nature of such action. A correct set of moral principles functioning as a decision procedure would (together with relevant factual information about whether the action has the features mentioned in the principle) provide us the means for reasoning our way to correct moral verdicts about the morality of suicide.

As we shall see in later chapters, some philosophers deny the claim that a moral principle that satisfies the theoretical aim must also satisfy the practical aim, given that agents are often in circumstances in which they lack the relevant factual information needed to reliably apply the principle to particular cases. Moreover, some moral philosophers deny altogether the idea that there can be moral principles of the sort featured in most moral theories and thus deny that morality can be systematized in the manner just explained. (The reader should therefore keep in mind that my introductory remarks are meant to capture traditional assumptions about moral theory and the roles of principles in any such theory, but that such assumptions have been challenged.)

Earlier, we noted that moral theory concerns questions about the morality of actions (what to do) as well as the morality of persons (how to be). And I have been saying that traditional moral theories are primarily in the business of formulating and defending principles about the morality of actions and of persons. Having explained the two main aims of moral theory and the role of principles in satisfying those aims, we need to say more about the basic concepts (and associated categories) featured in moral theory.

4. SOME BASIC MORAL CATEGORIES: THE RIGHT, THE GOOD, AND MORAL WORTH

As the opening quote from John Rawls indicates, the basic concepts in ethics are the concepts of the right, the good, and moral worth. Let us take a closer look.

The Right and Deontic Concepts

When we evaluate the morality of an action, we are primarily interested in whether the action is right or wrong. More precisely, we are interested in whether an action is *obligatory, wrong,* or *optional.* These are often called *deontic* concepts or categories (from the Greek term *deon,* which means duty) because they concern what one morally ought to do (and hence has a duty to perform) or morally ought not to do (and hence has a duty not to perform). Here is a brief description of these three fundamental deontic categories (which I will also call categories of right action):

Obligatory actions. An obligatory action is something one morally ought to do. Typically, we refer to actions that are obligatory as *duties.* Other terms used for this category include *"required"* and *"right."*5 (Use of the term "right" requires special comment. See below.)

Wrong actions. A wrong action is something that one morally ought not to do. Other terms often used for this category include "forbidden," "impermissible," and "contrary to duty."

Optional actions. An action is morally optional when it is neither obligatory nor wrong—one is morally permitted to perform the action, but not morally required to do so. Sometimes actions in this category are referred to as *"merely permissible"* ("merely," because unlike obligatory actions, which are permitted, they are not also required).

These characterizations are not intended as illuminating definitions. To be told that an obligatory action is one that morally ought to be done is hardly illuminating. However, the brief remarks made about each category are, I think, still useful for conveying an intuitive sense of the main categories of deontic evaluation.

What about the category of the right? Talk of right action has both a narrow and a broad use. When the term is used narrowly, it refers to the category of the obligatory, as when we say she did *the* right thing (meaning she did what she morally ought to have done). When the term is used broadly, right action is the opposite of wrong action: an action is right, in the broad sense of the term, when it is not wrong. For instance, to say of someone that what she did was right often conveys the idea that her act was morally in the clear—that it was all right for her to do, that what she did was not wrong. Since actions that are not wrong include those that fall either into the category of the obligatory or the category of the optional, talk of right action (in the broad sense) covers both of these categories.

Figure 1.1 summarizes what I have been saying, where "right" is used in its broad sense to mean simply "not wrong." In the chapters that follow, when I want to refer to the species of moral evaluation that we are now considering, I will speak indifferently about the *deontic status* of an action and of the *rightness or wrongness* of an action. These expressions are to be understood as shorthand for referring to an action's being obligatory, optional, or wrong.

The Good and Value Concepts

To speak of the value of something is to speak of its being either good or bad, or neither good nor bad (some things have no value, positive or negative). I have already mentioned that one concern of moral theory is with answering the question of what makes an individual a good or bad person. Goodness or badness of persons is not the only kind of value that is of concern to moral theory, as I will explain shortly. But let us begin to clarify the categories of the good and the bad by distinguishing the concept of intrinsic value from that of extrinsic value.

For something to have positive intrinsic value—for it to be *intrinsically good*—is for the goodness to be located in that thing.[6] One often finds intrinsic value being described as the value a thing has "in itself," or "for its own sake," or "as such." (Intrinsic negative value or badness is understood in an analogous way.) By contrast, to say that something is merely *extrinsically good* is to say that it possesses goodness because of how it is related to something that is intrinsically good. Here is an example.

Many people would agree that money is a good thing to possess. But what is the source of its goodness? It seems pretty clear that the goodness of money is not somehow internal to the pieces of paper and bits of metal that compose it. Rather, the goodness or positive value of money is explained by the fact that it is useful *as a means* for obtaining things and services that are either intrinsically good or contribute to what has positive intrinsic value. Thus assuming that money has positive value of some sort, its goodness or value, we say, is extrinsic. Given the means-ends relation obtaining in this particular example, this sort of external value has what is called "instrumental value."[7]

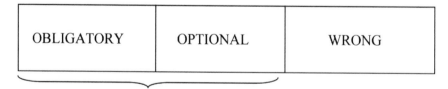

| OBLIGATORY | OPTIONAL | WRONG |

RIGHT
(in the broad sense)

Figure 1.1.   Basic Deontic Categories

In short, for something A to be extrinsically good in some way, there must be something B (to which it is related) such that B is intrinsically good and is the ultimate source of the goodness that is possessed by A. So the concept of intrinsic goodness is more basic than the concept of extrinsic goodness, and the same goes for the concepts of intrinsic and extrinsic badness.

Theories about the nature of the good are, therefore, theories about the nature of intrinsic value. And here again we find that there are three basic categories. In addition to the categories of the *intrinsically good* (or valuable) and the *intrinsically bad* (or disvaluable), there is the category of what we may call the *intrinsically value-neutral*. This third category comprises all those things that are neither intrinsically good nor intrinsically bad (though such things may have either positive or negative extrinsic value).

One historically important theory of intrinsic value is hedonism, according to which the only bearers of positive intrinsic value are experiences of pleasure and the only bearers of negative intrinsic value are experiences of pain. According to hedonism (at least as the theory is often developed), what explains why these experiences have the intrinsic value they do concerns the nature of the experiences in question—their introspective qualities of pleasantness and painfulness respectively. Contrast hedonism with the sort of view we find in classical natural law theory (see chapter 4) according to which human life, procreation, knowledge, and sociability are all basic intrinsic goods presumably because they are constituents of leading a life appropriate for members of the human species. There are other theories of intrinsic value, but this small sampling should be enough to give readers a sense of this branch of moral theory. The relevance of theories of intrinsic value to moral theory will be clarified below when we turn to issues of structure.[8]

Moral Worth and Aretaic Concepts

In addition to the concepts of the right and the good, Rawls mentions *moral worth* as among the basic notions in moral theory. This concept is a value concept, but it has specifically to do with the evaluation of responsible agents who can sensibly be held accountable for what they do and the kind of person they are, who can be praised or blamed. More precisely, the concept of moral worth has primarily to do with the evaluation of persons and their character.[9] We engage in this species of evaluation when we say of a person that he or she is a morally good or morally bad person where we mean to be saying something about the person's character. A morally good person, a person having positive moral worth—to use the term we are reserving for this species of evaluation—is someone who possesses and acts upon certain positive character traits that we call the virtues, a virtuous person. A morally bad person—someone who possesses negative moral worth—is one who has a vicious character, one who has and acts on certain negative character traits. Some of the commonly recognized virtues include honesty, beneficence, courage, and justice, whereas dishonesty, malice, cowardice, and injustice are among the commonly recognized vices. A theory of moral worth (often called a theory of virtue), then, aims to identify the virtues and the vices, and also explain what makes a trait either a virtue or a vice. In so doing, a theory of moral worth thereby aims to explain what makes a person overall a morally good or bad person. So while the theory of right conduct addresses moral questions about what to do, the theory of moral worth addresses questions about how to be.

The theory of value, as part of moral theory, thus has two main concerns. First, as noted in the previous section, it is interested in determining which things have intrinsic positive value (are intrinsically good) and which things have intrinsic negative value (are intrinsically bad), and why they have whatever intrinsic value they do have. On the basis of an account of intrinsic value, one can then determine what has extrinsic value. Second, the theory of value as part of moral theory is also concerned with the sort of goodness or badness that we attribute to persons in light of their character as revealed by their actions and attitudes. We are calling this kind of value moral worth. Notice that it is not being assumed that character traits possessing moral worth thereby possess intrinsic value. For example, the hedonistic theory of intrinsic value mentioned above denies that anything other than experiences of pleasure and pain possess intrinsic value. Since a trait of character (even if a virtue) is not itself an experience (though its exercise will involve having experiences), a trait of character for a hedonist is only a candidate for having extrinsic value. Some non-hedonistic theories of intrinsic value (including the one defended by W. D. Ross—see chapter 9), do recognize virtues as having intrinsic value.

5. MORAL THEORY AND ITS STRUCTURE

In the opening quote Rawls says that moral theory (understood as a branch of philosophical inquiry) is concerned with how the notions of the right, the good, and moral worth "may be arranged to form different structures." One way in which moral theories may differ from one another has to do with their overall structure—how they organize and relate their accounts of the right, the good, and moral worth.

To help clarify this point, let us say that an account of the nature of right and wrong action represents a *theory of right conduct*. An account of the nature of intrinsic value, then, represents a *theory of intrinsic value*, and an account of moral worth represents a *theory of moral worth*. Moral worth is a value concept, so we have two main branches of moral theory shown in figure 1.2 with theory of value having two sub-branches. Rawls's remark about structure, then, has to do with how a particular moral theory connects these branches. For instance, according to what are often called *value-based* theories, the concept of the good or intrinsic value is taken to be more basic than the concept of the right, and so right and wrong action are explained in terms of how actions bear on what has intrinsic value. The natural law theory (chapter 4) and versions of consequentialism (chapters 5 and 6) are representatives

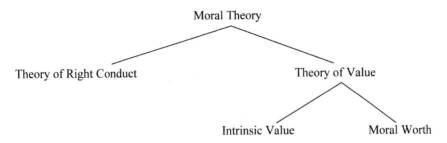

Moral Theory

Theory of Right Conduct

Theory of Value

Intrinsic Value

Moral Worth

Figure 1.2. Components of a Moral Theory

of this kind of theory. By contrast, according to *duty-based* theories, the concept of duty is taken to be more basic than value concepts or at least not less basic than value concepts.[10] The moral theory of Immanuel Kant (chapter 7) and the version of moral pluralism defended by W. D. Ross (chapter 9) are examples of this type of moral theory. Finally, there are *virtue-based* moral theories that take considerations of moral worth or virtue to be more basic than right action and attempt to explain right action (and deontic status of actions generally) in terms of virtue. These theories are featured in chapter 10.

6. BRIEF SUMMARY

Before going further, let us pause a moment to review some of what we have learned about moral theory. The main points are these:

- The moral evaluation of actions concerns their deontic status—their rightness and wrongness. One task of moral theory is to investigate the nature of right and wrong action.
- The moral evaluation of persons concerns their moral goodness and badness—their moral value or worth. And so another task of moral theory is to investigate the nature of moral worth.
- Because some moral theories make the deontic status of actions depend on considerations having to do with intrinsic value, an additional task for such theories is to investigate the nature of intrinsic value.
- The structure of moral theory is determined by how it relates the various branches of moral theory (and the categories these branches contain).
- In giving accounts of the nature of the right, the good, and moral worth, a moral theory aims to discover principles that will provide (if possible) both a unified theoretical account of the nature of such things and a decision procedure that can be used to reason correctly about matters of morality and thus serve as a guide to choice and action.

This concludes my introductory remarks about moral theory. Readers who are encountering moral theory for the first time may find some of what has been presented a bit much to absorb completely in one reading. However, as the book proceeds, the points I have been making will be illustrated by the theories we examine; this should help deepen the reader's understanding of the elements of a moral theory.

In the remainder of this chapter, I will briefly explain how to evaluate a moral theory and then make some general remarks about the field of ethics. I will conclude with a brief summary of the chapters to come.

7. EVALUATING MORAL THEORIES

In this section, I describe some of the main standards that are used to evaluate a moral theory. I recommend using this section for reference when, toward the end of each chapter, we turn to an evaluation of the theory being featured in the chapter.

Since a moral theory has the practical aim of providing a decision procedure for making correct moral judgments as well as the theoretical aim of providing moral criteria that explain the underlying nature of morality, it makes sense to evaluate a moral theory according to how well it satisfies these two aims. Here, then, is a list of seven desiderata—seven characteristics that it is ideally desirable for a moral theory to possess if it is to accomplish the practical and theoretical aims just mentioned.

Consistency

A moral theory should specify principles whose application yields consistent moral verdicts about whatever is being morally evaluated. One blatant way in which a moral theory might fail to be consistent is when its principles (together with relevant factual information) imply that some particular concrete action is both right and wrong. For example, if the principles of some theory were to imply that a particular instance of lying is both obligatory and not obligatory, it would fail the consistency standard.[11]

So, according to the *consistency standard,*

A moral theory should be consistent in the sense that its principles, together with relevant factual information, yield consistent moral verdicts about the morality of actions, persons, and other objects of moral evaluation.

The rationale for this standard can be easily explained by reference to the practical and theoretical aims of moral theory. Any moral theory that fails to yield consistent moral verdicts in a range of cases will fail (at least in those cases) to supply a decision procedure of the sort desired. To be told that some action is both obligatory and not obligatory is of no use in deciding what to do. Furthermore, if a theory of right conduct implies, for instance, inconsistent claims about the morality of certain actions, then the theory itself must be mistaken; it cannot be giving us a correct theoretical account of the nature of morality.

Determinacy

To say that a moral theory is determinate is to say that its principles, when applied to concrete cases, yield definite moral verdicts about the morality of whatever is being evaluated. One way in which a moral theory might fail to be determinate is when its basic principles are excessively vague and so fail to imply, in a wide range of cases, any specific moral verdicts. Suppose, for instance, that a moral theory tells us that an action is morally right if and only if it is respectful of persons. Unless the theory also defines fairly explicitly what it means to be respectful of persons, the theory will not yield definite moral conclusions about the morality of actions in a wide range of cases. For instance, does capital punishment respect persons? What about lying to save a life? And so on.

So, according to the *determinacy standard,*

> A moral theory should feature principles which, together with relevant factual information, yield determinate moral verdicts about the morality of actions, persons, and other objects of evaluation in a wide range of cases.

A moral theory that is grossly indeterminate will fail to provide a useful decision procedure, since in being indeterminate it will simply provide no guidance about what to do and what to believe regarding a wide range of cases. Again, if a theory is indeterminate, this may indicate that it is failing to explain properly the underlying nature of right and wrong or good and bad. Supposing that there is some feature of actions that makes them right or wrong, a theory that is indeterminate because it is vague has apparently failed to pinpoint exactly what it is about such actions that make them right or wrong. So, again, the determinacy standard is appropriate for evaluating moral theories in light of both the practical and the theoretical aims of such theories.

Applicability

A moral principle might satisfy the consistency and determinacy standards yet still fail to be very useful as a decision procedure. Suppose a moral theory makes the rightness of an action depend on how much happiness it would bring about for all of those who will ever be affected by the action. Presumably, this principle, together with relevant information, logically implies consistent moral verdicts that are determinate. Unfortunately, as human beings, we often are incapable of obtaining reliable information about the effects of our actions. In such cases, a principle like the one in question cannot be used as the basis of a reliable decision procedure, owing to limits on human knowledge about morally relevant facts; it lacks applicability. According, then, to the *applicability standard,*

> The principles of a moral theory should be applicable in the sense that they specify relevant information about actions and other items of evaluation that human beings can typically obtain and use to arrive at moral verdicts on the basis of those principles.

The remaining standards for evaluating a moral theory all have to do with wanting a moral theory in general and the principles they feature in particular to be appropriately related to (1) our beliefs about morality, (2) our considered moral beliefs, and (3) our nonmoral beliefs and assumptions.

Intuitive Appeal

In addition to moral beliefs (beliefs about what is right or wrong, good or bad) we have beliefs *about* morality. Beliefs of the latter sort include such ideas as: morality concerns the well-being of individuals, morality is rooted in facts about human nature, and morality represents an impartial standpoint for evaluating actions, people, and institutions. These ideas are vague, but as we shall see, moral theories often begin with intuitively appealing beliefs about morality and then go on to develop such ideas in a systematic way. So one kind of consideration that counts in favor of a moral theory is what I will call its *intuitive appeal*. According to this standard,

A moral theory should develop and make sense of various intuitively appealing beliefs and ideas about morality.

Internal Support

Despite the fact that people disagree about the morality of actions like abortion, animal experimentation, suicide, euthanasia, and other matters of moral controversy, most people do agree about the morality of a wide range of actions. We agree that killing innocent human beings against their will is wrong, that torturing someone for fun is wrong, and so forth. That is, there are many moral beliefs we have that are deeply held and widely shared and which we would continue to hold were we to reflect carefully on their correctness. Call these our considered moral beliefs.

One way to check the correctness of a moral principle is to test it against our considered moral beliefs about specific cases. When a principle, together with relevant information, logically implies one of our considered moral beliefs, we can think of the principle as having a correct moral implication. And having correct implications is one way a moral principle receives support, support that comes from moral beliefs—beliefs internal to morality.

On the other hand, moral theories whose principles have implications that conflict with some of our considered moral beliefs are (according to this standard) questionable if not mistaken. So according to the standard of *internal support*,

A moral theory whose principles, together with relevant factual information, logically imply our considered moral beliefs, receives support—internal support—from those beliefs. On the other hand, if the principles of a theory have implications that conflict with our considered moral beliefs, this is evidence against the correctness of the theory.[12]

Obviously, the rationale behind this standard has mainly to do with the theoretical aim of discovering moral criteria that underlie our moral evaluations.

Explanatory Power

A moral theory attempts to discover not only moral principles that support our considered moral beliefs but also principles that *explain* what it is about actions that *make* them right or wrong (or something good or bad). Clearly this is something we want in a moral theory that intends to satisfy the theoretical aim of providing moral criteria. Notice that a moral theory might provide good explanations of some moral obligations and not others. For instance, a moral theory might feature principles that provide a good explanation of our obligations of "fair play" involving taking on one's fair share of the burdens that are supposed to be shared by all, but fail to plausibly explain our obligations to family and friends. If so, it lacks what we might call "full" explanatory power. And it is full explanatory power that a complete moral theory hopes to provide.

We can express the standard of *explanatory power* this way:

> A moral theory should feature principles that explain our more specific considered moral beliefs, thus helping us understand why actions, persons, and other objects of moral evaluation are right or wrong, good or bad, have or lack moral worth.

Moral principles of right conduct that satisfy this standard are said to systematize morality because, in effect, they reveal the underlying nature of the various actions that are right (or wrong). Discovering principles that explain and thereby systematize morality directly reflects the theoretical aim of a moral theory.

External Support

The main idea behind the standard of external support was expressed by J. L. Mackie (1912–1982), who noted that "Moral principles and ethical theories do not stand alone: they affect and are affected by beliefs and assumptions which belong to other fields, and not least to psychology, metaphysics, and religion" (Mackie, 1977, 203). Whereas the standard of internal support has to do with the support a moral principle may receive from those considered moral beliefs it implies, the standard of external support has to do with the support that a moral theory in general, and its principles in particular, may receive from nonmoral views and assumptions, including those from the specific fields of inquiry Mackie mentions. The idea behind this standard is that a moral theory is more likely to represent a correct theory about the nature of morality (and thus satisfy the relevant theoretical aim of such theories) if its principles enjoy corroborative support from well-established beliefs and theories from other areas of thought.

As we shall see in the chapters to come, proponents of various moral theories attempt to defend their favored theory by appealing to nonmoral theories and assumptions. For instance, defenders of the divine command theory often appeal to religious theories and assumptions in support of their favored moral theory. Defenders of moral relativism are fond of appealing to certain findings from the field of anthropology in arguing that a relativist moral theory is correct. And other theories look to various other nonmoral views for support.

Whereas the fact that a moral theory is supported by some nonmoral theory is some evidence in its favor, the fact that a moral theory conflicts with certain well-established nonmoral views is evidence against it. I will not elaborate further; there will be plenty of examples in what is to come of how the standard of external support plays an important role in the overall evaluation of moral theories.

So, according to the standard of *external support*,

> The fact that the principles of a moral theory are supported by nonmoral beliefs and assumptions, including well-established beliefs and assumptions from various areas of nonmoral inquiry, is some evidence in its favor. On the other hand, the fact that the principles conflict with established nonmoral beliefs and assumptions is evidence against the theory.

This list is not complete; there are other desiderata (and associated standards) that philosophers invoke in evaluating moral theories. (In chapter 7, the standard of *publicity* is introduced.) The ones I have listed are among the most common that we find being used, and in the chapters to come they will figure prominently in our evaluation of the theories. For convenience, I have included an appendix that lists them all.

Let me close this section by making a few comments about these standards and their use. First, satisfying these standards is a matter of degree. For instance, a theory can be more or less determinate in its implications about the morality of actions. Again, the moral principles of a theory can vary in the extent to which they logically imply our considered moral beliefs, and so forth for the other standards on our list.

Second, it is worth keeping in mind that in addition to determining how well any one theory does according to these standards, part of evaluating moral theories involves comparing them with one another to see how well they do in satisfying the relevant standards. Since we are looking for several desirable characteristics in a moral theory, we may find that some theories possess some but not all of these characteristics to varying degrees. This means that evaluating a theory can be a very complex matter.

Finally, some of these standards are controversial, others are not. The standards of intuitive appeal and consistency are fairly uncontroversial, but others, such as the standard of internal support, are questioned by some moral philosophers. Questions about the proper standards for evaluating moral theories belong to a subfield of ethics called metaethics, which I will briefly describe in the next section.

8. SOME REMARKS ABOUT THE FIELD OF ETHICS

Ethics (often called moral philosophy) is the area of philosophy that inquires into morality. There are two main branches of ethics: normative ethics and metaethics. Normative ethics investigates moral questions, and it is common to distinguish between questions of theory and questions of application. Normative moral theory is what this book is all about; as we have seen, it attempts to answer very general moral questions about what to do and how to be. Applied moral theory investigates the morality of specific actions and practices, particularly those that are controversial. Books on applied ethics typically deal with such moral issues as abortion, the death penalty, euthanasia, and others, many of which we have already mentioned.

The relation between moral theory and applied ethics is somewhat like the relation between pure science (like physics) and engineering. Just as issues in engineering are matters of applying scientific principles to real-world projects and problems, issues in applied ethics are often thought of as matters requiring the application of the principles of a moral theory to real-world moral problems.

This way of conceiving the relation between the sorts of general moral questions that are raised in moral theory and the more specific moral questions that are raised in applied ethics suggests a natural order of inquiry, illustrated earlier by the controversy over suicide. Confronted with moral disputes about a variety of moral issues, a reflective person will be led to ask questions about the nature of right and wrong, good and bad, and thus will be led to raise the sorts of questions dealt with in moral theory. The hope is that by answering these more general, theoretical questions, one will then be able to use the results in correctly answering more specific moral questions about the morality of suicide, capital punishment, abortion, and other such issues.

However, as we shall see in the chapters to follow, competing moral theories give competing answers to the general questions raised in moral theory. This naturally raises questions about how one might come to know which moral theory is correct. Questions about knowledge belong to the area of philosophical inquiry called epistemology, from the Greek term *episteme*, or knowledge. So one important philosophical question concerns how one can come to know moral statements generally and moral principles in particular. The branch of epistemology that deals with such questions is called *moral epistemology*.

Of course, epistemological questions about knowledge in turn raise further philosophical questions about the meaning and truth of moral statements. To really come to know a moral principle, one must be justified in accepting the principle in question. But in order to be justified in accepting some claim, one must understand what the claim means, and this in turn requires that one know something about what makes the claim true or false. Questions about meaning and truth are semantic questions, and the branch of semantics that deals with such questions about moral thought and language is called *moral semantics*.

Questions about meaning and truth are related to metaphysical questions. Metaphysics is that branch of philosophy that inquires into the nature of reality—into what exists (what is real) and its ultimate nature. Questions about the existence and nature of space and time, about causation, about substance, and about events are all matters of metaphysical inquiry.

There are also metaphysical questions concerning morality. For instance, are there moral facts whose existence is what makes a true moral statement true? If so, what kind of fact is a moral fact? Is it the kind of fact that can be scientifically investigated? If so, what kind of scientific fact is it? Biological? Sociological? Anthropological? Perhaps a combination of these? Are moral facts (supposing that such facts exist) instead some sort of nonscientific fact? Perhaps moral facts are facts about the will of a deity. Some philosophers have been skeptical of the existence of moral facts, denying that there really are any. The branch of metaphysics dealing with such questions is called *moral metaphysics*.

These epistemological, semantic, and metaphysical questions about morality are typically referred to as metaethical questions. And the branch of ethics called metaethics ("meta" meaning "about") attempts to answer them. Figure 1.3 summarizes the main divisions of ethics.

I wish to make one final but very important comment about the distinction between normative ethics and metaethics. The description I have just given suggests a neat and tidy division between them. But, as we shall see, no such neat and tidy division really exists. A moral theory not only attempts to discover true or correct moral principles but is also concerned to justify or prove such principles. Thus questions about the proper way to justify or prove moral principles in particular, and moral claims in general, are necessarily involved in giving a normative moral theory. That is, epistemological questions about justification (as well as the sorts of semantic and metaphysical metaethical questions that naturally arise in connection with epistemological questions) are just beneath the surface when engaging in moral theory. Since the focus of this book is on moral theory, I have kept metaethical discussions to a minimum. However, as the reader will discover, metaethical questions arise throughout this book.

9. PREVIEW

In the chapters to follow, we shall examine representative versions of the following moral theories: divine command theory, moral relativism, natural law theory, consequentialism, egoism, Kant's moral theory, moral pluralism, virtue ethics, and moral particularism. Each chapter is devoted to one of these theories, though consequentialism is covered in two chapters, owing to the many varieties of this general type of view.

In each chapter I introduce readers to the main concepts involved in the theory being featured and then proceed to develop a version of the theory (sometimes I present both a classical and a more contemporary version), followed by a critical evaluation of the theory. The critical evaluation will typically involve an appeal to one or more of the seven basic desiderata explained above.

In presenting each theory, one main focus will be its theory of right conduct. And for some, but not all, moral theories we will also have to examine the theory of intrinsic value that is being proposed as a basis for understanding right action. (Some moral theories, as noted above, make the deontic status of an action depend

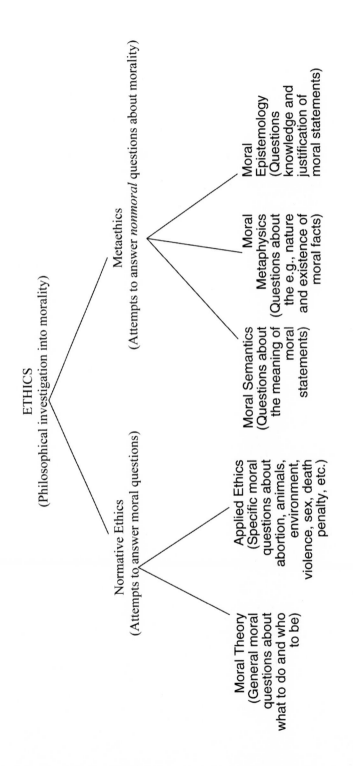

Figure 1.3. Main Divisions of Philosophical Ethics

on considerations of intrinsic value.) Theories of moral worth (virtue and vice), as we shall see, do not play a prominent role in many of the moral theories we shall examine (or at least they will not receive nearly as much attention in such theories). So in my treatment of some theories, moral worth is not mentioned, while in connection with others, it is mentioned only briefly.

A final comment: The moral theories featured in the following chapters all build on widely recognized ideas that will be familiar to most readers. (Recall the standard of intuitive appeal.) The idea that morality is based on God's commands is familiar and at the heart of the divine command theory. The idea that morality is simply relative to culture is likewise familiar and is the key idea in versions of moral relativism. The idea that morality requires that we not go against nature or do anything unnatural is related to the natural law theory. Versions of consequentialism and, in particular, utilitarian versions of this type of theory, work with the idea that the morality of an action depends on how it affects human happiness, while the idea that morality involves respecting persons is central to Kant's moral theory. One might think of these various theories, then, as attempts to develop these familiar ideas in a rigorous philosophical manner.

So although the study of these moral theories may be a new experience for many readers, many of the core ideas featured in them are familiar. This book is an invitation to explore ideas that are often taken for granted and often only vaguely understood.

NOTES

1. For instance, in 1997 the U.S. Supreme Court ruled that individuals do not have a Constitutional *right* to physician-assisted suicide but left open whether U.S. states may permit the practice.

2. Throughout, and merely for convenience, I use the masculine pronoun in referring to God.

3. Moral principles are often contrasted with moral rules. A moral rule (concerning right conduct) is less general than a principle and states that some specific type of action is right or wrong. Each of the Ten Commandments, for instance, expresses a moral rule. The role of moral rules in moral theory will be explored in later chapters.

4. In chapter 11, we will explore in more detail the relationship between moral principles and assumptions about the underlying unity of moral phenomena.

5. Talk of what one "morally ought" to do is here being used in the strong sense to mean what one morally *must* do. Sometimes the expression is used in a weaker sense so that actions that are supererogatory—"above and beyond the call of duty"—are referred to as actions one morally ought to do, even though they are not morally required.

6. Strict accounts of intrinsic value make such value depend on properties that are intrinsic to the thing or state possessing such value. Less strict accounts allow that something's intrinsic value can depend on its relational properties. For example, the fact that a coin is rare (a feature not intrinsic to the coin) can, on the less strict account of intrinsic value, make the coin intrinsically valuable.

7. Although being instrumentally valuable—valuable as a means to something that is intrinsically good—is one kind of extrinsic value, the means-ends relation is not the only relation that can figure in something being extrinsically valuable. For more on this, see Zimmerman, 2010.

8. For an illuminating overview of value theory, see Schroeder, 2008.

9. Some philosophers use the expression "*moral* goodness" to refer to what we are calling moral worth—the sort of value that can only be possessed by creatures who can be morally praised and blamed. I followed this usage in the previous edition, contrasting moral with nonmoral value. But this terminology can be confusing because it suggests that what has nonmoral value is not relevant to moral theory. It is also worth noting that moral worth is sometimes attributed to actions when they flow from a virtuous character trait. When used in this way, it is common to distinguish actions that merely comply with one's obligations but are not done out of a virtuous motive, from actions that not only comply with obligation but are done from a virtuous motive. In both cases one fulfills an obligation and thus does what is morally required, but in the latter case one's action also may be said to have moral worth.

10. These types of moral theory (duty-based) are sometimes called versions of deontology. But some moral philosophers classify some theories as value-based versions of deontology. This latter use is not consistent with using it to refer to duty-based theories. The term is also used to refer to theories according to which there are moral constraints (called "deontological constraints") on promoting good consequences, which is how I plan to use it. Deontological constraints come up in chapters 4 and 6.

11. Notice that a moral theory does not violate the consistency standard if its principles imply, for example, that in general lying is wrong and at the same time yields the verdict in some specific case that a particular instance of lying is not wrong (so long as the theory can account for the difference between lies that are wrong and those that are not).

12. In later chapters, it will be useful to distinguish between a strong sense and a weak sense of internal support. A moral principle receives strong internal support from considered moral beliefs when the principle (together with relevant factual information) logically implies the beliefs in question. A moral principle receives weak internal support when the principle is merely consistent with considered moral beliefs.

2

Divine Command Theory

In the minds of many people, there is a deep connection between morality and religion. Historically, of course, religious worldviews contain a moral outlook as part of an overall vision of the place and purpose of human beings in the world. People brought up in a religious community thus come to associate morality with religion. In addition to the historical connection between morality and religion, there are other possible connections between them. For instance, one might claim that moral knowledge requires revelation. However, in this chapter we are mainly interested in a particular way in which morality has been thought to depend on religion, or more precisely, on the commands of God. The thought, central to the divine command moral theory, is that morality itself—what is right and wrong, good and bad—depends on God's commands. It is God's act of commanding that we avoid certain types of action that makes those actions wrong, and similarly for other moral concepts.[1]

1. THE THEORY

The divine command theory about to be presented is what we may call an "unrestricted" view about the relation between God and morality because it proposes to explain the nature of both the right and the good in terms of God's commands. Later in the chapter (section 4), we will briefly consider a restricted version of the general idea that morality depends on God's commands—restricted because this version allows that some parts of morality do not depend on God's commands while other parts do.

In presenting the unrestricted divine command theory, let us begin with the theory of right conduct—that branch of moral theory that concerns the nature of right and wrong action. The main idea is that what makes an action right or wrong depends on (and thus can be expressed in terms of) God's commands. Theologian Robert C. Mortimer explains the view this way:

> From the doctrine of God as Creator and source of all that is, it follows that a thing is not right simply because we think it is, still less because it seems expedient. It is right because God commands it. This means that there is a real distinction between right and wrong that is independent of what we happen to think. It is rooted in the nature and will of God. (Mortimer, 1950, 8)

Mortimer mentions the rightness of actions being based on God's commands (by which he means an action's being obligatory), but all the other moral categories can be similarly characterized. In order to focus on the divine command theory, it will help if we express the essentials of the theory in terms of a set of basic principles.

Theory of Right Conduct

An action A is *obligatory* if and only if (and because) God commands that we A.

An action A is *wrong* if and only if (and because) God commands that we not A.

An action A is *optional* if and only if (and because) it is not the case that God commands that we A (thus, not obligatory), and it is not the case that God commands that we not A (thus, not forbidden). Less cumbersomely: An action A is optional if and only if (and because) God neither commands that we A nor that we not A.

If we turn for a moment to the divine command theory's account of value—the goodness and badness of persons, things, experiences, and states of affairs—it is, again, facts about God's commands that make certain things good and others bad (or evil). Typically, in presenting a theory of value we are concerned with the nature of *intrinsic* goodness and badness. However, in connection with the divine command theory, it would be misleading at best to talk about what is intrinsically good—good in itself—since the very idea here is that nothing is intrinsically good or bad. Rather, on this theory it is something extrinsic to whatever is good or bad that confers upon it the value it has, namely, God's commands.[2] With this in mind, we can set forth the divine command theory of value:

Theory of Value

Something S is *good* if and only if (and because) God commands that we bring about or preserve S.[3]

Something S is *bad* if and only if (and because) God commands that we refrain from bringing about or preserving S.

Something S is *value-neutral* if and only if (and because) God neither commands that we bring about or preserve S nor that we refrain from bringing about or preserving S.

What is crucial for understanding the divine command theory is the idea that what makes an action right or wrong, good or bad, is nothing but brute facts about God's commands. The fact that he commands that we not kill, rape, torture, and so forth is what makes such actions wrong; their wrongness consists entirely in the fact that he commands that we not engage in such actions.[4] We will come back to this point in section 3.

How might the theory be used? One obvious way involves appealing to some source, such as the Bible, that purports to contain evidence of God's commands. According to Mortimer, for example, the Bible provides moral guidance in three principal ways. First, "it recalls and restates in simple and even violent language fundamental moral judgments which men are always in danger of forgetting or explaining away. It thus provides a norm and standard of human behavior in the broadest and simplest outline" (1950, 15). For instance, the Ten Commandments of the Old Testament and Christ's teachings regarding love for fellow human beings in the New Testament provide general moral rules for all human beings.

Second, in addition to moral rules, which we might call the letter of the moral law as commanded by God, we find evidence of the proper spirit for following God's commands. Ideally, humans are to strive toward holiness by following God's commands, not out of fear or self-interest, but out of love for God. Because the moral worth of persons has to do with their motives, this point about the spirit of morality presumably reveals the divine command theory's account of moral worth: the moral worth (and hence moral virtue) of individuals is measured by how closely they come to fulfilling God's commands out of the motive of love for God.

Finally, according to Mortimer, biblical revelation "suggests new emphases and new precepts, a new scale of human values which could not at all, or could not easily, have been [otherwise] perceived" (1950, 16). As an example Mortimer notes that the Incarnation, signifying the restoration of fallen human nature, instructs us that God has equal concern for all human beings, including the outcast, downtrodden, and despised. This equal concern means that all human beings have a special dignity and that consequently all humans are to be treated as ends in themselves. The idea of human dignity is a moral idea that might otherwise be obscure to human beings except for revelation.

2. DEFENDING THE THEORY

Let us now consider why anyone might accept the divine command theory—or at least anyone who is already a theist. There are four arguments to consider.

According to what I will call the *linguistic argument*, the divine command theory is true simply because "obligatory," when used in its moral sense, just means "commanded by God" (and so on for the other moral concepts). Consider someone who would deny the truth of any of the theory's moral principles. According to the linguistic argument, such a denial would be like denying the general claim that all bachelors are unmarried. If one denies this latter claim, while also intending to use the term "bachelor" as it is ordinarily used, then one shows a lack of understanding of the concept of a bachelor. Similarly, so it might be claimed, if one denies the principles of the divine command theory, one thereby shows that one does not understand basic moral concepts of the obligatory, the good, and so on.

However, this appeal to meaning is implausible. Indeed, its implausibility is easily revealed by comparing the bachelor example with any of the divine command theory's principles. It certainly would show a lack of understanding on the part of someone to deny that all bachelors are unmarried, for it is manifestly clear that part of what we mean by the term "bachelor" is "someone who is unmarried." If we know that someone is a bachelor, the question of whether he is also unmarried is settled. Or to put it another way: if one claims that someone is a bachelor but then goes on to claim that he is married, one can be accused of contradicting oneself. But similar points cannot be made about moral concepts. If one claims that some action is obligatory but that the action is not commanded by God (perhaps because the speaker does not believe there is a God), one is not guilty of self-contradiction. So, the particular linguistic argument under consideration is not persuasive.[5]

Religious arguments for the theory appeal to theistic premises, for example, premises about the nature of God. Such arguments, then, attempt to provide support for this moral theory by appealing to nonmoral views, and thus represent an appeal to the standard of external support for evaluating moral theories that was explained in section 7 of chapter 1. We have already encountered one such argument in the first quote from Mortimer. He infers the truth of the divine command theory from the theistic claim that God is creator of all. We can elaborate Mortimer's line of thought as follows. God must be the creative source of morality and hence the divine command theory must be true, because if he were not the source of morality, then there would be some moral standards or principles independent of God. And if there are moral standards and principles independent of God, it follows that he would not be creator of all things. So, if God is creator of absolutely everything (except himself), then we are committed to the divine command theory.

I will pass over this argument for now since we return to it in the next section, where I will argue that the theist has good reason to question one of its basic assumptions.

According to the *argument from moral objectivity*, the only moral theory that provides an objective basis for a single true morality is the divine command theory. According to monotheism there is a single God, who issues a set of commands to all human beings, regardless of culture and historical setting. This means that, contrary to moral relativism, there is a single set of objectively true moral principles, and hence the kinds of problems that infect moral relativism do not apply to the divine command theory.[6]

An argument that is similar to the appeal to objectivity is the *authority of obligation argument*, according to which being under a moral obligation involves being subject to an authoritative demand. And this requires a divine authority in a position to issue commands. One way of developing this argument is to hold that obligation is an inherently interpersonal concept involving a relation between the party who is under an obligation and someone who has authority to place demands upon that party. The argument (that we will explore in more detail later in the chapter) is that the only being capable of placing human beings under an obligation—who has the authority to do so—is a divine authority. Thus, concludes the argument, to make sense of moral obligation, we must suppose that there is a divine authority—someone who issues commands and thereby creates obligations.

One major worry about the objectivity and authority arguments is that there may be ways of accounting for these features of morality without appeal to God. The other moral theories featured in this book (besides relativism) can be understood as attempting to defend a single true morality whose moral principles are objectively true and furthermore whose principles of right conduct in particular can explain obligation and its authority. So, in order for these arguments to have force, it would have to be that all other moral theories fail to do the job. This remains to be seen. Let us now consider challenges to the theory.

3. THE EUTHYPHRO DILEMMA

Many thinkers (both theists and nontheists) have claimed that the divine command theory should be rejected owing to a dilemma that takes its name from the title of one of Plato's dialogues, the *Euthyphro*. In this dialogue, Euthyphro professes to know what piety is, and Socrates questions him about it. After Euthyphro gives examples of what he takes to be pious actions, the dialogue continues:

> Socr: Remember, then, that I did not ask you to tell me one or two of all the many pious actions that there are; I want to know what is characteristic of piety which makes all pious action pious. You said, I think, that there is one characteristic which makes all pious actions pious, and another characteristic which makes all impious actions impious. Do you remember? (Plato, 1976, 7)[7]

After some discussion, we get Euthyphro's answer:

> Euth: Well, I should say that piety is what all the gods love, and that impiety is what they all hate. (11)

Socrates then poses the crucial question:

> Socr: Now consider this question. Do the gods love piety because it is pious, or is it pious because they love it? (11)

Here, Socrates is asking about the relation between piety and the love of the gods. But the same question can be raised in connection with the relation between morality generally and the commands of God: does God command that we perform obligatory actions because they are obligatory, or are some actions obligatory because God commands that we perform them? To fully appreciate the dilemma that results from having to choose between these two options, it will be useful to pause for a moment and review a few of the key tenets of traditional theistic belief.

According to many versions of theism, there is a single personal God who is an all-perfect being, possessing every perfection to the highest degree. God's perfections include omniscience (being all-knowing) and omnipotence (being all-powerful). In addition, the following three tenets further characterize God's nature:

Divine creator: God is creator of everything (other than himself). God's omnipotence ensures that he can bring about anything possible, and his being creator is a matter of his realizing his omnipotence in bringing about this particular world from among the possible worlds he might have created instead.

Divine rationality: God is a fully rational being; everything he does, he does for a good reason.

Divine moral perfection: God, as a being, is morally good in the fullest possible sense: he possesses every moral perfection to the highest possible degree. If we were to make a list of these perfections, we could begin by saying that he is all-just, omnibenevolent (all-loving), all-merciful, and so forth.

I won't pause to elaborate these tenets, hoping that my readers will find them clear enough for present purposes.

The Euthyphro dilemma is a dilemma for the theist who accepts these claims about the nature of God. And, as noted above, it arises in connection with the question: How is morality related to God's commands? There are two possibilities. Either morality depends on God's commands, or it does not. To be more precise, the two options are these. Either:

1. Morality depends entirely on God's commands: what makes an action right or wrong and what makes something good or bad are just God's commands.
   or
2. Actions have features that make them right or wrong, and states of affairs, experiences, and character traits have features that make them good or bad. There are thus standards of right and wrong, good and bad that specify those features of actions that make them right or wrong and those features of states of affairs, experiences, and character traits that make them good or bad. Being omniscient, God has complete knowledge of such standards, and being completely good (and caring for human beings) he issues commands to humanity that conform to this knowledge.

The first option represents the unrestricted divine command theory. The second option represents the rejection of this theory because it presupposes that, independently of God's commands, there are moral standards that specify those features of actions, character traits, and so forth that make them right or wrong, good or bad.

The dilemma can now be easily explained. In response to the question about how God and morality are related, either the theist accepts the divine command theory (option 1) or not (option 2). Whichever option one takes, one runs afoul of one or more of the basic theistic tenets mentioned above. Let us see why.

First, if one embraces the divine command theory, then one seems forced to give up the thesis of divine rationality, since it looks as if (contrary to this thesis) God does not have good reasons for the commands he issues. As I have been saying, according to the divine command theory, what *makes* an action obligatory is the fact that God commands that we do it; he does not command us to not kill and not steal because they are independently wrong. It is his commands, and his commands only, that make such actions wrong. But apparently this means that God's commands are arbitrary, mere whims; he might just as well command human beings to kill and steal as command humans to not kill and steal. After all, on this version of the theory, it isn't the fact that such actions are harmful to the victim, for example, that makes them wrong. But then if God's commands are not based on facts about actions that make them wrong, it looks as if he has no good reason whatsoever to issue one set of commands over another. Call this the *arbitrary whim* problem—a problem that is very commonly raised against the divine command theory. One challenge, then, to the divine command theorist (who wants to hold on to the divine rationality thesis) is to explain how this problem can be avoided.[8]

The arbitrariness worry concerns God's commands. The unrestricted divine command theory also has trouble with the claim that God (as a being) is perfectly good. According to this version of the theory, what makes someone a morally good individual (an individual having moral worth) is that he or she follows God's commands out of love for God. This would imply that God's own goodness or moral worth as a being is a matter of God's following commands that he gives to himself out of love for himself. But, as Philip Quinn notes in explaining what we may call the *divine goodness* problem, "since there is no moral value in always being obedient to self-addressed commands, the divine command theorist is unable to maintain that God is morally good" (Quinn, 2006, 75). And, of course, this means that the divine command theorist is forced to give up the thesis of God's divine moral goodness.

So we have before us one horn of the Euthyphro dilemma. If the theist accepts the divine command theory, then in light of the implications of the theory regarding arbitrariness and divine goodness, she must give up the theses of divine rationality and divine moral perfection. But clearly it would be too much for the theist to give up these theses, particularly the thesis of divine moral perfection, since it is the basis for devotion and worship. If this is correct, the theist must reject the divine command theory that we've been considering. But then if the theist rejects the theory, her view seems to require rejecting the thesis that God is creator of all. After all, if we admit that the right and the good are not a matter of God's commands, aren't we saying that there exists a moral code or standard that is independent of God? And if so, then he is not creator of everything. Mortimer's religious argument, recall, was to the effect that we have to accept the divine command theory in light of the idea of God as creator. This is the second horn of the dilemma. Call it the *divine creation* problem. So, whether the theist accepts the divine command theory (option 1) or not (option 2), it looks as if she must give up an important tenet of theistic belief about God. Hence, the theist faces a dilemma.

Now one way in which one might address the dilemma is to reject the divine command theory, claim that there are moral standards or principles that are independent of God—that God does not create—and argue that this option does not really compromise the divine creation thesis. How can this be? Many philosophers hold that fundamental moral standards, truths, and principles are not only true, but necessarily true. A truth is necessary when it is not possible for it to be false. Consider the mathematical proposition that $2 + 2 = 4$. This is not only true, but necessarily so: it is not possible for the equation to be otherwise. God couldn't make $2 + 2$ turn out to be 5 given the quantities designated by 2 and by 5 and given what "+" and "=" mean. But so what? As many theologians have argued, the fact that God cannot do or bring about what is impossible represents no genuine limit on God's omnipotence. So if we understand very basic moral principles to be necessarily true, we can likewise point out that it is no real limit on God's omnipotence that the truth of those principles does not depend on God's commands. If we reconsider the claim about God as creator, then we should reformulate it to say that, as omnipotent, God has power over everything that is not a matter of necessity. In particular, God is creator of the entire physical universe including human beings, whose existence is certainly not a necessary fact.

So one way to get out of the dilemma created by the tension between the theistic tenets and the divine command theory is to reject the theory, and refine one's understanding of what it means to say God is creator.

Can theists live with this solution to the dilemma? It is worth noting that many theists reject the divine command theory and embrace the sort of solution just proposed. For instance, Franz Brentano (1838–1917), who early in his life was a Catholic priest, wrote: "According to the Christian, the commandment to love our neighbor is right not in virtue of the fact that God requires it; God requires it in virtue of the fact that it is naturally right" ([1889] 1969, 41–42). But at this point it is important to remember that we have been examining an unrestricted view of the relation between God's commands and morality. Suppose one backs away from the claim that all of morality—the right *and* the good—depend simply on God's commands? As we are about to see, rejecting this assumption allows the theist a way to go through the horns of the Euthyphro dilemma without being impaled on either horn. Let us take a closer look.

4. RESTRICTING THE THEORY

There is a middle way for the theist that preserves the idea that God's commands play a foundational role in morality, while at the same time avoiding the problems just noted in connection with the Euthyphro dilemma. After all, even if it is implausible to suppose that all of morality depends on God's commands, it would be fallacious to immediately conclude that none of it is so dependent. Compare: it is not the case that all animals are carnivorous, but from this fact alone it does not follow that no animals are carnivorous. And indeed it is false that no animals are carnivorous. So, according to a restricted version of the theory, it is not the case that *all* of morality is based on God's commands. And this can be explained by the fact that goodness and obligation are importantly different so that the former is to be explained without appeal to God's commands, although a complete explanation of the latter requires reference to God's commands. Let us briefly consider the central ideas behind this version that I will summarize by stating four guiding ideas.[9]

First, on a restricted view, God's goodness is a matter of his possessing the various perfections to the greatest possible extent, including such perfections as being all-loving, all-merciful, and all-just. These characteristics are what *make* God supremely good. And as a supremely good being, God serves as the very paradigm of goodness. Thus, the problem of making sense of God's goodness that bedevils the unrestricted view does not arise on this view.

Second, God's goodness is a partial basis for an account of moral obligation. The idea is that certain actions such as torturing an innocent person for fun are incompatible with God's nature as an all-loving, all-just, all-merciful being; they are actions that necessarily God would never perform. Such actions therefore deserve the title of "bad actions." By contrast, actions whose performance God would necessarily not fail to perform owing to the moral quality of his nature are good actions. So, we have a conception of actions being good or bad owing to how they are related to the various excellences or virtues that constitute God's moral goodness.

But from the fact that an action is one that would be good to perform, it does not automatically follow that one has an obligation to perform the action. This is because the goodness of something only implies that the thing in question is worthy of being desired or, because we are concerned with actions, worthy of being performed. Something more is needed in order to explain why certain good actions (and not others) are not only good to do but required or obligatory. Even if we say that the sorts of actions that result from the exercise of one or another virtuous character trait are not only worthy of being performed, but ones whose performance would be excellent, we need more to explain obligation. After all, not all actions that would be worthy of being performed, indeed excellent—such as actions of supreme self-sacrifice—are also morally required. That is, it is common to recognize actions that it would be good to do but are "beyond the call of duty." Such actions are called "supererogatory."

Third, according to the restricted view, this additional obligation-making element has to do with the fact that the concept of moral obligation is arguably a social concept, in the sense that for one individual to be under a moral obligation to perform some action that action must be one that is demanded of her. And demands naturally presuppose some sort of relationship among rational agents: the one making the demand and the one upon whom the demand is being made.[10]

One might suppose that the moral conventions that have arisen in one's society constitute the social aspect of obligation—those conventions involve the society imposing demands upon its members. But the obvious problem with this proposal is that the moral conventions that a society happens to have may include "requirements" that are clearly morally outrageous, and may fail to include requirements that represent legitimate moral demands. Moreover, different societies may have conflicting moral norms—a theme to be explored in the next chapter on relativism. As Robert Adams remarks,

> These are all reasons for thinking, as most moralists have, that actual human social requirements are simply not good enough to constitute the basis of moral obligation. (Adams, 1999, 248)

So, fourth, the proposal by the restricted divine command theorist is that God and only God can play the role of the person to whom (at least ultimately) all moral demands are owed, as one who has the authority to demand of humans that they perform certain actions and avoid others. Moral requirements or obligations on this view depend (partly) upon God's commands. The fact that an action is not only a good action but one that God commands that we perform is what makes obligatory actions obligatory.[11]

We may now summarize the basic idea behind the restricted divine command theory of right conduct as follows:

RDCT An action is *obligatory* if and only if (and because) that act is morally good *and* it is commanded by God. Wrong actions are ones that are morally bad *and* which God commands that we not perform. All other actions are optional.

Notice three features of this view. First, it understands goodness and badness to be basic (within the realm of moral concepts) and defines or characterizes rightness and wrongness in terms of what is good and bad. With respect to the structure of moral theory, the theory of value is more basic than the theory of right. Second, as already mentioned, the view does not explain God's goodness in terms of his commands, so it avoids the divine goodness problem. But also, it avoids the arbitrariness problem because, as Adams (1999, 264) puts it, "those commands spring from God's character, which is the standard of goodness." God's commands are thus not arbitrary—his own nature serves as a basis for distinguishing good from bad actions which is in turn a basis for which actions he commands. Third, on this view God is the moral center of the universe for two reasons. First, as explained, God is the ultimate realization of moral goodness and stands as the paradigm of moral goodness. Second, it takes God's commands (together with facts about the relation between actions and moral goodness) to fully explain the deontic status of action.

What about the second horn involving God as creator? After all, it looks as if the restricted view implies that there are principles or standards of goodness including, for example, that being all-loving is a good character trait, that are independent of God; that do not owe their being correct to God's creative activity. God, being good, is subject to these standards, but he does not create them. Now we have already noted that it is open to a theist to say that basic moral standards are necessarily true and that there being such truths that God does not create does not really compromise God's creative power, properly understood. But the third point from the previous paragraph—about God being the moral center of the universe—seems to completely avoid any tension involving God as creator. This is because the proposal being suggested is that God *is* goodness. So as for the question "What makes these traits or features of God good-making ones?" the answer is "Just because they are features of God." If this makes sense and is correct, then the theist does not have to say that God is subject to independently existing standards.

We now have two versions of the divine command theory before us, an unrestricted and a restricted version, so let us turn to an evaluation of them.

5. EVALUATION OF THE DIVINE COMMAND THEORY

In evaluating the divine command theory, let us consider what can be said for and against the theory in both its unrestricted and restricted versions, making use of the standards for evaluating moral theories introduced in section 7 of chapter 1.

Consistency, determinacy, and applicability. First, if we assume that God's commands are consistent and that he has revealed enough detail about his commands to guide our moral decisions, then we may conclude that both versions of the theory satisfy the standards of consistency and determinacy. But it is worth noting that there are important issues about what constitutes a command of God and how determinate those commands are. If it turns out that the commands God has given to human beings are very general in their nature—the Ten Commandments suppose—then appealing to these rules in trying to determine the deontic status of a great many actions will require moral judgment. In this case, the theory will itself be limited in what conclusions can be drawn from a simple application of its principles; in this respect it will be much like the view of W. D. Ross that is featured in chapter 9.

While the standard of determinacy has to do with the range of actions whose deontic status is fixed by God's commands—the broader the range, the more determinate the theory—the applicability standard has to do with whether and how God's commands are accessible to human beings. If God issues a set of very determinate commands, but does not convey them to human beings, then the determinacy standard is met, but not the applicability standard. Regarding applicability, many if not most theists hold that God's commands are revealed to human beings through scripture, a point made by Mortimer. If this is correct *and* God's commands are reasonably determinate (an issue that we shall pass over) then all in all the divine command theory does reasonably well on the three criteria in question.

Intuitive appeal. Second, according to the standard of intuitive appeal, a moral theory should develop and make sense of plausible beliefs about morality. One such belief (held by many) is that there is a deep connection between morality and religion. Of course, this idea is what guides the development of the divine command theory, and so one might think that this standard favors the divine command theory—that the divine command theory, unlike competing theories, captures the belief in question. And so one might suppose that if one rejects the divine command theory, one has to reject what is surely a widely shared belief among theists.

But it would be a mistake to suppose that rejection of the unrestricted divine command theory is at odds with what religious people, including many fundamentalist Christians, really believe about the basis of right and wrong. In a very interesting study, psychologist Larry Nucci interviewed certain groups of fundamentalist Christian students about their understanding of the relation between God's commands, the Bible, and morality.

One group of subjects was composed of 64 fundamentalist Christian children and teenagers who were members of the Dutch reform Calvinist denomination attending Calvinist parochial school in Chicago. One of the questions he put to his subjects was this: "Suppose God has commanded [it is written in the Bible] that Christians *should* steal. Would it then be right for a Christian to steal?" (Nucci, 1986, 167). What Nucci found was that 69 percent of the subjects ages 10 to 13 and 81 percent of subjects ages 14 to 17 said no. Furthermore, when students in this study were asked whether God would ever command us to steal, students often gave the sort of response offered by a 15-year-old female subject who said that God would never issue such a command because "it's not the right thing to do, and he's perfect, and if he's stealing, he can't be perfect" (Nucci, 1986, 168). The idea that God's issuing such a command (and thus endorsing stealing and other such harmful actions) is not consistent with God's nature fits nicely with the basic tenets of the restricted divine command theory. But this leaves open the question of whether these subjects think that obligation depends in some way on God's commands. The study of another group of fundamentalist children addressed this question.

The group in question was composed of some Amish and some Mennonite children and teenagers ranging in age from 10 to 17 who attended the same fundamentalist school. Among other things, they were asked questions such as the following: "Suppose God had not given us a law about stealing, would it be all right to steal?" The result was that 70 to 100 percent of the subjects in each age category said that actions such as stealing, hitting, and slander would be wrong even if God had not commanded that we not perform them. Furthermore, when asked to justify this claim, most subjects gave reasons that made reference to the nature of the actions in question. For instance, one 17-year-old Amish teen, when asked why he thought slander would be wrong even if God or Christ had not told human beings to avoid slander explained, "it still wouldn't be right . . . [because] it is putting another person down . . . and I think no one has the right to do that" (Nucci, 1986, 165–66). The conclusion Nucci draws from this sort of evidence is that a majority of these fundamentalist Christians think that what makes certain actions wrong concerns the nature of the actions including their effects, period. And this in turn suggests that they do not think that obligation depends even in part on God's commands.

Suppose one takes the subjects of Nucci's study to be representative of fundamentalist Christian thinking about goodness and obligation. How does this bear on the correctness of divine command theory? Not much, one might think. After all, facts about what some people *believe* about the relation between God's commands and morality is not sufficient to show that a theory not in accord with such beliefs is incorrect. But remember, according to the criterion of intuitive appeal, it does count somewhat in favor of a theory if the theory captures people's beliefs about morality. And one might suppose that at least for Christians, and perhaps other monotheists, the divine command theory captures the Christian conviction that God "creates" morality in the way that Mortimer seems to advocate. And if so, then this counts at least somewhat in favor of the divine command theory. But in light of Nucci's study one has reason to doubt that the divine command theory really does capture the Christian's beliefs about God and morality. Perhaps Brentano's claim, quoted toward the end of the previous section, captures the thought of most Christians: God requires certain actions because they are "naturally" right.

External support. The attempt by Mortimer and others to argue from religious claims about God (he is creator of all) to the truth of the unrestricted version of the theory represents an appeal to the standard of external support. However, we have found reason to reject at least the unrestricted divine command theory.[12] In any case, I think what can be said is that for theists who think that God plays some essential role in explaining at least some aspects of morality, the restricted divine command theory fits with theistic belief and thus (to the extent that such beliefs are warranted) the theory thereby acquires some external support.

Internal support and explanatory power. Finally, let us suppose that the principles of right conduct and value can be used (together with facts about what God commands) to derive our considered moral beliefs. The theory will thereby satisfy the standard of internal support. But again, the Euthyphro dilemma helps us see that it is not God's commands alone that make something right or wrong, good or bad, and so the unrestricted divine command theory fails to plausibly explain what makes something right or wrong, good or bad; it fails to satisfy the standard of explanatory power. This means that it fails to satisfy the main theoretical aim of a moral theory of providing moral criteria for the right and the good.

The restricted version is far more promising on this count since it treats the nature of goodness and badness as being independent of God's commands and explains right and wrong partly in terms of goodness and badness and partly in terms of God's commands. The major worry that remains is whether God's commands are really essential in explaining the deontic status of actions. There are two questions here. First, is the concept of obligation an inherently social concept of the sort the restricted divine command theorist supposes? Some philosophers have argued that the sorts of demand characteristic of moral obligation are grounded in the sorts of reasons there are for performing some actions and avoiding others. For instance, that an action would cause a sentient creature gratuitous harm may fully explain why the act is morally wrong. No need to bring into the picture some additional agent cast in the role of demander.[13] But even if the social conception of obligation is correct, there is the second question of whether God and God alone can play the role of demander. For instance, Stephen Darwall (2006) defends a view that purports to explain obligation entirely in terms of certain interpersonal relations among human beings. His view attempts to avoid the relativist worries raised in the previous section about basing obligation on the moral norms that happen to be in force in a society at some time. Here is not the place to explore this matter further. In any case, Darwall's view has certain affinities to the moral philosophy of Immanuel Kant that we examine in chapter 8.

Suppose, finally, that the restricted divine command theorists are right, and for there to be genuine moral obligations there must be a God who issues commands. And suppose also that there is no such God. One immediate implication is that strictly speaking there would be no "genuine obligations," nor would there exist a being who fully and perfectly exemplifies the various good-making excellences of character. But nevertheless, moral virtue would still be possible for human beings, even if humans cannot realize such traits as generosity, love, and mercy as fully as could God. And virtue could serve as a basis for distinguishing good from bad actions. As for obligation, humans would be stuck with something less than the full-blooded kind that requires God and his commands.

6. CONCLUSION

Rejecting the divine command theory does not mean that religion generally, and God's commands in particular, are of no importance for morality. Certainly, assuming there is a God of the sort believed in by many theists, one can look to revelation for some moral guidance. Moreover, one can look to revelation for some indication of what makes an action right or wrong or some state of affairs good or bad. Christ's teachings concerning love might be construed as advocating an ethic of universal benevolence—the idea behind the consequentialist moral theory that we will consider in chapters 5 and 6. Mortimer, recall, claims that the Bible contains the idea that all humans possess a kind of dignity—an idea that is central in the moral philosophy of Immanuel Kant, which we take up in chapter 8. The idea that human beings are created by God and designed to fulfill certain purposes is, of course, an idea to be found in the Bible; this idea is featured in Thomas Aquinas's moral theory, which we examine in chapter 4.

Whereas the divine command theory attempts to ground morality (or at least obligation) on the will of God—his commands—the theory known as moral relativism attempts to ground morality on the will of society. Both views share the idea that morality is importantly connected to the dictates of some authority, but they are otherwise quite different. Moral relativism is the subject of the next chapter.

NOTES

1. The divine *command* theory is a species of a more generic type of moral theory often called "theological voluntarism," according to which morality depends on one or another volitional activity of God. For instance, instead of understanding the nature of right and wrong in terms of God's commands, other forms of the generic view make morality depend on what God *wills* or *intends* with regard to human action. For a discussion of the significance of such differences in the formulation of such theological views, see Murphy, 2008 cited in Further Reading.

2. We might attempt to capture something of the contrast between things with intrinsic value and things having extrinsic value by distinguishing those things with regard to which God issues commands—things having what we might call fundamental goodness or badness—from those things that, because they are instrumental in bringing about what is fundamentally good or bad, can be said to have derivative value. But since this complication does not matter for our purposes, I will ignore it.

3. Strictly speaking, this characterization makes everything that is intrinsically good something that human beings are in a position to do something about. But surely there could be things or states of affairs that are intrinsically good but are beyond the range of what humans can either bring about or preserve (perhaps because they are in some remote corner of the universe that we will never experience). (I thank Robert Audi for calling my attention to this problem.) To fix this defect, either we can restrict these characterizations to only those things, experiences, and states of affairs that humans can do something about, or we could replace reference to what God does and does not command with reference to what God does and does not approve of. (God may approve of all sorts of things that simply do not relate to human existence.) Since it is the divine command theory, I have chosen to express both the principles of right conduct and the principles of value in terms of God's commands. So we are to understand the principles of intrinsic value as restricted in the manner just explained.

4. Throughout, and merely for convenience, I use the masculine pronoun to refer to God.

5. This does not mean that all possible versions of the linguistic argument are as easily refuted. Sophisticated linguistic arguments that cannot be considered here are to be found in, e.g., Adams, 1973, 1979.

6. We study moral relativism and its problems in the next chapter.

7. All references to Plato's *Euthyphro* are from Plato, 1976 (translated version).

8. See for example Zangwill, 2011b.

9. For an elaboration and defense of the sort of view in question, see Adams, 1999.

10. Notice that the concept of goodness does not appear to be a social concept in the way obligation appears to be. This difference is supposed to help explain why the good and the right can be treated differently by divine command theorists. For a discussion of this point, see Adams, 1999, 233.

11. Of course, the arbitrariness problem will arise all over again unless God has some reason why he commands that we perform certain actions from among the ones that are good.

12. Indeed, reflection on the Euthyphro dilemma reveals why, despite initial appearances, the theory is at odds with some basic tenets of theism, giving the theist reason to reject this version of the theory. It might initially seem ironic that the divine command theory conflicts with certain religious tenets, but we just saw from Nucci's study that many (young) fundamentalists implicitly reject the divine command theory in favor of the idea that what is right or wrong is not just a matter of God's commands. Notice that in the Nucci study featuring Amish and Mennonite children who were asked about the deontic status of actions on the supposition that God had not commanded we refrain from doing those actions, their answers suggest that God's commands play no role in explaining the wrongness of actions in question.

13. See also Murphy, 2008, who raises worries about whether the restricted version of the divine command theory is well motivated, worries having to do with the alleged social nature of obligation.

FURTHER READING

Philosophical Literature

Adams, Robert M. 1973. "A Modified Divine Command Theory of Ethical Wrongness." In *Religion and Morality: A Collection of Essays*, ed. Gene Outka and John P. Reeder. New York: Doubleday. Reprinted in Helm, 1981. A sophisticated defense of the divine command theory.

———. 1999. *Finite and Infinite Goods: A Framework for Ethics*. Oxford: Oxford University Press. A defense of restricted divine command theory.

Alston, William P. 1990. "Some Suggestions for Divine Command Theorists." In *Christian Theism and the Problems of Philosophy*, ed. Michael D. Beaty. Notre Dame, IN: University of Notre Dame Press. Alston's main suggestion is to restrict the divine command theory in the manner explained in this chapter.

Berg, Jonathan. 1993. "How Can Morality Depend on Religion?" In *A Companion to Ethics*, ed. Peter Singer. Cambridge: Blackwell. Covers much the same ground as this chapter. Includes a select bibliography.

Hare, John. 2006. *God and Morality: A Philosophical History*. Oxford: Blackwell. Provides more historical detail than contained in his *Stanford Encyclopedia* article, as well as a defense of divine command theory.

———. 2009. "Religion and Morality." *The Stanford Encyclopedia of Philosophy*, ed. E. N. Zalta. http://plato.stanford.edu. An informative historical overview of views about the connection between morality and religion in Western thought.

Helm, Paul, ed. 1981. *Divine Commands and Morality*. New York: Oxford University Press. Twelve essays (many of them at an advanced level) by leading philosophers debating the divine command theory. Includes a useful introductory essay by the editor plus a bibliography.

Murphy, Mark. 2002. *An Essay on Divine Authority*. Ithaca, NY: Cornell University Press. An exploration of whether and to what extent God has authority over created rational beings.

———. 2008. "Theological Voluntarism." *The Stanford Encyclopedia of Philosophy*, ed. E. N. Zalta. http://plato.stanford.edu. Highly recommended as the next item on this list to read for a concise yet thorough overview of the various philosophical views that make God central to morality.

Quinn, Philip. 1978. *Divine Commands and Moral Requirements*. Oxford: Oxford University Press. A sophisticated defense of the divine command theory.

———. 2006. "Theological Voluntarism." *Oxford Handbook of Ethical Theory*, ed. David Copp. Oxford: Oxford University Press. Very readable overview and defense of a restricted form of divine command theory. Less comprehensive in its coverage of certain aspects of theological voluntarism than Murphy's article of the same title.

Sinnott-Armstrong, Walter. 2009. *Morality Without God?* Oxford: Oxford University Press. A short, lively defense of the view that morality exists independently of God. Highly recommended.

Wielenberg, Eric. 2005. *Value and Virtue in a Godless Universe*. Cambridge: Cambridge University Press. Chapter 2, "God and Morality," develops a thorough and penetrating critical examination of the attempt to establish a connection between God and morality. Of particular interest is the author's criticisms of various versions of divine command theory, including the sort of restricted view defended by Adams.

Empirical Literature

Nucci, Larry. 1986. "Children's Conceptions of Morality, Social Convention, and Religious Prescription." In *Moral Dilemmas: Philosophical and Psychological Reconsiderations of the Development of Moral Reasoning*, ed. C. Harding. Chicago: Precedent Press. Some results of this study are presented in section 5 of this chapter.

3

Moral Relativism

Studies of the moral beliefs and practices of various cultures reveal that different cultures often have very different moral beliefs and attitudes about the same sort of action. Consider a few examples.

- *Honor killings.* Members of some groups think that if an unwed woman becomes pregnant, it is the obligation of her family to kill her to restore family honor.
- *Parricide.* Anthropologists report that many cultures practice parricide—killing one's parents—once the parents become aged. It is a practice that members of the community, including the parents, take to be morally permissible and perhaps even morally required.
- *Premarital sex and wife sharing.* Some cultures do not think that there is anything wrong with premarital sex; indeed, it is condoned as an important and normal part of courtship. Moreover, in some cultures, it is considered a great honor if one's wife engages in sexual relations with other men.
- *Cannibalism.* There are numerous documented cases of cultures that engage in the eating of human flesh. Members of such cultures think the practice not only morally permissible but in some cases obligatory.
- *Treatment of animals.* Again, anthropologists report that many cultures are indifferent to the suffering of animals. For instance, in recent times there have been some groups who pluck live chickens in the belief that their meat will be particularly succulent. Other cultures condone "games" that involve inflicting intense pain on animals.

This short list is but a sampling of practices that are either permitted or required in certain cultures but are condemned as immoral in many others. The practices of infanticide, abortion, homosexuality, female circumcision, usury, and public

41

nudity also meet with different moral reactions among different cultures; this list could be extended. Such examples make clear not only that there are some intercultural differences in moral belief but also that many such differences are about matters of fundamental moral importance.

Reflection on such intercultural diversity in moral belief has led many anthropologists and some philosophers to embrace a moral theory typically called moral relativism. What is moral relativism? How exactly do cases of cultural diversity in moral belief lead to relativism? Is moral relativism plausible? Such questions are the main focus of this chapter. Let us begin our study of moral relativism with an explanation of this type of moral theory.

1. WHAT IS MORAL RELATIVISM?

Unfortunately, in ethics the term "relativism" is used as a label for quite a variety of views and ideas that differ in important ways. We shall consider some of these views and ideas as we proceed, but for the time being we are concerned with a normative moral theory that is appropriately called moral relativism (also referred to as ethical relativism). Again, there are different versions of moral relativism, but we shall be mainly concerned with the version according to which the rightness or wrongness of actions ultimately depends on the moral code of the culture to which one belongs. According to this view, then, the moral code of one's culture is the touchstone of moral truth and falsity when it comes to questions of right and wrong. And this implies that if two cultures differ in their moral codes, actions that are right for members of one of the two cultures may be wrong for members of the other.[1]

In the previous chapter on divine command theory, we distinguished unrestricted from restricted versions of the theory. We will be making a similar distinction in this chapter. Most of what follows will focus on an unrestricted version of moral relativism, a version which is sometimes referred to as "moral conventionalism." Later in the chapter, we will briefly consider a less radical, restricted version that gives up some of the claims featured in the unrestricted version. So, let us begin with an unrestricted version of relativism by explaining some of its central concepts. (For the time being, I will refer to this version simply as moral relativism.)

Moral relativism makes right and wrong depend ultimately on the moral code of a culture. What is meant by talk of a culture's moral code? Since cultures are made up of individuals, consider first the moral code of an individual. The very idea of having a *code* of some sort involves accepting a system of rules or norms. Most adults accept various codes for behavior, codes of etiquette and moral codes being the most obvious examples. We can understand an individual's moral code in the following way.

Individuals have moral beliefs about the rightness and wrongness of actions that vary in their generality. Some moral beliefs are about specific, concrete actions; others are more general beliefs about types of actions. Let us say that to have a general moral belief about the morality of a type of action is to accept a *moral norm* regarding such actions.[2] Typical moral norms might include *lying is wrong (unless one has a good reason)*, *intentionally killing a person is wrong (except in self-defense)*, and *one ought to help those in need of assistance when one can do so at little or no cost to oneself.*

Of the moral norms an individual accepts, we can plausibly suppose that some are more basic than others in the sense that some are (or can be) derived from others, while some are underived and represent an individual's basic moral commitments. For instance, one might accept a norm prohibiting embezzlement because one recognizes that embezzlement is a form of stealing and one accepts a moral norm to the effect that stealing is wrong. In this case, the norm about embezzlement is (for the individual in question) a nonbasic moral norm that can be derived from the more general norm about stealing. If the moral norm about stealing is not itself based on any other, more basic norm the individual accepts, it is basic for that individual.

Since, as noted above, a code for behavior is basically a set of rules or norms governing behavior, let us simply define an individual's moral code (that he or she possesses at some particular time) as the set of those moral norms that the individual accepts (at the time in question).

There is much more to having a moral code than simply accepting a bunch of norms. In addition, having a moral code involves being disposed to act in certain ways and to feel a certain range of emotions. For instance, if someone sincerely accepts a moral norm prohibiting gossip, then that person is disposed to avoid engaging in gossip. Moreover, such a person who knowingly violates the norm in question is likely to experience feelings of guilt or perhaps shame as a proper response to the violation. Such remarks only hint at a very complex phenomenon that we need not investigate here. Although having a moral code is not simply a matter of having general moral beliefs about types of actions, the norms that such beliefs express will be our main focus in what follows.

We can now define the notion of a culture's moral code by specifying how this code is a function of the moral codes of the individuals who are members of the culture. For each individual, we make a list that includes the types of actions morally prohibited and the types of actions morally required by that individual's moral code. We then compare these lists, looking for those moral norms that are widely accepted among the members of the culture in question. Having collected the widely shared moral norms of a culture, we select that subset of moral norms that represents the widely shared basic moral norms of individuals who are members of the culture. The set of basic moral norms represents the ultimate touchstone of rightness and wrongness for the culture in question, and so it is in terms of this set of norms that we can characterize moral relativism. So if we let C refer to a culture, we can spell out the principles of right conduct for moral relativism this way:

Theory of Right Conduct

An action A, performed by a member of C, is *obligatory* if and only if (and because), according to the basic moral norms of C, A is required.

An action A, performed by a member of C, is *wrong* if and only if (and because), according to the basic moral norms of C, A is prohibited.

An action A, performed by a member of C, is *optional* if and only if (and because), according to the moral norms of C, A is neither required nor prohibited.

In what follows, it will be useful to express the central idea of moral relativism as economically as possible; we can do this as follows:

MR What is right and what is wrong for the members of a culture depends on (is ultimately determined by) the basic moral norms of their culture.

In understanding what moral relativism is all about, it is important to note that the above moral principles are intended as moral criteria—as specifying what it is that *makes* an action right or wrong. The relativist makes parallel claims about goodness and badness. What makes something good or bad (for an individual who is a member of some culture) are the basic norms of goodness and badness that are part of the moral code of the individual's culture.

William G. Sumner (1840–1910), an anthropologist, nicely summarizes the basic idea of moral relativism when he writes:

It is most important to notice that, for the people of a time and place, their own mores are always good, or rather that for them there can be no question of the goodness or badness of their mores. The reason is because the standards of good and right are in the mores. (Sumner, [1906] 1959, 58)[3]

Notice that Sumner begins this passage with a remark that he immediately qualifies—in fact, corrects. It would be inconsistent for the moral relativist to say of a culture's basic moral norms (its basic mores) that they are good, because this would imply that there are norms of goodness that are independent of the mores in question and that can be used to evaluate those mores. But this is precisely what the relativist denies and what Sumner goes on to make explicit. With regard to the basic moral norms of the culture, one cannot sensibly raise questions about their goodness or badness (or their rightness or wrongness) since they represent the very standards of good and bad, right and wrong applicable in the culture that accepts them.

Thus, moral relativism is a moral theory that presents a positive account of the nature of right and wrong, good and bad. But there is more to the relativist's stance in ethics than is expressed in its theory of right conduct. Moral relativism is opposed to what we may call the universality thesis:

UT There are moral norms whose correctness or validity is independent of the moral norms a culture does or might accept, and thus they express universally valid moral standards that apply to all cultures.[4]

Notice that this thesis does not specify whether the universally valid norms in question serve to determine the rightness and wrongness of all or most all actions. The thesis that there are such moral norms is what may be called the single true morality thesis:

STM There is a single true morality for all human beings featuring moral norms that are universally valid and that specify for most if not all cases whether an action is right or wrong.

The universality thesis might be true, even if STM is false. And this point will come up when we turn in section 8 to a version of restricted moral relativism.[5] For the time being, what is important to note is that it is the denial of UT that prompts the (unrestricted) relativist's account of right and wrong action. After all, if there are no universally valid moral norms that apply to all cultures, then apparently the only standards available for determining what is right and wrong, good and bad are represented by the moral norms that individual cultures happen to accept. As we shall see, the denial of the universality thesis plays a crucial role in the main argument for moral relativism.

However, before we consider this argument, let us sharpen our understanding of moral relativism by contrasting it with what I will call the context sensitivity thesis.

2. THE CONTEXT SENSITIVITY THESIS

It is uncontroversial that what is right or wrong for someone to do can often depend on one's circumstances, including facts about one's culture. I am going to call such dependence the context sensitivity thesis. The important point about this thesis is that it is not equivalent to moral relativism, nor does it imply relativism. Since failure to understand this point leads to confusion, it is well worth our time to examine this thesis and compare it to moral relativism. Let us begin with some illustrations of the thesis in question.

What is right or wrong to do in a situation depends on certain facts about the situation in question. Suppose that you are an expert swimmer and one day while walking along a deserted beach, you see a young child flailing away in the water some twenty yards from shore, struggling for air, and obviously in immediate danger of drowning. You surely have a moral obligation to rescue the child. But suppose it is I who am walking along the same deserted beach—someone who can't swim. Since I would almost certainly drown if I tried to rescue the child, I do not have an obligation to go into the water to save the child (though I have an obligation to run or call for help). So here the particular type of action that you ought to do is not the same as the particular type of action that I ought to do.

Of course, the reason our specific obligations differ in this case is that there is a difference between us that in this case is morally significant: you can swim, I can't. And it is this fact about our situation that helps explain why you have an obligation to perform a certain specific action while I do not. So sometimes differences in facts about agents can affect what it is morally right or wrong to do in a particular context.

But the fact that what is right or wrong depends in this way on facts about agents has nothing to do with moral relativism.

The point I am making is often explained by pointing out that moral norms or principles have different implications depending on differences in situation or context. The following is a plausible moral principle of aid:

> One ought to help those who are in need of help when one is in a position to do so and can avoid serious risk of life and limb to oneself.

Suppose for the moment that this principle is universally valid—valid independently of the moral code of any culture. Still, this principle, when applied to the two cases just described, yields different moral verdicts about what each of us ought to do. In short, the application of moral principles will yield different moral verdicts in different contexts depending on the morally relevant details of the context. This is uncontroversial and something that is compatible with the denial of moral relativism.

For another example of this type of context sensitivity, consider the morality of insults.[6] It is plausible to suppose that it is morally wrong to insult someone. Let us suppose that this is true independently of the moral code of any culture. However, notice that what counts as an insult will vary from culture to culture. In some places, for a student to address a professor by her or his first name would be insulting to the professor. In other places, with different cultural norms for what counts as an insult, such address may not be considered an insult. This is yet another illustration of the thesis of context sensitivity and is compatible, like the previous example, with supposing that morality is not relative, that there are moral principles that are transculturally correct.

The point being made here is simple. The rightness or wrongness of particular actions performed in some specific context depends in part on certain nonmoral facts that obtain in the context in question. The same point can be made in connection with the application of moral principles. When we apply moral principles to particular cases, nonmoral facts about agents and their environment (including their culture) can be relevant in determining the morality of actions. For clarity's sake, let us formulate what I am calling the *context sensitivity thesis* as follows:

> **CS** The rightness or wrongness of an action (performed in some particular context) partly depends on nonmoral facts that hold in the context in question—facts concerning agents and their circumstances.

This thesis goes by other names, including *situational relativism, environmental relativism, application relativism,* and *circumstantial relativism.* I prefer to avoid using such terminology since using the term "relativism" invites confusion of this thesis with moral relativism.

In addition to the labels, what sometimes leads to confusion are such remarks as "What is right for me may not be what is right for someone else," and "What is right in one culture may not be right in another culture." These remarks are ambiguous—they can be interpreted in more than one way. Interpreted as saying something uncontroversial, they are most likely referring to CS: what is right in one culture may not be right in some other culture since, for example, specific actions or remarks that count as insulting and hence wrong for the members of one culture may not count as insults for the members of another culture. Again, we might interpret these remarks as referring to the facts of intercultural differences in moral belief: what is believed right in one culture may not be believed right in another. Again, this claim is uncontroversial.

But sometimes such remarks are intended to express moral relativism. The danger to be avoided, then, is sliding from the thought that the remarks in question express something uncontroversial and even enlightened about morality to the thought that moral relativism is true.

What about the truth of moral relativism?

3. THE MORAL DIVERSITY THESIS

As already noted, diversity in moral belief across cultures is responsible for leading some thinkers to accept moral relativism. In the following three sections, we will examine the attempt to infer relativism from such diversity, but let us first consider more closely the issue of intercultural diversity in moral belief.

The thesis that some cultures accept moral beliefs that conflict with the moral beliefs of other cultures is often called *descriptive relativism* because it purports to state an anthropological fact about cultures that can be scientifically investigated and described. What is of particular interest here is the two-part thesis that (1) there are deep-going, fundamental conflicts in moral belief across cultures—conflicts at the level of basic moral norms—and (2) that such conflicts are widespread.[7] This idea can be expressed by what I will call the *moral diversity thesis*:

> **MD** (1) The moral codes of some cultures include basic moral norms that conflict with the basic moral norms that are part of the moral codes of other cultures. (2) Such fundamental conflicts are widespread.

One main argument for moral relativism is based on this thesis. Before considering this argument, however, let us consider the idea of moral norms in conflict.

In order to represent moral conflicts as involving conflicting moral norms, we need to impute to a culture's moral code norms of permission. Let me explain. Moral norms are typically of two sorts: (1) norms of prohibition, which are concerned with actions that are wrong or forbidden, and (2) norms of requirement, which specify obligatory actions. For actions that are neither wrong nor obligatory—for actions that are morally optional—we normally don't formulate what might be called norms of permission. Actions that we are permitted but not required to perform are simply all of those actions not mentioned in either norms of prohibition or norms of requirement.

Now whenever the moral code of one culture includes a norm requiring that actions of certain sorts be performed (e.g., the eating of human flesh under certain circumstances) while the moral code of some other culture includes a norm forbidding such actions, we have a conflict of moral norms. But there are also cases in which the norms of one culture include either a norm of prohibition or a norm of requirement regarding some type of action while another culture simply lacks a moral norm regarding such an action. To be able to represent such cases as involving a conflict of moral norms, I am suggesting that we impute to the second culture a norm of permission.

Thus, when it comes to intercultural conflicts of moral norms, there are three types of case to consider. First, it may be that with regard to some type of action, one culture accepts a norm of prohibition while the other culture accepts a conflicting norm of requirement. For example, one culture may prohibit the eating of human flesh, while another culture may (under certain circumstances) require such an action. Second, there are cases in which, with regard to some type of action, one culture may accept a norm of requirement (e.g., that its members render aid to strangers in need) while the other culture may only (implicitly) accept a norm of permission regarding such action. Finally, there may be cases in which, with respect to some type of action, one culture accepts a norm of prohibition (e.g., regarding homosexuality) while the other culture accepts a conflicting norm of permission.

We have just been focusing on cases where a moral conflict is due to conflicting norms about the deontic status of actions. But another form of conflict or disagreement, and one that is perhaps more widespread, involves cases in which two cultures share many or most of the same moral values, say a respect for privacy and a respect for freedom of speech, but where the cultures differ in the importance they attach to these values. Here we have what I will call "moral priority conflict." Later in this chapter (see section 8), we will revisit conflicts of this sort. For the time being, most of what follows will feature examples of conflicts of moral norms of the sort illustrated in the previous paragraph.

Having explained the idea of moral norms in conflict featured in the moral diversity thesis, let us now begin to explore how the moral diversity thesis and moral relativism are related. In the next three sections, we will consider whether the moral diversity thesis, if true, provides good, or perhaps conclusive, evidence for the truth of moral relativism. But to help sharpen our understanding of moral relativism, let us consider whether the truth of moral relativism commits one to the moral diversity thesis.

Our first question is: If moral relativism is true, does it follow that the moral diversity thesis must also be true? One might initially think so, but strictly speaking, moral relativism is compatible with widespread agreement in the basic moral norms accepted by different cultures. Moral relativism, as I have explained, makes a dependency claim: it says that what makes some action right or wrong (for the members of some culture at a time) depends ultimately on the moral code (in particular, the basic moral norms) of the culture in question. Whether or not different cultures accept different and conflicting basic moral norms is an empirical matter and does not affect the truth of relativism. Thus, even if it turns out (now or sometime in the future) that all cultures accept the same set of basic moral norms, moral relativism might still be true.

To see this more clearly, let us consider an analogy. We all know that when it comes to driving a vehicle, different countries have different rules, and that these different rules are equally valid. According to the rules that govern driving a vehicle in the United States, one is supposed to drive on the right side of the road. In England, the corresponding rule requires that one drive on the left side of the road. It would be silly to ask which rule expresses the truly correct way to drive on roads, as though one of these rules must be mistaken. Rather, the rules in question are purely conventional. Now if, in the future, England were to change its rule about driving and accept the same rule as the United States, and indeed, if every country were to adopt the same rule about driving on the right side of the road, the universal acceptance of such a rule would not count against such a rule being purely conventional.

The same point applies to moral relativism. If we find out that all cultures accept the same basic moral code (or if in the future, this comes to pass), this would not show that relativism is false. What the moral relativist would say in light of this possibility is that even though as a matter of fact all cultures at the present time happen to embrace the same moral code, it is possible for there to be a culture whose moral code differs from the one enjoying widespread currency. And, adds the relativist, for any such culture, what is right and wrong, good and bad would depend on its moral code.

But even though it is possible for moral relativism to be true when MD is false, the most powerful reason for accepting relativism is the belief that MD is true. Reasons for supposing that MD is true come from the field of anthropology, so let us consider the connection between anthropology and moral relativism.

4. ANTHROPOLOGY AND MORAL RELATIVISM

The bearing of work in anthropology on moral theory in general, and moral relativism in particular, is more complex than one might initially suppose. My plan is to begin with a rather simple argument for moral relativism based on anthropology that, despite the appeal and popularity of the argument, is flawed. Since I think the flawed argument in question does not adequately express the real motivation leading from work in anthropology to moral relativism, I want to consider how the relativist might best express the core idea that prompts relativism. Doing so will lead us, in the following section, to clarify the sorts of intercultural moral disagreements that are offered in support of moral relativism; then in section 6 I will present what I take to be the strongest version of the anthropologist's argument.

The work of anthropologists makes clear that moral beliefs and attitudes vary across cultures and, in some cases, the differences are quite striking. We began the chapter with some examples of intercultural differences in moral belief and attitude, and reflection on such differences may prompt the following line of reasoning.

The Anthropologist's Argument (version 1)

1. Different cultures have different moral codes; in particular, the moral codes of some cultures include basic moral norms that conflict with the basic moral norms of other cultures, and such fundamental conflicts are widespread (= MD).
2. If MD is true, then there are no universally valid moral norms applying to all cultures (= denial of UT).
3. If there are no universally valid moral norms applying to all cultures (= denial of UT), then what is right and what is wrong for the members of a culture depends on the basic moral norms of their culture (= MR).

Thus,

4. Moral relativism (MR) is true.

Because this argument attempts to support moral relativism by appeal to nonmoral claims from anthropology—factual claims about moral diversity—it represents an appeal to the standard of external support (explained in section 7 of chapter 1). Is the argument a good one?[8]

One source of difficulty is premise 2, which asserts that intercultural disagreement or conflict about some matter of fundamental moral importance entails that there is no single truth about the matter in question. But why should mere difference in belief over some issue entail that there is no single correct belief about that issue? Different cultures have had (and may still have) different beliefs about the shape of the earth, some believing that it is flat, others believing that it is spherical, others perhaps believing something else. But from the fact that there are differences in belief about the shape of the earth, we do not first conclude that there is no single truth about its shape and then (as in the above argument) go on to conclude that the truth about the shape of the earth is relative—that it is literally flat for those who believe it is flat, spherical for those who have this belief, and so on. In other words, in general we do not suppose that mere difference in belief about a subject means that there is no single truth about that subject. So unless we are given some reason why we should suppose that a disagreement in moral belief is a legitimate basis for thinking that there is no single truth about morality, we should deny the second premise of this argument.

Some critics also raise questions about the truth of the first premise. It is clear that there are cross-cultural differences in moral belief about certain actions. Some cultures, for example, find nothing wrong in the practice of wife sharing; others do. But the thesis of moral diversity claims not merely that there are differences across cultures in their moral beliefs about various types of action but also that we find differences in the *basic* moral norms accepted by different cultures. To understand the significance of the thesis of moral diversity and why, despite the fact that cultures may disagree about the morality of certain types of actions, they may not really disagree in their basic moral norms, we need to consider the phenomenon of moral disagreement in more detail.

5. UNDERSTANDING MORAL DISAGREEMENTS

The thesis of moral diversity asserts that there is some intercultural conflict at the level of basic moral norms. And moreover, it asserts that such conflict is widespread. Now one might suppose that the work of anthropologists in describing different moral beliefs, attitudes, and practices of different cultures easily and plainly establishes the moral diversity thesis. However, this issue is more complicated, and hence more controversial, than it may at first appear. To see why, we need to distinguish what may be called *fundamental moral disagreement* from *nonfundamental moral disagreement.*

Nonfundamental Moral Disagreements

Imagine that you and I disagree about the morality of capital punishment: I think it is morally wrong, and you do not. Our disagreement may stem from the fact that we disagree about certain nonmoral factual matters. Suppose, then, that I believe that capital punishment has no positive social benefits and, in particular, that it is not an effective crime deterrent. And suppose that I accept as a basic moral norm the following:

1. In response to violations of its laws, a society ought to employ only those punishments that have overall beneficial consequences for society (= P).

This norm, together with my nonmoral belief about the effects of capital punishment,

2. Capital punishment does not have overall beneficial consequences for society.

lead me to conclude that

3. Capital punishment ought to be abolished.

Now like me, you accept the above basic moral norm P, but you disagree with me about the deterrent effects of capital punishment, so you reason as follows:

1. In response to violations of its laws, a society ought to employ only those punishments that have overall beneficial consequences for society (= P).
2. Capital punishment, because it is an effective crime deterrent, does have overall beneficial consequences for society.

Thus,

3. It is not the case that capital punishment ought to be abolished.

This simple example is supposed to illustrate a *nonfundamental moral disagreement*. You and I agree in our basic convictions about the morality of punishment; our disagreement about the morality of capital punishment is due to differences in nonmoral beliefs about this kind of punishment. The thing to notice about this disagreement is that were one of us to change our mind about the overall social benefits of capital punishment—were you to become convinced by relevant empirical research that this practice is not an effective crime deterrent and that it possesses no other social benefits—then you should come to agree with me about the morality of capital punishment. Because our disagreement here is rooted in a disagreement about a nonmoral factual matter that is suitable for scientific investigation, it is one that is rationally resolvable. It gets resolved once we find out the truth about the social effects of capital punishment.

Fundamental Moral Disagreements

A *fundamental moral disagreement* between two parties is one rooted in the basic moral norms of the parties in question. It is thus a disagreement that would persist even if both parties agreed about all of the relevant nonmoral facts about the disputed issue. Again, consider a moral disagreement over capital punishment. Only this time suppose that you and I agree about the social consequences of this practice; we agree, let us suppose, that it has no significant deterrent effect on crime. Still, we disagree about the morality of capital punishment because we accept different moral norms concerning punishment. To see this more clearly, suppose that instead of P, you accept the following norm:

P* Punishments for crimes ought to involve, whenever possible, inflicting harm on the wrongdoer that is equivalent to the harm that the wrongdoer inflicted on his or her victim(s).

This principle, together with the belief that in cases of murder the death of the murderer is the only penalty equivalent to the crime, leads to the conclusion that capital punishment is obligatory in such cases and hence not morally wrong. Now if the moral conclusion I reach about capital punishment is based on P and the conclusion you reach is based on P*, then our disagreement results from a disagreement in our basic moral norms. And when a moral disagreement stems from a disagreement over basic moral norms, the moral disagreement is fundamental.

Is the Moral Diversity Thesis True?

Recall that the moral diversity thesis is composed of two claims. The first claim says that there are cases of intercultural moral disagreement that are fundamental (that the basic moral norms of some cultures conflict with those of other cultures), and the second claim says that such disagreements are widespread. So, having illustrated and explained the difference between a nonfundamental and a fundamental moral disagreement between individuals, let us focus on the first claim of the MD thesis. The main thing to notice is that the fact that two cultures disagree about some moral issue does not automatically mean that the disagreement stems from a disagreement over basic moral norms. Consider the practice of putting one's parents to death once they reach a certain age. Suppose that most, if not all, of the members of some culture believe that this practice is morally obligatory. Our own culture does not hold such a moral belief and, in fact, holds that it is morally wrong to engage in such killing. Because this intercultural disagreement is rather striking, one might be tempted to conclude that our culture accepts as a basic moral norm something like the following:

> One ought to treat one's elders with respect, no matter their age.

Furthermore, it may seem that the other culture in question rejects this moral norm and that this is what explains the intercultural difference in moral belief about killing one's parents. It may seem that we have here an example of a fundamental moral disagreement, indicating a conflict of basic moral norms.

However, this diagnosis of the disagreement is too hasty. To see this, suppose that the culture in question believes in an afterlife full of activities like hunting and playing and that one has the body in the afterlife that one last had in this life. This nonmoral belief about the afterlife, together with the above norm of respect, would lead one to conclude that one ought to kill one's parents once they get to be a certain age, before their bodies become too decrepit to enjoy the afterlife. Thus, what may at first appear to be a case of fundamental moral disagreement between two cultures may turn out to be nonfundamental.[9]

With this in mind, let us now briefly reconsider the thesis of moral diversity. It says that the *basic* moral norms of some cultures often conflict with those of other cultures. If there are such differences, the cultures in question will disagree fundamentally about the morality of certain actions. Now clearly different cultures do sometimes disagree over the morality of actions, but the crucial question is: How many such disagreements are fundamental, thus indicating intercultural conflicts in basic moral norms? This brings us to the second claim of the MD thesis.

Perhaps intercultural moral disagreements can almost always be explained in terms of intercultural differences in the relevant nonmoral beliefs, as in the case of the treatment of one's parents. If so, and the second claim of the MD thesis is false, that is, if all or most intercultural disagreement is nonfundamental, and so can be traced to differences in nonmoral factual beliefs, then the overall two-part thesis of moral diversity would turn out to be false. Granted, the first part of the thesis may be true, but if there are very few fundamental moral conflicts across cultures, then arguably they can be explained as being about moral issues that are extremely difficult to resolve, even though there is a single moral truth about these few disputed issues. It is the belief that there is *widespread* intercultural conflict in basic moral norms that leads some anthropologists and philosophers to embrace moral relativism. Is there such widespread conflict in basic moral norms across cultures?

The issue is an empirical one, to be decided by available evidence. Although some anthropologists, particularly those who embrace moral relativism, have stressed intercultural differences and conflicts in moral norms, other anthropologists have wanted to stress intercultural similarities. So, for example, anthropologist Clyde Kluckhohn (1905–1960) noted that

> Every culture has a concept of murder, distinguishing this from execution, killing in war, and other "justifiable homicides." The notions of incest and other regulations upon sexual behavior, of prohibitions upon untruth under defined circumstances, of restitution and reciprocity, of mutual obligations between parents and children—these and many other moral concepts are altogether universal. (Kluckhohn, 1955, 672)

Writing in 1959, philosopher Richard Brandt (1910–1997), having examined the anthropological evidence for the thesis of moral diversity as well as for the thesis, expressed by Kluckhohn, that there is widespread intercultural agreement over basic moral norms, concluded that

> no anthropologist has offered what we should regard as really an adequate account of a single case, clearly showing there is ultimate disagreement in moral principle. Of course, we must remember that this lack of information is just as serious for any claim that there is world-wide agreement on some principle. (Brandt, 1959, 102)

More recently, Michele Moody-Adams has argued that there are deep methodological problems that stand in the way of establishing the moral diversity thesis (what she refers to as "descriptive relativism"). She writes:

> The most serious obstacles to formulating contrastive judgments about the moral practices of particular human groups, and to establishing the truth of descriptive relativism, reflect a difficulty peculiar to the study of cultures: that of deciding who—if anyone—has the "authority" to represent the defining principles, especially the basic moral principles, of a given culture. (Moody-Adams, 1997, 43)

Moody-Adams goes on to argue that because of the complexity of cultures and the problem of determining a moral authority for a culture, it is extremely difficult, if not impossible, to gather the kind of empirical evidence that would be needed to support the moral diversity thesis.

Arguably, the methodological obstacles Moody-Adams is pointing to can be overcome by those investigating the moralities of various cultures. And very recent work in the social sciences may present us with cases of fundamental moral disagreement. For instance, some research of recent vintage does seem methodologically sound and also seems to support claim 1 of the moral diversity thesis. For instance, Richard E. Nisbett and Dov Cohen (1996) have investigated certain patterns of violence in the U.S. South that appear to be more common than in the North, as well as Southern versus Northern attitudes toward violence and insults. Their data includes: homicide rates of White male Southerners compared to their White Northern counterparts resulting from arguments compared to homicides that occur in other contexts (e.g., robberies), surveys of both groups about when violence is justified, legal scholarship comparing North and South about when the use of violence is justified in defense of oneself or one's property, and a controlled laboratory study involving levels of cortisol and testosterone in saliva samples (hormones associated with high levels of stress, anxiety, and aggression) taken from Northerners and Southerners after subjects had been verbally abused. In assessing this data as it bears on the moral diversity thesis, John Doris and Alexandra Plakias (2008) argue that the data points to a fundamental disagreement between many Northerners and many Southerners over the permissibility of interpersonal violence. Many Southerners seem to embrace an "honor ethic" that is significantly more permissive in the use of violence in cases of insult or trespass compared to norms governing the use of violence accepted by many Northerners. Of course, even if Doris and Plakias are correct in arguing that the disagreement here is fundamental (they consider and reject various explanations which, if true, would show that the disagreement is likely nonfundamental), it is but one case. To establish the moral diversity thesis would require evidence of widespread fundamental disagreements, which (as yet) is apparently far from being firmly established.

6. THE ANTHROPOLOGIST'S ARGUMENT RECONSIDERED

But let us suppose that the thesis of moral diversity is true and there is significant intercultural conflict in the basic moral norms across many cultures. We noted in section 4 that there is a problem going from the thesis of moral diversity (MD) to the denial of the universality thesis (UT). Just because different cultures accept different and conflicting basic moral norms, and so work with different basic moral assumptions, the claim that there are no universally valid moral norms does not logically follow. After all, as we pointed out earlier, differences in belief about the shape of the earth or about the movements of the planets do not tempt us to conclude that there is no single truth about such matters and that it is all just a matter of what your culture believes. So why accept this kind of inference in the case of morals?

Suppose the advocate of the anthropologist's argument were simply attempting to infer the denial of the universality thesis from MD as represented in the second premise of version 1 of the argument. Then this point would be decisive against the argument. However, there seems to be more to the argument than is expressed in the formulation from section 4. Let me explain.

Those who are impressed with what they take to be deep-going, fundamental moral disagreements across cultures are also likely to hold the view that such disagreements cannot be resolved in the way in which disagreements about, say, the shape of the earth or the movement of the planets can be resolved. With respect to differences in belief about the shape of the earth, we have ways of explaining why one party to the disagreement is mistaken. Prescientific cultures lacked the kind of evidence we now possess about the earth's shape and so came to accept a false belief based on limited evidence. This kind of mistake—inference based on limited evidence—can be corrected in principle by rational means. Thus, disagreements between two cultures over the shape of the earth, and many other such scientific matters, are capable of being resolved by rational means. In the case of scientific disputes, rational means include the various methods and procedures characteristic of good science. Furthermore, the fact that such disagreements are rationally resolvable is to be expected given two further assumptions. First, we assume that with regard to matters like the shape of the earth, the movements of the planets, and many more such matters about the universe, there is some single set of facts or truths about our universe out there waiting to be discovered. And, second, we assume that we are capable of getting at the truth. These assumptions would explain why, over time at least, there is convergence in scientific belief about our universe.

The moral relativist will now insist that there is a crucial difference between disagreements over scientific matters, on one hand, and moral disagreements, on the other. As just explained, the former are in principle resolvable by rational methods and procedures, but (so the relativist claims) this is not so in the case of many moral disagreements—in particular those involving a conflict between basic moral norms. So, it is not merely the fact that there are fundamental moral disagreements between cultures, but that such disagreements are (unlike disputes in science) rationally irresolvable. Moreover, what this indicates, according to the relativist, is that when it comes to such disputes, there is no single moral truth about the matter being disputed, for if there were, we would expect more intercultural moral agreement at the level of basic moral norms than the anthropological evidence suggests. Thus, moral truth is plausibly relativized to the basic norms of individual cultures. In short, the irresolvability by rational means of certain moral disagreements indicates that there are no culture-independent moral norms to be discovered.

So, based on these reflections, here is an improved version of the anthropologist's argument that captures this idea about irresolvability.

The Anthropologist's Argument (version 2)

1. Different cultures have different moral codes; in particular, the moral codes of some cultures include basic moral norms that conflict with the basic moral norms of other cultures, and such fundamental conflicts are widespread (= MD).
2. Such conflicts cannot be resolved by rational means.

Thus,

3. There are widespread and rationally irresolvable intercultural conflicts over basic moral norms.
4. The best explanation for such irresolvable conflicts is: there are no universally valid moral norms applying to all cultures (= denial of UT).
5. If there are no universally valid moral norms applying to all cultures (= denial of UT), then what is right and what is wrong for the members of a culture depends on the basic moral norms of their culture (= MR).

Thus,

6. What is right or wrong depends on the basic moral norms of the culture in which the action is performed (MR).

This version of the anthropologist's argument is an improvement over the first version. In the first version, premise 2 just claims, without explanation, that the denial of the universality thesis follows immediately from the moral diversity thesis, which, as we have seen, is problematic. In the new version, the denial of the universality thesis is being proposed in premise 4 as the best explanation of the apparent irresolvability of the sort of deep-going conflict mentioned in the moral diversity thesis. This way of arguing for the denial of the universality thesis allows the relativist to plausibly explain why moral disagreements differ importantly from scientific disagreements. So, if we grant the thesis of moral diversity, the case for moral relativism (based on anthropological evidence) depends on whether such disagreements in basic moral norms can be rationally resolved.

A Nonrelativist Response

In responding to this argument, then, the nonrelativist, who accepts the universality thesis, is going to question premise 2. In doing so, she will have to explain how such disagreements about moral issues can be rationally resolved, at least in principle. What means of rational resolution might be available in ethics?

The topic is a large and complex one; indeed, attempts by philosophers to elaborate and defend nonrelativist moral theories of right conduct and value can be viewed as attempts to answer this question. For instance, you may recall from the last chapter that according to the divine command theory, rational resolution of moral disagreement involves appealing to facts about God's commands. According to the natural law theory (which we take up in the next chapter), fundamental moral disagreements can in principle be resolved by appeal to facts about the nature of human beings. Other theories to be considered, including consequentialism, Kant's moral theory, and virtue ethics, make other proposals regarding the rational resolution of moral conflicts. Thus, a full answer to this question would involve an examination of the sorts of moral theories featured in this book.

However, for the time being, we can indicate, if only very briefly, how a nonrelativist might attempt to respond to the above argument. To focus our thinking about this matter, let us ask how an individual's basic moral norms might be rationally criticized. Suppose we encounter someone who does not think it is morally wrong for people to engage in activities that inflict pain on lower animals and condones "games" like "chicken pull," described by Richard Brandt.

> In this "game," a chicken is buried in the sand, up to its neck. The contestants ride by on horseback, trying to grab the chicken by the neck and yank it from the sand. When someone succeeds in this, the idea is then for the other contestants to take away from him as much of the chicken as they can. The "winner" is the one who ends up with the most chicken. (Brandt, 1959, 102)

Let us suppose further that the individual who finds nothing morally objectionable about this game and other such treatment of animals does not have nonmoral beliefs about animals that differ from ours. For example, the individual does not believe that chickens and other animals are just nonconscious automata, cleverly designed to emulate genuine pain behavior. Nor does the individual believe that such activities are necessary to please the gods and thus ensure a good harvest. Rather, this individual shares all of our nonmoral beliefs about animals, it is just that his moral code does not include a norm prohibiting such treatment of animals; the individual in question sees nothing wrong with games like chicken pull.

The question is: Can we make sense of the suggestion that this individual is mistaken in thinking that there is nothing morally wrong with painful treatment of animals? Here is one way of doing so. We might begin by noting that proper moral thinking about some issue may require that one have the capacity for thinking sympathetically about the effects of one's actions on creatures that are affected by them and that one engage this capacity in contemplating various courses of action. So, although the person who does not see anything wrong with games like chicken pull may have correct beliefs about the pain caused to animals, he might not properly appreciate such facts owing to a lack of proper sympathy. If exercise of sympathy is involved in properly reasoning about matters of morality, then failing to engage sympathetically with the victims of chicken pull will lead one to mistaken moral convictions about such treatment.

This is but a sketch of how a nonrelativist might attempt to show that individuals can be mistaken in their basic moral convictions. Much more would have to be done in elaborating and defending any such view about proper moral methodology. But the important point here is that we should not assume that the relativist is correct in claiming that in ethics there is no method for rationally resolving moral disagreements, even fundamental ones.

On the basis of what has been said thus far, I think we must conclude that the final verdict is still out on the cogency of the anthropologist's argument.

7. THE PRICE OF MORAL RELATIVISM

What about the plausibility of moral relativism—and remember, we have been examining unrestricted moral relativism, the view that makes all of morality completely dependent on the basic moral norms of a culture? Although I do not think there is a decisive refutation of this type of moral theory, I do think that in accepting unrestricted moral relativism, one must pay a heavy price. Here, I want to focus on three challenges facing this version of relativism: (1) problems having to do with formulating the theory that affect the theory's consistency and determinacy; (2) problems having to do with what I shall call our critical practices concerning moral issues that bear on the standard of intuitive appeal; and, finally, (3) problems having to do with the standard of internal support and explanatory power. Let us take these up in order.

Problems of formulation: consistency and determinacy. According to moral relativism, the rightness or wrongness of actions depends on the moral code of the culture to which the agent belongs. (Similar remarks apply to what is good or bad.) But what counts as one's culture? This question is perhaps not difficult when it comes to small groups that exhibit a high degree of social cohesion. But what counts as the culture of people living in the United States, a country exhibiting a great deal of nonuniformity in moral belief and practice? Should we suppose that all citizens of the United States are members of one, single culture, the American culture? Or perhaps we should carve up cultures by smaller geographical regions of the United States, so that we would have midwestern culture, southern culture, northeastern culture, and so on. Or perhaps culture can be specified in terms of religious affiliation (at least for those who have such an affiliation) since religions involve moral codes. Again, political organizations, like the U.S. Democratic and Republican Parties, would seem to count as cultures. The point is that there is a plurality of ways in which we might conceive of a culture, and the relativist needs to provide a principled account of what counts as one's culture for purposes of moral evaluation. Failure to do so means that the relativist has failed to specify what it is that makes an action (done by a particular person at a particular time) right or wrong and thus has failed to provide a determinate moral criterion. This means that the theory fails the standard of determinacy as explained in chapter 1.

There is another aspect of this problem worth bringing out. In our pluralistic society, there are many cultures (or subcultures, as they are often called) and at any given time most individuals are members of more than one of them. Unless the relativist specifies which culture is relevant for moral evaluation, it can turn out that moral relativism implies inconsistent moral evaluations of the same action. Suppose, for example, that Susan is a member of the Roman Catholic Church, which forbids almost all abortions, but that she is also a member of the Democratic Party, whose moral code does not forbid abortion and in fact condones it in a wide variety of cases. If one accepts moral relativism, it appears that one must conclude that for Susan, having an abortion (at least under certain conditions) would be both right and wrong! This means that the theory fails to satisfy the standard of consistency for moral theories explained in chapter 1. So the problem of specifying, in a nonarbitrary way, what is to count as one's culture for purposes of moral evaluation is not just some technical point that the relativist can push aside.

Unless the moral relativist can plausibly deal with these problems of formulation, the theory fails both the determinacy and consistency standards for evaluating moral theories.

Moral relativism, our critical practices, and intuitive appeal. More serious problems for moral relativism concern our critical practices. We normally think that it makes sense to evaluate the moral codes of different cultures and claim that in some respects the moral code of some particular culture is mistaken. We also suppose that the moral code of our own culture (whatever that is) can improve or become worse. And we normally think that moral reformers are sometimes correct in their critical evaluations of the moral codes of the culture to which they belong. But, if moral relativism is correct, then none of these assumptions about our common critical practices is correct. Let us consider these problems in order.

The problem of intercultural evaluation. Consider the case of critically evaluating the moral codes of different cultures. Notice first of all that it is possible, according to the version of moral relativism we have been examining, to sensibly raise objections to nonbasic moral norms of a culture. Suppose, for example, a culture accepts as basic a moral norm to the effect that killing sentient creatures—creatures with a developed capacity to experience pleasure and pain—is wrong. Suppose they also have the nonmoral belief that a certain species of plant is sentient and thereby come to accept the derived moral norm that killing this species of plant is morally wrong. If they are mistaken in their nonmoral belief, then we can say that their derived moral norm is (for them) mistaken. However, if moral relativism is true, the basic moral norms of a culture set the standard for right and wrong conduct for the members of the culture in question. And, if these norms set the very standard for right and wrong, then it makes no sense to question the correctness of those norms—they just are the ultimate standards for the relevant culture.

To really fix on this idea—which goes to the heart of relativism—consider the meter bar. (And, remember, we are examining *unrestricted* moral relativism.) The meter bar is a bar, located in France, which represents the standard for the meter.[10]

Suppose you and a friend are looking at the meter bar and your friend turns to you and asks, "How do we know that it's a meter long?" Now your friend might be wondering how we can be sure that the bar has remained the same length since the time it was first established as the standard for a meter. But suppose your friend is wondering whether the bar was ever a meter long. In wondering about this, your friend shows that he doesn't understand what the meter bar represents: it is the standard for something's being a meter in length, and questions about whether it—the very standard—is (or was originally) a meter long make no sense.

The parallel with moral relativism should be obvious. According to unrestricted moral relativism, the basic moral norms of a culture represent the moral meter bar, so to speak, for the culture. Thus, questions about the correctness of those standards for the members of the relevant culture cannot be sensibly raised. But surely it makes sense to question the correctness of the basic norms of culture. Consider a culture some of whose basic norms are racist. Surely it makes sense to criticize such norms and claim that they are mistaken. But if we accept moral relativism, engaging in such criticism makes no sense. Clearly, having to accept this implication is a high price to pay for being a moral relativist.

The problem of intracultural evaluation. Consider now the practice of comparing the moral code of a culture at one time in its history with its code at another time. We have all heard preachers and politicians talk about how, with regard to some practices, morality has declined. It is sometimes said, for instance, that widespread acceptance of homosexuality marks a change for the worse in the morality (or moral code) of contemporary culture and so in this respect at least today's moral code is worse than the moral code accepted a generation ago.[11] Similarly, we have all heard claims to the effect that in some ways our moral code has improved over the course of time with respect to racial and gender equality, as well as the treatment of animals.

But can such comparative claims make sense for the moral relativist? Clearly not, since if at some time in our history, say 1950, it was part of our moral code that homosexuality is wrong, then it was wrong (for members of the culture at that time) to engage in such sexual activity. If we find that now our moral code has changed so that homosexuality is no longer condemned, then such activities are no longer morally wrong. For the moral relativist, one cannot make sense of the idea that the basic norms of a moral code of a culture have gotten better or worse, that it has improved in some ways or degenerated in others. Rather, all the relativist can say is that over time what is right or wrong has changed for members of some culture.

The moral reformer problem. Finally, consider the very idea of a moral reformer. A moral reformer is someone who attempts to change the moral beliefs and attitudes of a culture, possibly her own. So imagine someone who thinks that the practice of honor killing (mentioned earlier) is morally wrong and who, as a member of the culture in question, publicly opposes the practice as morally wrong. According to relativism, if this practice really is part of the moral code of the culture in question (it is required or permitted by its basic moral norms), then the moral reformer in question is necessarily saying something false when she says, "The practice of honor killing is wrong." But this implication of relativism just seems completely mistaken. We don't think that the claims of a moral reformer that go against the moral grain of her culture are necessarily mistaken. Indeed, we normally think that moral reformers are sometimes correct in their moral opposition to certain practices of their own culture.

These various critical practices reflect beliefs about morality to the effect that criticism of the moral norms of other cultures as well as one's own culture is possible. As we have seen, moral relativism implies that such intuitively appealing beliefs about morality are mistaken. Recall from chapter 1 that according to the standard of intuitive appeal, a moral theory should make sense of various intuitively appealing beliefs about morality. Thus, moral relativism (at least the version under consideration) can be criticized for not accommodating such beliefs.

Internal support and explanatory power. If we accept moral relativism, then if a culture's basic moral norms either condone or require the torture and killing of certain human beings just because of their ethnic background or whatever, we have to conclude that such behavior really is right (perhaps even obligatory) for that culture. The example of Naziism is often brought up as an example. It was part of the Nazi value system that Jews should be exterminated. But no one should conclude that therefore the torture and killing of Jews was morally right for the dedicated Nazi. The reader can no doubt think of other examples where moral relativism conflicts with our considered moral beliefs. Thus, moral relativism fails to satisfy the standard of internal support for evaluating a moral theory.

Finally, the fact that moral relativism conflicts with various considered moral beliefs indicates that it also fails to provide a correct explanation of what makes an action right or wrong, or something good or bad, and thus that it fails the standard of explanatory power. Appealing to the moral code accepted by a culture may explain why many members of the culture have the moral beliefs they do in fact have. But we are interested in explaining what makes something have the moral quality it has, and mere facts about the moral norms accepted by cultures fail to give us the desired explanation.

As I mentioned earlier, these observations do not decisively refute moral relativism, if only because there are more sophisticated versions that avoid at least some of the problems we have just reviewed. Recently, for instance, David Wong has defended what I call *restricted moral relativism* that backs away from the radical claim that all of morality is entirely culture dependent. Space does not permit the sort of elaboration and examination this view deserves. But because the restricted version is far superior to its unrestricted cousin, it is well worth considering, even if only briefly, before moving on.

8. RESTRICTED MORAL RELATIVISM

What entitles this view to the label "restricted" is the idea that there are culture-independent constraints on a moral code being true or correct. These constraints have to do with (1) intrapersonal as well as interpersonal functions of morality, together with (2) facts about human nature, including the nature of human cooperation. So, consider first, the intrapersonal function of morality which Wong describes as having to do with "shaping character and specification of worthwhile lives." If we consider this function in light of facts about human nature,

> There are a limited number of goods that human beings seek, given their nature and potentialities. The satisfaction of their physical needs, the goods of intimacy, sociability, and social status and approval, perhaps the opportunity to discharge aggressive energy, . . . and knowledge either of the physical world or of the human world are goods sought across many different cultures. (Wong, 2008, 44)

As Wong goes on to say, morality is not "determined" by these facts about human nature, that is, there is no *one* moral code the following of which satisfies all of these human needs and provides for these goods. However, if any morality or moral code is going to count as a true or correct moral code for human beings, it must respect these needs and promote these goods.

The interpersonal function of morality, according to Wong, has to do with promoting and regulating cooperation among human beings. This function, together with facts about human nature and human cooperation, also yields constraints on what can count as a true or correct morality. For instance, the strength of human self-interest requires that a true morality include a norm of reciprocity so that the morality in question can perform its interpersonal function. Speaking very generally, a norm of reciprocity is one that has to do with returning proportional good for good, which is important since human beings need the help and cooperation of others in order to live well. Such norms encourage other-regarding behavior, but at the same time any such norm, to be effective, must allow individuals some leeway to freely pursue their own projects and interests. But, there is no *one* norm of reciprocity that fits with facts about human self-interest and the interpersonal function of encouraging cooperation; there is a plurality of such norms.

Another constraint on a true morality having to do with its interpersonal function is that its moral norms must be seen by those who are to be governed by them as justifiable and thus not dependent on falsehoods. This constraint would rule out moral norms that allow or require aggression against and subordination of certain targeted groups where the basis for such aggression and subordination rests on falsehoods about the targeted group.

There is much more to say about these constraints, and readers are referred to Wong's book for more detail. For present purposes, two points should be reasonably clear. First, according to Wong, not anything goes when it comes to morality. There are universal constraints on what can count as a true or correct morality. This is why the view is appropriately thought of as restricted. Second, the resulting account of morality is still a form of relativism because there is no one set of moral norms that uniquely satisfy the constraints in question, rather there is a plurality of true or correct moral codes. Wong calls his view "pluralistic relativism."

To convey the general idea of this type of relativism, consider, for instance, a society A whose morality gives more weight to considerations of freedom of speech compared to protection of personal privacy in cases where these considerations conflict, and which otherwise conforms to the above constraints, and so counts as a true morality. Consider too a society B whose morality counts as one of the true ones, but gives priority to privacy over freedom of speech in cases where these considerations conflict. Here we have a case of what we earlier called a moral priorities conflict or disagreement: both societies place value on freedom of speech and privacy, but in cases of conflict they prioritize them differently.[12] Now consider a case of someone publishing insulting or embarrassing remarks about public officials. In society A, we are supposing, this action would be permissible, because even though publishing such things can infringe upon a person's privacy, considerations of freedom of speech are taken to outweigh considerations of privacy when the two conflict. The reverse is true of the moral code of society B. So the idea is that within the limits represented by the constraints on a true morality, there can be equally correct or true moral codes that imply different moral verdicts about what are intuitively the same types of action.

Let us encapsulate this restricted version of moral relativism as follows.

> **RMR** What is right and what is wrong for the members of a culture depends on (is ultimately determined by) the basic moral norms of their culture, but only in cases where those norms are consistent with those universal constraints on an adequate morality that properly reflect the functions of morality as well as facts about human nature. Such constraints do not pick out one complete set of moral norms as being uniquely correct or true (so there is no single true morality), but they constrain the range of moral norms (and thus entire codes) that can count as a true or correct morality.

One obvious advantage of restricted over unrestricted relativism is that it avoids what is perhaps the major objection to the latter view having to do with conflicts with considered moral judgments (recall the case of so-called Nazi morality). But what is important to notice is that Wong's restricted moral relativism features a nonrelativist core, namely, the culture-independent constraints on what can count as a true morality given the functions of morality together with facts about human nature. So the restricted view represents an important departure from the unrestricted and rather crude "conventionalist" version of moral relativism discussed earlier. The restricted version embraces the universality thesis (UT) presented in section 1, but denies the strong single true morality thesis (STM). It thus represents a compromise view of sorts. Before concluding, there is one more issue about moral relativism that is worth clearing up.

9. RELATIVISM AND TOLERANCE

Some anthropologists who infer moral relativism from facts about intercultural differences in moral convictions have also apparently thought that a relativist stance in ethics commits one to a principle of tolerance. Ruth Benedict, for instance, claimed that on the basis of moral relativism,

> We shall arrive then at a more realistic social faith, accepting as grounds of hope and as new bases for tolerance the coexisting and equally valid patterns of life which mankind has created for itself from the raw materials of existence. (Benedict, 1934, 278)

The suggestion seems to be that moral relativism commits one to tolerance regarding the moral beliefs and convictions of other cultures since, after all, what is right or wrong is simply a matter of the basic moral norms of one's society. So if a culture, on the basis of its moral code, engages in honor killing, parricide, or games like chicken pull that members of other cultures might find abhorrent, there is no basis for these outraged cultures to interfere with the practices of other cultures, at least if moral relativism is true. In engaging in honor killings, the culture that takes this practice to be morally right is engaging in actions that really are morally right for members of the culture in question. And if the members of a culture are engaged in practices that are morally right (at least for them), then there is no moral basis for interfering with such practices. Thus, according to this line of argument, moral relativism is committed to a principle of tolerance:

> It is morally wrong for any culture to interfere with moral practices of another culture.

Perhaps this principle needs to be qualified to allow that under certain conditions interference in the practices of other cultures is permitted—particularly in cases where those practices threaten the welfare of members of one's own culture. However, the question to be considered here is whether moral relativism commits one to accepting this principle of tolerance.

It takes little reflection to see that *unrestricted* moral relativism involves no such commitment. Notice that the above moral principle is intended to state a moral requirement that is valid for all cultures. It would in fact be inconsistent for an unrestricted relativist to advocate the principle in question as a universally valid moral norm. After all, according to this version of moral relativism, what is right or wrong depends on the moral code of one's culture. This implies that whether it is morally wrong for some culture C to interfere with the practices of another culture depends on the moral code of C. Clearly, if one accepts unrestricted moral relativism, then the truth or validity of any principle of tolerance is relative: it is true or valid for those cultures whose basic moral norms include or imply this principle, false or invalid for those cultures that do not.

But now consider restricted moral relativism. On this view, if the culture-independent constraints on a correct moral code require acceptance of a norm of tolerance, then this form of relativism is compatible with there being a culture-independent and thus nonrelative principle of tolerance. For anthropologists like Benedict, this would no doubt be a welcome feature of the restricted view, and a reason to prefer it over any unrestricted version.

In addition, it should be noted that nonrelativist moral theories do not commit one to the denial of a principle of tolerance like the one above. One might think that unless one accepts moral relativism, one will be committed to the idea that one's own culture ought to engage in a moral campaign to convert other cultures with different moral codes to one's own moral outlook. But again, this inference is clearly mistaken. According to the divine command theory, the morality of interfering with the practices of other cultures depends on God's commands, and those commands may condemn all sorts of interference. A similar remark applies to the other nonrelativist moral theories featured throughout the rest of this book.

In summary, according to unrestricted moral relativism, then, whether we ought to be tolerant of the moral practices of other cultures depends on the moral code of our own culture. And, of course, whether members of other cultures ought to be tolerant in this way depends on the moral codes of their cultures. By contrast, a restricted form of moral relativism like Wong's may provide a basis for defending a culture-independent principle of tolerance. And finally, tolerance may be required by the moral principles featured in nonrelativist moral theories.

10. CONCLUSION

The topic of relativism in ethics is complex and potentially very confusing. Our main focus has been on a normative moral theory that I have been calling moral relativism. And most of the chapter was spent discussing an unrestricted version of relativism. Perhaps the most appealing feature of this theory (recall the standard of intuitive appeal from chapter 1) is the fact that it coheres nicely with the idea that there are deep-going differences in the moral codes of different cultures, an idea that perhaps seems to be supported by the work of anthropologists. However, the theory faces serious problems.

We have discovered that the main argument for this type of theory—the anthropologist's argument—faces certain challenges. More importantly, unrestricted relativism encounters serious objections concerning its formulation, and consequently has difficulty satisfying the standards of determinacy and consistency for evaluating moral theories. Furthermore, the theory is seriously at odds with the standards of intuitive appeal, internal support, and explanatory power. We briefly considered David Wong's restricted version of relativism that allows for a plurality of equally true or correct moral codes, but imposes nonrelativist restrictions on what can count as a correct moral code. Wong's version of moral relativism involves a nonrelativist core that takes account of deep facts about human nature. And this fits nicely with the views of some anthropologists who have suggested that facts about human nature may provide a basis for a universally valid set of moral norms. Consider what Kluckhohn says:

> While specific manifestations of human nature vary between cultures and between individuals in the same culture, human nature is universal. All value systems have to make some of the same concessions to the natural world of which human nature is a part.

Some needs and motives are so deep and so generic that they are beyond the reach of argument. (Kluckhohn, 1955, 676)

If, as Kluckhohn says, there is a universal human nature, then since morality has to do with what to do and how to be, it makes sense to consider grounding morality in facts about universal human nature. And this is exactly a guiding idea behind the natural law moral theory featured in the next chapter. The version we shall consider is meant to be a thoroughly nonrelativist moral theory, and so contrasts with Wong's restricted, pluralistic relativism, despite the fact that both views appeal to similar facts about human nature in theorizing about morality.

NOTES

1. The moral relativist gives a similar account of goodness and badness in terms of the moral codes of cultures. Since the theory of value offered by the moral relativist is parallel to the relativist theory of right conduct, we shall focus almost exclusively on the theory of right conduct.

2. Talk of moral norms, then, is being used to cover both very general moral principles as well as more specific moral rules.

3. In another place, Sumner writes: "The notion of right is in the folkways. It is not outside of them, of independent origin, and brought to them to test them" ([1906] 1959, 28).

4. This thesis is often called moral absolutism. But since the term "absolutism" is also commonly used to refer to certain moral rules like "Do not lie, regardless of what good may come about from lying" (an idea that we take up in the next chapter), I am avoiding that label here.

5. As we shall see, a restricted version of relativism rejects STM but accepts UT.

6. I thank Tom Nenon for this example.

7. The idea of a fundamental conflict or disagreement in moral belief will be explained in section 5.

8. In what follows, premises 1 and 2, but not 3, are subjected to critical scrutiny because they tend to be the premises that attract the most critical attention in the debate over moral relativism. However, premise 3 has been challenged by those who defend versions of moral skepticism, and by those who defend so-called expressivist views about moral thought and language. Consideration of skepticism and expressivism would take us too far into metaethics and so will not be treated in this book.

9. Notice that in this example, unlike the one about capital punishment used to illustrate nonfundamental moral disagreements, the disagreement may turn out to be rationally irresolvable if there are no rational procedures for deciding factual questions about the afterlife, including whether there is one.

10. Strictly speaking, this bar represented the standard from 1889 to 1960 but has since been replaced by a measure in terms of time and the speed of light.

11. Such claims about the erosion and decline of the moral codes of such countries as England and the United States are explored in Himmelfarb, 1995.

12. This example is roughly based on a 2010 *New York Times* article, "When American and European Ideas of Privacy Collide," by Adam Liptak. The article can be accessed at http://www.nytimes.com.

FURTHER READING

Philosophical Literature

Brandt, R. B. 1959. *Ethical Theory*. Englewood Cliffs, NJ: Prentice-Hall. Chapters 5 and 11 are both notable for an informed discussion of anthropological data bearing on relativism.

Cook, John W. 1999. *Morality and Cultural Differences*. New York: Oxford University Press. A useful attempt to examine the issue of moral relativism bringing together both philosophical and anthropological sources. Cook is critical of relativism.

Doris, John M., and Alexandra Plakias. 2008. "How to Argue about Disagreement: Evaluator Diversity and Moral Realism." In *Moral Psychology*, vol. 2, ed. W. Sinnott-Armstrong. Cambridge, MA: MIT Press. An illuminating examination of the controversy over the nature and likely extent of fundamental moral disagreement.

Gowans, Christopher. 2000. *Moral Disagreement: Classic and Contemporary Readings*. London: Routledge. A collection of essays, including some by anthropologists, on the topic of moral disagreement and its significance for moral objectivity. Includes an extensive bibliography and excellent introductory essay.

———. 2009. "Moral Relativism." *The Stanford Encyclopedia of Philosophy*, ed. E. N. Zalta. http://plato.stanford.edu.Very helpful overview of the disputes over moral diversity and moral relativism.

Harman, Gilbert. 1975. "Moral Relativism Defended." *Philosophical Review* 84: 3–22. An important statement and defense of moral relativism.

———, and Judith Jarvis Thomson. 1996. *Moral Relativism and Moral Objectivity*. London: Blackwell. Harman defends relativism, and Thomson defends nonrelativism. Included also are lively responses by both authors to the views of the other.

Ladd, John. 1985. *Moral Relativism*. Lanham, Md.: University Press of America. A collection of writings from anthropologists and philosophers debating relativism.

Moody-Adams, Michele M. 1997. *Fieldwork in Familiar Places: Morality, Culture, and Philosophy*. Cambridge, MA: Harvard University Press. A critique of moral relativism and a defense of the claim that morality is objective. Of particular interest is Moody-Adams's view on the obstacles that stand in the way of obtaining reliable anthropological evidence about a culture's moral code. But see the 2008 article by Doris and Plakias for discussion of Moody-Adams on this issue.

Moser, Paul, and Thomas L. Carson, eds. 2001. *Moral Relativism: A Reader*. New York: Oxford University Press. A wide-ranging collection of essays with a useful introduction and bibliography by the editors.

Paul, Ellen F., Fred D. Miller, and Jeffrey Paul. 1994. *Cultural Pluralism and Moral Knowledge*. Cambridge: Cambridge University Press. Contains some important essays on moral relativism.

Stewart, Robert M., and Lynn L. Thomas. 1991. "Recent Work on Moral Relativism." *American Philosophical Quarterly* 28: 85–100. An overview of some work on moral relativism from the 1970s and 1980s. Includes a useful bibliography.

Wong, David. 1984. *Moral Relativity*. Berkeley and Los Angeles: University of California Press. A sophisticated defense of a version of moral relativism that differs importantly from the unrestricted version examined in this chapter.

———. 2008. *Natural Moralities: A Defense of Pluralistic Relativism*. Oxford: Oxford University Press. In addition to refining his earlier view, Wong's book draws on different moral traditions as well as the fields of psychology, anthropology, and evolutionary theory in exploring the sources of moral disagreement as well as potential for agreement and accommodation.

Empirical Literature

Benedict, Ruth. 1934. *Patterns of Culture*. New York: Houghton Mifflin. A classic defense of moral relativism by a noted anthropologist.

Brandt, Richard. 1954. *Hopi Ethics*. Chicago: University of Chicago Press. A field study of the ethical code of Hopi Native Americans, on the basis of which Brandt attempts to address certain philosophical questions about ethics.

Ladd, John. 1957. *The Structure of a Moral Code*. Cambridge, MA: Harvard University Press. A field study of the ethics of Navajo culture.

Nisbett, Richard E., and Dov Cohen. 1996. *Culture of Honor: The Psychology of Violence in the South*. Boulder, CO: Westview Press. The data from this book are used by Doris and Plakias in their 2008 discussion of the moral diversity thesis.

Schweder, Richard A. 1991. *Thinking through Cultures*. Cambridge, MA: Harvard University Press. An examination of cross-cultural similarities and differences in conceptions of mind, person, emotion, and morality.

Sumner, William G. [1906] 1959. *Folkways*. New York: Dover. Classic discussion of the habits and customs of groups that influence moral attitudes.

Westermark, Edward. 1960. *Moral Relativity*. New York: Humanities Press. Of particular interest is chapter 7, which contains a brief overview of the anthropological evidence for diversity in moral belief.

4

Natural Law Theory

On April 15, 1989, seventeen-year-old Tony Bland was attending a soccer match at Hillsborough Football Stadium in Sheffield, England. As thousands of fans were hurrying to enter the stadium, some of them were smashed against a barrier, leaving ninety-five people dead and many others seriously injured. Bland was injured in the incident, and although he did not die, his lungs were crushed by the pressure of the crowd, resulting in a loss of oxygen to his brain. The unhappy result was that the cortex of his brain was destroyed, causing permanent loss of consciousness, though his body was kept alive by machines and feeding tubes. Tony Bland's family and the attending physician, Dr. J. G. Howe, were prepared to withdraw life support, since his continued existence was (so they thought) pointless. To avoid the possibility of criminal charges, the hospital treating Bland applied to the Family Division of the High Court for permission to withdraw treatment. The case stirred moral and legal controversy and was eventually settled in the British courts in a decision that held that physicians are not under a legal obligation to continue treatment that does not benefit a patient. However, there were those who were morally and legally opposed to withdrawing life support from Bland. They argued that since withdrawing treatment would be the intentional killing of an innocent human being, such action would be wrong, even in tragic cases like Bland's.

The idea that there are certain types of action that are morally wrong in all circumstances is characteristic of the natural law theory of ethics, a moral theory that represents the moral teachings of the Roman Catholic Church. Other types of action which, according to this theory, are always wrong include homosexuality, artificial means of birth control, suicide, abortion, and artificial insemination. Are such types of action always morally wrong? If so, what reason can be given for such restrictions? The natural law theory represents an attempt to work out a systematic answer to these questions and will be the focus of this chapter.

71

As we shall see, the natural law theory—at least the version of it that we will examine—involves some interesting complexity, and so it will be presented in stages. We begin, in the first section, with some general remarks about natural law ethics and then proceed in sections 2 through 11 to examine the version of natural law suggested in the writings of Saint Thomas Aquinas. In section 12 we consider various objections to this moral theory.

1. WHAT IS NATURAL LAW?

In many contexts, talk of natural law refers to laws of nature—the sorts of law that are investigated by the sciences. Such laws are descriptive—they describe certain regularities in nature. Boyle's law, for example, states that the pressure and volume of a gas vary inversely at a given temperature. Of course, in English, the term "law" is also used to refer to the sorts of norms and rules that characterize a legal system. Such civil laws are prescriptive: they express norms and rules for how citizens are supposed to behave. In ethics, natural law refers to moral laws (or principles) which, like the laws of a legal system, prescribe how individuals ought to behave.

However, there is an important contrast between natural law in ethics and the laws of a legal system. The term "natural" in natural law ethics indicates that moral laws have a source and authority that distinguish them from the civil laws of any society. At the end of the last chapter, I quoted a passage from the work of anthropologist Clyde Kluckhohn in which he suggests that a possible basis for a nonrelativist, universally valid set of moral principles is our common human nature. The idea that there is an objective set of moral principles based in human nature is central to the natural law theory. Moral laws (or principles), according to this theory, are natural in the sense that they are grounded in human nature and thus represent universally valid norms for the behavior of all human beings. In this respect, natural law ethics contrasts sharply with moral relativism.

Thus, according to the natural law theory of ethics, there are moral laws (or principles) that express requirements on behavior that, because they are grounded in human nature (and because human nature is the same for all human beings), are valid and hence apply to all human beings, regardless of culture.

However, this characterization does not capture what is distinctive about natural law ethics. Other nonrelativist moral theories that we shall study in the following chapters set forth moral principles that are grounded at least partly in facts about human beings and that purport to be universally valid. Unfortunately, the theories representative of the natural law tradition, because they differ over what is and is not essential to natural law ethics, make it difficult to provide a definitive characterization of this type of moral theory. Perhaps the best way to proceed in examining natural law ethics is simply to consider the version we find in Aquinas—arguably the greatest proponent of this type of theory—and let this version be representative of the natural law tradition. In any case, there are elements of Aquinas's view that we do not find in rival moral theories and which therefore make his view worth studying.

Let us begin our study of natural law theory with some general remarks about some of its basic elements. We will then be ready to examine the version we find in Aquinas.

2. THREE COMPONENTS OF NATURAL LAW MORAL THEORY

As I will present the theory, it has three main components. First, there is what I will call the theory's core, which involves a *perfectionist theory of value* that is the basis for understanding right and wrong conduct. This is a *value-based* moral theory, since the value concepts are more basic than the deontic concepts. Aquinas grounds his perfectionist theory of value in facts about human nature: it is because we are creatures of a certain sort, sharing a common human nature, that certain kinds of states of affairs and activities are intrinsically valuable. It is also part of Aquinas's view that acting morally—doing the right thing—is a matter of acting rationally, and so moral principles of right action represent basic requirements of practical rationality.

The second component of this theory addresses the question of whether it is ever morally permissible to do or bring about what is bad or evil in order to promote what is good. The theory's answer to this question is expressed in the *principle of double effect*, which raises interesting issues about the moral importance of intention and foresight in action.

The third component of traditional natural law ethics is its commitment to *moral absolutism*—the idea that certain kinds of action are always morally wrong, regardless of whatever good might result from them. Such actions are featured in absolutist moral rules—rules that, for example, absolutely prohibit such acts as killing innocent human beings, lying, and homosexuality.

Let us now proceed to examine these three components in more detail. Following the thought of Aquinas, the next two sections outline the theory's core.

3. AQUINAS'S PERFECTIONISM

The essential features of the moral theory of Thomas Aquinas (1224–1274) are contained in a few short sections of his massive work, *Summa Theologiae* (*Summary of Theology*). This theory, like all of Aquinas's philosophical work, was strongly influenced by the ideas of the Greek philosopher Aristotle (384–322 BC). (The moral theory of Aristotle is featured in chapter 10.) Though there are important differences in the moral theories of Aquinas and Aristotle, they do share a certain conception of the connection between human nature and the good in relation to humans that is a natural starting point in coming to understand their moral theories. To understand this conception of

the human good, it will be useful to begin with some general remarks about the relation between a thing's essential nature and the good of that thing.[1]

Purpose, Perfection, and Goodness

The essential nature, or essence, of a thing is what makes that thing what it is.
According to Aquinas (following Aristotle), a thing's purpose, or end, is crucial for
understanding its essence. (In this context, the terms "purpose," "end," "function,"
and "goal" all refer to the same thing.) This is easiest to understand in relation to
human artifacts. Consider a knife. To understand what a knife is—to understand its
essence—one must understand its purpose, or function, which is to cut.[2] Of course, a
knife might or might not be useful for the purpose of cutting owing to such things as
the sharpness of its blade, its size, and so forth. Knives with dull blades are difficult,
if not impossible, to use for the purpose of cutting. This means that the state a knife
is in with respect to its end or purpose can vary. A knife that can be used to perform
its cutting function well is in a state of perfection or excellence (for that sort of knife).
And it is the perfection of a knife that constitutes its goodness. The goodness of a
knife, then, is its being in a state of perfection, and to be in a state of perfection is
for it to be able to perform its function well. Since there are different types of knives,
designed for different jobs—bread knives, paring knives, butcher knives, steak knives,
and so on—a good knife of a certain type is one that cuts certain sorts of things well.
A good bread knife, for example, is one that can be used to cut bread well.

According to a teleological worldview (from the Greek word *telos*, meaning end
or goal), which Aquinas inherited from Aristotle, all things in nature have purposes,
and thus to understand the essence of anything requires that one understand a thing's
purpose (or purposes, in the case of things with complex natures). So for instance, to
understand a plant—its essence—one must understand its purposes, which include
taking in nutrition, growth, and reproduction. The perfection, and hence the good,
of a plant, then, is its taking in nutrition, growing, and reproducing well.

Again, nonhuman animals are to be understood in terms of their purposes, which,
in addition to those characteristic of plants, also include (at least for many animals)
such capacities as locomotion and sense perception. The perfection of an animal
with such capacities is for it to be in a state in which its capacities are fully developed
and engaged. In general, with regard to organisms, we can say that their good is a
matter of their flourishing as the types of organisms they are.

Human Nature and the Good for Humans

The same general point about purpose, perfection, and goodness applies to humans: the perfection, and hence good, of a human being is a matter of its being in
a state in which those purposes characteristic of human beings are fully developed
and engaged. However, unlike plants and lower animals, human beings are rational
agents with free will. This means, first of all, that it is up to humans (in a way that it
is not up to plants and lower animals) to come to understand their essential nature

and thus come to understand their good through the use of reason. It also means that humans are then to exercise free will in fully achieving their good or perfection based on their understanding of their good. In short, it is up to human beings to understand and develop those capacities whose development perfects human nature and hence represents the good for humans.

Value Perfectionism

We are now in a position to explain Aquinas's theory of intrinsic value for human beings. The basic idea, as just presented, is that the good of a thing is a matter of its fully developing those capacities that are essential to its nature, which, in turn, results in that thing's having or achieving its ends or purposes. For something to achieve such ends or purposes is for it to achieve a state of perfection.

In ethics, *value perfectionism* is the view that goodness in relation to a thing is a matter of its fully developing those capacities that are essential to it. Aquinas's theory of value is thus a version of perfectionism.

Moral perfectionism is the view that a perfectionistic account of value is central in understanding the nature of right and wrong action. Aquinas, as we shall see, is also a moral perfectionist.[3] We can now set forth the basic principles of Aquinas's theory of intrinsic value in relation to human beings as follows:

Theory of Intrinsic Value

Some state of affairs S is *intrinsically good* in relation to human beings if and only if (and because) the realization of S is part of what perfects human nature.

Some state of affairs S is *intrinsically bad* in relation to human beings if and only if (and because) S involves the hindrance or destruction of those states of affairs that perfect human nature.

Some state of affairs S is *intrinsically value-neutral* in relation to human beings if and only if (and because) S is neither part of what perfects human nature nor involves the hindrance or destruction of those states of affairs that perfect human nature.

The Four Basic Human Goods

This perfectionist account of the human good is hardly illuminating until we specify something about the essential nature of human beings. Doing so requires that we specify those ends or purposes characteristic of such beings. Which purposes or ends are essential to human beings? According to Aquinas, we can discover essential human purposes or ends by observing our natural inclinations:

> Since good has the nature of an end and evil its opposite, all the things to which man has a natural inclination are naturally apprehended by reason as good and therefore as

objects to be pursued, and their opposites as evil to be avoided. Therefore the order of the precepts of the natural law follows the order of our natural inclinations. (*ST*, 49)[4]

Furthermore, according to Aquinas, observation and reflection upon the natural inclinations of human beings reveal four basic human goods (basic values): *life*, *procreation*, *knowledge*, and *sociability*. The idea is that human beings have certain capacities and powers—capacities and powers that are part of the very essence of humanity. By nature, we are living creatures with powers of rationality, and these facts about us ground certain basic values.

As living creatures, we are naturally inclined to preserve our own lives as well as assure the continuation of the species through procreation. Thus, with respect to individual human life Aquinas writes:

> There is in man, first, an inclination to the good that he shares by nature with all substances, since every substance seeks to preserve itself according to its own nature. Corresponding to this inclination the natural law contains those things that preserve human life and prevent its destruction. (*ST*, 49–50)

In addition to human life, procreation is a basic good, as indicated by the fact that there are certain inclinations we share with nonhuman animals:

> Secondly, there is in man an inclination to certain more specific ends in accordance with the nature that he shares with other animals. In accordance with this, the natural law is said to contain what nature has taught all animals, such as the union of man and woman, the education of children, etc. (*ST*, 50)[5]

As rational creatures we are inclined to seek knowledge about ourselves and the world in which we live as well as to form various kinds of social bonds, and hence knowledge and sociability are basic goods.

> Thirdly, there is in man a natural inclination to the good of the rational nature which is his alone. Thus man has a natural inclination to know the truth about God and to live in society. Thus the things that pertain to inclinations of this kind belong to the natural law, such as that man should avoid ignorance, that he should not offend others with whom he must associate, and other related actions. (*ST*, 50)

We can summarize this discussion in three main points: (1) Aquinas embraces a perfectionist theory of value according to which the good in relation to human beings is a matter of their achieving a state of perfection by fully realizing those ends or purposes that are essential to being human. (2) Those ends or purposes that are essential to human beings are reflected in natural human inclinations and dispositions, and so we can consult such inclinations and dispositions in coming to a more precise understanding of what constitutes human perfection. (3) Upon investigation we find that life, procreation, knowledge, and sociability are the basic ends of human nature whose realization perfects human nature and thus count as the most basic goods for human beings.

4. RATIONALITY AND RIGHT CONDUCT

I mentioned in section 2 that the natural law theory is value-based in the sense that value concepts are more basic than the concepts of right and wrong. We now must consider how the concepts of right and wrong are related to the concepts of good and bad in the natural law theory in general and in Aquinas's thought in particular.

According to Aquinas, human beings are rational creatures, and there are two realms or spheres of rationality. Theoretical (speculative) reason has to do with knowledge of how things are, while practical reason has to do with how we ought to behave. Just as in our quest for understanding the world around us we need reason to properly guide our inquiries, so in our efforts to live our lives properly we need reason to determine what is good and hence worth pursuing and how to go about pursuing such goods.

In both of these realms, there are very general propositions expressing truths that are the proper basis for inferring more specific propositions, forming a hierarchy of ordered propositions. With regard to knowledge about the world—about being—Aquinas tells us (again, following Aristotle) that the most basic proposition is the principle of contradiction: "something cannot be affirmed and denied at the same time" (*ST*, 49). Moreover, such basic propositions that guide the use of theoretical reason are self-evident in the sense that their truth can be grasped, and hence they can be known, on the basis of rational reflection upon the proposition in question. Such knowledge is knowledge on the basis of reason. So, one can come to know the principle of contradiction as a result of coming to understand the relation among the concepts mentioned in the principle. Knowledge on the basis of self-evidence contrasts with coming to know a proposition's truth as the result of learning it from direct sense experience or inferring it from some other proposition. The principle of contradiction and other general principles, then, represent the most basic first principles that can be grasped through the use of theoretical reason.

Moral propositions expressing truths about right conduct and value can be arranged in a hierarchy, with the most general propositions being the basis for deriving more specific ones. The most fundamental moral propositions are self-evident: their truth can be grasped, and hence they can be known, on the basis of rational reflection.

The most general such truth concerning right conduct is "Good is to be done and pursued, and evil is to be avoided" (*ST*, 49). This principle of right conduct, combined with Aquinas's account of the basic goods for humans, implies the following basic principle of right conduct:

NLT Life, procreation, knowledge, and sociability are to be preserved and promoted; their hindrance and destruction are to be avoided.

As we shall see, this principle will have to be refined and qualified, but before going further, let us pause for a moment to see what this principle implies about various ethical issues. In order to use this principle to arrive at specific conclusions about the morality of actions, we need to say more about the four basic goods. Let us briefly consider them one by one.

- *Life.* Human life has intrinsic value and is to be preserved. Hence, we are obligated to protect and promote our own lives and the lives of others. For instance, since our lives require that we maintain our health, we have an obligation to promote our own health and the health of others. Since suicide and murder involve the intentional taking of human life, it follows that such actions are wrong.[6]
- *Procreation.* Procreation involves both the having and the rearing of children. Actions that are necessary or otherwise crucial for having and raising children are morally required. This includes, for example, providing for their education. According to Aquinas, actions that hinder or destroy this value include adultery, artificial means of birth control, and homosexuality.
- *Knowledge.* In the final passage quoted in the previous section, Aquinas mentions knowledge of God in particular as something to be promoted and maintained because, as a theist, he maintains that such knowledge is of the highest, most perfect kind. However, this value also includes the pursuit of knowledge about the world in which we live. Actions that would interfere with the pursuit of knowledge such as suppression of religious and scientific ideas are wrongs to be avoided.
- *Sociability.* This basic good concerns the ways in which human beings are inclined to live together and cooperate for mutual benefit. Thus, such bonds as friendship, marriage, and civil society are to be pursued. Actions that destroy such bonds, such as lying, slander, and treason are wrong.

The types of action mentioned in connection with each of these basic values represent but a few instances of some of the more specific moral requirements that allegedly follow from Aquinas's basic principle of right conduct (NLT). Obviously, the specific conclusions one can infer from NLT depend crucially on how one interprets the four basic values. For instance, since skydiving involves certain life-threatening risks, does it violate the value of human life? What about smoking? Can civil disobedience intended to challenge certain laws be justified, or do such actions violate the value of sociability? What about divorce and the value of procreation? One might answer such questions by claiming that in certain cases divorce, smoking, and the rest are not in violation of the basic values featured in natural law theory and hence not wrong. This answer will no doubt generate legitimate disagreement over where to draw the line between permissible and impermissible instances of such actions.

These remarks are not meant as criticisms of the natural law theory, but they do serve to bring into focus Aquinas's view about the degree of certainty that attaches to moral claims of various sorts. According to Aquinas's vision of moral theory, the most general moral propositions of the theory—its fundamental principles—are self-evident and hence can be known with certainty. These principles, together with claims about human nature, yield conclusions about the morality of specific sorts of actions expressed by moral rules—rules against suicide, killing others, lying, and so forth. And again, these rules, because they are supposed to follow deductively from the basic principles, can be known with certainty.[7] However, in order to arrive at moral conclusions about specific concrete actions, one must apply the rules to oftentimes complex moral situations, and such applications will often involve uncertainties. I have mentioned a few such uncertainties in the previous paragraph. Figure 4.1 illustrates the levels and ordering of moral truths.

Thus far in this chapter I have been describing what I call the core of Aquinas's natural law theory—a core consisting of a perfectionist theory of value that is central in his account of what makes an action right or wrong. But there is more to the theory than its core; indeed, there must be more if the theory is to deal with cases of moral conflict. In what follows, we shall complete our presentation of Aquinas's natural law theory by first explaining the problem of moral conflict that looms for the theory and then explaining how this problem is avoided.

5. THE PROBLEM OF MORAL CONFLICT

The basic principle of natural law ethics instructs us to do good and avoid evil, where human life, procreation, knowledge, and sociability represent the basic goods to be brought about and maintained, and the evil to be avoided is the hindrance or destruction of such goods. But there is an obvious problem with the theory as so far presented having to do with cases in which it is not possible both to do good and to avoid evil, and so it appears as if the fundamental principle of natural law theory sometimes yields contradictory moral evaluations of the same action.

To illustrate the problem, let us consider a few cases. Suppose that in order to preserve one's own life against an unjust aggressor, one must kill the assailant; there

Particular Moral Verdicts
(about specific actions)

Moral Rules
(about suicide, lying, adultery, etc.)

Fundamental Moral Principles
(of intrinsic value and right conduct)

Figure 4.1. Levels of Moral Truth

is just no other way. In this sort of kill-or-be-killed situation, may one kill in self-defense? The natural law theory requires that we promote and maintain the basic goods, one of which is human life. Since, in the situation imagined, the only way of protecting one's own life is by taking the life of another human being, the theory yields the conclusion that we ought to take the life in question. On the other hand, the natural law theory tells us that we are to avoid bringing about evil, and since intentionally taking the life of a human being is an evil, the theory apparently yields the conclusion that we ought not to kill the assailant. So, the natural law theory, as so far explained, yields the contradictory moral conclusion that we ought to kill the assailant and that we ought not to kill the assailant.

Here is another case of moral conflict in which the natural law theory yields apparently contradictory moral judgments. Suppose a woman has cancer of the uterus and therefore needs to undergo a hysterectomy (an operation in which the uterus is removed) to safeguard her life. Suppose also that she is pregnant and that because she is in the early stages of pregnancy, the fetus cannot be removed without bringing about its death. If we assume that the fetus counts as a human being with full moral standing, we are led by the natural law theory (as so far presented) to contradictory moral judgments.[8] On the one hand, the woman ought to undergo the hysterectomy in order to preserve her life. But, on the other hand, this surgical procedure will inevitably bring about the death of her unborn child and hence violate the basic good of human life. So she ought not to have the operation. This case, like the previous case, involves the prospect of bringing about the death of a human being, though unlike the assailant in the previous case, the fetus is completely innocent.

While both the self-defense and hysterectomy cases involve a single basic value—human life—other problematic cases involve multiple basic values. Consider this example. Suppose that I am hiding an innocent person being hunted by a band of killers who are now asking me about the location of their intended victim. If I tell them the truth (or refuse to answer), they will find the person I'm hiding; if I lie to them, I can very likely save this innocent person (at least for the time being). Lying, recall, violates the value of sociability. So, it is only by engaging in the evil act of telling a lie that I can bring about the good result of preserving a human life. In this situation it looks as if I ought to do what I can to save an innocent human life (so I ought to lie), but since I am to avoid evil, I ought not to lie.

Because these situations of moral conflict that arise for the natural law theory (as so far presented) yield inconsistent moral verdicts, the theory fails to satisfy the consistency standard for evaluating moral theories. Thus, we must either reject the theory (since a theory that yields inconsistent moral judgments cannot be correct), or we must find some way to qualify or revise the theory so that it avoids inconsistency.

One way (and apparently Aquinas's way) of qualifying the theory involves attaching moral importance to the difference between what one strictly intends in acting and what one merely foresees as a result of acting. This distinction and its moral importance are expressed in the principle of double effect that we consider in section 7. But before turning to such matters, it will be useful to consider one possible solution to the problem of moral conflict—a solution that natural law theorists reject—because it will help bring out another important feature of classical natural law thinking.

6. A NON-CONSEQUENTIALIST APPROACH TO THE PROBLEM OF MORAL CONFLICT

The natural law theory directs us to promote what is good and avoid evil. But in the cases of moral conflict just described, in order to promote what is good, the agent must do something that will bring about bad or evil effects. Now it would certainly appear that in these cases, it would not be wrong to kill in self-defense, have a hysterectomy, or lie to save an innocent life. So we can pose the question about moral conflict this way: According to natural law theory, is one ever morally permitted to do or bring about what is bad or evil in order to promote or bring about something good? One straightforward way of answering this question (rejected by the natural law theory) is to focus on *how much* good and *how much* evil or bad would result from the action in question, compared to how much good and how much evil or bad would result from taking some alternative course of action, and then perform the action that will produce the best overall results. Such an approach is embraced by *act consequentialist* moral theories—moral theories that make the deontic status of actions depend entirely upon the value of the consequences of alternative courses of action. (Chapters 5, 6, and 7 are devoted to versions of consequentialism.) To see how a consequentialist would approach questions about cases of conflict, let us revisit some of our examples.

In the self-defense case, then, the current proposal for resolving the conflict would be to estimate the amount of good and the amount of evil that would result from the act of killing in self-defense and compare the net value of killing with the net value of refraining from such an act. The option that has the highest net value is, on the current proposal, the morally right option. Granted, whether one refrains from killing the assailant and thereby allows one's life to be taken or kills in self-defense, a human life will be lost. But obviously such facts as that the assailant is an unjust aggressor and the would-be victim is innocent are morally relevant in this case, and one way this might be reflected in our moral thinking is to suppose that the innocent life is worth more than the life of the aggressor. We might, that is, compare the values of these different human lives on some sort of scale and then reason as follows. Since the life of an unjust aggressor is worth less than the life of someone who is innocent, the good to be preserved in an act of self-defense is greater than the bad or evil result of bringing about the death of the assailant. Hence, all things considered, one is permitted, and perhaps even morally obligated, to kill in self-defense.

Consider the case in which one must lie to save an innocent life. Isn't it clear that, in the situation as described, whatever evil is brought about by telling a lie to the would-be killers is far less of an evil than would be brought about by the murder of their intended victim? Granted, in the situation described, one cannot avoid performing an action that violates one of the basic values. Still, if we compare the value attached to an innocent life with the value attached to not telling a lie (and if we suppose that these are cases where no matter what we choose, some evil will result), shouldn't we act to minimize the *amount* of evil?

Hence, by calculating *degrees* of goodness and badness of the consequences of these various actions and then requiring that in cases of moral conflict we act to bring about the best consequences, don't we have a solution to cases of moral conflict?

However, natural law theory is opposed to any such solution. According to natural law thinking, the deontic status of an action is not just a matter of the goodness and badness of the consequences of actions. Rather, as we shall see, one's *intentions* are an important element in what makes an action right or wrong.

7. THE PRINCIPLE OF DOUBLE EFFECT

The principle (or doctrine) of double effect provides a set of guidelines for dealing with cases of moral conflict of the sort we have been considering. It provides an answer to the question we have been asking: Is one ever morally permitted to do or bring about what is bad or evil in order to promote or bring about something good?

To explain adequately the principle of double effect (PDE) and how it figures into natural law thinking, it will be useful to explain some basic concepts and distinctions involved in it.

Some Preliminary Distinctions

The PDE makes use of the distinction between means and ends of our actions. Often, when we act, we act for some ultimate goal or end that we hope to bring about through what we do. The ultimate end shapes our subsequent choices. So, for instance, if one of my ends is to earn a skydiving certificate, then there are other, related ends that I must set for myself as means to my main end of earning the certificate. For instance, I must accumulate so many hours of instruction, I must pass a written test, and so forth. Of course, in setting myself these derivative ends, there may be other tasks I must complete and so other ends I must achieve. And in pursuing these derivative ends, I will have to engage in various actions. Clearly, the derivative ends and the actions I will perform in achieving them all count as means to my ultimate end of earning a skydiving certificate.

Another important distinction featured in PDE is between what we intend and what we merely foresee as resulting from our actions. That is, with regard to our efforts, we can distinguish between those effects of our actions that are intended and those that are not intended but merely foreseen. A few examples will help make the distinction clear. When I drive my car either for pleasure or to get to some destination, it is not part of my purpose to wear down my tires as I drive. I do, however, foresee that as a result of driving my car, I inevitably cause tire wear, but tire wear is not an integral part of my plan.[9] Here, we can say that my driving has the wearing down of my tires as one of its effects; but this effect, although foreseen, is not intended. Here is another example. I may know enough about one of my students to know that if she receives any grade in my course other than an A, this will cause her to be severely depressed. In giving her the B that she deserves, I can foresee her depression as an effect of my assigning this grade, but I do not thereby intend this effect. Since the tire wear and the student's depression are not an integral part of the plan of action and hence not intended, they are referred to as "side effects."

A Formulation of the Principle

Some actions bring about two (or more) effects, one good and one bad, which are both foreseen—hence a "double effect." The principle of double effect sets forth conditions under which it is morally permissible to perform such actions.

> **PDE** Whenever an action would produce at least one good effect and one bad or evil effect, then one is permitted to perform the act if and only if all of the following conditions are met:

1. *Intrinsic permissibility.* The action in question, apart from its effects, must not be wrong.
2. *Nonintentionality.* The bad effect must not be intended by the agent. There are two principal ways in which an effect might be intended:
   a. Any effect that is a chosen end of action is intended.
   b. Any effect that is a means for bringing about some intended end is also intended.
3. *Proportionality.* There is a proportionally grave reason for bringing about the evil effect. For example, there is no feasible alternative course of action (of which the agent is aware or should be aware) that would bring about the good effect without causing as much evil. Moreover, the disvalue of the bad effect is not disproportionate to (does not greatly outweigh) the positive value of the good end being sought.[10]

To understand this complex principle, let us work with the previously mentioned example involving a hysterectomy. In that example, recall, a woman with cancer of the uterus is pregnant. Her choices are to have the uterus removed, which will unavoidably cause the death of the fetus, or to refuse the operation, in which case both she and her unborn child will die. Since the operation would have the good effect of saving the woman's life and the bad effect of bringing about the death of a human being, we can apply PDE to determine whether the operation is nevertheless permissible.

First, the operation—removal of cancerous tissue—is not itself morally wrong. Second, for a well-intentioned physician the bad effect is not the ultimate end of the operation; the ultimate end is to save the woman's life. Nor is the bad effect a means for bringing about the good effect. After all, it is not the fetus but the cancer that poses a threat to her life, and so the death of the unborn child is not part of the means for saving her life. She would have the operation even if she were not pregnant. Third, since we are assuming that both woman and fetus are human beings with full moral standing, we may assume that the decision to engage in actions that would terminate one human life in order to save another (given that the other conditions are met) satisfies the requirement of the proportionality clause. This includes the assumption that the physician knows of no other feasible course of action (nor is there one that she ought to be aware of) that could save the mother's life while not bringing about the death of the fetus. Since all three conditions of the PDE are satisfied, we may conclude that the hysterectomy in question, performed by a well-intentioned physician, is morally permissible according to the natural law theory.

By applying the PDE to this case, we have thus resolved the problem of moral conflict involving the hysterectomy case. More generally, the PDE represents an answer to our question of whether, in ethics, it is ever morally permissible to do or bring about what is bad or evil in order to bring about a good result. As we have seen, the principle does allow that in some cases one may bring about a good effect in the knowledge that bad effects will result from what one does. However, the principle, in effect, accepts the directive of Saint Paul (Romans 3:8) that one may not do evil that good may come about, and so yields a negative answer to our question. Good ends do not justify using evil means to obtain them! But why not? One answer, offered by Thomas Nagel, is that in acting to intentionally bring about an evil effect one is being "guided by evil" (1986, 181). And, as we noted earlier, on Aquinas's view, evil is something to be avoided. So, although we are sometimes permitted to do what we can foresee will have bad or evil effects, we are never permitted to bring about such effects intentionally.[11]

8. MORAL ABSOLUTISM

In natural law thinking, there is a greater emphasis on avoiding wrong acts—acts that no moral person should do—than there is on promoting in a positive way what is good. The claim that there are certain very general types of action that are always morally wrong to perform, even when performing them would bring about good results, is called *moral absolutism*. Such types of action that are thus absolutely prohibited represent what are often called "deontological constraints" and are featured in such moral rules as the following:[12]

It is wrong to intentionally kill human beings, regardless of any good effects that may result.

It is wrong to torture, regardless of any good effects that may result.

It is wrong to engage in adultery, regardless of any good effects that may result.

It is wrong to engage in homosexual behavior, regardless of any good effects that may result.

Many versions of natural law ethics embrace moral absolutism. What is important to notice about such absolutist versions is that the PDE, by prohibiting the intentional bringing about of bad effects, makes it clear that what is absolutely prohibited is not just any action that, for example, kills a human being. After all, were there an absolute prohibition on actions that bring about the death of human beings, we would still be stuck with those cases of moral conflict illustrated earlier in section 5. Rather, the PDE helps the natural law absolutist make clear that it is the intentional taking of human life that is absolutely prohibited. Moral absolutism, then, represents the third main component in the natural law theory.[13]

9. THE THEORY OF RIGHT CONDUCT

In explaining some of the ideas in the moral theory of Aquinas, we began with his basic principle of right conduct (NLT), according to which we are required to do good and avoid evil, where good and evil have to do with the basic human goods of life, procreation, knowledge, and sociability. We then noted that, unless the theory is somehow qualified, there will be cases of moral conflict in which it yields inconsistent moral verdicts about particular cases. We have just seen how the principle of double effect serves to importantly qualify the theory's core and how some versions of natural law accept moral absolutism.

Let us now bring together the main components of natural law thinking—its core, the PDE, and moral absolutism—in order to present its theory of right conduct. We can do so by distinguishing direct from indirect violations of the basic values.

> **D** An action directly violates a basic value if and only if (1) the action will seriously hinder or destroy a basic value, and (2) that action cannot be justified by the principle of double effect.

Actions that satisfy the first clause of D but can be justified by the principle of double effect count as *indirect violations*. Now we can present the theory of right conduct for the natural law theory.

Theory of Right Conduct

An action A is *obligatory* if and only if (and because) failing to perform A would result in a direct violation of one or more of the basic goods.

An action A is *wrong* if and only if (and because) performing A would result in a direct violation of one or more of the basic goods.

An action A is *optional* if and only if (and because) neither performing A nor failing to perform A would result in a direct violation of one or more of the basic goods.

Thus, on the natural law theory, what *makes* an action right or wrong depends on whether it involves a direct violation of one or more of the basic human goods.

10. SOME SAMPLE APPLICATIONS OF THE THEORY

It will solidify our understanding of natural law thinking if we examine its implications in a range of cases.

Craniotomy

In some rare cases, a pregnant woman with a heart condition will die unless her unborn child is aborted. In such cases, the method of abortion involves performing a craniotomy—crushing the skull of the child—so that the fetus can be removed. What does the natural law theory imply about this case? Since the craniotomy has both a good effect (preserving the life of the woman) and a bad effect (the death of the unborn child), we can invoke the PDE to determine whether this sort of surgical procedure is morally permissible.[14]

First, as in the case of the hysterectomy, the operation is not itself morally wrong,[15] and there is a proportionally grave reason for bringing about the evil effect. Thus, the first and third parts of the PDE are satisfied. But consider the second clause requiring that the bad effect not be intended. In the hysterectomy case, it is reasonably clear that the death of the unborn is a mere unintended side effect (if performed by a well-intentioned physician), since it is the cancer that is life-threatening and so its removal, and not the death of the child, is the means for saving the woman's life. But the craniotomy case is apparently different. It is the presence of the unborn that poses the threat to the woman's life, and so its removal (involving its inevitable death) is integral to saving her life. Hence, the death of the unborn child is a means to saving her life, and so this bad effect is intended. And since the bad effect is intended, the operation in question cannot be justified using the PDE. If the operation cannot be justified by the PDE, the craniotomy involves a direct violation of the value of human life and is thus prohibited by the natural law theory.

If we compare the hysterectomy and craniotomy cases, we see that they both involve choices whose immediate outcomes are the same. In both cases, performing the operation will bring about the death of the unborn child and save the woman's life. In both cases, refraining from such procedures will result in the deaths of both individuals. Assuming that the PDE has been correctly applied in both cases, we see how, according to the natural law theory, an individual's intentions are crucial in determining the moral quality of the action. Actions whose outcomes are the same might still differ in their moral qualities owing to the agent's intentions (the diagram of the two cases shown in figure 4.2 may help).

Hysterectomy

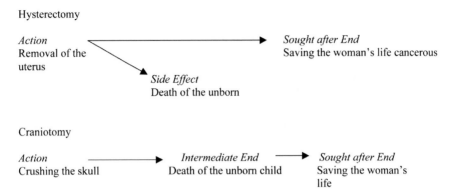

Craniotomy

Figure 4.2.   Hysterectomy and Craniotomy Compared

For some, this result is hard to accept. After all, as just pointed out, in both cases, either there is medical intervention that will save one life or there is not, in which case two lives are lost. So aren't they morally on a par? We will return to this matter in our critical discussion of the PDE in the final section.

End-of-Life Medical Decisions

In 1998, Dr. Jack Kevorkian assisted Thomas Youk in taking a lethal injection of drugs, an incident that was videotaped and broadcast on CBS's *60 Minutes.* Youk had been suffering from Lou Gehrig's disease and decided that he preferred death to the kind of painful life one experiences in the advanced stages of this disease. He enlisted the help of Kevorkian, who was later found guilty of second-degree murder for his active role in Youk's death—a case of physician-assisted suicide.

If we examine this case in light of the PDE, it is clear that what Kevorkian did was not morally justified. Although the ultimate, sought-after end was the cessation of the patient's pain, the means for bringing about this end was death. Here is the associated diagram:

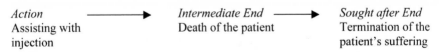

Figure 4.3.   Active Euthanasia

This case is to be distinguished from cases in which a patient with a terminal disease must take a particular drug (it is the only one available) in order to ease unbearable pain, but where a foreseeable side effect of the drug is a shortening of the patient's life. If we assume that the easing of pain provides a proportionally serious reason for taking the drug, then the PDE implies that this sort of action is morally permissible. So, the appropriate diagram for this case is:

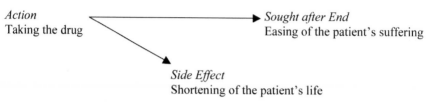

Action   ▶ *Sought after End*
Taking the drug   Easing of the patient's suffering

                          Side Effect
                          Shortening of the patient's life

Figure 4.4.   Life-Shortening Drug

Self-Defense

As a final sample application, let us return to the self-defense case described earlier, because it was in connection with such cases that Aquinas explicitly invoked the PDE. In answering the question of whether self-defense is morally permissible, Aquinas wrote:

> The action of defending oneself may produce two effects—one, saving one's own life, and the other, killing the attacker. Now an action of this kind intended to save one's own life can not be characterized as illicit since it is natural for anyone to maintain himself in existence if he can. An act that is prompted by a good intention can become illicit if it is not proportionate to the end intended. This is why it is not allowed to use more force than necessary to defend one's life. (*ST*, 70)

Here, Aquinas is saying that in cases of self-defense, if one's primary aim is to save one's own life, and if one does not use more force against the attacker than is essential in protecting oneself, then one may use force to bring about the good end being intended. With regard to the proportionality requirement, the idea is that if one can escape the threat of the attacker by running away or otherwise stopping that person by use of no or little force, then one is not allowed, for example, to maim or kill the attacker.

But what about killing the aggressor if doing so is the only way to save one's own life? Although Aquinas thinks that it can be morally correct for a proper public authority to carry out a sentence of death against a justly accused and tried criminal, he denies that a private individual may intentionally kill in self-defense.

> However, because killing is only allowed by action of public authority for the common good, it is not lawful for someone who is acting in self-defense to intend to kill another man. (*ST*, 71)

So, Aquinas's moral stance is that although one is allowed to use force against an unjust aggressor in defense of one's own life, one may not intend the aggressor's death, although one may foresee that death as an inevitable side effect of using a certain amount of force. Here is the relevant diagram:

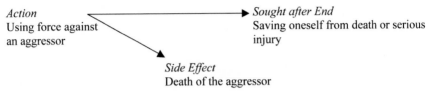

Action
Using force against
an aggressor

Sought after End
Saving oneself from death or serious
injury

Side Effect
Death of the aggressor

Figure 4.5. Self Defense

This use of the PDE may seem a bit strained since it requires that we distinguish between an action that involves a certain kind of harm to a victim and the effect of killing the victim. Suppose that all I have available to defend myself is a stick of dynamite. Are we to suppose that in lighting it and throwing it at my assailant I intend to blow him to bits, but that I only foresee his death as an unintended side effect? This raises a serious question, to which we will return in section 12, about how we are to distinguish between what one intends and what one merely foresees.

11. BRIEF RECAP

We now have before us a version of the natural law theory derived mainly from the writings of Aquinas. Before we turn to its evaluation, it will perhaps help the reader's philosophical digestion if we pause for a moment to briefly review its three main components.

- The core of the theory involves a perfectionist account of the human good that is the primary basis for a theory of right conduct. Such value-based moral theories are versions of moral perfectionism. Aquinas defends his version of moral perfectionism—featuring life, procreation, knowledge, and sociability as the most basic human goods—by appealing to facts about human nature and, in particular, by appealing to facts about basic human inclinations.
- Because there is a plurality of basic values and the theory requires that we both promote these values and avoid the evil of their destruction, the natural law theory needs to address cases in which these values come into conflict. In particular, the theory must address the question of whether one is ever permitted to bring about or promote the good by doing or bringing about what is bad or evil. The principle of double effect (the second component) addresses this question by setting forth guidelines that permit some actions aimed at promoting good results even when some bad or evil effects will inevitably result. However, one is never permitted to intentionally do or bring about evil in order to promote what is good.

- In addition to these two components, the classical version of natural law ethics embraces moral absolutism—the idea that there are certain very general types of action that are morally wrong regardless of any good consequences which would occur (or are likely to occur) were one to perform one of them.

Putting this all together, the natural law theory makes human perfection the primary value to be respected and requires that we never act so as to directly violate any of the basic human values (life, procreation, knowledge, and sociability) whose realization perfects human nature. Thus, what makes an action right or wrong, on this view, are facts about whether an action directly violates one or more of the basic goods.

12. EVALUATION OF THE NATURAL LAW THEORY

Because of the theory's complexity, its evaluation will likewise be somewhat complex. In what follows, I consider the three major components of the theory: (1) moral absolutism, (2) the principle of double effect, and (3) its core. Proceeding in this manner is necessary because, as I will explain, it is possible to accept any one of these elements while rejecting the other two. Before turning to the criticisms, let us pause for a moment to consider some of the advantages of natural law ethics that concern four of the standards for evaluating a moral theory.

Intuitive appeal, consistency, determinacy, and applicability. The natural law theory has the following apparent advantages; the first two concern the standard of intuitive appeal. First, the theory develops the intuitively appealing idea that morality is grounded in facts about human nature. This makes sense, since one would expect that questions about what has worth for human beings and questions about what humans ought to do must reflect the essential nature of such beings.

Second, natural law ethics represents a nonrelativist moral theory, another intuitively appealing characteristic of the theory. The basic principles of value and right conduct featured in the natural law theory are supposed to be correct or valid for all individuals, in all historical and cultural contexts, and at all times. John Finnis expresses this point nicely when, in commenting on such principles, he writes:

> Principles of this sort would hold good, as principles, however extensively they were overlooked, misapplied, or defied in practical thinking, and however little they were recognized by those who reflectively theorize about human thinking. That is to say, they would "hold good" just as mathematical principles of accounting "hold good" even when, as in the medieval banking community, they were unknown or misunderstood. (Finnis, 1980, 24)

Having examined moral relativism in the previous chapter, we are in search of a theory that avoids its problems, and natural law ethics offers an initially promising nonrelativist account of value and right conduct.

Third, once properly qualified, the theory apparently satisfies the consistency standard. Moreover, given the specifications of the PDE, the theory also seems to yield fairly determinate moral verdicts in cases of conflict; so, again, the theory seems to satisfy the determinacy standard.

Fourth, with regard to the standard of applicability—the standard having to do with whether the principles of the theory specify morally relevant information about action that human beings can typically obtain—again, the theory seems to do reasonably well. To avoid absolute prohibitions, one needs to know something about the nature of what one has done or is proposing to do. To apply the principle of double effect, one must have in mind the various basic goods, understand what one intends to do, and have a sense of whether there is a proportionally serious reason for engaging in some course of action that will bring about some bad or evil effects.

Having noted some of the positive aspects of natural law ethics, let us consider problems the theory encounters beginning with moral absolutism.

Moral Absolutism

Moral absolutism is the thesis that there are some general types of action that, in all circumstances, it would be morally wrong to perform. Such moral prohibitions can be expressed by moral rules, according to which certain types of action are wrong regardless of any good effects particular instances of such acts may bring about. As we have seen, such rules are interpreted in light of the principle of double effect, which limits the scope of what the rules prohibit. The rule against killing and harming, for instance, absolutely prohibits intentional killing or harming individuals, thus allowing that under certain conditions nonintentionally causing death or harm may be permissible. The main challenge for the defender of moral absolutism is to provide a rationale or justification for such rules. Why suppose there are any such moral rules? Aren't there going to be exceptional cases in which one would be justified in breaking one of these supposedly absolutist rules?

To examine these questions, let us simply focus on the moral rule against killing human beings. And to make the rule as plausible as possible, let us specify that it is the intentional taking of innocent human life that is absolutely prohibited.[16] After all, if there are any absolute moral prohibitions, the rule against killing surely expresses one of them. So, are there any clear cases in which it would be morally permissible to intentionally kill an innocent human being?

Arguably there are. Cases of active voluntary euthanasia and assisted suicide strike many reflective people as morally justified cases of intentionally killing the innocent.[17] For instance, many people, including the family of Thomas Youk, think that Kevorkian was morally justified in helping his patient to commit suicide. Before the Youk incident, Kevorkian was arrested and tried four times for his role in cases of assisted suicide, but no jury would convict him. Since Youk consented to his dying with the help of Kevorkian, one might amend the rule so that the absolute prohibition concerns the intentional bringing about of the death of an innocent human being without their consent. But in the Tony Bland case—a case of *nonvoluntary* euthanasia—the British justices who decided that it was lawful to disconnect Bland from his feeding tubes judged that bringing about the death of an individual who can no longer benefit from treatment should be legally permitted, despite the fact that Bland was not able to give his consent to the discontinuation of his only means of nourishment.[18] These attitudes toward such cases indicate that upon reflection, many people see nothing wrong with intentionally killing the innocent in at least some cases. Thus many people see certain cases of euthanasia and suicide, which involve the intentional killing of innocent human beings, as morally justified exceptions to the rule against killing.[19]

The defender of the absolute prohibition in question might argue at this point that the alleged counterexamples should not be given too much weight. After all, reasonable people disagree about such cases, and so the critic has not provided clear evidence of permissible cases of intentional killing of innocents.

But in addition to apparent counterexamples to the absolutist rule against killing, a commitment to this rule (and other similar absolutist rules) seems to be irrational. A way of bringing out the apparent irrationality involved in such rules is to consider cases in which, by engaging in a single violation of the rule, one can prevent a great number of violations of that same rule. Here is a well-known example from Bernard Williams that will help illustrate the point.

> Jim finds himself in the central square of a small South American town. Tied up against the wall are a row of twenty Indians, most terrified, a few defiant, in front of them several armed men in uniform. A heavy man in a sweat-stained khaki shirt turns out to be the captain in charge and, after a good deal of questioning of Jim which establishes that he got there by accident while on a botanical expedition, explains that the Indians are a random group of the inhabitants who, after recent acts of protest against the government, are just about to be killed to remind the other possible protestors of the advantages of not protesting. However, since Jim is an honored visitor from another land, the captain is happy to offer him a guest's privilege of killing one of the Indians himself. If Jim accepts, then as a special mark of the occasion, the other Indians will be let off. (Smart and Williams, 1973, 98)

If, on the other hand, Jim refuses the offer, then the captain will proceed as originally planned and order that all twenty captives be shot. Jim must choose between killing one (presumably innocent) person and allowing all twenty captives to die. His killing one of them would be a violation of the rule against killing, but his refraining from this killing would result in many more violations of the same rule.

So we have a case in which a single violation of the rule will result in fewer violations of that same rule. If, by killing one innocent person, one can prevent the killings of nineteen other innocent persons, isn't it paradoxical, and thus irrational, to accept a rule against killing that, if followed in this case, would ensure many more violations of the rule? What rationale can be provided for such an absolute prohibition against killing?

Perhaps those sympathetic to absolutist moral rules will attempt to defend them by appealing to the claim that individuals are more responsible for what they do than for what they allow to happen, and so it is more important for Jim to avoid violating the rule against intentional killing than it is for him to prevent others from violating that principle. This rationale may sound reasonable, but upon closer inspection, it does not work. After all, the claim that individuals are more responsible for what they do than for what they allow to happen is a moral doctrine that is in just as much need of justification as the absolutist moral rules. Why are individuals more responsible for what they do than for what they allow, especially in cases where they can prevent a great number of violations of some rule?

There are certainly other ways in which one might try to justify absolutist moral rules, but it is doubtful that any of them will succeed.[20] So I think we may conclude that absolutist versions of natural law theory are implausible.

The Principle of Double Effect

Suppose that no plausible defense of moral absolutism can be given. Still, one might hold on to the rest of the natural law theory by accepting its core together with the principle of double effect. The result would be a nonabsolutist version of the theory. According to this version, there is no absolute prohibition against intentionally violating any of the basic goods. However, given the PDE, there is a morally relevant difference between acts that intentionally violate one or more of the basic goods and actions that foreseeably but nonintentionally result in the violation of one or more of these goods. Consider the morality of killing human beings. According to a nonabsolutist version of natural law theory, it is not always wrong to intentionally kill an innocent human being; however, in cases where such killing would be wrong, it is sometimes permissible (in otherwise similar circumstances) to bring about someone's death so long as the death is not intended. Since this nonabsolutist version of the theory depends on the PDE, let us proceed to examine the principle of double effect.

Moral Nativism, Trolley Cases, and PDE

One interesting question about PDE is whether it is part of a normal human being's natural endowment, and if so, what to make of this fact. Let us begin, then, with the proposal that the principle of double effect is "natural" in the sense that rather than being a principle that human beings happen to learn from their parents or teachers, it is innate. The hypothesis that certain general moral principles are innate is called *moral nativism*.[21] One argument in favor of the nativist view about PDE comes from cross-cultural studies involving trolley cases, the most famous of which are the following two.

An out-of-control trolley is hurtling down a track headed toward five adult male workers who are not able to get out of the way and will certainly be killed if the trolley smashes into them. But there is a switching station between the trolley and the workers where there happens to be a man who sees what is unfolding and can pull a lever that will send the trolley onto a side track, thus saving the lives of the five workers. Unfortunately, there is a lone adult male worker on the side track who will be hit and killed by the trolley if the lever is pulled. Call this the "bystander case." Should the bystander pull the lever? Now consider the "footbridge case" in which there is a footbridge going over the track and located between the oncoming trolley and the five workers. Two men are standing on the footbridge, one of them very large, the other fairly slight. The large man is just large enough so that if his body were to be pushed onto the track just before the trolley passes under the bridge, it would stop the trolley and thus save the workers. So by pushing the large man onto the track at the right time the workers' lives can be saved. Unfortunately, the man would die as a result of the trolley hitting him. (We assume for both scenarios that all of these persons are strangers to each other, of roughly the same age—in other words, that there is no particular basis not mentioned in the stories that would be morally relevant in deciding what to do.)

Along with a sizable majority of people who have responded to these questions in various studies, you probably judge that it would be morally permissible for the bystander to pull the lever, but that it would be wrong for the man on the footbridge to push the large person onto the track. In both cases the choice is between the loss of five lives versus the loss of one, so what explains this common pattern of judgment? This is a descriptive question about people's moral psychology, and here is what the moral nativist says.

> An ordinary person was never taught the principle of Double-Effect . . . and it is unclear how such a principle might have been acquired from the examples available to the ordinary person. This suggests that the relevant principle is built into [a person's] morality ahead of time. (Harman, 1999a, 225)

The moral nativist hypothesis (regarding PDE) is this. When presented with the bystander and footbridge scenarios, people's judgments about these cases are spontaneous or intuitive. They don't have the experience of consciously bringing to mind the PDE (most people are unaware of the principle) and then applying it to these cases. So when presented with the bystander case, they don't have an inner monologue like the following:

> "Well, pulling the lever and sending the trolley down the side track will have a bad effect, but the death of the lone worker is not the bystander's end nor is it a means for saving the other five. And since there is a proportionally grave reason to bring about the evil effect, I guess that it is morally permissible for the bystander to pull the lever."

But people do spontaneously and automatically judge that pulling the lever is permissible, while they spontaneously and automatically judge that pushing the large man onto the tracks is wrong. As Harman says, people who make these judgments are not taught the PDE. So the moral nativist hypothesis is that this principle is part of a human being's moral hardwiring, so to speak; not something one learns in childhood.

This nativist explanation of people's judgments has been challenged by nonnativists who defend the view that moral rules are learned rather than innate.[22] This is not the place to consider this debate in moral psychology. Rather, let us suppose (merely for the sake of discussion) that the moral nativist hypothesis about PDE is correct. What bearing would this have on the correctness of this principle? Granted, the nativist story would vindicate the idea that in one sense the PDE is "natural." But the supposed fact that we come equipped with PDE which then is operative in generating various moral judgments does not mean that the principle is true or correct. After all, upon reflection, we might decide that this prewired principle involves an unjustified moral bias; that there is no good reason to suppose that whether a bad outcome is intended or merely foreseen is morally relevant in determining the moral permissibility of an action.[23] The point here (about which all sides to the nativist/nonnativist debate are fully aware) is that it would be a mistake to infer that a moral principle is true or correct simply from the supposed descriptive fact that it is innate. (We will revisit this general point in the next section when we consider NLT's core.) In any case, regardless of whether PDE is innate in the way proposed by the moral nativist, we can ask whether it is true or correct.

Is PDE a True Moral Principle?

According to the standard of explanatory power (see chapter 1, section 7) for evaluating the truth or correctness of a moral principle, if a moral principle, together with relevant factual information, not only implies our considered moral beliefs about particular cases, but also provides an *explanation* of why certain actions are right and others are wrong, we have excellent reason to think that the principle in question is true. Now consider the intuitive moral judgments that people make about the trolley cases. The moral beliefs those scenarios prompt seem to be widely shared and deeply held (at least by a great majority of those who have been presented with these cases). If we assume that people's moral beliefs about the bystander and footbridge cases are true or correct, how can we explain their correctness? Why is it permissible to do what one knows will bring about the death of the one person in the bystander case, but not in the footbridge case? One answer is that the PDE is true. Its truth or correctness would seem to explain, perhaps better than any other proposed explanation, why the moral beliefs about the trolley cases are correct.

But this best explanation defense will only hold up if the principle makes intuitively correct moral discriminations in a wide range of cases that cannot otherwise be explained. So, let us ask whether this principle makes intuitively correct moral discriminations in the cases to which it is typically applied.

Consider once more the hysterectomy and craniotomy cases. In both cases the possible outcomes of operating compared to refraining from medical intervention are the same: operating in both cases will save the life of the woman and cause the death of the unborn child, while refraining will result in the death of both. But the verdict reached about the craniotomy case using PDE is that performing the craniotomy would be morally wrong. To many this verdict will seem clearly mistaken. After all, whether or not one performs the craniotomy, the unborn child will die. Since by performing the operation the woman's life can be saved, it seems clear that the operation is not morally forbidden and is perhaps even obligatory. And if the verdict in such cases is mistaken, then there must be something wrong with the principle. Critics have raised similar worries about the euthanasia and life-shortening cases as well.[24]

Of course, the fact that many individuals upon reflection will judge that performing the craniotomy is not wrong does not prove conclusively that PDE is mistaken. After all, such cases are of interest partly because they are controversial. And so the defender of the PDE might well respond by insisting that it does give the correct moral verdict in this case and others as well. However, other defenders of the PDE argue that its correct application to the craniotomy case does not yield the conclusion that this medical procedure is wrong. These friends of the principle argue as follows. The death of the unborn is a merely foreseen, unintended side effect of the craniotomy because, strictly speaking, it is altering the shape of the unborn's skull that is the means for saving the woman's life. Of course the death of the unborn is an inevitable result of crushing its skull, but this result (say the defenders) is not part of the means but only a foreseen side effect of the craniotomy. Thus, contrary to how the PDE is standardly applied in this case, the principle does not yield the result that the craniotomy is morally wrong.

This response depends on being able to discriminate finely between what one strictly intends and what one merely foresees. But many critics find this way of handling the craniotomy case deeply problematic. Is it really plausible to claim that one can intend to crush someone's skull and yet not intend to kill him? Is it plausible to claim that one can intend to blow someone to bits with a bomb but that the resulting death is a merely foreseen side effect of being blown to bits? Is it plausible to suppose that one can intend to shoot someone through the heart and yet not intend to kill the individual?

None of these suggestions is plausible. Rather, the act of crushing someone's skull can also be described as killing him; blowing someone to bits can also be described as killing him; and shooting someone through the heart can be described as killing him. What we have here are alternative ways of describing the same action. This point helps reveal what seems deeply suspicious about the attempt to show how the PDE yields the correct result in the craniotomy case. If we describe the action of the physician one way—as the crushing of the unborn's skull, with the result that it dies—then it appears that the death of the unborn is not part of what the physician does but rather some separate effect of the act. But, of course, we can and often do correctly describe our actions in terms of what results from our basic bodily movements. If I move my finger so as to flip the light switch and thus cause the light in the room to go on, what I have done can be described in various ways: I moved my finger; I flipped the switch; I turned on the light.

Similarly, the physician who performs a craniotomy does what may be described as using a certain surgical instrument; crushing the skull; killing the fetus. It is quite proper, then, to describe the physician's intentional action as killing the fetus. So describing the action of the physician in one way yields the verdict that her action is an intentional killing, but when the action is described another way, the PDE yields the verdict that her action is not an intentional killing. This means that the verdict we get using the PDE depends on how we describe the physician's action. (See figure 4.3.) Clearly, something is wrong here. Either the physician's action is morally wrong or it is not morally wrong. What the defender of the PDE owes us is a way of distinguishing intention from mere foresight in a way that marks a difference that is morally relevant for determining the rightness and wrongness of actions. This has proved difficult to do. Let us consider a few proposals.

1. *Temporal proximity.* One proposal is to claim that an effect is part of one's intention if it is temporally close to the action that brings it about; that is, if the action and effect occur simultaneously, or if the temporal gap between the action and the effect is very small. Because the death of the unborn follows immediately after (or occurs at the same time as) the crushing of the skull, it is to be counted as part of what one intends.

But little thought is needed to see that this proposal does not help draw a morally relevant distinction between intention and mere foresight. For one thing, since the death of the unborn in the hysterectomy case is temporally close in time to the medical procedure of removing the uterus, its death would count as intended. But the hysterectomy case seems to be one of the clearest cases where the death of the individual is not intended. Furthermore, on this proposal, were I to give you a very slow-acting poison, my causing your death would be unintended; but clearly it isn't. The temporal immediacy of an effect following an action does not mark a morally relevant distinction.

2. *Close causal connection.* Another proposal focuses on there being a close causal connection between action and effect. The idea is that if an effect is an inevitable causal result of the action, then one intends the effect. The death of the fetus is an inevitable causal result of the act of crushing the skull, so it is an intended effect.

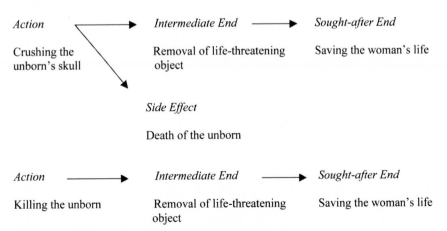

Figure 4.6. **Alternate Descriptions of the Craniotomy Case**

Again, however, this proposal will not do. The PDE clearly allows that there can be inevitable and foreseen effects of our actions that are not intended. In the hysterectomy case, the death involved is an inevitable causal result of the action in question, but it is not supposed to be intended. In general, if one accepts this causal proposal, then one will not be able to draw a morally relevant distinction between the sorts of cases used to illustrate the moral significance of the principle.

The proposals just discussed appeal to temporal and causal relations respectively—objective relations in the external world between actions and effects. The next two proposals attempt to understand the distinction between intended and merely foreseen by appeal to an agent's psychology.

3. *Desired effects.* One such proposal is that an effect is intended if it is desired by the agent—if the agent who performs the action welcomes the effect. But again, there is an immediate problem with this proposal. If the distinction between what one intends and what one merely foresees is based on what one happens to desire, then if the physician performing a hysterectomy involving a pre-viable child does not want or welcome the death of the child, then the death is not intended. On the other hand, if, for whatever reason, she does want the death of the child, then the child's death would be intended. But this makes things too subjective. Why should an agent's desires with respect to some effect make a difference in the rightness or wrongness of the action that produces that effect?

4. *Counterfactuals.* Another attempt to draw the desired distinction that might have occurred to readers involves appealing to a counterfactual claim about the physician's disposition toward the unborn. A counterfactual statement (also called a contrary-to-fact conditional) is a conditional "if . . . , then . . ." statement that has a false antecedent. Here is an example: Had Gore won the state of Florida in the 2000 presidential election, then he would have been elected president of the United States. Presumably, this counterfactual is true. So consider the following counterfactual claim: If the physician could perform the craniotomy without killing the unborn child, then she would do so. Now granted, given how things really are in the world, it is not possible to crush someone's skull and not kill them. Nevertheless, the proposal is that whenever a counterfactual of this sort is true, the effect is merely foreseen. The idea here is that if we would be willing to avoid a certain state of affairs if it were possible to do so, then that state of affairs is not intended.

This proposal may sound promising, but unfortunately it will not do, because it would imply that any means that produces an unwanted effect would not be intentional. Specifically, it would imply that if it were possible for the physician to save the woman's life without crushing the skull, then her action of crushing is not intended. But according to the PDE, one necessarily intends both the ends and one's chosen means of action. So this counterfactual test cannot be used by the defender of the principle to mark a morally relevant difference.

These proposals for distinguishing what is intended from what is merely foreseen do not exhaust the possibilities. But until the proponent of the PDE provides a criterion for making this distinction that marks a morally relevant difference, we may tentatively conclude that this principle is not sound.[25]

But what about the claim that PDE is the best explanation of the truth or correctness of the moral beliefs people have about trolley cases? Perhaps we should hold onto this principle and take up the challenge just mentioned, at least if it really is the *best* available principle for explaining certain moral beliefs. But there are competing explanations of the correctness of those trolley beliefs. For instance, in the trolley cases it is plausible to suppose that we have a conflict between various moral rules including a rule that prohibits assaulting persons, and a moral rule that requires we minimize the loss of human life (at least when doing so involves little cost or sacrifice by the agent). In most cases, the no assault rule is more stringent than the helping rule, and so in the footbridge case it would be wrong to push the man to his death. But in the bystander case, pulling the lever does not constitute assault, and moreover the helping rule is applicable and favors pulling the lever in the bystander case. Admittedly, this is but a bare sketch of an alternative explanation of the truth or correctness of the trolley judgments. And questions remain about what counts as assault (why isn't sending the train down the side track toward the lone worker a case of assault?), as well as questions about why the assault rule is more stringent than the helping rule.

In any case, given the problems with finding a suitable articulation of the intended/merely foreseen distinction that is the backbone of the PDE, I think we are justified in setting it aside.

The Core

Even if we reject moral absolutism and the PDE, we need not reject natural law theory's core. We may, that is, embrace moral perfectionism by (1) giving a perfectionist account of the human good and then (2) using it as a basis for characterizing right and wrong action. In exploring the prospects for developing this sort of view, I want to consider three issues. First is the issue of how one might attempt to justify value perfectionism and, in particular, Aquinas's project of grounding a theory of value on facts about human nature. Second, any version of moral perfectionism that rejects moral absolutism and the PDE will have to deal with cases of moral conflict. Finally, there is the issue of whether a plausible moral theory can be based on considerations of human perfection. Let us take these up in order.

The grounding project. Aquinas is often read as attempting to justify his list of basic values by inferring them from facts about human inclinations. Perhaps this reading is encouraged when he writes:

> [A]ll the things to which man has a natural inclination are naturally apprehended as good and therefore objects to be pursued, and their opposites to be avoided. Therefore the order of the precepts of the natural law follows the order of our natural inclinations. (*ST*, 49)

He then goes on, as explained earlier, to refer to natural human inclinations toward self-preservation, preservation of the species, knowledge, and sociability in specifying the four basic human goods. Suppose for the time being that Aquinas meant to infer basic values from claims about human inclinations. What are we to make of such attempted inferences?[26]

Let us first of all be clear about the aim or point of such inferences and how they are supposed to work. Presumably, the idea here is to provide an objective basis for morality—a basis grounded in nonmoral descriptive facts about human nature. Aquinas (on the reading under consideration) is assuming that facts about human inclinations—inclinations characteristic of the species—are a proper basis for inferring claims about basic human goods. So, without making assumptions about the good in relation to human beings, we are to observe such beings, make note of species-wide inclinations, and then on the basis of our observations, infer basic human goods. The key idea here is that such inferences are supposed to feature only premises that make nonmoral factual claims about human nature and conclusions that make reference to what is intrinsically good.

There are two main problems with this project. One problem concerns a logical gap between statements of nonmoral fact and statements of value, and the other concerns a worry about circularity in reasoning from fact to value. Let us take these in order.

To infer a claim about what is good or valuable directly from a premise about some matter of fact is invalid: the conclusion does not follow logically from the premise. Thus, in the following argument:

1. Human beings are inclined by nature to preserve their own lives;

therefore,

2. Human life is intrinsically good

the conclusion does not follow logically. In order for the conclusion to follow, one would need to add this premise,

3. If human beings are inclined by nature to preserve their own lives, then life is intrinsically good.

To avoid the logical gap between statements of nonmoral fact and statements of value, one must add a "bridge premise" to the sort of argument displayed above that connects facts about human nature with value. But then, one needs to provide a justification for this premise. And now the question becomes, why suppose that the claims expressed by such bridge premises are true? In general, why suppose that if human beings are naturally inclined toward some end or goal, then the end or goal in question is intrinsically good?[27] After all, there seem to be other widespread human inclinations—inclinations toward selfishness and aggression—that one would not be tempted to use as a basis for deriving human goods. So not just any old human inclination can be used as a basis for drawing a conclusion about what is intrinsically good. This point leads to the worry about circularity.

If there are such inclinations toward selfishness and aggression that are part of human nature, then in appealing to human inclinations as a basis for inferring what is good, one must be selective. But on what basis does one select some human inclinations (and not others) for purposes of inferring what is good? It begins to look as if the procedure is circular. The plan was to observe human inclinations without making any assumptions about what is good or bad and then use such information as a basis for inferring what is good (and bad). But, given the need to be selective in one's choice of human inclinations, it appears that one must first make assumptions about the human good in selecting those human inclinations that are to be a basis for inferring what is good. We thus go in a circle!

Perhaps there is a way of inferring claims about the human good from facts about human nature that does not involve arguing in a circle.[28] In any case, there is a general lesson here that we noted above in connection with the moral nativist proposal that PDE is innate, namely, that it is not legitimate to conclude that a moral principle or rule is true or correct based merely on facts about human nature, including facts about human inclinations and claims about moral principles being innate. But even if this kind of grounding project is doomed to failure, two points are worth keeping in mind.

Some critics make this sort of grounding project essential to any version of natural law ethics and therefore reject all versions of the theory because they think the grounding project is hopeless.[29] However, John Finnis, a contemporary advocate of natural law ethics, denies this characterization.[30] Moreover, Finnis claims that it is not even true of Aquinas's version of the theory that claims about morality are supposed to be derived from facts about human nature. On his reading of Aquinas, moral propositions identifying basic goods are not derived at all. So

> for Aquinas, the way to discover what is morally right (virtue) and wrong (vice) is to ask, not what is in accordance with human nature, but what is reasonable. And this quest will eventually bring one back to the underived first principles of practical reasonableness, principles which make no reference to human nature, but only to human goods. (Finnis, 1980, 36)

According to Finnis's reading of Aquinas, claims about what are the basic human goods are self-evident in the sense that anyone of sufficient maturity, and thus able to understand the relevant concepts involved, can, by the use of reason, come to grasp the truth of such claims as "Life is intrinsically good," "Knowledge is intrinsically good," and so forth. I am calling attention here to the fact that there is some dispute about whether all versions of natural law ethics (including even Aquinas's) must involve the attempt to infer basic moral principles from facts about human nature.

My second observation is that even if it is not possible to infer values from non-moral facts about human nature, this does not mean that we should reject moral perfectionism, which is at the core of natural law ethics. We should not confuse the perfectionist core of natural law ethics with a supposedly failed attempt to justify it by the sort of grounding project we have been examining. There may be other ways to justify moral perfectionism.

Revisiting the problem of moral conflict. In presenting the version of natural law ethics we find in Aquinas, we proceeded in stages. We began with the perfectionistic account of the human good together with an initial account of right action but found that there are cases in which the view (unless qualified) leads to inconsistent verdicts about the morality of actions. As we also saw, the core of the theory, when augmented by moral absolutism together with the PDE, results in a theory that avoids inconsistency. If we now give up absolutism and the PDE but want to hold on to the core, we need a way of handling the problem of inconsistency generated by cases of moral conflict.

One proposal for developing the core so as to avoid inconsistency is to claim that the various intermediate moral rules—rules concerning killing, lying, and the rest—that are featured in the theory state presumptive moral reasons for engaging in or avoiding certain forms of behavior. Thus, the rule against lying is not absolute but can be expressed as follows:

> It is wrong to lie unless, in particular circumstances, there is some moral reason to lie that outweighs in importance the moral reason for not lying.

Suppose that the other moral rules featured in traditional natural law moral theory are similarly formulated. As before, we still have to deal with cases in which two rules apply to the same situation, one rule favoring doing some action while the other favors not doing the action. In other words, in cases of conflict, we have to decide which rule, in the particular circumstance under consideration, is overriding and thus should be followed.

One possibility would be to find some sort of nonarbitrary rank ordering of the rules so that, whenever there is a conflict, the rule higher on the list should always be followed. But suppose it is not possible to come up with a fixed ranking of this sort. In that case, another possibility is to claim that in cases of conflict we simply must appeal to the details of the case at hand and use good moral judgment to decide which rule, in that particular case, should be followed. For instance, if the situation is such that in order to save an innocent life, one must lie, then one must use good moral judgment to determine whether saving a life is a good moral reason for lying that outweighs the moral importance of not lying. The key idea here is that in cases of conflict, there is no supreme moral principle or super rule that determines what we are to do; rather, in such cases, moral judgment must take over.[31]

I maintain that the best way to develop the remaining core of the natural law theory—the way hinted at in the previous paragraph—will result in the theory being both pluralistic and limited in its power to generate verdicts about the morality of specific actions. The view will be pluralistic because it will feature a plurality of moral rules. It will be limited because the moral rules that make up the theory will not themselves determine (in cases where the rules conflict) which action is morally right. When, for example, in some circumstance, the rule against lying conflicts with the rule requiring that we help others in need, there is no higher rule or principle that can settle what we are to do in that circumstance. This is where theory is powerless to dictate some right answer to the question of what ought (or ought not) to be done in a particular circumstance and so lacks a measure of determinacy.

If we follow my suggestion for interpreting the core of the natural law theory, we end up with a kind of moral theory that I will refer to as a limited, pluralist moral theory. Moreover, I shall argue that the most plausible versions of the theories to be considered in the remaining chapters will be versions of moral pluralism that are limited in the way I've described. (The idea of this type of theory will become clearer as we go, especially when we come to the moral theory of W. D. Ross in chapter 9.)

Moral perfectionism? But is the project of developing the perfectionistic core of the natural law theory worth pursuing? Moral perfectionism, recall, is the view that (1) considerations of value are conceptually prior to considerations of right conduct, and (2) the sort of value that is central to ethics is perfectionistic value. Thus, versions of moral perfectionism purport to explain the nature of right and wrong action in terms of how actions bear on perfectionistic value. But this view has been challenged by philosophers who would agree with the first claim made by the moral perfectionist but deny that perfectionistic value is central to morality. These critics would thus reject moral perfectionism's way of explaining what makes actions right or wrong and thus (appealing to the standard of explanatory power) reject it as a correct moral criterion.

Some moral philosophers hold the view that it is welfare—one's life going well for one—that is of primary concern in ethics and that one cannot understand the welfare of a human being (or other creature) solely in terms of its perfection. Their main reason for saying this is that the idea of the perfection of something is the idea of its being a good or excellent specimen of its kind. Arguably, this is an objective matter; it does not depend on the attitudes of the creature whose perfection is in question. By contrast, the notion of welfare or well-being is importantly subjective because it essentially involves the perspective of the agent in question. My life might satisfy the conditions for being a good or excellent specimen of humanity—I might be healthy and be quite knowledgeable about a range of issues—but it is still possible that from my perspective my life is not going well. But my well-being or welfare requires that from my perspective, my life is going well for me. Thus, achieving perfection does not guarantee my welfare. So, we can and should distinguish between perfectionist value and welfare (or what is often called prudential value). Here is how L. W. Sumner explains the contrast:

> [Y]ou can easily imagine yourself, at the end of your life, taking pride in your high level of self-development but none the less wishing you had got more out of your life, that it

had been more rewarding or fulfilling, and thinking that it might have gone better for you had you devoted less energy to perfecting your talents and more to just hanging out and diversifying your interests. Whatever we are to count as excellences for creatures of our nature, they will raise the perfectionist value of our lives regardless of the extent of their payoff for us. There is therefore no logical guarantee that the best human specimens will also be the best off. (Sumner, 1996, 24)

If one takes welfare (or prudential value) to be central to ethical concerns, then if Sumner is correct and welfare cannot be understood in terms of perfectionist value, we must reject moral perfectionism as giving us a correct moral criterion.

One type of moral theory that does take considerations of welfare to be central to ethical concerns is consequentialism, which will occupy us in the next three chapters.

13. CONCLUSION

I have argued that there is reason to reject moral absolutism and the principle of double effect, which are associated with the natural law tradition in ethics. However, if we reject these components, we still are left with the core of the theory. The core consists of a perfectionist account of intrinsic value and an account of right conduct according to which we are to promote such value and not hinder or destroy it. Since there is a plurality of basic human goods, the remaining core instructs us to promote these goods and to avoid hindering or destroying them. For each of the basic goods, we can formulate moral rules that prohibit some forms of conduct and require others. I have suggested that in cases where these rules come into conflict, there is no supreme moral principle that will tell us which rule one should observe; rather we must rely on our moral judgment in deciding what ought to be done in such situations of conflict. Understood in this way, the natural law theory—its remaining core—is limited in its powers to tell us what ought to be done in many specific circumstances and so lacks a measure of determinacy. In the end, developing the theory in this way will yield a limited, pluralist moral theory.

NOTES

1. Aquinas, of course, was a theist, and his version of natural law theory is embedded in a theological framework. However, it is possible to interpret Aquinas's natural law ethic without relying on theological assumptions. See Lisska, 1996, chapter 5 for a defense of this claim. In general, there are secular versions of the natural law theory, and so attempts to reject this type of theory on the basis of rejecting a religious outlook are a mistake.

2. To be precise, I am thinking of a certain category of knives that does not include such knives as butter knives and putty knives, neither of which is designed to cut.

3. It is important to distinguish these two types of perfectionism because it is possible to recognize value perfectionism as one kind of value but then go on to deny that this sort of

value is central or even relevant to questions about right and wrong behavior. We will return to this matter at the end of the chapter.

4. Passages quoted from *Summa Theologiae* will be abbreviated *ST* followed by the page numbers from Paul Sigmund's translation of Saint Thomas Aquinas, *On Politics and Ethics* (New York: Norton, 1988).

5. Since what is distinctive of human beings is their rational capacities (both theoretical and practical), and since perfecting one's human nature would seem to concern developing those capacities, one might wonder whether the values of life and procreation belong on a list of perfectionist goods. For instance, life (including the maintenance of one's health) is certainly necessary for perfecting one's human nature, but should it be included among the human perfections? Of the four basic goods, knowledge and sociability seem most clearly to relate to our rational natures and thus count as perfectionist goods.

6. In connection with suicide, Aquinas points out that it is wrong not only because it violates the value of life but also because it violates sociability, since "Man is part of the community and the fact that he exists affects the community. Therefore if he kills himself he does harm to the community" (*ST*, 70). In general, a type of action may be required or forbidden by more than one of the basic values.

7. If such rules can be known with certainty through deduction, then the premises from which they are deduced must be known with certainty, including claims about human nature featured in such deductions.

8. This claim about the moral status of the human fetus is widely accepted by members of the Catholic Church, including Catholic moral philosophers. While it is certainly controversial, let us grant it here and throughout the rest of this chapter.

9. However, it might be, if, for example, someone has offered to buy me a new set of tires once mine are worn out and I want those new tires as soon as possible.

10. This proportionality clause allows that the values of the consequences of actions figure in the determination of whether a proposed course of action is morally permissible according to PDE. But such consequences only figure in if the other clauses of PDE are met. It is worth noting that one finds different formulations of this clause by various authors who discuss PDE. For instance, T. A. Cavanaugh, in his 2006 book *Double Effect Reasoning*, formulates it as follows: "The agent has proportionally grave reasons for acting, addressing his relevant obligations, comparing the consequences, and, considering the necessity of the evil, exercising due care to eliminate or mitigate it" (36).

11. The claim that we are *never* permitted to intentionally bring about bad effects represents an absolutist interpretation of PDE, which is how the principle is standardly interpreted. But some defenders of PDE embrace a nonabsolutist interpretation according to which there is normally a stronger reason against an action whose performance intentionally brings about a bad effect than if the action has the bad effect as an unintended effect. See, for example, Quinn, 1989 and Wedgwood, 2011b.

12. Defenders of moral absolutism may disagree over which types of action are absolutely prohibited.

13. As I will explain in section 12, moral absolutism is not an essential component of natural law ethics. But since it is an interesting and important doctrine in moral theory, it is worth considering, even if natural law ethics is not firmly committed to it.

14. Here, as in the hysterectomy case, we are assuming that if the operation is not performed, both the woman and her child will die. Sometimes the cases are described so that the choice is between saving the woman and saving her child. I prefer to work with the cases as I

have described them because it helps bring out certain implications of this principle that we will consider in section 12.

15. Is performing a craniotomy on a living fetus a morally permissible act, apart from its effects? If not, then the procedure is ruled out as impermissible by clause 1 of PDE.

16. In doing so, we sidestep any problems there might be in having to use the PDE (as does Aquinas) to justify killing in self-defense, since an unjust aggressor is not, by definition, innocent, and the rule only prohibits intentional taking of innocent human life.

17. See Buchanan, 1996 for a discussion of the bearing of cases of voluntary euthanasia and assisted suicide on the prohibition against intentionally killing the innocent.

18. See Singer, 1994 for an extensive critical treatment of the sanctity of life ethic, which upholds the absolute moral prohibition against intentionally killing the innocent. Singer discusses the Bland case in chapter 4.

19. What about a rule that prohibits the intentional killing of innocent human beings against their consent? Some would argue that if such a killing were the only way to avert a catastrophe in which a million innocent people died, then breaking the rule in question would be justified. The example in the following text from Bernard Williams is relevant here.

20. For a critical discussion of a range of possible justifications, see Scheffler, 1982, chapter 4.

21. Moral nativism represents a research program in moral psychology that is often presented as the idea that human beings have a moral faculty, understood (roughly) as a specialized innate system whose job it is to generate moral judgments. Some inspiration for moral nativism comes from a suggestion by John Rawls, 1971 that there might be a parallel between attempts to characterize the moral sensibility of individuals and groups on one hand and the attempt by linguistics to characterize one's sense of grammaticalness on the other. This general idea, taken by at least some moral nativists as a suggestion about moral psychology, involves the thought that just as individuals come equipped with rules or principles that are operative in the ability of a native speaker of a language to produce grammatical sentences (without having explicitly learned the rules of grammar for her language) so it may be that individuals come equipped with a set of general moral principles that are operative in the ability of human beings to produce moral judgments. For an articulation and defense of this so-called linguistic analogy on behalf of moral nativism, see Hauser, Young, and Cushman, 2008 and Hauser, 2006. It is important to note that there is a variety of importantly different nativist theses about morality, and not all of them propose that moral norms or rules are innate. For discussions of the varieties of moral nativism see Nichols, 2005 and Sripada, 2008.

22. For a critique of moral nativism and defense of nonnativism see Prinz, 2008a, 2008b, 2009. See also Nichols, 2005 for a critical discussion of the descriptive hypothesis that the innateness of PDE is the best explanation of the fact that people's judgments seem to conform to PDE.

23. Judith Jarvis Thomson, 1999 and T. M. Scanlon, 2008 both argue that the advocates of the PDE mistakenly suppose that it is relevant in connection with explaining what makes an action morally permissible, while in fact this principle is better understood as bearing on the moral evaluation of agents. For a response to Thomson and Scanlon, see Wedgwood, 2011a, 2011b. See also FitzPatrick for a recent defense of PDE.

24. Here, of course, we are appealing to the standard of internal support.

25. For a critical survey of attempts to draw the intended/merely foreseen distinction, see Davis, 1984 and Marquis, 1991.

26. Notice that the attempt to base a theory of value on facts about human nature is an attempt to satisfy the standard of external support.

27. Here is one place where Aquinas might appeal to God's design in creating human beings. In one place he writes, "God has implanted a natural appetite for such knowledge in the minds of men" (*Summa contra Gentiles*, in Aquinas, 1988, 4). However, appealing to God's design will not, of course, help salvage the attempt to infer claims about intrinsic value solely from claims about human inclinations.

28. For a recent attempt to ground a version of moral perfectionism on nonmoral facts about human nature, see Hurka, 1993. Hurka's grounding project is trenchantly criticized by Kitcher, 1999.

29. See O'Connor, 1967, 68.

30. Finnis, 1980, 33.

31. Moral judgment involves going beyond the application of rules in coming to correct moral verdicts. More will be said about moral judgment in the chapters to come, especially chapter 9.

FURTHER READING

Aquinas and Natural Law Theory

Buckle, Steven. 1991. "Natural Law." In *A Companion to Ethics*, ed. Peter Singer. Oxford: Blackwell. A useful historical overview of natural law theorizing in ethics.

Finnis, John. 1980. *Natural Law and Natural Rights*. Oxford: Oxford University Press. One of the most important contemporary defenses of natural law theory.

———. 1998. *Aquinas*. New York: Oxford University Press. A penetrating study of the moral, legal, and political doctrines of Aquinas.

———. 1998. "Natural Law." In *Routledge Encyclopedia of Philosophy*, vol. 6, ed. Edward Craig. London: Routledge. A helpful characterization of the rudiments of natural law theory.

———. 2005. "Aquinas's Moral, Political, and Legal Philosophy." *The Stanford Encyclopedia of Philosophy*, ed. E. N. Zalta. http://plato.stanford.edu. Excellent overview.

Fried, Charles. 1978. *Right and Wrong*. Cambridge, MA: Harvard University Press. A defense of moral absolutism.

George, Robert P. 1992. *Natural Law Theory*. Oxford: Oxford University Press. Essays by various authors on contemporary natural law theory in ethics and law.

Haakonssen, Knud. 1992. "Natural Law." In *Encyclopedia of Ethics*, vol. 2, 2nd ed., ed. Lawrence C. Becker and Charlotte B. Becker. New York: Routledge. Brief overview and critique of natural law ethics.

Lisska, Anthony J. 1996. *Aquinas's Theory of Natural Law*. New York: Oxford University Press. A detailed interpretation of Aquinas's natural law theory of ethics. Includes discussion of contemporary versions of natural law ethics.

Murphy, Mark. 2008. "The Natural Law Tradition in Ethics." *The Stanford Encyclopedia of Philosophy*, ed. E. N. Zalta. http://plato.stanford.edu. Excellent overview.

Double Effect

Bole, Thomas J. 1980. "Toward Understanding the Principle of Double Effect." *Ethics* 90: 527–38. A restatement and defense of the traditional principle.

——, ed. 1991. *Journal for Medicine and Philosophy* 16. A special issue, "Double Effect: Theoretical Function and Biomedical Implications," featuring various authors debating the PDE.

Cavanaugh, T. A. 2006. *Double Effect Reasoning.* Oxford: Oxford University Press. A defense of PDE, including a history of its development and use.

Davis, Nancy. 1984. "The Doctrine of Double Effect: Problems of Interpretation." *Pacific Philosophical Quarterly* 65: 107–23. Criticism of various attempts to draw the intended/merely foreseen distinction.

FitzPatrick, William. 2013. "Intention, Permissibility, and Double Effect." In *Oxford Studies in Normative Ethics*, vol. 2., ed. M. Timmons. Oxford: Oxford University Press. An interpretation and defense of PDE according to which, contrary to standard interpretations, the principle is not best understood as appealing to an agent's *actual* intentions in determining the permissibility of actions. FitzPatrick's defense is usefully compared to Ralph Wedgwood's defense of PDE in the article listed below.

Foot, Philippa. 1967. "The Problem of Abortion and the Doctrine of Double Effect." *Oxford Review* 5: 1–15. Important critical discussion of PDE.

Marquis, Donald B. 1991. "Four Versions of Double Effect." *Journal of Medicine and Philosophy* 16: 515–44. Features criticisms of four versions of the PDE including those to be found in the writings of Boyle and Quinn.

McIntyre, Alison. 2009. "Doctrine of Double Effect." *The Stanford Encyclopedia of Philosophy*, ed. E. N. Zalta. http://plato.stanford.edu. Excellent overview.

Quinn, Warren. 1989. "Actions, Intentions, and Consequences: The Doctrine of Double Effect." *Philosophy & Public Affairs* 18: 334–51. A nonabsolutist interpretation and defense of the PDE that attempts to justify it in terms of the idea of respecting persons.

Scanlon, T. M. 2008. *Moral Dimensions.* Cambridge, MA: Harvard University Press. In chapter 1, "The Illusory Appeal of Double Effect," Scanlon argues that the DDE, despite appearances, does not bear on the moral permissibility of actions; rather it pertains to assessments of agents.

Schroth, Jörg. Current. "Bibliography on the Principle of Double Effect." Extensive list, updated regularly. http://www.ethikseite.de/bib/bpdw.pdf.

Thomson, Judith Jarvis. 1985. "The Trolley Problem." *Yale Law Journal* 94: 1395–1410. Important discussion of the complex set of issues raised by the trolley problem.

Uniacke, Suzanne. 1998. "Double Effect." In *Routledge Encyclopedia of Philosophy*, vol. 3, ed. Edward Craig. London: Routledge. A useful overview of the role, development, and problems for the PDE.

Wedgwood, Ralph. 2011. "Defending Double Effect." *Ratio* 24: 384–401. Illuminating interpretation and defense of a nonabsolutist version of PDE.

Woodward, P. A., ed. 2001. *The Doctrine of Double Effect: Philosophers Debate a Controversial Issue.* Notre Dame, IN: University of Notre Dame Press. An excellent resource that includes nineteen essays, including those by Boyle, Davis, Marquis, and Quinn listed above.

Empirical and Empirically Focused Literature

The following items concern the debate over moral nativism, most of them giving some attention to the principle of double effect.

Dwyer, Susan. 1999. "Moral Competence." In *Philosophy and Linguistics*, ed. K. Murasugi and R. Stainton. Boulder, CO: Westview Press. A defense of moral nativism.

Harman, Gilbert. 1999. "Moral Philosophy and Linguistics." In *Proceedings of the Twentieth World Congress*, vol. 1, *Ethics*, ed. K. Brinkmann. Bowling Green, OH: Philosophy Documentation Center. A defense of moral nativism.

Hauser, Marc. D. 2006. *Moral Minds*. New York: HarperCollins. An extended defense of the nativist idea that humans come equipped with a dedicated moral faculty.

———, Liane Young, and Fiery Cushman. 2008. "Reviving Rawls' Linguistic Analogy." In *Moral Psychology*, vol. 2, ed. W. Sinnott-Armstrong. Cambridge, MA: MIT Press. A very helpful overview and defense of moral nativism.

Nichols, Shaun. 2005. "Innateness and Moral Psychology." In *The Innate Mind: Structure and Content*, ed. P. Carruthers, S. Laurence, and S. Stich. New York: Oxford University Press. A critique of the nativist proposal that PDE is innate.

Prinz, Jesse J. 2008. "Is Morality Innate?" In *Moral Psychology*, vol. 1, ed. W. Sinnott-Armstrong. Cambridge, MA: MIT Press. A critic of moral nativism.

Roedder, Erica, and Gilbert Harman. 2010. "Linguistics and Moral Theory." In *The Moral Psychology Handbook*, ed. J. M. Doris. Oxford: Oxford University Press. Overview and examination of the analogy between language and morality.

5

Consequentialism 1: Classical Utilitarianism

In the previous chapter, we considered two cases featuring a woman and an unborn child, one involving a hysterectomy and the other a craniotomy. In the former case, a pregnant woman's life can be saved from cancer by removing her uterus, while in the latter case, a pregnant woman's life can be saved only by performing a craniotomy on the fetus. As the cases were described, the consequences of intervening to save the women's lives were essentially the same (the woman's life is saved, but the fetus dies), as were the consequences of not intervening (both woman and fetus die). Upon reflection, these cases strike many thoughtful individuals as being morally on a par; it seems reasonably clear (to many) that the right thing to do in both cases is to intervene and save the woman's life. In other words, there does not seem to be a morally relevant difference between the two cases, mainly because the choices involved are equivalent in the effects upon the lives of the individuals involved. Certainly, the effects or consequences of actions upon human beings and other sentient creatures are important considerations in determining the morality of actions. This thought introduces *consequentialism*, a species of moral theory that explains the deontic status of actions and other items of moral evaluation entirely in terms of the values of consequences of actions or other items being morally evaluated.

Because the consequentialist approach to morality has resulted in a variety of importantly distinct versions of this type of moral theory, it will be useful to break up our examination of this approach into two chapters. Utilitarianism is historically perhaps the most prominent form of consequentialism and the views of two of its most historically influential proponents, Jeremy Bentham and John Stuart Mill, will be the main focus of this chapter. Examining the elements of their views will lead us to consider the objection that the utilitarian theory is useless in contexts of moral decision making and thus cannot satisfy the main practical aim of such theories.

Utilitarian modes of response to this sort of objection can be found in the writings of Bentham and especially Mill.

In the following chapter, we continue our examination of utilitarianism by considering various theoretical objections to it that challenge the idea that it represents a correct moral criterion. Examining such objections will lead us to consider some developments in contemporary moral theorizing that have resulted in more sophisticated versions of both utilitarianism and non-utilitarian species of consequentialism.

1. CONSEQUENTIALISM CHARACTERIZED

Consequentialism, as a theory of right conduct, most generally speaking, is the view that an action's deontic status is ultimately explained on the basis of the *value* of states of affairs that constitute the consequences (or outcomes) that are in some way associated with the action.[1] There are many varieties of this species of theory, but what makes all of them versions of consequentialism is their commitment to the following two theses:

- *Value is independent of the right.* It is possible to give an account of the value of states of affairs and thus a comparative ranking of alternative states of affairs without appeal to the concept of right action. The states of affairs relevant in a consequentialist theory of right action are consequences (or outcomes) related in some way to the action.
- *Explanatory priority of value.* A full and proper explanation of what makes an action right (or wrong) can be given in terms of the value of the consequences that are related in some way to the action.

In addition, most consequentialist theories are concerned with what is called *personal value*—value having to do with the quality of the lives of persons (and perhaps sentient creatures generally). If there are some things that have intrinsic value independently of their contribution to the lives of persons and sentient creatures generally, they are said to have *impersonal value*. For example, one might hold that natural beauty has intrinsic value independently of how such beauty affects the lives of sentient creatures. If so, then a consequentialist could include the value of such items as among those that are relevant in determining the deontic status of actions. But most consequentialists include only personal value as deontically relevant. So, let us add a third thesis to our characterization of consequentialism, even if it is not a strictly necessary element:

- *Personal value alone as relevant.*[2] The states of affairs having value that are relevant in explaining right action concern the value that can be realized in the lives of individuals.

This generic characterization leaves two important questions wide open which must be addressed to make the generic view more precise. First, since consequentialism as a theory of right conduct is a *value-based* theory, one question any consequentialist must address is which theory of value is to serve as the basis for explaining right and wrong action. Different theories of value can be used as a basis for different versions of consequentialism. Those that embrace welfarist theories of value (to be explained shortly) are versions of utilitarianism, the topic of this chapter and the most well-known type of consequentialism.

Second, a consequentialist must also address the question of exactly how right action is related to and thus explained by the value of consequences. The most direct way of answering this question is to say that the deontic status of some particular action is explained by the intrinsic value of the consequences *of that action*. Relating actions and consequences in this direct way yields what is called *direct act consequentialism*.[3] However, there are more indirect ways of relating the deontic status of actions to the values of consequences. For instance, according to *rule consequentialism*, rules for behavior are evaluated in terms of the value of consequences associated with them, and then the deontic status of particular actions are explained, not in terms of the consequences of those particular actions, but in terms of whether they conform to the rules selected on the basis of the value of the consequences associated with those rules.[4] The deontic status of actions is thus indirectly related to consequences and their value. The distinction between act and rule versions of consequentialism is taken up in the next chapter.

Determining whether the consequences of individual actions or of rules are relevant in explaining the deontic status of actions is not the only issue that must be addressed in explaining how consequences are relevant. There are questions, for example, about whether the *expected* consequences as opposed to the *actual* consequences are relevant in determining the rightness or wrongness of actions—a topic that comes up later in this chapter. Still other questions and issues about the relation between right action and consequences need to be addressed. But rather than list them here at the outset of the chapter, let us turn our attention to a classical version of act utilitarianism that will provide a case study of how various questions and issues about the relation between an action's deontic status and consequences have been answered.

2. ACT UTILITARIANISM

Act utilitarianism makes the deontic status of an action depend entirely on the value of the action's consequences. (Henceforth, and for purposes of brevity, I will just refer to act utilitarianism as utilitarianism.) But, as lately noted, there is more to say. In addition, utilitarianism makes specific claims about (1) how actions are related to their consequences in determining their deontic status, (2) which kinds of valuable consequences count morally, (3) the scope of concern regarding such consequences, and (4) the relative importance of the welfare of those individuals affected by one's actions. Let us take these up in order.

First, utilitarianism is characteristically understood to involve a *maximizing* conception of right action: right actions are those which, compared to the alternative actions open to one in a situation, would produce the greatest total amount of value. The theory thus directs us to maximize the good (or at least minimize the bad); actions that do so are right, those that do not are wrong.

Second, as noted above, the sorts of consequences that utilitarianism is interested in have to do with the welfare of individuals (including persons but also perhaps including other sentient creatures). The actions we perform can, and often do, have effects on the welfare or well-being of ourselves and others, and it is the goodness or badness of the consequences of our actions in relation to the welfare of individuals that determines the rightness or wrongness of an action. Thus, utilitarianism accepts *welfarism*—the view that the only kind of value that is of fundamental relevance for ethical evaluation is welfare.

Third, the utilitarian theory under consideration in this chapter is *universalist* in the sense that the effects of one's actions on the welfare of *all* individuals who will be affected by what one does figure in determining the deontic status of one's actions. Of course, one might consider the welfare of all those who will be affected by one's action and yet give special weight to the welfare of one's family, friends, and associates. Or one might give special weight to the members of some group even though those individuals are not specially related to you. But the present utilitarian theory rules out such cases of special weighting.

And so, fourth, utilitarianism is an *impartialist* theory in the following way: the benefit (or loss) to one person counts just as much as the same size benefit (or loss) to anyone else affected by one's action. This idea really involves two distinct claims. First, the fact that the agent, her family, friends, or associates would benefit a certain amount from her action is not to be given more weight in determining the deontic status of her act than the same size benefits her action would produce for those to whom she has no special connection.[5] This idea is sometimes put by saying that utilitarianism is an *agent-neutral* moral theory.

But it is possible for a theory of value to be agent-neutral in the way just described but still assign more weight to the consequences of an action as it affects some particular group of individuals compared to other groups. For instance, one might hold the view that the welfare of individuals whose level of welfare is far below average ought to be given more weight in determining right action than the welfare of those who are reasonably well off. The idea would be that a benefit to someone who is among the disadvantaged is of more value than an equivalent benefit to someone who is well off. Such views are *prioritarian* versions of consequentialism, according to which (roughly) one morally ought to maximize utility, where the utility of an action represents the result of giving a certain amount of extra weight (and thus priority) to the welfare of the disadvantaged in determining the overall utility associated with the action.[6] Classical utilitarianism is *nonprioritarian*. The universalist and impartialist elements of utilitarianism are encapsulated in Bentham's memorable slogan "Everyone to count for one, no one to count for more than one."

Thus, on the utilitarian theory, the deontic status of an action is determined entirely by how much intrinsic value the action would produce (compared to other alternative actions one could perform instead), where intrinsic value has to do with welfare, and where equal consideration is given to all individuals who will be affected by the action in question.

"Utility" is a technical term featured in utilitarianism that refers to the values of the consequences of actions. More specifically, I will be using the term to refer to the overall net intrinsic value of the consequences of actions. The idea is this. An action can, and often will, have both good and bad effects upon the welfare of individuals. My making difficult paper assignments in my courses will predictably have good consequences: students will be challenged to extend themselves and many will in fact (I hope) improve their philosophical acumen thus contributing positively to their overall welfare. However, my making such assignments also results in an increased level of stress for many students, which, given the mental anguish involved, counts as a bad effect of my action. We might say, then, that my making tough paper assignments has some positive, or good, consequences and some negative, or bad, consequences. If one were to consider how much positive value (good) compared to how much negative value (bad) my action would produce, the overall net intrinsic value of the consequences of my action is what we mean by referring to the utility of the action. The idea can be made a bit more precise as follows. Let us consider an action whose performance results in both positive and negative effects on the welfare of a number of individuals. Then the utility associated with this action is the result of (1) summing the positive welfare-related consequences or effects of the action on all of those who are positively affected in some way by the action, which yields a positive value, (2) summing the negative welfare-related consequences or effects of that action on all of those who are negatively affected in some way (some individuals may be both positively and negatively affected) which yields a negative value, and then adding the positive and negative values together to obtain the overall net total utility of the action. This way of determining the utility of an action is often referred to as *aggregation* for obvious reasons.[7]

Notice that if some action were to produce a greater aggregate negative than positive value, then its utility would be negative. Indeed, in some cases, it might turn out that all of the alternative actions open to an agent have negative utilities. In this case, the utilitarian theory directs one to perform the action having the least amount of negative utility. This point helps make clear the guiding idea behind utilitarianism: one is always permitted, if not required, to bring about the best state of affairs bearing on welfare that one can in the particular situation in which one finds oneself. In some situations, the theory will direct us to make the best of a bad situation. The general idea (characteristic of utilitarianism and all versions of act consequentialism) that it is always at least permissible for one to bring about the best available results is often referred to as the view's *compelling idea*.[8]

Here, then, is the theory of right conduct for utilitarianism:

Theory of Right Conduct

An action A is *obligatory* if and only if (and because) A would produce a higher level of utility than would any other alternative action that the agent could perform instead.

An action A is *wrong* if and only if (and because) A would produce less utility than would some other alternative action that the agent could perform instead.[9]

An action A is *optional* if and only if (and because) (i) A would produce as high a utility as would any other alternative action that the agent could perform instead, but (ii) there is at least one other alternative action that would produce as high a utility as A. (In other words, an action is optional if and only if (and because) in terms of utility production it is tied for first place with at least one other action.)

As we proceed in this chapter and the next, it will be convenient to be able to refer to a single principle that encapsulates the utilitarian theory just presented. So, making use of the category of right action (which includes both the obligatory and the optional), we can express the basic idea of the theory by what I will call the *generic principle of utility*:

GPU   An action A is *right* if and only if (and because) A would produce as high a utility as any alternative action that the agent could perform instead.

Utility, as we have said, refers to the value—the intrinsic goodness and badness—of the consequences of actions as they bear on the welfare or well-being of individuals. But how are we to understand welfare?

3. HEDONISTIC ACT UTILITARIANISM: THE CLASSICAL VIEW

The classic utilitarians, Bentham and Mill, accepted the following two claims:

1. One's welfare (how one is faring in life) is a matter of one's level of happiness.
2. Happiness is constituted by experiences of pleasure (and the absence of experiences of pain).

Individual welfare for these philosophers, then, was understood in terms of pleasure and pain. The resulting moral theory is called *hedonistic utilitarianism*. Let us consider it in a bit more detail.

In ethics, *value hedonism* is the view that experiences of pleasure alone are intrinsically good and experiences of pain alone are intrinsically bad.[10] All other things that have value are extrinsically good or bad. Money, health, power, knowledge, beauty, and other such desirable things are only good as means to the production of pleasure. To be more precise, it is specific uses of money, power, and knowledge that are good as a means (and hence extrinsically good) whenever their possession or use promotes pleasure, while their possession or use on some occasion is bad as a means (extrinsically bad) when such possession or use promotes pain. Otherwise they are intrinsically value-neutral.

As mentioned earlier, utilitarianism is committed to welfarism, according to which welfare is the only type of value that is of fundamental relevance in ethics. If we now combine welfarism with a hedonist account of welfare, we get *ethical hedonism*:[11]

> **EH** Experiences of pleasure are intrinsically good and experiences of pain are intrinsically bad, and they are the only items of intrinsic value with which ethics is concerned.

In connection with ethical hedonism it is important to stress that talk of pleasure and pain is to be understood broadly and includes not only bodily pleasures resulting from eating, drinking, getting a massage, and so forth, but also intellectual and aesthetic pleasures. Solving a difficult mathematical puzzle or viewing one of Edward Hopper's paintings can be a source of pleasure, and the pleasures so produced are to be included in the utilitarian's calculations of utility.

Hedonistic utilitarianism, then, is the result of plugging ethical hedonism into the basic utilitarian conception expressed above in GPU. Bentham was an advocate of this brand of utilitarianism, and Mill, on some readings, was as well. We can begin our study of hedonistic versions of utilitarianism by defining a hedonistic conception of utility (net intrinsic value) as follows:

> **HU** The utility of an action = the overall balance of pleasure versus pain that would be produced were the action to be performed.

If we now reformulate our generic principle of utility (GPU) to reflect a hedonist account of welfare, we have the basic principle of hedonistic utilitarianism:

> **PHU** An action A is *right* if and only if (and because) A would produce at least as high an overall balance of pleasure versus pain as would any other alternative action open to the agent.

How might we go about determining the utility of actions given this hedonistic theory of utility? This question is addressed in Bentham's "felicific calculus," to which we now turn.

4. BENTHAM'S FELICIFIC CALCULUS

Jeremy Bentham (1748–1832), who was among the most distinguished of the early proponents of utilitarianism, defended his version of the view in his 1789 work, *An*

Introduction to the Principles of Morals and Legislation. As just mentioned, Bentham (like many utilitarians) accepts ethical hedonism. Of particular interest for our purposes is Bentham's so-called felicific calculus, which provides a checklist of seven features to be used in calculating the utilities of actions and thereby arriving at reasoned conclusions about their deontic status. Here is the list:

1. Intensity
2. Duration
3. Certainty and uncertainty
4. Propinquity and remoteness
5. Fecundity
6. Purity
7. Extent

Let us take a closer look.

The two items on Bentham's list that directly concern the calculation of the utilities of actions (where utility concerns episodes of pleasure and episodes of pain) are the *intensity* of such experiences and their *duration.* The key idea here is that pleasures and pains can be measured. That is, in principle at least, we can assign numerical values to episodes of pleasure and of pain based on their intensity and duration. Doing so allows us to add and subtract their values. Engaging in such hedonic arithmetic in turn allows us (again, in principle) to assign numerical values to the utilities of actions for purposes of arriving at judgments about their rightness and wrongness. Let us briefly elaborate this idea.

To carry out these calculations, we need to settle on some unit of measure for both episodes of pleasure and episodes of pain. Consider the pleasure one experiences from drinking lemonade over the course of one minute on a hot day when one is thirsty. Let us stipulate that this will represent our unit for calculating pleasures. Thus, if drinking a beer yields pleasure that is twice as intense as drinking lemonade under the conditions specified, then drinking a beer for one minute equals two units of pleasure. Now we do a similar thing for experiences of pain: we stipulate some unit in terms of which all other pains can be assigned a numerical value. The idea, then, is that all experiences of pleasure (bodily, aesthetic, and intellectual) can be assigned a numeric value using our stipulated scale of measure, and the same can be done for experiences of pain. This means that such values are *commensurable,* which means that there is a common unit measure that can be used to rank values.

The third entry on Bentham's list—*certainty* and *uncertainty*—has to do with the likelihood that an action will have some particular pleasurable or painful outcome. This dimension of utilitarian calculation will come up again in section 6, so we will skip over it for now.

Propinquity and *remoteness* have to do respectively with episodes of pleasure and pain that follow more or less immediately from an action and those that follow some time after the action. Since the utility of an action depends upon all of its consequences—including those that do not occur until some time has elapsed after the action—Bentham has us consider the propinquity and remoteness of episodes of pleasure and pain that an action would produce if performed.

In taking account of the long-range consequences of our actions, Bentham has us consider the *fecundity* and the *purity* of pleasures and pains in determining the utility of actions. Fecundity refers to the likelihood that episodes of pleasure will be followed by further episodes of pleasure, and similarly for pain. For instance, for many individuals the act of reading a fine novel will not only result in the immediate pleasures involved in the reading but also is likely to result in further pleasures experienced in reflecting on themes from the novel. For such individuals, the act of reading such a novel is fecund.

The purity of a pleasure or pain refers to the likelihood that such experiences will not be followed by experiences of the opposite sort. For instance, the immediate result of eating a chocolate bar may be one of pleasure. But suppose that as a result of eating the candy, one will experience a severe stomachache two hours later. In that case, eating the chocolate lacks, in Bentham's terminology, purity.

As I have explained these features, fecundity and purity have to do with calculating the remote effects of actions, and remoteness just has to do with considering all of the episodes of pleasure and pain that flow from some action. So, the intensity and duration of the episodes of pleasure and pain are fundamental in determining the utility of an action.

Finally, *extent* concerns the number of persons whose welfare will be affected by one's action. In describing a procedure for morally evaluating actions, Bentham recommends that we begin our calculations by considering any person who seems directly affected by the action in question. For this person, we consider all of the episodes of pleasure (both immediate and remote) that he will experience as a result of the action, and similarly for the episodes of pain.[12] We can then determine how much utility would accrue to this individual were the action to be performed. As Bentham explains, we next

> [t]ake an account of the *number* of persons whose interests appear to be concerned; and repeat the above process with respect to each. *Sum up* the numbers expressive of the degrees of good tendency, which the act has, with respect to each individual, in regard to whom the tendency of it is *good* upon the whole: do this again with respect to each individual, in regard to whom the tendency of it is *bad* upon the whole. Take the *balance*; which, if on the side of pleasure, will give the general *good tendency* of the act, if on the side of pain, the general *evil tendency*, with respect to the same community. (Bentham, [1789] 1948, 31)

Calculating the utility of a single action is not sufficient for determining its deontic status for the utilitarian. Utilitarianism is a maximizing theory, and we are to perform the action with the highest utility. So we must calculate the utilities of the alternative actions open to us in some situation. We are morally required by the theory to perform the action with the highest utility (which might be negative); all other actions are forbidden. In cases where two or more actions are tied for first place in terms of their utilities, we are required to perform some one action from among this select alternative set, although each such action, taken individually, is optional.

This may all seem very tidy, but one may question whether such a calculus is possible even in principle. Is it theoretically possible to assign numerical values to episodes of pleasure and of pain that would allow the kind of hedonic arithmetic mentioned above? We explained this sort of measurement in terms of the duration of the experience and its intensity. The duration of pleasures and pains can, of course, be measured, but what about intensity? Consider the intensity of the pleasure involved in drinking a fine Bavarian pilsner beer, and compare it to the intensity of the pleasure involved in reading a good mystery novel. Can the intensities of these two very different experiences be put on some common scale of cardinal measurement? Of course, the problem is aggravated when we consider coming up with some unit of measure for making interpersonal comparisons of utility. Whether it is possible in principle to assign numerical values to episodes of pleasure and pain so that they can be added and subtracted will largely depend on the nature of such mental states. This is a difficult topic that we cannot pursue here.

But even if no such scheme of cardinal measurement is possible, this does not spell disaster for hedonistic utilitarianism. So long as there is some way to compare the levels of pleasure and pain experienced by different individuals, the utilitarian has all she needs for her theory. And we do seem to be able to make such comparisons. Consider first the comparisons we make in our own case. I judge that going to eat at Los Olivos would be a more pleasant experience than going to eat at Pink Pony. I judge that staying home this evening and reading a Graham Greene novel would be more pleasant and yield more personal happiness than would going to Beale Street and being in a crowd. We make such *intra*personal comparisons of actual, remembered, and prospective pleasures and pains all the time.

Interpersonal comparisons also seem quite possible. That is, there seems to be no problem in comparing how much enjoyment I would derive from going to the restaurants in question with how much you would derive. And the same applies to reading a Graham Greene novel and going to Beale Street. I can sensibly judge, for example, that you would derive far more pleasure in going to Beale Street this evening than I would and that you would not enjoy reading a Graham Greene novel nearly as much as I. Such *inter*personal comparisons of pleasure and pain are commonplace and seem to be all one needs to make sense of interpersonal comparisons of utility.

Of course, in practice it may be difficult, if not impossible, to make interpersonal comparisons of utility for purposes of moral decision making, especially when one's action affects many people (a point that we consider in more detail in section 6). And even if the sort of felicific calculus envisioned by Bentham were possible, we could only hope to roughly approximate the rigor prescribed by his procedure. But our discussion of utility in terms of pleasure and pain has, thus far, taken for granted that the hedonic value of experiences of pleasure and pain is exhausted by considering their intensity and duration. This feature of Bentham's view prompted a certain criticism of the utilitarian doctrine that Mill was anxious to rebut. Mill's rebuttal involved rejecting Bentham's purely quantitative conception of utility, as we shall see in the next section.

5. MILL'S UTILITARIANISM

The moral and political writings of John Stuart Mill (1806–1873) continue to be extremely influential in the field of ethics in general and in the utilitarian tradition in particular. His 1863 *Utilitarianism* is as important for its forceful presentation and defense of utilitarianism as it is short. Two significant elements of Mill's theory are his conception of welfare and his attempted proof of the principle of utility. Let us briefly examine them.

Qualitative Hedonism

Like Bentham, Mill was committed to ethical hedonism as an account of welfare:[13]

> By happiness is intended pleasure, and the absence of pain; by unhappiness, pain, and the privation of pleasure. To give a clear view of the moral standard set up by the theory, much more requires to be said. . . . But these supplementary explanations do not affect the theory of life on which this theory of morality is grounded: namely, that pleasure, and freedom from pain, are the only things desirable as ends. (Mill, [1863] 1979, 7)

However, Mill's version of hedonism makes an important departure from the version advocated by Bentham.

Bentham's hedonistic conception of the good for human beings (and other sentient creatures) is properly described as purely *quantitative*. As we have seen, the two aspects of experiences of pleasure in virtue of which such mental states have positive value are their intensity and their duration—properties of such states that can (so Bentham assumed) be measured in units. Bentham's quantitative hedonism (and hence the utilitarian theory generally) was attacked as being a moral philosophy unfit for humans, being more appropriate for lower animals like pigs. In response to this criticism, Mill refined Bentham's purely quantitative version of hedonism by insisting that considerations of quality, along with quantity, represent an aspect of pleasurable mental states that help determine their value. Let us review the objection that prompted Mill's refinement and then consider his reply to it.

Here is how Mill characterizes what has come to be known as the *doctrine of swine objection*:

> Now such a theory of life [utilitarianism] excites in many minds, and among them in some of the most estimable in feeling and purpose, inveterate dislike. To suppose that life has (as they express it) no higher end than pleasure—no better and nobler object of

desire and pursuit—they designate as utterly mean and groveling, as a doctrine worthy only of swine. (Mill, [1863] 1979, 7)

The idea behind this objection is clear enough. Human beings are certainly capable of many fine and noble pursuits—we have capacities for intellectual and aesthetic endeavor, as well as a capacity for moral pursuits, that are quite beyond any capacities possessed by lower animals, which can experience only those pleasures associated with, for example, eating, drinking, sex, and (at least for pigs) wallowing in mud. Hedonistic utilitarianism, however, seems to ignore these facts about human beings, setting forth a life of pleasure and reduction of pain as the highest good for human beings and the end of moral conduct.

Now certainly, one sensible requirement of any plausible moral theory is that it reflect somehow the nature of human beings. A moral theory that sets forth severely demanding moral requirements might be fit for saints or some other superhuman creatures, but it would hardly be a theory fit for humans. Similarly, a moral theory that puts forth requirements that in effect represent human beings as creatures on a par with pigs errs in the other direction. Hedonistic utilitarianism does just that, according to the critics.

One obvious response to this criticism is that nothing in Bentham's version of hedonistic utilitarianism requires or advises human beings to pursue only those types of bodily pleasures that can also be experienced by lower animals. Certainly, given the enlarged capacities of humans compared to those of lower animals, nothing in Bentham's view conflicts or fails to comport with facts about distinctive human capacities. The fact that we are capable of intellectual and aesthetic endeavors means that we are capable also of experiencing the pleasures that typically result from pursuing such things. And furthermore, it is open to Bentham to claim that more often than not the pursuit of intellectual and aesthetic ends will yield longer-lasting pleasures and hence, on the whole, pleasures of greater quantity compared to pleasures resulting from such activities as drinking and eating.

Nevertheless, there is still a worry that can be raised against a purely quantitative hedonism that is brought out in a vivid and imaginative way by Roger Crisp in his story about Haydn and the oyster.

> You are a soul in heaven waiting to be allocated a life on Earth. It is late Friday afternoon, and you watch anxiously as the supply of available lives dwindles. When your turn comes, the angel in charge offers you a choice between two lives, that of the composer Haydn and that of an oyster. Besides composing wonderful music and influencing the evolution of the symphony, Haydn will meet with success and honor in his own lifetime, be cheerful and popular, travel and gain much enjoyment from field sports. The oyster's life is far less exciting. Though this is a rather sophisticated oyster, its life will consist only of mild sensual pleasure, rather like that experienced by humans when floating very drunk in a warm bath. (Crisp, 1997, 24)

Haydn will die at the age of seventy-seven, but the angel in charge offers you the life of an oyster for as long as you like—hundreds, even thousands, of years. Clearly, the variety and intensity of the pleasures that fill Haydn's life far exceed the pleasures that the oyster will experience in that same seventy-seven year span of time. But on the sort of quantitative view held by Bentham, if the oyster lives long enough, eventually the total quantity of pleasure it will experience will exceed the total quantity experienced by Haydn. If the only thing that counts in deciding matters of personal welfare is the product of the intensity and duration of one's pleasures (as Bentham's version of hedonism implies), then it follows that the extended life of the oyster is to be preferred over a life like Haydn's. But this seems to be an absurd result.

What the Haydn-oyster example reveals is that we normally think that there is more to the value of pleasure than mere intensity and duration: facts about *kinds* of pleasure also matter. And this is precisely what Mill's version of hedonism—his *qualitative hedonism*—is intended to reflect.

> It is quite compatible with the principle of utility to recognize the fact, that some kinds of pleasure are more desirable and more valuable than others. It would be absurd that while, in estimating all other things, quality is considered as well as quantity, the estimation of pleasures should be supposed to depend on quantity alone. (Mill, [1863] 1979, 8)

It might help to understand Mill's position if we reflect a bit more on hedonism as a theory of value. This sort of view makes two claims, sometimes not clearly distinguished. First, hedonism makes a claim about what sorts of items have intrinsic value: certain mental states and, in particular, mental states of pleasure are intrinsically good, and mental states of pain are intrinsically bad. Second, the view offers an explanatory claim about what *makes* such states intrinsically good or bad: certain properties possessed by states of pleasure make them intrinsically valuable, and similarly for states of pain. According to Bentham's quantitative hedonism, the only good-making properties of pleasures and pains are their intensity and duration. On Mill's qualitative version, not only intensity and duration but also facts about the very nature of the pleasure—its quality as a pleasurable experience—are good-making features of such states. (Again, similar remarks apply to states of pain.)

Of course, if we enrich hedonism in the way Mill suggests, we must have some way to determine the relative qualities of pleasures. Mill's proposal for dealing with this matter is that we are to consult the opinions of competent judges.

> If I am asked, what I mean by difference in quality of pleasures, or what makes one pleasure more valuable than another, merely as a pleasure, except its being greater in amount, there is but one possible answer. Of two pleasures, if there be one to which all or almost all who have experience of both give a decided preference, irrespective of any feeling of moral obligation to prefer it, that is the more desirable pleasure. If one of the two is, by those who are competently acquainted with both, placed so far above the other that they prefer it, even though knowing it to be attended with a greater amount of discontent, and would not resign it for any quantity of the other pleasure which their nature is capable of, we are justified in ascribing to the preferred enjoyment a superiority in quality, so far outweighing quantity as to render it, in comparison, of small amount. (Mill, [1863] 1979, 8–9)

What do the experts have to say about matters of quality? According to Mill:

> Now it is an unquestionable fact that those who are equally acquainted with and equally capable of appreciating and enjoying both do give a most marked preference to the manner of existence which employs their higher faculties. (Mill, [1863] 1979, 9)

Thus, according to Mill, the best evidence we have concerning the relative qualities of pleasures are the verdicts of those who have experienced a full range of types of pleasures, including bodily, intellectual, and aesthetic pleasures. Moreover, the experts apparently agree that, by and large, the pleasures flowing from the use of our intellect and from our aesthetic sense (the pleasures of the higher faculties) are more desirable and hence of a higher quality than those resulting from our lower, bodily faculties.

What is particularly important to recall from our previous discussion is that on a purely quantitative conception of utility, pleasures (and pains) of any sort could be put on a common numerical scale for comparison. So, for example, regardless of the fact that the pleasures that Haydn will experience are of far greater sophistication and intensity than the ones experienced by the oyster, it is possible, on a purely quantitative scale, to equate the total amount of pleasure that Haydn will experience in his lifetime with the total amount of pleasure that the oyster will experience during its lifetime. In short, on a purely quantitative version of hedonism, pleasures and pains are fully and completely commensurable.

The introduction of quality disrupts such commensurability: some types of pleasure cannot be equated with other types, whatever the quantity involved. In the very last sentence of the first of the above two passages, Mill claims that competent judges will rank some pleasures higher in value than others "and would not resign [them] for any quantity of the other pleasure." According to Mill, then, various types of pleasures are *incommensurable*—they can't be put on a cardinal scale of measurement.

How does the addition of quality help answer the doctrine of swine objection? Presumably, doing so blocks the claim that, for example, the extended life of an oyster is better (represents a greater source of welfare) than the life of Haydn. Haydn's life was filled with all sorts of non-bodily pleasures of a higher quality than the sorts of pleasures that would be experienced by the oyster. Take any one of Haydn's higher pleasures, such as the pleasure derived from composing a symphony. No amount of pleasure of the sort experienced by the oyster will outrank in quality this pleasure of Haydn's. Thus, by factoring in considerations of the quality of various pleasures, we can conclude that the life of a Haydn is certainly more desirable than the life of an immortal oyster.

I have been using the Haydn-oyster story for purposes of vivid illustration, but the point of Mill's qualitative hedonism can be brought to bear on the choices that human beings actually face. One can easily imagine having to choose between two paths in life. One path will result in a life of relative ease that will not put much strain on one's current intellectual abilities. The other path will be a life in the pursuit of scientific knowledge, which will no doubt involve many sacrifices and setbacks. Assuming the scientist enjoys some intellectual pleasures as a result of her scientific inquiries her life is to be preferred to the life of the ne'er-do-well. By making quality one of the properties of experiences of pleasure and pain that determine the value of such experiences, Mill's moral theory fully respects the fact that humans have greater capacities than pigs and are thus "higher" than such beasts. Thus, Mill's qualitative hedonism helps the utilitarian theory avoid the charge that it is a moral philosophy fit for swine.

Objections to Qualitative Hedonism

Mill's qualitative hedonism has been roundly criticized. I shall mention two of the objections; the first challenges its intelligibility, the other raises worries about the appeal to experts.

A common objection to Mill's version of hedonism is that it faces a dilemma. Either quality has to do with the intrinsic nature of mental states of pleasure, or it does not. If it does, then it has to do with the pleasantness of experiences of pleasure, in which case the only basis for distinguishing various pleasures is their intensity and duration, and Mill ends up a pure quantitative hedonist after all. However, if quality does not have to do with the intrinsic nature of pleasure and has rather to do with something other than the pleasantness of the experience, Mill has forsaken hedonism. (You may recall that the second claim made by the hedonist is that it is intrinsic properties of pleasures and pains that make them good and bad respectively.) Thus, there is no distinct position that can be described as qualitative hedonism.

The reply to this objection is that it begs the question against Mill's view. The first horn of the dilemma simply assumes without argument that the only aspects of pleasures that can affect their ranking are quantifiable. Mill would insist that the intrinsic nature of a pleasure—the quality of its pleasurableness—makes it more or less valuable than other types of pleasure. Also, appealing only to the pleasurableness of such states means that he can avoid the second horn of the dilemma. The idea might be put this way: for Mill it is a basic fact that the intrinsic nature of certain kinds of pleasures (apart from their intensities and durations) confers on them a value that is higher than the value conferred on other, "lower" pleasures of equal intensity and duration.

Critics have also raised doubts about Mill's use of competent judges as a basis for distinguishing higher from lower pleasures. As I have explained Mill's qualitative hedonism, the judgments of the experts do not make some pleasures higher than others; rather the role of the experts is evidential: their preferences represent the best evidence we have for judging the relative qualities of pleasures. Now, presumably, to be competent in judging matters of quality, one must have the developed capacities to enjoy the types of pleasures to be ranked. An uneducated individual, who is not able to appreciate works of literature and other works of art, is not competent to make comparative rankings between bodily pleasures and aesthetic pleasures. Only a select group will have the requisite competence. But how can Mill be so sure that those who are competent in the way he requires will reach universal or nearly universal agreement over matters of quality?

Consider Joe, a philosopher and avid football fan. One can imagine that Joe, under the appropriate conditions for making comparisons, may well rank the pleasure derived drinking beer and watching professional football on television to be of a higher quality than the pleasure derived from reading (and contemplating) book Zeta of Aristotle's *Metaphysics*. If Joe is thereby disqualified from being among competent judges, the worry is that appeal to the experts is a cheat. That is, if it turns out that in order to qualify as a "competent" judge you must agree that the intellectual and aesthetic pleasures are of a higher quality than the bodily pleasures, then Mill's appeal to the experts is circular. We are supposed to appeal to the experts for unbiased testimony as to the comparative rankings of pleasures. But to count as an expert (so it seems) you must antecedently agree with a certain preferred ranking.

Despite such worries, there is something both plausible and attractive about Mill's attempt to sophisticate hedonism with the introduction of quality as a dimension of pleasure and pain. However, the main task seems to be one of blending such considerations of quality with considerations concerning the quantity of pleasures in arriving at judgments of overall relative value. It is simply not clear how considerations of both quantity and quality are to figure in determining the utilities of actions. Whether there is some way it can be done I will leave for the reader to ponder.

Mill's "Proof"

Bentham claimed that the principle of utility could not be proved, since "that which is used to prove every thing else, cannot itself be proved: a chain of proofs must have their commencement somewhere" (Bentham, [1789] 1948, 4). The idea is that since the principle of utility is fundamental in the sense that all other moral claims are justified ultimately by appeal to it, there can be no further principle to which we can appeal in attempting to prove it. If there were, the principle of utility would not be fundamental. The assumption here seems to be that any genuine proof of a moral principle must appeal to some further, more basic *moral* principle.

Opposed to Bentham, many philosophers have thought that it is possible to prove, or at least provide justifying evidence for, a fundamental moral principle by appealing to nonmoral theories and assumptions.[14] However, Mill agrees with Bentham that "questions of ultimate ends do not admit of proof, in any ordinary acceptation of the term" (Mill, [1863] 1979, 34). Nevertheless, Mill thinks that:

> We are not, however, to infer that its [the principle of utility's] acceptance or rejection must depend on blind impulse or arbitrary choice. There is a larger meaning of the word, "proof" in which this question is as amenable to it as any other of the disputed questions of philosophy. . . . Considerations may be presented capable of determining

the intellect either to give or withhold its assent to the doctrine; and this is equivalent to proof. (Mill, [1863] 1979, 4–5)

Mill's "proof" (in the larger meaning of the term) is not so much an argument for the principle of utility as it is an argument for the claim that the general happiness is alone of intrinsic value. Mill assumes that if this can be shown, then since morality requires that we perform actions that produce as much positive value or goodness as possible, the principle of utility will have been (in the broad sense of the term) proved.

Mill's proof proceeds by attempting to establish three conclusions. First, he argues that each individual's happiness—that is, each individual's pleasurable experiences—is intrinsically good for that individual; second, that the general happiness (the happiness of all individuals) is an intrinsic good for the aggregate of individuals; and finally, that happiness is the only intrinsic good. Let us take a closer look at each stage.

Stage 1. Mill writes:

> The only proof capable of being given that an object is visible is that people actually see it. The only proof that a sound is audible is that people hear it; and so forth for the other sources of our experience. In this manner, I apprehend, the sole evidence it is possible to produce that anything is desirable is that people actually do desire it. (Mill, [1863] 1979, 34)

We can elaborate Mill's line of thought as follows:

1. People desire their own happiness for its own sake.
2. If something is desired for its own sake, then it is desirable.

Thus,

3. Each person's own happiness is desirable for that person.
4. If something is desirable, then it is intrinsically good (by definition).

Thus,

5. One's own happiness is an intrinsic good for oneself.

Stage 2. Mill continues:

> No reason can be given why the general happiness is desirable, except that each person, so far as he believes it to be attainable, desires his own happiness. This, however, being a fact, we have not only all the proof which the case admits of, but all which it is possible to require, that happiness is a good, that each person's happiness is a good to that person, and the general happiness, therefore, a good to the aggregate of all persons. Happiness has made out its title as one of the ends of conduct and, consequently, one of the criteria of morality. (Mill, [1863] 1979, 34)

So, the argument continues:

6. One's own happiness is an intrinsic good for oneself (conclusion of stage 1).
7. If each person's own happiness is an intrinsic good for that person, then the general happiness is intrinsically good for the aggregate of persons.

Thus,

8. The general happiness is an intrinsic good for the aggregate of persons.[15]

Before proceeding to stage 3, let us pause to consider the argument thus far. Both stages allegedly involve some basic logical fallacies. The argument of stage 1 seems to commit the fallacy of equivocation. This fallacy occurs when a line of reasoning trades on a word or expression being used with more than one of its meanings in the context of the argument. For instance, consider this bit of sophistry:

1. Philosophy is an art.
2. Art is studied by art historians.

Thus,

3. Philosophy is studied by art historians.

The problem here is obvious: the word "art" in English has more than one meaning. In the first premise, to say that philosophy is an art is to say that engaging in the activity of philosophy involves a kind of skill. But in the second premise, the word is referring to things like paintings, music, and film. Thus, the argument commits the fallacy of equivocation.

Now the word "desirable" has at least two meanings. It can mean "able to be desired" but it can also mean "worthy of being desired." Given the analogy Mill is drawing between what is visible and audible, on the one hand, and what is desirable, on the other, the occurrence of "desirable" in premise 2 is plausibly understood as meaning *able* to be desired. After all, to say that something is visible is to say that it is something people are able to see. But in order for step 4 in the argument to be true, the term must mean *worthy* of being desired. And certainly, from the fact that something is capable of being desired (a great many things are *capable* of being desired), it does not follow that it is worthy of being desired. Thus, stage 1 of Mill's argument commits the fallacy of equivocation. At least this is how it has often been read.

But notice that although the visible/desirable analogy is problematic, the conclusion of the argument is something that many are inclined to accept. And the fact that most everyone finds themselves desiring their own happiness as an end in itself might plausibly be said to be some evidence (though not ironclad) that happiness is very likely something intrinsically good.

But more problematic than the first stage is the second stage of the argument. There just seems to be a huge gap between the claim that my happiness is an intrinsic good to me, and your happiness is an intrinsic good to you (and so on for each and every person), to the conclusion that the total sum of happiness of all individuals (the general happiness) is something intrinsically good to the aggregate of individuals. An egoist would admit the premise, but why should he accept the conclusion?

The argument is typically understood to be an instance of the fallacy of composition involving reasoning about parts and wholes. One commits this fallacy when one illegitimately infers that some property possessed by each part or member of a whole is thereby also possessed by the whole itself.[16] From the fact that some machine is made up of parts and each part weighs less than five pounds, it does not follow that the machine taken as a whole weighs less than five pounds. To make such an inference is to commit the fallacy in question. Of course, no one would be tempted by this particular argument about machines and their parts since it is so obviously fallacious. But, consider this more subtle example of the fallacy.[17] "Every member of this basketball team is the second best player in the league at her position; therefore the team is second best in the league." One might be tempted by this line of argument, but it too commits the fallacy of composition. Similarly, Mill's argument here is diagnosed as going illegitimately from a claim about each member of the aggregate of human beings to the same sort of claim about the aggregate. Whether this is a proper diagnosis of Mill's argument, the problem of bridging the gap between the conclusion of stage 1 and the conclusion of stage 2 remains.[18]

Stage 3. Mill recognizes that having argued that happiness is an intrinsic good is not sufficient to secure his position; he also needs to provide reasons for claiming that it is the *only* thing of intrinsic value. Mill recognizes that people do desire various things and states of affairs like virtue, knowledge, and power for their own sakes; and according to the mode of reasoning featured in the first stage of Mill's argument, this is evidence that these items are intrinsically good. So the task that Mill sets for himself is to show that although virtue and the rest are often desired as intrinsically valuable, it is nevertheless the case that such items are really a part of an individual's happiness. If he can show this, then happiness after all is the only thing of intrinsic value. Continuing the argument, then:

1. All other things besides happiness that are desired for themselves are really only desired as parts of the end of happiness.

Thus,

2. Happiness is the sole intrinsic good.

Again, let us examine a passage from Mill:

The ingredients of happiness are very various, and each of them is desirable in itself, and not merely when considered as swelling an aggregate. The principle of utility does not mean that any given pleasure, as music, for instance, or any given exemption from pain, as for example health, is to be looked upon as means to a collective something termed happiness, and to be desired on that account. They are desired and desirable in and for themselves; besides being means, they are a part of the end. Virtue, according to the utilitarian doctrine, is not naturally and originally part of the end, but it is capable of becoming so. (Mill, [1863] 1979, 35–36)

In addition to virtue, Mill makes similar remarks about money, power, and fame and concludes that such items are, or can be, "included in happiness. They are some of the elements of which the desire for happiness is made up. Happiness is not an abstract idea but a concrete whole; and these are some of its parts" (Mill, [1863] 1979, 36–37).

To make sense of Mill's claim here, we should not understand him as claiming that virtue, power, money, and fame are themselves literally a part of happiness. Happiness is composed of pleasurable experiences, and these items are not identical to mere pleasurable experiences. Rather, the idea must be that our happiness is constituted of various types of pleasant experience, and so when people find virtue, power, or fame desirable in themselves, what they are really finding desirable are the pleasures that can be experienced from practicing virtue, from obtaining and making use of money and power, and from attaining and enjoying fame.

Again, we cannot pause here to enter into the scholarly debates that surround Mill's obviously complex conception of happiness. However, if we stand back from the details of Mill's proof and ask ourselves about the overall plausibility of his view, we can note two rather obvious things. First, the claim that happiness is the sole item of intrinsic value is not implausible. Many philosophers would agree (though philosophers differ in their conceptions of happiness). Second, the idea that taking the moral point of view requires that we take an impartial view of matters and, in particular, that we be concerned with the welfare of individuals regardless of whose welfare it is is also initially plausible. Finally, the idea that it is rational to produce as much intrinsic value as possible (the basic idea behind the principle of utility) is also initially plausible. Combining these ideas naturally leads one to embrace some form of utilitarianism. So, whatever the verdict on Mill's proof, there are considerations that favor this sort of moral theory.

Having presented the basic elements that go into a utilitarian moral theory, as well as having examined some of the doctrines of Bentham and Mill, I will now turn from presentation to criticism.

6. PRACTICAL OBJECTIONS TO UTILITARIANISM

One objection to utilitarianism that may have occurred to many readers is that the principle of utility is not directly useful for effectively guiding deliberation and action. In order to apply it in a concrete situation in an effort to correctly determine the deontic status of an action, one would have to figure out the utilities of all of the available alternative actions one might perform in the situation. Given how many individuals might be affected by an action, and given that we don't have direct access to the experiences of other people, the calculation of utility seems beyond our powers. For instance, how many individuals do I affect in giving a lecture on Mill's utilitarianism to my students? Perhaps some of them, as a result of what I say, will tell others who are not in the class about some point I made. Perhaps my presentation will make a deep impression on one of my students and over time she will become a practicing utilitarian. Her conversion to this moral view may lead her to become an advocate for the underprivileged, eventually leading her to assume a prominent role in an organization devoted to famine relief, and on and on. Of course, it is also possible that the effect that my presentation has on this student has some negative effects on her life and the lives of others with whom she comes into contact. Whatever the effects of my presentation on this student and others, I can't possibly foresee such effects, so there is no chance that I can use the principle of utility to determine the morality of my actions.

The problem is one of ignorance or uncertainty about the actual outcomes of the available actions and their associated utilities in contexts calling for moral decision making, and so concerns the standard of applicability explained in chapter 1. According to this standard, a moral theory, in providing a decision procedure, ought to specify a procedure that human beings, with their various limitations, can actually use in moral deliberation and in guiding our actions in general. As just explained, the utilitarian theory as so far developed fails to do this. There is a related problem of fairness. If one is ignorant or uncertain about the actual consequences of one's alternative actions in a situation, then in many cases it will be a matter of sheer luck if one happens to perform an action that has the highest utility; in a great many cases, a conscientious utilitarian moral agent will just fail to do what is right. In failing to do so, one's action counts as morally wrong. If we link moral wrongness with blame, then one will be blameworthy for failing to perform an act which, among one's alternatives, has the highest utility. But to be blameworthy in cases where successfully performing a right action is a matter of luck seems unfair.

The Principle of Utility as a Moral Criterion, Not a Decision Procedure

The points featured in this objection are well taken, but utilitarians have ways of deflecting their force. In the first place, we need to recall the difference between the theoretical and practical roles associated with moral principles. In an investigation into the nature of the right and the good, many moral philosophers are primarily interested in the theoretical goal of providing principles that correctly express the most fundamental right-making and good-making features of actions, persons, institutions, and so on. That is, they are primarily interested in providing moral criteria—criteria that specify what makes an action right or wrong or something good or bad. But a moral principle functioning as a criterion of right action need not also serve as a decision procedure and so need not fill the practical role sometimes associated with such principles. In response to the above complaint, the utilitarian will point out that the principle of utility is intended as a moral criterion, and so the fact that it is not useful in practice (and thus does not satisfy the practical role of a moral principle) does not matter. But even so, one expects a moral theory to address practical questions about moral decision making and moral guidance in general. What does the utilitarian have to say about practical guidance? However the utilitarian addresses this question, it would seem that an adequate answer must factor into account the agent's perspective in confronting moral choices.

In what follows, let us briefly examine this question, beginning with a distinction between two versions of the generic principle of utility that differ over the kind of consequences being put forth as a basis of right conduct.

Actual versus Expected Consequences

Notice that in explaining the utilitarian moral theory, I have been presenting what is called *actual consequence utilitarianism,* which makes the deontic status of actions depend on the actual consequences of the alternative actions. In this context, talk of actual consequences of actions refers, then, to those consequences that would (actually) occur were the action to be performed. However, an alternative way to have the value of consequences figure in determining right action makes use of the idea of expected consequences. To explain the difference between a utilitarian principle that refers to actual consequences and one that refers instead to expected consequences, let us consider the following case described by Derek Parfit:

> *Mine Shafts:* A hundred miners are trapped underground, with flood waters rising. We are rescuers on the surface who are trying to save these men. We know that all of these men are in one of two mine shafts, but we don't know which. There are three flood-gates that we could close by remote control. . . . Suppose next that on the evidence available as we believe, it is equally likely that the miners are all in shaft A or all in shaft B. (2011, 159)

Let us replace reference in the story to what we should do with reference to what Phil should do, the lone person who is in a position to rescue the miners by using the remote control. We are assuming, by the way, that Phil knows that the flood-gates are in excellent working condition. Here, then, is the chart summarizing Phil's alternatives:

The miners are in

		Shaft A	Shaft B
	Gate 1	Phil saves 100 lives	Phil saves no lives
Phil closes:	Gate 2	Phil saves no lives	Phil saves 100 lives
	Gate 3	Phil saves 90 lives	Phil saves 90 lives

Figure 5.1. Mine Shafts Example

If Phil closes either gates 1 or 2, his evidence indicates to him that he has a 50 percent chance of saving 100 lives, and he knows that if he closes gate 3 he will save 90 lives regardless of the miners' location. Suppose as a matter of fact that the miners are trapped in shaft A. Then the act with the highest *actual utility* is closing gate 1—the utility that would actually result were the action in question to be performed. But, of course, in the story, Phil doesn't know this fact. And because he doesn't, and in light of what he takes to be the likelihood of the various outcomes, it seems intuitively clear that he ought to close gate 3 and not take the risk of losing all 100 miners. This verdict is reflected by taking into consideration the various likelihoods, and then calculating what is typically called the *expected utility* of each of these options. The expected utility of an action is the result of multiplying the likelihood of each possible outcome of the action (as judged by the agent) by the value of that outcome and then summing the resulting products. To illustrate using the mine shafts example, let us suppose just for the sake of illustration (and simplicity) that the value of each man's life is +1. Then the expected utilities associated with the various gate closings from the example are as follows:

The miners are in

	Shaft A		Shaft B	Expected Utility
Close Gate 1:	(.5 x 100) = 50	+	(.5 x 0) = 0	+50
Close Gate 2:	(.5 x 0) = 0	+	(.5 x 100) = 50	+50
Close Gate 3:	(.5 x 90) = 45	+	(.5 x 90) = 45	+90

Figure 5.2.   Mine Shafts Example with Expected Utilities

Given the expected utilities we can formulate a version of the generic principle of utility that expresses a principle of *expected consequence utilitarianism*.

> **ECU** An action A is *right* if and only if A has as high an expected utility as any alternative action that the agent could perform instead.

And, of course, ECU applied to the mine shafts case yields the intuitively correct verdict.

Because this principle yields what we take to be the intuitively right verdict in this case, one might be tempted to replace ACU with ECU as a criterion of right action, and therefore insert "and because" into the formula. But many utilitarians will resist this, and for good reason.

We are interested in what, objectively speaking, makes an action right or wrong, and arguably ACU captures this objective notion for the utilitarian. Support for this comes from retrospective judgments. Suppose that after Phil closes gate 3, he finds out that in fact the miners were trapped in shaft A. It makes sense and seems entirely appropriate for him to think, "I ought to have closed gate 1, and then all 100 would have been saved." And it would make sense for him to regret not having made that decision, at least in hindsight. This reaction suggests that what, objectively speaking, was the right action to have performed is the closing of gate 1 associated with the highest actual utility. Of course, on the other hand, viewing things from the perspective of Phil, it also seems appropriate to say that there is a sense in which, in the circumstances, he did the right thing in closing gate 3. In the situation, with his uncertainty about the location of the miners, it would have been morally foolhardy and arguably outrageous for him to have closed either gates 1 or 2. He would have been subject to appropriate moral blame.

In response to these reactions, and keeping in mind that we are addressing the is-sue of making decisions and guiding choices in conditions of uncertainty, we can and should distinguish between the *objective rightness* of actions and an action's *subjective rightness*. Utilitarians can, and arguably should, stick with ACU as a criterion of ob-jectively right action.[19] But then they can make use of the idea of expected utility in fashioning a utilitarian principle of subjective rightness that can guide deliberation and subsequent action in conditions of uncertainty:

> **SPU** An action A performed in circumstances C is (presumptively) *subjectively right* if the agent believes that A has as high an expected utility as does any of the available alternative actions that she believes are open to her in C. In cases where only one act is judged to have the highest expected utility, that action is subjectively obliga-tory, all others are subjectively wrong.

This principle is deliberately formulated in terms of what the agent believes both about her options and the expected outcomes, which is what is needed for purposes of deliberation and action guidance, at least in cases where the agent has time and it is otherwise appropriate for her to consider the expected utilities of her various options. Indeed, you may recall that Bentham's felicific calculus, which he proposed as part of a decision procedure for estimating the overall utility of actions, included consideration of the "certainty" and "uncertainty" having to do with the likelihood of outcomes. The important point, noted at the outset of this discussion, is that any principle that can be used by an agent to guide moral deliberation will have to reflect the agent's first-person, and typically limited perspective on her moral options and their (subjectively) likely outcomes.[20]

Four comments are in order. First, the principle formulates only a sufficient ("if") condition, and so not also a necessary ("only if") condition for a utilitarian-based principle of subjective rightness, because, as a number of philosophers have pointed out, any moral theory of objective deontic status is going to require a series of related subjective principles in order to address a complete range of cases in which an agent suffers from uncertainty about relevant nonmoral matters. If a utilitarian-committed agent lacks beliefs about expected outcomes of the sort featured in the mine shafts case, then SPU will not suffice as a guide. The agent will need another principle of subjective rightness to guide her. How those principles might be formulated is a topic we cannot pursue here.[21]

Second, SPU is formulated as providing only a *presumptively* sufficient condition for an action's being subjectively right because the fact that an agent believes that action A has as high an expected utility as does any alternative action she believes is open to her is not always sufficient for an act's being subjectively right.[22] For instance, suppose we alter the facts of the original mine shafts case so that by closing gate 3, Phil can save only 50 of the 100 miners. The believed expected utility associated with closing gate 3 is now +50 and so equal to the believed expected utilities of the other two options. But it is, I think, counterintuitive to conclude that the subjectively right act for Phil is to close any one of the three gates since they are equal in believed expected utility. Why? Because of the great risk in lives lost were he to close either gate 1 or gate 2. Suppose that he can only save 49 by closing gate 3 so that now this potential action of his has a lower expected utility than the other two options. Ordinarily, actions whose believed expected utilities are lower than those of some alternative the agent believes she has are subjectively wrong. But intuitively it would still be subjectively wrong for Phil to fail to close gate 3 even if the believed expected utility of doing so is slightly lower than the believed expected utilities of the other options. One might try to formulate a more complicated version of SC that would build into it various exceptions like the ones I've just mentioned so that the principle expresses an all-things-considered sufficient condition for an action's being subjectively right. However, I will not try to do so.

Third, we began this discussion with the observation that if a utilitarian holds on to ACU as the correct criterion of objective rightness and wrongness, then it seems that blame in the sense of being blameworthy is out of place in cases where an agent is not in a position to know the actual utilities of the various alternative actions she might perform on some occasion. Because considerations of moral praise and blame are sensitive to how morally conscientious a person is in choosing to perform an action, which in turn is sensitive to what the person believes about her circumstances and the options she faces, the utilitarian can and should tie praiseworthiness and blameworthiness to standards of subjective rightness. So, Phil is not blameworthy even though as a matter of fact he performed an action which, according to ACU, was objectively morally wrong.

Finally, alert readers may have noticed a perhaps surprising element of Parfit's mine shafts case, namely that here we have a case in which Phil (a committed utilitarian) realizes that in not closing either gates 1 or 2 he will be performing an objectively wrong action in closing gate 3. So long as we distinguish what Phil subjectively ought to do from what he objectively ought to do, and keep in mind that blameworthiness is tied to the subjective notion of moral obligation, then the surprising element in question should not strike one as both surprising *and implausible*. Here, the utilitarian will insist that there can be cases of knowingly engaging in blameless (objective) wrong-doing.

So far, in dealing with the practical objection to utilitarianism, we have been focusing on situations allowing for some moral deliberation. And SPU is a principle that human beings can use in many contexts of moral deliberation. However, one might wonder whether, on utilitarian grounds, the principle ought to be used in all contexts calling for moral decision. Moral deliberation (whether guided by utilitarian principles or not) is, after all, itself an activity whose deontic status depends, for the utilitarian, on the overall value of its consequences. And clearly there are situations in which it would be morally wrong to engage in moral deliberation. If, for instance, I see that a child is about to be run over by a fast-moving car and I am close enough to pull the child to safety, I morally ought to spring into action and save the child. What I should not do is pause to consider various alternative courses of action I might perform (grab the child, look the other way, yell at the child, run away and hide, etc.) and consciously estimate the expected utilities of all the alternatives. Of course, it is a mistake to suppose that the utilitarian theory requires that we use a principle like SPU as a decision procedure on every occasion in life.

The Two-Level Approach to Moral Thinking

This raises a question about the value of employing conscious utilitarian deliberation in other, nonemergency contexts. Should a utilitarian be in favor of a system of moral education in which individuals would be brought up so that they consciously, whenever possible, guide their behavior by reference to a principle like SPU? The answer to this question depends, of course, on whether doing so would be best from a utilitarian perspective, and no doubt it is difficult to say one way or the other with any degree of conviction. But it seems plausible to suppose that overall utility will not be maximized by training people to always directly apply SPU and like principles of subjective rightness in figuring out what to do. Not only is there no time for such calculation, but the likelihood of miscalculation owing to self-interest will likely be high when one's own welfare is importantly affected by one's actions.

Therefore, many utilitarians, Mill included, have thought that when it comes to most situations in life, the moral responses of most individuals are properly guided by moral rules—rules having to do with lying, theft, killing, and so forth—that we learn in our early years. Such thought is properly so guided because, as Mill explains, over time humans have "acquired positive beliefs as to the effects of some actions on their happiness; and the beliefs which have thus come down are the rules of morality for the multitude" (Mill, [1863] 1979, 23). These rules of commonsense morality are thus by and large good utilitarian guides for individuals to learn and follow in a great many situations in life where applying a principle like SPU would be wrong or otherwise not feasible.

Still, there is obviously a role for utilitarian moral principles in moral thinking. Mill points out that, inevitably, we will confront situations in which the moral rules of common sense come into conflict. Indeed, Mill cautions that we "must remember that only in cases of conflict between [moral rules] is it requisite that first principles should be appealed to" (Mill, [1863] 1979, 25). And, of course, his claim about such contexts is that "If utility is the ultimate source of moral obligations, utility may be invoked to decide between [moral rules] when their demands are incompatible"

(Mill, [1863] 1979, 25). Of course, given what was said about contexts of deliberation under conditions of uncertainty about actual utilities, a principle like SPU (or some other principle of subjective rightness) would be called for in determining what to do in conflict situations of the sort Mill is considering. When, for example, a rule against lying conflicts with a rule against hurting others (because telling someone the truth about some matter will cause them great mental stress), it would make sense, given one's estimates of the expected utilities, to make use of SPU to adjudicate the conflict.

Utilitarians who advocate this approach to moral thinking distinguish two levels of moral thought.[23] First-level moral thinking, or what is called the intuitive level, proceeds (perhaps unreflectively in most cases) according to moral rules that we learn early on and that help us negotiate our social world. Such rules are taken to be more or less reliable guides to maximizing actual utility. Second-level moral thinking involves cases like the one just mentioned where ordinary moral rules come into conflict and we must deliberate about what to do. It is here at this second, critical level that utilitarians like Mill advocate employing, for example, SPU for purposes of moral decision making.

What is crucial to notice about this two-level approach to moral thinking is the role that moral rules play. Here, they are taken to be generally reliable guides to morally correct behavior in most situations where we are not confronted with moral conflict. However, even in those non-conflict situations, the objective rightness or wrongness of actions does *not* depend on whether they conform to these rules; objective rightness or wrongness for the act utilitarian always depends on the actual utilities of actions. (When we consider rule consequentialism in the next chapter, it will be important to bear this point in mind.)

Let us sum up. The main practical challenge to utilitarianism has to do with how the theory addresses questions about practical guidance. We have made the following observations.

- The utilitarian is going to insist that the principle of utility, ACU, which refers to actual consequences, is to be understood as a moral criterion and not as a decision procedure.
- Further, the utilitarian distinguishes moral principles like ACU, which set forth the standard for objectively right and wrong action, from principles like SPU that can figure in first-person deliberation and serve to offer guidance to agents in conditions of uncertainty. Such principles are interpreted as principles of subjective rightness and wrongness, a kind of deontic status that is properly associated with moral praise-worthiness and blameworthiness.
- Finally, the utilitarian may propose a two-level approach to moral thinking that allows the rules of commonsense morality to provide moral guidance in many circumstances, particularly those in which the agent does not have time (or should not take time) to deliberate in responding to those circumstances in morally appropriate ways.

7. CONCLUSION

This chapter has been devoted to a presentation of the elements of the utilitarian approach to moral theorizing, including an exposition of some of the main ideas and arguments of the classical utilitarians, Bentham and Mill. We ended the chapter with an examination of a kind of practical objection to the utilitarian theory and saw how the utilitarian can plausibly defend against this sort of objection. In the next chapter, we consider some of the developments in the utilitarian approach to moral theory that involve discussion of various theoretical objections to the theory. Additionally, non-utilitarian versions of consequentialism will receive some attention.

NOTES

1. Readers should be aware that one finds importantly different definitions of "consequentialism" in the ethics literature. My characterization is broad enough so that versions of ethical egoism, the subject of chapter 7, count as versions of consequentialism. Some philosophers define the view to include the requirement that it is only consequences considered impartially that determine the deontic status of actions, a requirement that excludes ethical egoism.

2. The category of personal value is to be understood broadly so that it includes not only considerations having to do with individual welfare or happiness but also considerations having to do with individual perfection.

3. Some direct act consequentialists consider the action itself to be included among the consequences of performing the action, so that any intrinsic value that might be possessed by the action may figure in determining the deontic status of that action. However, for a utilitarian consequentialist, since the state of affairs having value is welfare, and since actions are what causally produce welfare, actions are not themselves constituents of welfare. So, utilitarians have typically not included actions as part of the consequences whose value determines the deontic status of actions.

4. There are other forms of indirect consequentialist accounts of right action including, for instance, motive utilitarianism articulated by Adams, 1976, according to which an action is right just in case (and because) the motive behind the action is such that acting on that motive generally produces good consequences.

5. Agent-neutral theories are contrasted with agent-relative theories. A theory is agent-neutral if an assignment of value to whatever items have value does not make essential reference to the agent. A theory is agent-relative if an assignment of value to whatever items have value does make essential reference to the agent. Ethical egoism, which we take up in the next chapter, is agent-relative because in determining the deontic status of actions, an agent is to consider the value of the consequences of her actions as they bear exclusively on *her* well-being. For a thorough overview of the agent-neutral/agent-relative distinction in ethics, see Ridge, 2010. Some philosophers, including Amartya Sen, 1982 and Douglas Portmore, 2001, 2007 have defended nonegoistic versions of agent-relative consequentialism. Unfortunately, space does not permit consideration of this important species of the view.

6. For a general discussion of prioritarian views, see Parfit, 1997. Arguably, on the most plausible versions of prioritarian moral theory, the priority given to those suffering severe de-

privation of basic goods is not absolute. That is, on such views, benefits to the worst off could be outweighed by sufficiently great benefits to those better off.

7. For moral issues relating to population, it is important to distinguish *total* net utility from *average* net utility, where the latter is obtained by dividing the total net utility by the number of persons affected. For reasons of space, we are only going to be concerned with total net utility. For an overview of the topic of consequentialist aggregation, see Driver 2012, chapter 3.

8. What counts as "the best available outcome" will depend on exactly how a consequentialist theory of right conduct specifies this notion. I count ethical egoism as a form of consequentialism (see chapter 7), but in that theory the value of outcomes is determined entirely in terms of what is *good for the agent*, rather than what is good considered from an agent-neutral perspective.

9. It turns out the question of which alternative actions are genuinely open to an agent on some occasion is a complicated matter that we shall not have space to take up. For discussion, see Dorsey, forthcoming.

10. Value hedonism makes claims about what is intrinsically valuable. It should be distinguished from *psychological hedonism*, which claims that all human actions are ultimately motivated by concern for pleasure and avoidance of pain. The two forms are independent. One can embrace the former yet deny the latter, and vice versa. Psychological hedonism is discussed in chapter 7. It should also be noted that a hedonist need not hold that all experiences of pleasure are intrinsically good. A hedonist can restrict the range of pleasures that have intrinsic value, claiming, for instance, that the pleasure experienced by someone performing a sadistic act does not possess any intrinsic value.

11. Strictly speaking, ethical hedonism does not imply value hedonism, because one might embrace the former (and think that pleasure and pain are the only things having intrinsic value that are relevant for ethical evaluation) and yet deny that they are the only things having intrinsic value, thus denying the latter.

12. Of course, some actions may only result in episodes of pleasure for some affected individual, while some may only result in episodes of pain.

13. This claim has been disputed by some recent interpreters. For a brief critical overview of such interpretations, see Donner, 1998.

14. Recall from chapter 1 that the standard of external support for evaluating moral theories assumes that nonmoral theories and assumptions can be used to support (and to criticize) moral principles. We have seen this assumption at work in the divine command theory, moral relativism, and natural law theory.

15. Here, in stating the conclusion in this way, I am following what Mill says. One might think that what Mill needs as a conclusion is the claim that the general happiness is of intrinsic goodness for each individual. One of Mill's critics, Henry Jones, thought so, but Mill (in a letter quoted by Crisp) denies that his argument should be reinterpreted that way. See Crisp, 1997, 77–78.

16. Not all arguments involving wholes and parts are fallacious. From the fact that each piece of a jigsaw puzzle is uniformly the same shade of red, it does follow that the puzzle as a whole is uniformly red.

17. Thanks to Michael Gill for this example.

18. I have been rehearsing the standard objections to Mill's proof. In defense of Mill against the charge of committing logical fallacies, Geoff Sayre-McCord argues that "the apparently rampant fallacies [attributed to Mill's argument] . . . are due to rampant misunderstandings of

the argument" (2001, 2). What Sayre-McCord finds problematic about Mill's argument has to do with facts about human psychology.

19. This claim is controversial and not all utilitarians will agree. For a defense of the claim that consequentialists generally should embrace so-called objective principles, like ACU, as moral criteria of right action, see Driver, 2012 and 2013. What makes a consequentialist principle objective in the relevant sense is that it does not tie the deontic status of actions (1) to the agent's psychology, such as her beliefs about consequences, (2) or to matters concerning the evidence an agent does possess or might acquire about likely consequences. Consequentialist principles that tie rightness to an agent's actual beliefs about outcomes of actions are subjective principles of rightness, while consequentialist principles that tie rightness to what it would be reasonable for an agent to believe (given her epistemic limitations) are called prospectivist principles of rightness. For a view that favors rejecting ACU and other objectivist consequentialist principles as representing moral criteria of right action in favor of prospectivist principles, see Zimmerman, 2008 and Mason, forthcoming. Prospectivists like Mason argue that ACU should be understood as a principle stating what makes an action *objectively best* from a consequentialist perspective rather than what makes an action morally right.

20. This principle is formulated in terms of what an agent believes about expected utilities rather than in terms of what she might be expected to believe given, for example, evidence about likely outcomes of her actions that is available to her and that she ought to have acquired. Smith, 2010 persuasively argues, I think, that if we keep our focus on principles that can be used by the agent to derive deontic verdicts in every situation the agent confronts, then we will want to formulate principles of subjective rightness in terms of what the agent in fact believes.

21. But see Smith, 2010 for an illuminating and nuanced discussion of this matter.

22. The point here is not just about SPU, but an issue about expected utility theory. Such a theory may not always be the best way to deal with cases involving risk. (Thanks to Elinor Mason for this observation.)

23. See Hare, 1981 for a developed version of this two-level approach.

FURTHER READING

Brink, David O. 1989. *Moral Realism and the Foundations of Ethics.* Cambridge: Cambridge University Press. See chapter 8 for a defense of utilitarianism that makes critical use of the distinction between a moral principle functioning as a criterion and as a decision procedure.

———. 2006. "Some Forms and Limits of Consequentialism." In *The Oxford Handbook of Ethical Theory*, ed. David Copp. Oxford: Oxford University Press. An authoritative overview of consequentialist moral theory.

Crisp, Roger. 1997. *Mill on Utilitarianism.* London: Routledge. A lucid introduction to Mill's moral philosophy.

Donner, Wendy. 1998. "Mill's Utilitarianism." In *The Cambridge Companion to Mill*, ed. John Skorupski. Cambridge: Cambridge University Press. A concise overview of Mill's moral theory, including an illuminating discussion of Mill's qualitative hedonism.

Driver, Julia. 2009. "The History of Utilitarianism." *The Stanford Encyclopedia of Philosophy*, ed. E. N. Zalta. http://plato.stanford.edu. Very helpful overview of the history of utilitarianism, including discussion of Bentham and Mill, as well as Henry Sidgwick (1838–1900), and G. E. Moore (1873–1958).

Hare, R. M. 1981. *Moral Thinking*. Oxford: Oxford University Press. Chapter 1 defends the two-level approach to moral thinking mentioned in section 5.

Mason, Elinor. Forthcoming. "Objective and Subjective Utilitarianism." In *Cambridge Companion to Utilitarianism*, eds. B. Eggleston and D. E. Miller. Cambridge: Cambridge University Press. Very helpful overview of the varieties of and debates about objective and subjective utilitarian conceptions of right action.

Mulgan, Tim. 2007. *Understanding Utilitarianism*. Stocksfield, UK: Acumen. A very useful introductory overview of the utilitarian tradition in ethics, combining discussion of historical sources with a critical discussion of the varieties, problems, and resources of this tradition.

Quinton, Anthony. 1973. *Utilitarian Ethics*. Chicago: Open Court Press. A mainly historical treatment of the utilitarian tradition with chapters devoted to Bentham and Mill.

Scarre, Geoffrey. 1996. *Utilitarianism*. London: Routledge. Includes a historical overview of the development of utilitarian doctrine.

Schneewind, J. B., ed. 1968. *Mill: A Collection of Critical Essays*. Garden City, NY: Anchor Books. Includes some classic essays on Mill's moral philosophy.

Sinnott-Armstrong, Walter. 2011. "Consequentialism." *The Stanford Encyclopedia of Philosophy*, ed. E. N. Zalta. http://plato.stanford.edu. A state-of-the-art overview of consequentialism in its many varieties.

6

Consequentialism 2: Contemporary Developments

In this chapter, we consider some developments in consequentialist moral thinking that have been largely prompted by certain objections to classical versions of the theory—act utilitarianism in particular—that we examined in the previous chapter. The objections in question—theoretical objections—challenge the idea that utilitarianism represents a correct moral criterion of right action. The next two sections explain these objections, and the remaining sections consider utilitarian responses to them, including, as we shall see, versions of utilitarianism, and consequentialism more generally, that differ importantly from the views of Bentham and Mill.

1. THEORETICAL OBJECTIONS

Theoretical objections to utilitarianism (often referred to as moral objections) have to do with the main theoretical aim of a moral theory—the aim of providing a theoretical account of the nature of right and wrong and thereby providing a moral criterion of right action. This section will be concerned with certain stock-in-trade objections to the theory that challenge its theoretical correctness.

A very common method of criticizing utilitarianism involves thinking up cases in which the theory is dramatically at odds with ordinary moral thinking about the issue at hand. Appealing, then, to the standard of internal support for evaluating moral theories, the claim is that since the utilitarian theory conflicts with our considered moral beliefs in a wide range of cases, it fails to be a correct moral criterion. There are two general sorts of cases; cases involving deontological restrictions where the theory presumably clashes with people's moral intuitions concerning justice and rights, and cases where the clash is with people's moral intuitions about the limits of what morality properly demands.

Deontological Constraints: Justice and Rights

You may recall from chapter 4 that a deontological constraint represents a moral restriction that prohibits agents from engaging in certain actions even if by doing so they can produce better outcomes than by conforming to such constraints.[1] As noted above, these constraints typically involve considerations of justice or rights that are at odds with utilitarianism. Here are four cases of the sort often featured in this kind of objection.

Punishment and retributive justice. Suppose a series of horrible unsolved crimes has been committed and the townspeople are up in arms, demanding that the culprit be found and brought to justice; otherwise they will riot. The foreseeable result of a riot would be a great loss in overall utility, given the predictable loss of life, injury, and damage to property. Unfortunately, the police have no suspects. The chief of police is pondering the situation and, as a good utilitarian, is considering alternative courses of action he might take.

One option would be to do what one can to quell the rising fear and anger, and intensify the investigation. But another, more devious option is to frame someone who is innocent of the crimes in question—someone with no family or friends, preferably a social outcast with a long police record. The chief happens to know of just such a person against whom a plausible case could easily be concocted. He is also quite certain that this individual is innocent of the crimes in question. Of course, taking this second alternative would result in severe hardship for the outcast, but when one considers the overall utility of such a course of action compared to the other main alternative, it seems pretty clear to the chief that as a good utilitarian he ought to proceed with the case against the innocent outcast. Let's suppose that the police chief is correct in his assessments of the utilities of his options. Utilitarianism thus implies that the chief has a moral obligation to proceed with framing and punishing the innocent person. But, so the objection goes, it would clearly be morally wrong for him to bring punishment upon someone known to be innocent of the crimes in question. Thus, the utilitarian theory yields an incorrect moral verdict in this case.

Medical sacrifice and the right to life. A physician with a strong utilitarian conscience finds herself in the following situation. A perfectly healthy patient has been admitted to the hospital for alcohol abuse. The physician knows about the personal history of this patient. She knows, for example, that the patient has no family, is homeless, and so forth. Except perhaps for the patient's liver, his bodily organs are in excellent shape. Now suppose that under the physician's treatment are three individuals who need an organ donor, each needing a different organ. Moreover, time is quickly running out for these patients. You see how the story goes from here. Our physician does some utilitarian calculation and concludes that since it would be easy and (let us suppose) not at all risky for her to cause the death of the alcohol abuser, she ought to do so, since she would then have at her disposal the needed organs for her three patients. (We are assuming that there is a match in blood types so that the transplants are medically feasible.) Suppose the chances of successful transplant are very high and that proceeding would in fact yield success. From the utilitarian perspective (whether we consider the probable or the actual consequences) our physician ought to kill the one patient to save the other three. But doing so would be murder! Again, the theory leads to obviously incorrect moral conclusions.

Distributive justice. Distributive justice has to do with how the benefits and burdens of society are spread among its citizens. Now consider two schemes of distribution for a society as they bear on two groups that together compose the society.

Scheme 1			Scheme 2		
Group 1	Utility =	+500	Group 1	Utility =	+1,300
Group 2	Utility =	+500	Group 2	Utility =	-200
	Total =	+1,000		Total =	+1,100

Figure 6.1. Distributive Justice Schemes

Suppose that the numbers for each group represent the total amount of utility that would be produced within the group given the relevant scheme. Assume also that within each group utility is fairly evenly distributed and that at a level of +500, the members of such a group can live comfortably. According to scheme 1, the members of both groups can live comfortably. However, members of groups having a total utility below 0 are below poverty level and must struggle against disease, poor education, poor job opportunities, and other social ills. So, were scheme 2 implemented, the members of group 1 would be well enough off, but not the members of group 2.

Since the utilitarian theory is only concerned with total aggregate utility, it clearly favors the second scheme, ignoring considerations of equal distribution of benefits and burdens across the members of society. In doing so, the theory runs afoul of our sense of fairness. Certainly, considerations of equality are morally important, and scheme 1 is to be morally preferred over scheme 2, contrary to utilitarianism. (Some critics like to employ this same mode of reasoning to show how, at least in principle, utilitarianism could, under the right conditions, morally require that a certain segment of the population be enslaved in order to produce the greatest total aggregate utility in society.)

Promising. It is often pointed out that utilitarianism does not square with our considered moral beliefs about promising. Suppose that Jones, who is terminally ill, has secretly entrusted to me, his financial adviser, a large sum of money that I have promised to give to his young daughter when she turns twenty-one. I am to keep tabs on her until then. In the meantime, the daughter comes into a huge fortune by winning her state's Powerball lottery and by the time she is twenty-one has no need of the money her father has entrusted to me. However, my own situation is financially desperate. My wife is suffering from a debilitating disease that has eaten away at our savings and has forced us to sell our house. I am on the brink of financial ruin and realize that the money entrusted to me by Jones would essentially bail me out. So it appears as if the correct thing to do from the utilitarian perspective is to keep the money and thereby break my promise. But can this be right? Wouldn't it be morally wrong to break my promise to Jones?

All of these examples involve actions that, at least as the cases are described, are intuitively morally wrong but morally obligatory according to utilitarianism. However, other counterexamples involving actions that we judge to be morally optional reveal that utilitarianism is too demanding. Let us consider some of them.

Demandingness: Supererogation and Special Obligations

Utilitarianism is often criticized as being excessively demanding. There are various ways in which this kind of objection can be pressed. What is referred to as the demandingness objection is typically cast in terms of one's duty of beneficence. The idea is that a plausible principle of beneficence should not require too big a personal sacrifice in order to help strangers (that is, persons other than family and friends and other close associates). The idea is that the utilitarian requirement to maximize utility impartially assessed conflicts with one's considered moral beliefs about actions that are optional, even though performing them would (in general) be morally admirable. We consider this objection immediately below in the sub-section on supererogation. A closely related objection concerns special obligations having to do with close personal relationships. Before turning to these objections, we should begin with a clarification.

Morality is demanding. Moral constraints are often at odds with what we want to do. Any moral theory that adequately captures and makes sense of what we take to be moral obligations will sometimes impose demands on agents that they do not welcome. So the objection to utilitarianism under consideration is not that it is demanding but that it is *overly* demanding. Let us take a closer look.

Supererogation. In describing some of the general characteristics of utilitarianism (chapter 5, section 1), we noted that it is both universalist, holding that everyone whose welfare will be affected by one's action counts morally, and impartialist—everyone's welfare counts equally in determining the deontic status of an action. Here is a passage from Mill in which he comments on this kind of strict impartialism:

> I must repeat, what the assailants of utilitarianism seldom have the justice to acknowledge, that the happiness which forms the utilitarian standard of what is right in conduct, is not the agent's own happiness, but that of all concerned. As between his own happiness and that of others, utilitarianism requires him to be as strictly impartial as a disinterested and benevolent spectator. (Mill, [1863] 1979, 16)

This kind of universal impartialism places extreme demands on us. Let us take a simple example. Suppose that one of my favorite activities is gardening; it is a hobby I love doing. I thus have a reason, based on my own "partialist" concerns, to do some gardening in my spare time. But suppose also that I could spend my spare time on a

Sunday afternoon doing some volunteer work for the city, which, from an impartial perspective, would be the best course of action to engage in at the time in question. I thus have a reason, based on the sort of impartialist perspective represented in utilitarianism, to do the volunteer work.

So far, we have simply noted the possibility of a clash between two sorts of reasons for action. But add to this two further claims. First, moral requirements are typically taken to be *supremely authoritative* in the sense that they provide individuals with overriding reasons for action. Anytime we have a moral reason to perform some action and a nonmoral reason for not performing that same action, the former trumps the latter. Second, seemingly there are many occasions in life where there is a clash between our partialist concerns (and the reasons for action they generate) and impartialist reasons flowing from the perspective represented by utilitarianism.

Putting all of this together, the implication is that utilitarianism is extremely demanding—so much so that according to its standard of right conduct, we are often doing something morally wrong in pursuing our own personal projects and interests. Thus, many actions that strike us intuitively as morally optional are forbidden according to utilitarianism.

In the case just described, choosing to volunteer one's time seems to be supererogatory. We have not had occasion to refer to supererogatory actions until now, but this moral category of action is familiar. We sometimes hear about someone who performed an action that was "above and beyond the call of duty." As this description suggests, such actions, because they are beyond the call of duty, are not, strictly speaking, one's duty and so they are not obligatory; they are, strictly speaking, optional. Because they are above the call of duty, agents who perform such actions typically deserve moral praise. Since the actions in question are neither obligatory nor forbidden, they are optional actions—but, of course, optional actions of a very special sort. Such actions are called supererogatory (from the Latin *erogare*, meaning "to demand").

One particularly memorable example of supererogation concerns the January 1982 crash of a jet liner into the icy waters of the Potomac River. Among the nearby witnesses were Lenny Skutnik and Roger Olian. Skutnik jumped into the river risking his life to save one passenger from drowning. Olian too, at some risk to his life, swam out to the wreckage to encourage and aid passengers waiting for rescue helicopters to arrive on the scene. This story made newspaper headlines, was featured on television news shows, and was dramatized on the made for TV movie, *Flight 90: Disaster on the Potomac*. The attention these individuals received in the media is certainly due to the fact they were going beyond the call of duty in doing what they did.

It cannot be said of every supererogatory action that, from among the agent's options, it has the highest utility. After all, some acts of supererogation are not successful. Suppose Skutnik had actually drowned while trying to rescue one of the passengers, and so his efforts proved entirely fruitless—he tried but saved no one and consequently lost his own life. However, it is a good bet that in many cases in which the right opportunities present themselves, the supererogatory action will maximize utility. But if so, then such actions are, according to the utilitarian, morally obligatory and not, according to the definition, supererogatory after all. But any theory that turns many (if not all) of what we ordinarily suppose to be supererogatory actions into obligatory actions, is overly demanding. Call this the *supererogation objection*.

The overly demanding nature of utilitarianism prompted J. L. Mackie to complain that this theory represents an "ethics of fantasy": a theory that sets standards of right action that are simply too high for normal human beings, given our deeply ingrained concern for ourselves, friends, and family.

Personal relationships and special obligations. The remark by Mackie about our deeply ingrained concern for friends and family is worthy of further comment. Classical utilitarianism presumably cannot make room for so-called special obligations we have to family, friends, and loved ones because of its strict impartiality in determining the value of the consequences. The goodness and badness of consequences, on this view, is conceived "agent-neutrally," that is, from an impartial perspective—the perspective of a non-favoring neutral observer rather than the perspective of the agent. To illustrate the objection, consider a case in which I can either use some of my savings to put my son (an average student) through college or I can use that money to put a neighbor's more promising student through college whose parents cannot afford the cost. If the consequences of my using the money to send the neighbor's child to college would be better than if I use that money for my own child's education, then (assuming there is no better way to use the money from the utilitarian perspective) I am obligated to use the money for the education of the neighbor's child. But clearly, so the objection goes, it is not morally wrong to give special weight to the welfare of one's own children in such cases. But giving special weight in this way is contrary to the impartialist element of the utilitarian theory. Similar remarks apply to various special relationships involving bonds of love and friendship—relationships between parents of their offspring, between spouses, between lovers, between good friends, between colleagues, and so on. So the objection here is that the utilitarian theory is seemingly at odds with special obligations owing to the bonds involved in personal relationships.

These demandingness objections, like the other theoretical objections, have been presented as variations on a central critical theme, namely, the utilitarian theory has implications regarding the deontic status of various actions that are at odds with our considered moral beliefs about those actions. The punishment, medical sacrifice, distributive justice, and promising scenarios all concern actions that are forbidden but are classified as obligatory or optional (depending on how the utilities work out) by utilitarianism. The demandingness objections involving supererogation focus on actions that strike one as optional though on the utilitarian theory are obligatory. The demandingness objection focused on special relationships involving family and friends focuses on actions that strike one as obligations but which are not recognized as such by the utilitarian, at least in a great range of cases.

So the objection to utilitarianism as a moral criterion based on such examples is just this. One way of testing the correctness of a moral criterion is to see whether it implies, or is at least consistent with, our considered moral beliefs about a range of cases. This way of testing the correctness of a theory appeals to the standard of internal support for evaluating moral theories, which was explained in section 7 of chapter 1. Now we need not insist that our considered beliefs—our moral intuitions—about such cases are always correct; if a moral theory is otherwise very attractive but conflicts with our considered moral beliefs in a few cases, then we might have good reason to revise our beliefs about the specific cases in question. But in connection with utilitarianism, the theory seems to conflict with a whole range of very deeply held and widely shared moral beliefs. Thus (so this objection goes) the theory fails the standard of internal support and gives us reason to reject it as providing a correct moral criterion.

2. VARIETIES OF RESPONSE

Utilitarians and consequentialists generally have deployed a variety of types of response to this battery of theoretical objections. You may recall from the previous chapter that classical utilitarianism is first of all a species of consequentialism according to which the deontic status of an action is explained entirely in terms of the value of the consequences of outcomes associated with the action in question. What distinguishes utilitarianism as a species of consequentialism is its welfarist theory of value, and the classic utilitarians embraced a hedonistic account of welfare or happiness. In addition, the classical view, as presented in chapter 5, included the following structural features:[2]

- It is *direct*: individual actions are evaluated on the basis of the utility associated with the action being evaluated.
- It is *maximizing*: whether an individual action is right or wrong depends upon whether it produces the highest level of net value (utility) compared to alternative actions open to the agent.
- It is *impartialist*: the value of the consequences of an action is to be assessed from an impartial point of view; the value of the consequences on all who are affected are given equal weight in determining the deontic status of an action.

If a consequentialist focused on theory of right action wants to defend utilitarianism against the various theoretical objections lately described, she has a number of options. First, she can attempt to rebut the objections directly by challenging their probative force in one way or another. This option is explored in the following section. Second, she can defend an alternative theory of welfare. Third, she can reject one or more of the three structural features, replacing it (or them) with some alternative. Another option for the consequentialist is to reject utilitarianism (and possibly some of the structural features) by replacing welfarism with an alternative theory of value.[3] A select set of the second and third options are explored below in sections 5–7. Let's begin, then, with attempts by utilitarians to give direct, non-concessive responses to the injustice, rights, and demandingness objections.

3. BOLD DENIAL AND REMOTE EFFECTS

One way of responding to such objections is to challenge some of the claims made in the examples. Either the utilitarian can deny the moral verdict being offered about the case under consideration, or she can challenge the claims made about the utilities of the various options. And, of course, she can appeal to both sorts of response. Let us briefly consider these responses in order.

Bold Denial

In responding to the objections in question, the utilitarian might just boldly deny the moral verdicts made by the critic. Go back for a moment to the example about promising in which I can either keep my promise and inform the intended beneficiary of her inheritance or break the promise and keep the money for myself. In that example, the critic first of all claims that the action of breaking the promise would have the highest utility in the imagined circumstances but that, contrary to what the utilitarian theory implies, this action would be morally wrong.

But is it so clear that it would be wrong for me to break my promise (under the circumstances) and keep the money? Remember, I need the money desperately, but the intended heir has all the money she will ever need. I suspect that this case will prompt a good deal of disagreement among thoughtful individuals, and so the critic's objection is somewhat blunted because the anti-utilitarian moral verdict in the case at hand is questionable. Indeed, a very bold utilitarian might also go on to deny the moral verdicts being passed on the actions featured in the punishment, medical sacrifice (see below), and distributive justice examples.

This form of response is arguably bolstered by appealing to some empirical claims which have been used to challenge the reliability of moral intuitions (what we have been calling considered moral beliefs). For instance, Joshua Greene has marshaled neuroscientific evidence concerning people's reactions to trolley cases to argue that so-called "deontological," non-consequentialist moral intuitions that are evoked by the case of pushing the large man off of the footbridge in order to stop the runaway trolley from killing 5 trapped workers, are driven by arational emotional responses that likely result from our evolutionary history. (Trolley cases were briefly discussed in chapter 4, section 12.) According to Greene, "We have strong feelings that tell us in clear and uncertain terms that some things *simply cannot be done* and that other things *simply must be done*. But it is not obvious how to make sense of these feelings, and so we, with the help of some especially creative philosophers, make up a rationally appealing story" (2008, 63). Among prominent rationally appealing stories that Greene is attacking are Kantian moral theories that reject consequentialism in part because of the intuitive responses people generally have to the sorts of cases featured in punishing, medical sacrifice, and other cases described earlier. Here is not the place to delve into the work of Greene and others that attempt to debunk people's moral intuitions—work that has gained much attention from philosophers and psychologists alike in recent years. The point is that utilitarians and consequentialists generally, who wish to challenge the moral intuitions featured in the various theoretical objections we have been considering, need not be viewed as flat-footedly denying the intuitions in question. They can bring empirical evidence to bear on the reliability of people's moral intuitions.[4]

Appeal to Remote Effects

Utilitarianism makes the rightness or wrongness of an action depend on the values of all of its consequences, including both immediate and long-term consequences. (Recall from the last chapter that Bentham's felicific calculus includes propinquity and remoteness as one dimension of utilitarian calculation.) A second strategy for answering at least some of the theoretical objections is to challenge the critic's claims about the utilities of the options featured in the examples. The critic more or less stipulates, for example, that in the case of the threatening mob, utility will be maximized by framing and then punishing an innocent person. But how plausible is this stipulation, give the possible long-term consequences of engaging in such behavior? How easy will it be for the police chief to keep his deed a secret? Realistically, won't he need some cooperation from a prosecuting attorney? Won't he have to engage in a whole web of lies and deception, which again will, realistically speaking, be uncovered eventually?

Once we begin to think through this case (and the others) by factoring in plausible empirical assumptions about likely consequences of punishing innocent persons (and the disutility associated with such consequences), it is no longer clear that the police chief's best option (on utilitarian grounds) is to engage in such obviously unjust, immoral behavior. Similar remarks can be applied to the other cases as well. By questioning assumptions about utilities in this way, the defender of utilitarianism hopes to deflect theoretical objections to her theory.

How successful are these two strategies in combating the alleged counterexamples to utilitarianism? Here is a quick (mixed) assessment. On one hand, the utilitarian is correct in demanding that potential counterexamples to her theory involve plausible real-world assumptions and that the moral judgments being rendered in such cases be as uncontroversial as possible, as well as contrary to the utilitarian theory.

On the other hand, it does seem in principle possible that cases of the sort the critic aims to describe can (and probably do) turn up in the real world. Granted, in complex social settings like hospitals and law enforcement agencies, the kinds of immoral actions featured in the examples are very unlikely to maximize utility. But consider this variation on the medical sacrifice case described by Katarzyna de Lazari-Radek and Peter Singer:

> [A] surgeon has to do a delicate brain operation on a patient who happens to be the ideal organ donor for four other patients in the hospital, each of whom will die shortly unless they receive respectively, a heart, a liver, and—for two of them—a kidney. The doctor is highly skilled, and is confident of her ability to carry out the brain surgery successfully. If she does, the patient will lead a more or less normal life. But because the operation is a delicate one, no one could blame her, or have any reason to suspect anything, if the patient were to die on the operating table. Moreover, the hospital is experienced in organ transplantation and the surgeon knows that if the patient were to die, the recipients of the patient's organs would soon be able to go home and lead a more or less normal life. The surgeon knows no other details about her patient or the other patients, such as whether they are married, have children, or are about to discover the cure for cancer. (2010, 40)

Lazari-Radek and Singer are discussing a certain implication of act consequentialism (including act utilitarianism), namely, that there are cases (however rare) in which it would be morally right to do in secret what it would otherwise not be right to do publically. What they go on to say about the case just described is that "the consequentialist must accept that, in these circumstances, the right thing for the surgeon to do would be to kill the one to save the four, but [they continue] we do not agree that consequentialism should be rejected" (2010, 40). They go on to say that in this and like cases, the widespread damage that would occur were the surgeon's action to become public, and the fact that such cases are extremely rare in the real world, provide strong consequentialist grounds for a rule that absolutely prohibits doctors from making such decisions. They admit there is seeming paradox for the consequentialist in saying that the right action is for the surgeon to sacrifice her patient, since to say an action is right seems to recommend the action, and yet such actions by doctors are not to be recommended. But they think that this is something that the act consequentialist must accept by emphasizing the unlikelihood of the facts about the outcomes of the doctor's options being just like the ones stipulated in the example and a doctor ever having the knowledge of those facts that the hypothetical surgeon is stipulated to possess. So what we find here is an appeal to both bold denial in judging the particular case as described, and an appeal to remote effects in explaining why, from the perspective of consequentialism, it is a good thing that doctors adhere to one of the core principles of medical ethics, namely, "do no harm." I will leave it to readers to reflect on the plausibility of this kind of response to theoretical objections to act consequentialism.

We turn next to more radical kinds of response to these objections—more radical in the sense that they depart from one or another of the commitments of classical utilitarianism as summarized above in section 2. Since the responses featured in the next two sections are available to non-utilitarian consequentialists as well as to utilitarians, I will refer to such views as versions of consequentialism. Non-utilitarian versions will be discussed later in section 7.

4. SATISFICING CONSEQUENTIALISM

Another way in which one can depart from the classical version of utilitarianism (and standard versions of consequentialism generally) is to replace the maximizing conception of the relation between the value of consequences and the deontic status of actions by something less demanding. So, one way to preserve the basic consequentialist approach to right action—making right action depend entirely on the value of consequences—is to replace maximizing with what is called "satisficing." Roughly, to satisfice in this context is to perform an action that is "good enough" with respect to its consequences, even if some alternative action would have even better consequences were it to be performed.[5] Talk of "good enough" is vague and can be made precise in various ways for purposes of developing a satisficing view. Let us consider one of those ways.

We determine some level of utility and let that be our "satisficing threshold": in those situations in which more than one alternative action meets or exceeds the threshold, one is permitted to perform any one of the actions in question. Let us suppose that the appropriate threshold level is +10. And suppose that from among one's options, there are three actions that meet the threshold: Action A: +20, action B: +35, action C: +10. Suppose all of one's other options fall below the threshold. Then, according to the satisficing version of utilitarianism, actions A, B, and C are good enough, and one is permitted to perform any one of them. Suppose that on some Saturday afternoon, I could either pursue my hobby of gardening whose associated utility would be +20 or I could do some volunteer work whose associated utility would be +30. Given the proposed threshold, one is permitted to garden instead of doing what would maximize utility. Because the volunteer work would bring about even better consequences than gardening, and would require some level of self-sacrifice, this option can comfortably be classified as supererogatory. So, relaxing the requirement on morally permissible action in this way can help the utilitarian overcome the demandingness objections.

What about cases in which all of one's alternative actions have associated utilities that are below the threshold? One proposal would be to say that in these cases, one should maximize. The resulting satisficing conception of utilitarianism (and consequentialism generally) can be expressed as follows:

SC An action A performed in circumstances C is morally *right* (not wrong) if and only if (and because) the utility of A meets or exceeds the specified threshold utility. (In cases where A is below the threshold but has the highest utility among one's options, then A is morally required.)

A satisficing conception of right action might seem like a promising way to deal with demandingness, but as some critics have noted, SC (and arguably all other versions of satisficing consequentialism) have unacceptable implications in a range of cases. Here is one. Suppose I collect money for a charity organization and the donations I have received over the course of the past month can be used to raise the level of utility by +200, far in excess of the threshold. However, were I to keep a portion of the money for myself and give the rest to the charity, the result would be +150 in overall utility, which would still be in excess of the threshold. According to SC, both actions are morally permissible, but clearly it would be morally wrong for me to keep a portion of the money and fail to do what would maximize utility in this case—I'm engaging in theft.

There are other examples that are problematic for SC that do not involve immorally benefitting oneself while still producing outcomes at or above the satisficing threshold. Here is one.

> *Ian's Options.* There are two groups of campers, 6 in one group and 2 in another, both groups camping in a ravine but at some distance from one another. Heavy rains have caused a nearby dam to break and water is flooding into the ravine. Ian, a helicopter pilot, knows the location and size of each group, but he can save only one of the groups before the flood waters reach the campers. The members of the group who aren't rescued will drown. Being experienced at such missions, he knows that he will be successful in rescuing one group or the other. Ian does not have any special connection to any of the campers, and he knows this.

Let us suppose that saving the members of either group would produce utility in excess of the satisficing threshold, though, of course, saving the 6 will produce triple the utility compared to saving only 2. According to SC, if Ian chooses to save the 2 instead of the 6 he is doing nothing wrong—both of his rescue choices are merely morally permissible. But, so the objection goes, it would be wrong for Ian to save only 2 when he could just as easily save 6.

In light of such examples, one might think that all they show is that the particular version of satisficing consequentialism—SC—is problematic and that a more sophisticated version might avoid such problem cases. Perhaps so, but it is up to the fan of satisficing to formulate such a view.[6]

5. RULE CONSEQUENTIALISM

So far in this and the previous chapter, we have been focusing on direct versions of act consequentialism, according to which the utilities of individual concrete actions that might be performed in some situation directly determine the deontic status of those actions. Versions of *indirect consequentialism* that concern the deontic status of actions, consider the consequences of something other than individual actions as a basis (indirect, of course) for explaining the deontic status of actions.

The most well-known version of indirect consequentialism is *rule consequentialism* that was developed in the 1950s and 1960s, and put forward and defended as superior to its direct act consequentialist cousin. Again, the alleged superiority of this version of the view has to do with its ability to avoid the various theoretical objections presented earlier. What is rule consequentialism? How does it avoid the objections?

The basic idea behind the view can be summarized by two claims.

- Alternative codes of rules for conduct aimed at governing the behavior of a society's individuals can be evaluated according to the value of the consequences associated with each of the alternative codes. A code of rules associated with the production of at least as much overall intrinsic value as any alternative code is an "ideal code."
- The rightness or wrongness of an action depends on whether it is required or prohibited by an ideal code of rules.

Thus, as a basic formulation of the view, we have:

RC An action A is *right* (not wrong) if and only if (and because) A is not prohibited by an ideal code of rules. By implication, obligatory and wrong actions are, respectively, those required by and those prohibited by an ideal code.

Mention of the value of consequences "associated with" a code of rules is deliberately vague because there is more than one way to understand the relation between rules and the production of consequences. For our purposes, it will be enough if we consider one prominent version of RC.

Although RC refers to codes of rules, it will be useful for purposes of exposition to focus on individual rules and their associated value. What we may call the *acceptance value* of a rule is defined as the overall level of value that would result if individuals were to accept, in the sense of internalize, the rule in question. To internalize a rule is to have one's behavior be guided by and thus largely conform to the rule. An ideal code, then, would be a set of rules whose acceptance value would be at least as great, if not greater, than alternative sets of rules. With regard to internalization, the rule consequentialist must specify whether RC is best formulated with reference to complete acceptance, so that the ideal code is supposed to be accepted by each and every competent member of a society, or whether instead, it is best formulated supposing less than complete acceptance. Brad Hooker, a prominent defender of rule consequentialism, argues that it is most realistic to formulate the view with reference to acceptance by an "overwhelming majority" of society, arguing in particular that the majority in question ought to be in the 90 percent range. So let us follow Hooker on this point. There are other details of formulation to be addressed including "transition costs"—the costs involved in getting various rules accepted in the first place. I won't pause here to go into these details. For a concise discussion of these finer points, see Hooker 2008a, sections 6.2 and 6.3.

To convey a basic understanding of RC, let us work with a very simple example involving a single rule. Suppose that I have promised to help you clean out your garage on Saturday. Saturday comes and among my options are these:

A1 Keep my promise and help you out
A2 Break my promise and do something I'd prefer to do instead

Now for each alternative action, we can formulate a rule that mentions the action in question (and thus a rule that applies to the situation). Thus,

R1 Whenever one has made a promise, one is to keep the promise.
R2 Whenever one has made a made a promise, one may break the promise if one prefers to do so.

We now consider the acceptance value for each of these rules. That is, we consider the value that would result were an overwhelming majority of individuals in society to internalize R1, and compare it to the utility that would result were an overwhelming majority of individuals to internalize R2. Given the great value of trust and coordination of efforts by the members of society and the role promise keeping plays in promoting such values, it is pretty clear that R1 has associated with it a higher acceptance value than is associated with R2, thus (restricting our alternatives to just these two rules) R1 is favored over R2. Finally, the rule consequentialist theory tells us that the action of keeping my promise is obligatory in this particular situation, since it will figure in a code of rules having a higher acceptance value than a code that includes R2.

Now suppose that in the situation just sketched, if I break my promise and shoot pool with some friends at the local pub, I would thereby bring about a greater amount of value than if I were to keep my promise. Direct act consequentialism implies that the objectively right act is to shoot pool and thereby break the promise. But intuitively, this seems incorrect. Rule consequentialism, by contrast, has us calculate, not the values of the consequences of individual actions available to one in the circumstances, but rather the value resulting from whole patterns of rule-governed action, and so in this case yields what strikes one as an intuitively correct moral verdict.

Return now to the examples featured in the various theoretical objections. The rule consequentialist theory gives us morally correct results when applied to those cases. Individual actions of punishing an innocent person, committing murder to benefit others, unequally distributing benefits and burdens in society, and breaking promises, though they may, in rare instances, maximize value, nevertheless are morally wrong according to RC. For instance, a rule that permits physicians to sacrifice innocent people in cases where they know that by doing so they can save a few others would predictably have a lower acceptance utility than a rule prohibiting such courses of action. The general acceptance of a rule permitting such sacrifice would produce much distrust and anxiety in society about doctors and hospitals generally, causing people to put off or avoid needed treatments for illness and disease.

In a similar manner, RC can avoid the problems associated with demandingness because part of determining which code would be ideal requires that one consider the costs of successfully getting people to internalize a rule that requires people to be completely impartial in their decisions that affect their own welfare and the welfare of family and friends. If it is unreasonable, given the fact that human beings are very strongly disposed from an early age to favor themselves and those close to them, then the costs of getting individuals to internalize a rule requiring strict impartiality would be greater than the costs of getting individuals to internalize a rule that allowed a large measure of partiality but with some concern for the welfare of strangers including distant peoples.

Moreover, RC helps make sense, from a consequentialist perspective, of the very common idea that breaking promises is wrong because of the kind of act it is—an act of promising that violates a moral rule against such actions. And the same goes for other actions like murder and lying. Of course, the rule consequentialist offers an account of why such actions are wrong in terms of consequences associated with rules, but the view allows moral weight to attach to moral rules in terms of which we often justify our actions.

A full evaluation of rule consequentialism is not possible here.[7] We will have to make do with a brief assessment. In what immediately follows, let us first consider the worry that rule consequentialism collapses into act consequentialism. This worry has, I think, been adequately addressed in the literature, but it worth considering nonetheless. More worrisome are objections based on the criteria of internal support, explanatory power, and determinacy, which will be taken up in order after considering the threat of collapse.

Does Rule Consequentialism Collapse into Act Consequentialism?

Let us return to our example of promise keeping. Although R1 has a higher acceptance value than R2, we can expect that a more complex rule concerning promising will have a greater acceptance value than either of these two. For instance, in situations where I can save an innocent life by breaking a promise, the rule

R3 Whenever one has made a promise, one will keep the promise unless by breaking it one can save innocent lives

would no doubt have a higher acceptance value than R1. After all, in cases where there are no innocent lives to be saved, R3 would agree with R1 in implying that one ought to keep one's promises. But in those rare cases in which one can save lives by breaking a promise, acceptance of R3 would no doubt produce a greater amount of good than would acceptance of R1. Thus, overall, R3 would have a higher acceptance value than R1.

It is clear that there are other circumstances in which breaking one's promise and performing some competing action would (in general) produce better results than acceptance of a rule like R3 with only one exception built into it. Thus, some rule more complex, probably much more complex, than R3 would apparently have the highest acceptance value for situations having to do with keeping promises.

But now one might suspect that the following rule will have the highest acceptance value for situations involving promises:

R4 Whenever one has made a promise, one will keep it unless there is some alternative action open to the agent which, in the situation, would produce a greater amount of value.

But R4 in effect prescribes that in such situations we perform the action that would maximize value. And, of course, for every situation, there will be, from among the set of alternative rules, a rule like R4. But then one is led to the conclusion that rule consequentialism is "extensionally equivalent" to act consequentialism; that is, it will necessarily agree with act consequentialism about the deontic status of actions. And this result means that rule consequentialism cannot, after all, avoid the kinds of theoretical objections described in the previous section!

Now some versions of rule consequentialism are indeed extensionally equivalent to act utilitarianism, but the version under consideration is not one of those.[8] You may recall from section 5 of the previous chapter that it is very unlikely, given how human beings are, that a rule requiring individuals to maximize utility would, if consciously followed, actually yield as much utility as would simpler rules that are easier to follow and less likely to encourage self-interested biases from inappropriately affecting one's moral decisions. In other words, rules like R4 have arguably less acceptance value than other, more easily and reliably applied rules, and so the version of rule consequentialism under consideration does not reduce to act consequentialism.

So rule consequentialists hold that an ideal code will be one which, in light of human limitations of various sorts, will "favor a code of rules without too many rules, too much complication within the rules, or rules that are too demanding" (Hooker 2008a, section 8). Of course, there may be cases in which it is very clear that in order to prevent a complete disaster from occurring one must break one or more of the not-so-complicated rules in question. One such case is the often-discussed ticking bomb terrorist case in which a series of very powerful bombs are set to be detonated in a large city which would kill or seriously injure many thousands of innocent people. The police have apprehended the terrorist who knows where and when the bombs are to go off, and having exhausted all other methods of extracting the information, they are left with the option of torture. Suppose that the rule regarding torture that has the highest acceptance value is one that prohibits all torture. In the ticking bomb terrorist case it would clearly be irrational from a consequentialist perspective to conform to a rule that prohibits torture and allow the disaster to occur. So, to avoid this problem, the rule consequentialist builds in a "prevent disaster" rule according to which one is required to break one of the other rules of the code if doing so is necessary to prevent a disaster. Since the prevent disaster rule only becomes relevant when there is a huge difference in the value of consequences between conforming to the rule and breaking it, again, RC does not just collapse into act consequentialism.

Assuming, then, that RC represents a moral theory that is truly distinct from act consequentialism, how plausible is it?

The Problem of Partial Compliance

As just noted, rule consequentialism is supposed to overcome the demandingness objections to act consequentialism. But does it? Consider the extent of today's world hunger and extreme poverty. What does RC require of those living in relative affluence in light of such miserable living conditions of so many? Wouldn't RC include a rule to the effect that those of us living in relative affluence (with money to spend on such luxuries as concert tickets, nice cars, vacations, and so on) are required to come to the aid of others so long as the benefit to those in desperate need is far greater than the sacrifice an affluent person would have to make? As Hooker points out, such a rule would make very heavy demands on those of us with money in excess of what is required to live a *much* less affluent life. And such a rule would be demanding indeed. Hooker's response to this threat of demandingness is that his version of RC only "calls for an amount of self-sacrifice that is not unreasonable. If each relatively well-off person contributed some relatively small percentage of his or her income to famine relief, there would be enough food to feed the world. Perhaps ten percent from each of the well-off would be enough" (1990, 72). Hooker goes on to say that giving this much is somewhat demanding, but not unreasonably so. Rule consequentialism is thus presumably able to escape the demandingness objection.

But problems with this solution emerge in light of the so-called partial compliance problem, according to which following the moral code that would be ideal in a world in which everyone (or nearly everyone) internalized the rule can be counterproductive if not outright disastrous in circumstances in which very few are complying with the rule. Of course, if the ideal code includes a rule that one is to prevent (or do what one can to help prevent) great harm or disaster, then one may permissibly break one of the (other) relatively simple rules, conformance to which in real life circumstances would either produce or fail to prevent great harm. Now suppose (which is easy to do) that in fact very few in a position to donate ten percent or more to famine relief are in fact doing so. Given the "prevent disaster" rule, the implication would seem to be that I should give more than ten percent of my income and that I should keep on giving until I am living a non-affluent life, though above poverty line, since donating a very high percentage of my income and greatly reducing my standard of living would arguably save the lives of some others in danger of death from starvation, thus preventing great disaster at least to those individuals.

The upshot is that there is an apparent tension in Hooker's version of RC: a rule permitting or requiring one to avoid great harm if the only way of doing so is to break one of the other rules of the ideal code is needed to save the theory from being overly demanding. But this very move seems to impose great demands in at least some situations of partial compliance. To be fair, Hooker has attempted to respond to this worry, but in his 2001 book *The Demands of Con-*

sequentialism Tim Mulgan convincingly develops this particular demandingness worry in some detail. He argues that Hooker's rule consequentialism is subject to counterexamples that undermine the hope that RC (or some rule version of consequentialism) can really avoid at least some of the theoretical objections to direct act consequentialism. If this charge sticks, then rule consequentialism has difficulties with the standard of internal support.

The Wrong Explanation Objection

According to the standard of explanatory power, a correct moral theory should not just imply moral verdicts that are consistent with considered moral beliefs, but its principles should provide moral criteria that correctly explain why this or that action has the deontic status it has. Although what I am about to say is fairly controversial, it seems to me that rule consequentialist explanations of the morality of certain types of action are misguided. Consider a particular act of someone intentionally killing an innocent person for reasons of greed—a case of murder. Granted, any ideal code of rules will likely include an absolute rule against such killing, and the rationale for the rule will have to do with its comparative level of acceptable value. But apparently for the rule consequentialist what *ultimately explains* why a particular murder is wrong is that a rule prohibiting such behavior has a higher acceptance value than alternative rules. But is this fact—the fact that a rule prohibiting murder has a higher acceptance value of alternative rules—what explains why a *particular* murder is wrong? The explanation here seems too indirect. A better explanation is just in terms of what the killing does to the particular victim: it unjustly deprives her or him of life and the valuable experiences a continued life would bring.

The worry being raised here is perhaps more forceful in connection with special obligations to family and loved ones. What best explains why a daughter or son has special filial obligations to her or his parents? What best explains why spouses, particularly those who have been through much together, have special obligations to one another? Intuitively, the answer to these questions will have to do with the special bonds between such individuals. But according to rule consequentialism, what ultimately explains such obligations has to do with facts about the benefits to society of everyone in special relationships fulfilling their obligations to parents, spouses, and friends. However, the fact that everyone (or most everyone) fulfilling such obligations will have good overall consequences for society seems not to be the ultimate ground of one's obligation to a parent, spouse, or friend. The proper ground and thus ultimate explanation of such special obligations arguably has to do with the particular bonds of love and friendship that relate people in certain intimate ways. So even if rule consequentialism can provide an intuitively correct explanation of certain moral obligations such as the obligation not to cheat on one's taxes, it seemingly lacks the power to properly explain obligations having to do with special interpersonal bonds.[9]

Problems with Determinacy

Another worry concerns conflicts of rules and the issue of whether rule consequentialism provides a method or principled way of resolving such conflicts. If not,
then the theory will be limited in its ability to yield determinate verdicts in a range
of cases. As explained above, rule consequentialists like Hooker insist that the rules
included in an ideal code must be relatively simple in order that they can be learned
and readily applied. This means that a system of rules in which all sorts of exceptions
are built into the rules would likely have a lower acceptance value than systems with
simpler rules. But then what does rule consequentialism say in cases where rules
come into conflict in particular cases, as they inevitably will? Lack of a good answer
to this question will mean that the theory is seriously lacking in determinacy. One
might consider a lexical rank ordering of the rules so that in cases of conflict a higher
ranking rule always trumps lower ranking rules. But for reasons we will explore in
chapter 9 on moral pluralism, this will not work. Sometimes a rule requiring that
we keep promises will trump a rule requiring that we help those needing immediate assistance, but sometimes it will be the other way around. Hooker, following
a proposal by R. B. Brandt, suggests that in cases of conflicts of rules, one should
conform to the rule that "whatever course of action would leave morally well-trained
people less dissatisfied" (Brandt, 1963, 134).[10] But for this proposal to work, one
would need to argue for two claims: (1) well-trained people would largely converge
in their reactions to particular cases of conflict, and (2) the moral sensibility of a
morally well-trained person is more determinate than the moral code he or she has
internalized (otherwise appealing to the reactions of a morally well-trained person
will not help determine which rule an agent should follow). Both claims are highly
dubious however.[11]

Let me conclude this discussion of rule consequentialism with a caveat and an
observation. The caveat (now familiar) is that there may be a version of rule consequentialism that avoids the problems we have been considering (as well as ones we
haven't). The observation is that Hooker recognizes that there are limits in resolving
conflicts among moral rules which "limits the theory's ability to resolve our moral
uncertainties. Here is a place where rule-consequentialism comes up short" (2000a,
136). It is a place where his theory comes up short, but in my view, any plausible
moral theory is going to be limited in its determinacy.

6. ALTERNATIVE THEORIES OF VALUE

According to utilitarianism, right acts maximize the good, and the good to be
maximized is the welfare of individuals. As we saw in the last chapter, classical
utilitarianism understands welfare in terms of happiness and understands happiness
hedonistically. A happy life is one filled with experiences of pleasure and lacking (so
far as possible) experiences of pain. But even granting that pleasure and pain are

among the items that have intrinsic value and disvalue respectively, and granting also that they are at least part of what makes a person's life go well, are they the only items that have this status? Many moral philosophers reject hedonism as an account of welfare. One reason for the rejection is nicely illustrated by a thought experiment devised by Robert Nozick:

> Suppose there were an experience machine that would give you any experience you desired. Superduper neuroscientists could stimulate your brain so that you would think and feel you were writing a great novel, or making a friend, or reading an interesting book. All the time you would be floating in a tank, with electrodes attached to your brain. Should you plug into this machine for life, preprogramming your life's experiences? (Nozick, 1974, 42)

If the only items of positive intrinsic value are mental states of pleasure, why not plug in?

But, of course, most people (and maybe all people whose lives are not utterly miserable) will not plug in. Presumably this reveals that there are items other than experiences of pleasure that we take to have intrinsic value and that are an important part of what makes an individual's life go well for her. Nozick points out that there are things we want to do, and not just think we are doing. We also want to be persons of a certain sort, and not just think we are. A fantasy life in which I merely think I have written a great novel or have many friends is clearly inferior in value to a life in which such things really occur. But if what matters is how everything seems from the inside, then there is no difference in value between my thinking I have done something and my truly having done it. In short, hedonism does not do justice to our considered moral beliefs about what it is in life that makes up a person's welfare. Pleasure may be one item that has intrinsic value and contributes positively to one's welfare, but it does not seem to be the only kind of thing that does.

As explained in the last chapter, the generic principle of utilitarianism

> **GPU** An action is *right* if and only if (and because) A has as high a utility as any alternative action that the agent could perform instead

does not itself specify a theory of utility or value and so it does not commit one to hedonism. Because value hedonism seems implausible, contemporary versions of utilitarianism (and consequentialism generally) typically embrace some nonhedonistic theory of welfare.

One prominent nonhedonist account of welfare to be developed and defended in the last half of the twentieth century is the *desire fulfillment theory of welfare*. Its basic idea is that what makes a person's life go better is the fulfillment of her desires, and what makes it go worse is the nonfulfillment or frustration of her desires. This view can be understood as making the two following claims.

- What is of intrinsic value for a person contributing to her welfare is her desires being fulfilled, and what is of intrinsic disvalue for a person detracting from her welfare is her desires not being fulfilled.
- Insofar as the objects of one's desires are properly said to have value, they have it only because they are the objects of one's desires.

The first claim can be (and typically is) qualified by restricting the range of desires that figure in the account of intrinsic value and we will come back to this point in a moment. But first, there are two important points about this theory to avoid misunderstanding it. First, the view should not be confused with hedonism because it is the fulfillment of a desire—the fact that it is fulfilled—that constitutes a benefit to the person, apart from whether she experiences any pleasure as a result of the desire being fulfilled. Similarly, the frustration of one's desires, apart from whether one experiences displeasure as a result, is what constitutes a reduction in one's welfare. Second, people desire a variety of things, including pleasure, friendship, good food, world peace, knowledge, and so on. On the desire fulfillment view, the objects of desire are not themselves intrinsically good; rather, as the second bullet point attempts to make clear, they have value for a person *because* she desires them. But, again, notice that on the desire-fulfillment view, what contributes to the welfare of a person and thus what has intrinsic value is the fulfillment of a person's desires—the fact that the objects of one's desires are realized.

If we plug this theory of welfare into the generic utilitarian scheme, we have desire fulfillment utilitarianism. Utilitarianism, of course, is concerned with the general welfare, and hence desire fulfillment, of all those affected by one's action. So we can formulate this version of the theory as follows:

> **DFU** An action A is *right* if and only if (and because) A would result in at least as much general desire fulfillment as any alternative action that the agent could perform instead. (Talk of "general desire fulfillment" refers to the net balance of aggregated desire fulfillment versus aggregated desire frustration for all those affected by the action.)

One attractive feature of this theory is that it avoids the main objection to hedonism. Many of our desires are for things and activities other than pleasurable experiences. I desire to write a best-selling novel that will be at least nominated for the Nobel Prize in Literature, and not just think I've done so when I really haven't. Thus, because my actually writing the novel and its being nominated for this prize fulfills one of my desires, all this has intrinsic value for me and contributes positively to my welfare. So on this theory of welfare, how things really are—what I am really doing and how I really am—is important for one's welfare; I am not doing well if I am merely hooked up to Nozick's experience machine (unless, of course, all I really desire is to have the kinds of experiences that the machine can deliver).

However, the desire fulfillment theory of welfare has its share of problems. I will mention three of them. First, some restrictions must be placed on those desires whose fulfillment plausibly contributes to one's welfare. After all, I might desire that the music of the Beatles still be popular in the twenty-second century, long after I am gone. It is hard to see how the fulfillment (or nonfulfillment) of this desire could contribute in any way to my welfare. Presumably, the theory needs to make welfare depend only on those desires whose fulfillment (or nonfulfillment) will affect one's own life.[12]

A second, more serious problem for the theory is that desire fulfillment as such does not necessarily seem to contribute to one's welfare. Suppose that someone's guiding desire in life is to count blades of grass.[13] The pleasure this person derives from counting contributes to his welfare, but it is hard to see how the mere fact that his desire is being fulfilled contributes to his welfare.

A third, related problem concerns horrendous desires, such as a desire to torture children. Do we really want to grant that the fulfillment of a person's horrendous desires contributes to that person's welfare? Certainly one would not want to count the fulfillment of such desires as figuring in an account of right action.

It would seem, then, that it is only when the "right" desires are fulfilled that our welfare is enhanced. But what are the right desires? Aren't they for things and activities that have value for us independently of our desiring them? If so, then the desire fulfillment theory cannot be a correct account of the nature of welfare.[14]

Both hedonism and desire-fulfillment views of welfare that we have considered are often classified as *subjectivist theories of intrinsic value*. Hedonism is subjectivist in the sense that the bearers of intrinsic value are subjective mental states alone. And desire-fulfillment theories are considered subjectivist both because they make a person's welfare depend entirely on fulfillment of one's desires—a certain kind of mental state—and because the value that anything possesses for a person is dependent on being an object of that person's desires.

By contrast, *objectivist theories of intrinsic value* maintain that such things as knowledge, achievement, appreciation of beauty, and friendship, are intrinsically good. The list of such items is not narrowly restricted to mental states (unlike hedonism) even though such a list might include pleasure as an intrinsic good and even though friendship, knowledge, and appreciation of beauty involve the possession of certain attitudes. Nor is their value dependent on being the object of an individual's desire, contrary to desire-fulfillment views. Such views are often called "objective list" theories of intrinsic value and represent a kind of *enumerative value pluralism*—they recognize a plurality of equally basic goods.[15]

In light of problems with the two sorts of subjectivist theory of value, let us consider versions of consequentialism that work with objectivist theories of value. One option for a consequentialist is to accept welfarism as an account of intrinsic value, but reject any subjectivist theory of intrinsic value and hold an objectivist account instead. (In the next section, we will examine just such a view.) According to how I have been using the terminology, such views (because they embrace a welfarist theory of value) are versions of utilitarian consequentialism.

But there are non-welfarist versions of consequentialism. One such view is *perfectionist consequentialism* that embraces a perfectionist theory of value according to which certain states make a person's life good without such states necessarily contributing to a person's welfare or happiness. Knowledge and achievement, for instance, are often understood as perfectionist goods—goods the obtaining of which concerns what makes for a good human life in general. (We encountered a version of value perfectionism in chapter 4 when we examined the version of natural law theory associated with Aquinas. You may recall the quote from W. L. Sumner at the end of that chapter in which he contrasts a welfarist conception of the good life with a perfectionistic conception.) As a form of act consequentialism, the view is that the deontic status of an action depends entirely on its contribution to, if not realization of, those states that constitute human perfection. Another form of non-utilitarian consequentialism would be a hybrid view of intrinsic value that combined welfare values such as pleasure with perfectionist values.[16]

The importance of taking note of these various theories of intrinsic value is twofold. First, there are pluralistic theories of welfare that many consequentialists favor because arguably they help the theory overcome the various theoretical objections regarding justice, rights, the significance of personal relations, and demandingness. Second, many who find the generic consequentialist idea attractive—that the right depends in some way on the value of consequences or outcomes—embrace one or another non-welfarist conception of value, either embracing a fully perfectionist conception of personal good or a hybrid view featuring a mixture of welfarist and perfectionist elements. Again, one driving motivation toward such non-welfarist views is to develop versions of consequentialism that can adequately respond to the theoretical objections. Let us consider how value pluralism can come to the aid of act consequentialism.

7. VALUE PLURALIST CONSEQUENTIALISM

If none of the strategies explained above in sections 4–6 succeed in answering the various theoretical objections to act consequentialism, there is a strategy that may work. It involves two key ideas.

First, the view in question embraces an objective pluralist theory of intrinsic value of a special sort—what I will call *morally constrained value pluralism*—in attempting to show how the consequentialist theory can be made to fit with our considered moral beliefs about punishment, sacrifice, promising, distributive justice, and the level of sacrifice morality demands. The strategy, then, is to develop and defend a particular pluralistic theory of intrinsic value and then show how a consequentialist theory that makes use of this particular theory of value fits with our considered moral beliefs about the sorts of cases discussed above.

Second, one of the structural elements of classical utilitarianism is its commitment to a certain form of impartiality: *the value of the consequences of an action is to be assessed from a strictly impartial point of view; the values of the consequences on all who are affected have equal weight in determining the deontic status of an action.* Many of the theoretical objections to classical act utilitarianism can be traced to this demanding form of impartiality. This is particularly clear with the problems having to do with distributive justice, the moral significance of personal relationships, and demandingness. So, one option for a consequentialist is to reject the utilitarian conception of impartiality by either allowing that the value properly associated with outcomes that affect oneself and one's associates may be given more weight than the value of the outcomes that affect strangers, or by allowing that the welfare of disadvantaged individuals be given more weight and thus a certain priority in determining the value of consequences. We have seen how consequentialists have tried rejecting other structural elements of classical utilitarianism by rejecting maximizing in favor of satisficing and rejecting direct versions in favor of indirect versions. The version of consequentialism about to be described retains the maximizing and direct focus elements of the classical view. It also retains the universalist thesis that the effects of one's actions on all individuals is morally relevant in determining the deontic status of actions. What it rejects is the sort of strict impartial weighting of consequences expressed by the above thesis of impartiality.

In what follows, I will briefly explain the pluralist theory of value in question and how it works to the advantage of the consequentialist. Then I want to suggest (if not fully argue) that embracing this strain of consequentialism will be at the cost of determinacy in the resulting theory and will, in effect, be an instance of a limited, pluralistic moral theory.

The version of consequentialism under consideration is developed and defended by David Brink.[17] According to Brink's pluralist theory of value, there are three main components of an individual's life that have intrinsic value and thus contribute to her or his personal good: (1) reflective pursuit of one's reasonable projects, (2) realization of those projects, and (3) certain personal and social relationships, including family relations, friendships, and other social connections. In addition, Brink's view recognizes extrinsic goods that are necessary conditions for the intrinsic goods and include the goods of basic well-being (health, nutrition, and shelter), liberty, and education. These goods contribute causally to an individual's welfare. But it is crucial to Brink's theory of intrinsic value that for the pursuit (and realization) of a personal project to be truly valuable, and for personal and social relationships to be truly valuable, they must respect persons. Since the notion of respect for persons is a moral one, it is morally constrained pursuit (and realization) of personal projects and personal and social relationships that have intrinsic value in the first place. Here is how Brink puts the point (he refers to his theory as "objective utilitarianism" "OU" for short):

> [T]here are moral constraints on valuable projects; in order for the pursuit and realization of a project to be of value, that project must, among other things, respect other people at least in the minimal sense of not causing significant and avoidable harm. Moreover, personal and social relationships involving mutual concern and respect form an important part of human good, according to OU's theory of value. (Brink, 1989, 264)

If value is attached to the pursuit of any personal project, no matter what, then a racist's project of genocide would have to count as having positive value. And if there are enough such racists and few enough members of the group targeted by the racists, it might turn out that maximizing utility would justify racist activity. Obviously, this result is blocked on Brink's version of consequentialism. Since racist projects fail to respect persons, those projects do not have value in the first place.

As an example of how this version of consequentialism can avoid the various sorts of moral objections we have examined, let us consider Brink's response to the distributive justice objection. According to that objection, utilitarianism and other forms of consequentialism can in principle require patently unjust, and hence immoral, allocation of benefits and imposition of burdens whenever the greatest aggregate utility would thereby be produced. For instance, the theory would justify gross inequalities in such basic goods as health, nutrition, and shelter in the interests of maximizing overall welfare. In short, utilitarianism is insensitive to matters of distribution.

In response to this objection, Brink argues that according to his version of consequentialism,

> inequalities in basic goods cannot be justified as maximizing the total amount of welfare. It will always be better (i.e., more valuable) to give basic goods to one more person than to increase someone else's supply of nonbasic goods. Moreover, OU's insistence on respect for persons constrains accepting inequalities in nonbasic goods. In order for pursuit or realization of one's personal projects to be valuable, they must respect the interests of others, and the development and maintenance of personal and social relationships involving mutual concern and commitment are intrinsically valuable. For distributions of goods and services to respect persons, they must express fair terms of social cooperation. . . . OU's theory of value is thus itself distribution-sensitive. (Brink, 1989, 272)

Because Brink's view is distribution sensitive, it in effect rejects the sort of strict impartiality characteristic of classical utilitarianism and counts as a form of *prioritarian consequentialism*—a view that was briefly mentioned in the previous chapter (section 2). In general, then, by embracing a morally constrained account of intrinsic value, Brink is able to argue plausibly that his version of consequentialism fits nicely with our considered moral beliefs about punishment, promising, distributive justice, and the importance of personal projects and thereby nicely satisfies the standard of internal support for evaluating a moral theory.

Now the observation I wish to make about such value pluralist versions of consequentialism is that they seem to lack the kind of determinacy possessed by more classical versions of the theory. Let me explain.

The classical version of utilitarianism, involving value hedonism, makes the deontic status of an action depend on how much overall utility would be produced by the action (compared to how much would be produced by alternative actions). Utility is a matter of the net balance of episodes of pleasure over episodes of pain. Thus, the classical principle of utility enjoys a high degree of determinacy since (in a wide range of cases) there is going to be a determinate fact of the matter about the utilities of actions, and the principle of utility specifies how such utilities determine the deontic status of actions.

Although I cannot fully argue the case here, I believe that Brink's version of utilitarianism will lack the kind of determinacy characteristic of the classical version. The reason for this is that in order for the pursuit of personal projects, their realization, and the realization of personal and social relationships to have positive value at all, they must respect persons. Sometimes, for instance, when the choice is between pursuing one's own projects and maintaining or promoting certain social relationships, the pursuit of personal projects would fail to respect persons. Suppose a young woman, interested in pursuing her artistic ambitions, strongly desires to move from the United States to Paris to study art. However, suppose she has a sick family member whose care falls to her, thus requiring that she stay in the United States indefinitely. Arguably, in this context, consideration of respect for persons favors the promotion of the good of a family relationship. In other cases, it may be the other way around. But I doubt there are any principles or methods that fix or determine what counts as respecting persons in many contexts. And if not, then moral principles that make substantial use of this notion will lack a measure of determinacy both as decision procedures and as criteria for right action. In making this claim I am anticipating what I will be arguing in the chapter on Kant's moral theory—a moral theory that makes the idea of respect for persons central in its account of right conduct.

But notice what I am not claiming. I am not claiming that on a theory like Brink's there is no determinate fact of the matter about level of intrinsic value possessed by the outcomes of actions. What I'm claiming is that the theory does not provide any principles or method of determining how much overall morally constrained value an action would (if performed) produce. The manner in which the various components of intrinsic value may combine in determining the overall net value of some state of affairs may be too complex to capture in some principle or set of principles, thus requiring a large role for judgment about particular cases in arriving at deontic verdicts about alternative actions and policies.[18] On this point, value pluralist versions of consequentialism stand in contrast to simpler hedonistic versions. The contrast is nicely put by Richard Brandt:

> Matters are more complicated [on pluralist versions compared to hedonic versions], of course, if we go along with some utilitarians and say that knowledge, autonomy, deep personal relations, and accomplishment are important intrinsic goods. We then do not have the evidence for a definite conclusion that we theoretically would have if hedonistic utilitarianism were true—provided measurement and interpersonal comparison of pleasure were possible. We must simply make some large judgments. (Brandt, 1988, 353)[19]

In chapter 4, I argued that the natural law theory, once it is purged of implausible elements, lacks determinacy as a moral theory and is plausibly interpreted as a limited, pluralistic moral theory. I am making the same point about plausible versions of act consequentialism, a point that I will go on to make about Kant's moral theory.[20]

W. D. Ross's version of moral pluralism and what I take to be the most plausible version of virtue ethics, which we take up in chapters 8 and 9 respectively, are clear versions of moral pluralism, though limited in their determinacy: limited, pluralistic moral theories. Thus, one of the main themes to emerge from this book is that plausible versions of many of the theories we examine are indeterminate in what the principles of the theory imply about the deontic status of a wide range of actions. This fact about those theories is not so much a defect to be somehow overcome as an acknowledgment of the limit on the degree of determinacy we can expect from any plausible moral theory, given the complexity of moral phenomena.

8. EVALUATION OF CONSEQUENTIALISM

An overall evaluation of consequentialism is difficult because there are many versions of the theory that vary in their plausibility, and because consequentialists under fire have met the various challenges with responses that have some degree of plausibility (so I think). Some critical comments have already been made about versions of act utilitarianism, satisficing consequentialism, and rule consequentialism. However, a few general observations can be made in coming to a tentative evaluation of the theory, focusing on value pluralistic versions of direct act consequentialism.

Intuitive appeal. Consequentialism, in at least some of its varieties, captures three intuitively plausible ideas about morality. First, it is based on a very plausible view of practical rationality. When it comes to rationality in the realm of choice and action, the idea that we ought to bring about as much good as possible seems irresistible. Second, consequentialism captures the idea that impartiality is at the heart of morality (at least it captures a certain conception of impartiality). Finally, utilitarian versions committed to welfarism accommodate our sense that morality has to do with human well-being (and perhaps the well-being of other sentient creatures). Thus, according to the standard of intuitive appeal, consequentialism has a lot going for it.

Consistency and applicability. Since act consequentialism makes the deontic status of action depend entirely on consequences, there does not seem to be any problem with satisfying the standard of consistency. For the theory to be inconsistent it would have to be the case, for example, that some action, if performed, would both bring about the highest net aggregate value compared to the value that would be produced by an agent's alternative actions, and that it not do so. This doesn't seem possible.

As for the standard of applicability, in the last chapter we saw how the act utilitarian can deal with the main practical objection to the theory by denying that it represents a decision procedure. We also saw how actual consequence utilitarians (and consequentialists generally) have proposed principles of subjective rightness that can plausibly address the applicability standard. As for the fact that the actual consequence utilitarian principle cannot (and should not) be used in cases where trying to calculate utilities is not possible or advisable, an advocate of this theory can follow Mill by adopting a two-level approach to moral thinking and decision making. These options serve to blunt objections based on the applicability standard.

Internal support and explanatory power. However, the theoretical objections that challenge the claim that utilitarianism represents a correct moral criterion are not so easily dealt with. In this chapter, we have explored five strategies that utilitarians have offered in response: (1) the strategy of bold denial, (2) the strategy of appealing to remote effects, (3) satisficing (4) the move to rule consequentialism, and (5) the strategy of appealing to a morally constrained pluralist theory of welfare. I have suggested that the fifth strategy seems to work best in helping the consequentialist square her theory with our considered moral beliefs and thus overcome the various theoretical objections. Value pluralist consequentialism does seem to satisfy the standard of internal support. What is questionable is whether the theory adequately satisfies the standard of explanatory power by providing correct explanations of the deontic status of actions and practices. Is it true that the rightness and wrongness of all actions is entirely explained by appeal to consequences? As we shall see in the coming chapters, the answer to this question is hotly disputed.

External support. In presenting Mill's version of utilitarianism we examined his attempt to offer a proof of the principle of utility based on an appeal to nonmoral claims about what people desire. We noted that according to a standard interpretation of Mill's proof, it involves various fallacious inferences. Had Mill's proof worked, then according to the standard of external support, Mill's theory would enjoy some level of confirmation. However, this standard can also be used to criticize a theory. For instance, one challenge to standard versions of consequentialism is that it fails to comport with a realistic understanding of human psychology. Human beings are, by nature, strongly self-interested and partial to their circle of family and friends. Shelly Kagan remarks that "Given the parameters of the actual world, there is no question that [maximally] promoting the good would require a life of hardship, self-denial, and austerity" (1989, 360). The point is that the impartialist demands that are characteristic of standard forms of act consequentialism are deeply at odds with how human beings really are. This is what led Mackie to complain that act utilitarianism is an "ethics of fantasy"—fantasy, because the sacrifice involved in maximizing the good impartially assessed is beyond what can reasonably be expected of human beings. This tension between facts of human psychology and at least certain forms of act consequentialism is a basis for claiming that such views are implausible.

But the consequentialist has a reply to this worry. If the consequentialist theory is understood as a decision procedure, the charge sticks. But the consequentialist is not proposing her theory as decision procedure—how one should conduct their moral lives depends on what motives would be overall best for human beings with our psychologies to have, given the aim of maximizing good outcomes. Mill and Brink argue that by and large, conforming to the rules of conventional morality will be productive of the best outcomes.

Determinacy. We have noted that value pluralist versions of act consequentialism are motivated by the desire to avoid the battery of theoretical objections raised at the outset of this chapter. But, as the above quote by Richard Brandt makes clear, compared to classical versions of act utilitarianism that featured a comparatively simple and highly determinate theory of value and thus a highly determinate account of right action, pluralist versions (in order to deal with the theoretical objections) lack simplicity and determinacy. Again, some degree of indeterminacy in moral theory is, I think, only to be expected.

9. CONCLUSION

In closing I want to consider briefly a claim often made against consequentialism that is supposed to reveal something that is deeply wrong with it. But consequentialists are a resourceful lot, and I also want to indicate how some contemporary versions of the view attempt to sidestep the particular worry I am about to describe. Here is the complaint. Consequentialism, so the complaint goes, fails to respect the separateness of persons. Presumably, this fact about the theory underlies its problems with punishment, distributive justice, demandingness, and other such cases.

We normally take ourselves to be, in some deep sense, distinct from one another. We have separate identities and think of ourselves as separate centers of care and concern. Moreover, we think that this fact about ourselves ought to be respected by a sensible moral theory. Now the way in which utilitarianism supposedly fails to respect the separateness of persons is often explained by noting that the theory can be viewed as taking a perfectly plausible method of prudential choice and decision making and extending it to moral choice and decision making. Prudential rationality seems to require that we maximize our own welfare over time by discounting, as it were, temporal considerations. In maximizing one's own welfare, that is, it is rational to make intrapersonal trade-offs in which one forgoes indulging in an immediate pleasure in order to enjoy something more worthwhile at a later time. In short, in cases of intrapersonal rational choice, if we look at our temporally extended lives as a series of stages of a single individual, it makes perfect sense that my welfare at one stage be sacrificed for my greater welfare at some other stage.

Now the idea is that consequentialism takes this conception of rational intrapersonal choice and extends it to social choice by treating different individuals as though they were parts of one great big person. Just as prudence is indifferent with respect to different times at which one experiences welfare, so the utilitarian theory, in its approach to social choice, is indifferent toward individuals, allowing the welfare of some individuals to be sacrificed for the good of the whole. Thus, so the complaint goes, utilitarianism does not respect the separateness of persons.[21]

Moreover, its failure to do so explains why it has counterintuitive implications about the sorts of cases considered previously. For instance, the utilitarian theory is susceptible to the objection based on distributive justice because it allows (and even sometimes requires) that for the greater overall good we impose unequal burdens on some individuals that intuitively seem grossly immoral. It allows for such treatment because it does not respect the separateness of persons. And because it does not properly respect persons, it ultimately fails to explain why right actions are right and wrong ones wrong: it thus fails to satisfy the standard of explanatory power. One way around this objection is to follow Brink and build into the utilitarian theory considerations of respect for persons. Whether doing so results in a moral theory that represents a fully adequate moral criterion, I will not try to determine here. There is little doubt, however, that the idea that morality, and moral requirements in particular, must reflect respect for persons is a very intuitively appealing belief about morality that most of us share. It is at the very center of the moral theory that we consider in chapter 8 when we turn to Immanuel Kant's moral theory.

Another way to avoid the worry about separateness of persons is to reject the strict impartiality that is characteristic of some forms of consequentialism. You may recall that the thesis of strict impartiality involves both a non-prioritarian account of the weight to be given to the welfare of individuals, which rules out distribution-sensitive theories, and the thesis of agent-neutrality, according to which an assessment of the value of consequences is to be made from an impartial point of view and thus without reference to the agent's perspective. But as we have noted, one can reject either one of these impartialist theses and remain a consequentialist. Brink's view is a version of prioritarian consequentialism. Ethical egoism, the topic of the next chapter, rejects the agent-neutrality component of strict impartialism and so represents a strictly partialist moral theory. Its partialism reflects a robust conception of the separateness of persons.

NOTES

1. *Absolutist* deontological constraints prohibit performing certain actions regardless of the consequences of performing them. *Nonabsolutist* deontological constraints allow that if the consequences of complying with the constraint are catastrophic, or at least bad enough, only then is one justified in not complying with the constraint. Absolutist deontological constraints were featured in chapter 4.

2. As noted in chapter 5, it is also *universalist* in that the effects of an action on the welfare of all who will be affected by the action figure in determining the deontic status of the action. Although a consequentialist could question this structural feature, the versions we go on to consider do not.

3. Taking this option does not mean that the consequentialist must reject the idea that welfare or happiness (however conceived) has intrinsic value that figures in explaining the deontic status of actions. One could defend a pluralist account of intrinsic value in which welfare or happiness is among the fundamental goods to be promoted.

4. See Singer, 2005, a consequentialist, who does appeal to evolution and recent empirical evidence from neuroscience and social psychology in an effort to debunk non-consequentialist-favoring moral intuitions.

5. Slote, 1985 is credited with first proposing satisficing as a way for consequentialists to avoid problems with demandingness.

6. There is reason to be pessimistic, however. Bradley, 2006 discusses eight versions of satisficing consequentialism and argues that all of them, in one way or another, are subject to counterexamples.

7. For a thorough critical discussion, see Mulgan, 2001, chapter 3.

8. If we define utility in terms of the results of everyone actually conforming their behavior to a rule—call this *conformance utility*—then RU turns out to be extensionally equivalent to act utilitarianism. After all, for any situation, if we consider the values of the consequences were everyone actually to conform to some rule (regardless of whether or not such rules are understood or accepted), the result will be that rules like R4 will always have the highest (conformance) utility. Hence we get extensional equivalence between rule and act utilitarianism.

9. This point about special obligations and indirect forms of consequentialism is forcefully argued by Zangwill, 2011a.

10. Why not just say that in cases of conflict among rules one should just perform the action that will produce (or likely produce) the best consequences? Because (as Hooker, 2000a, 90 n.21 notes) this would have the effect of partially collapsing RC into a two-levels version of act consequentialism of the sort defended by Hare, 1981 that was introduced toward the end of the previous chapter, thus undermining RU's distinctiveness. More importantly, it would leave RU open to many of the objections raised against versions of act utilitarianism.

11. See Eggleston, 2007 who presses the indeterminacy objection to Hooker's rule consequentialism.

12. See Sumner, 1996, chapter 5 for further discussion.

13. This example is from Rawls, 1971, 432.

14. Defenders of desire fulfillment views (also sometimes called "preference" views) can attempt to filter desires by appealing to "informed" desires—desires one would have were they to survive a process of scrutiny. But the worry is that spelling out the notion of informed desire so that, intuitively, only fulfillment of the "right" desires possess intrinsic positive value will have to rely on an antecedent conception of what objects of desire are good. This would make the account circular. For discussion of such accounts see Brandt, 1979 and Griffin, 1986, chapter 2.

15. Enumerative value pluralism is to be distinguished from *explanatory value pluralism*. According to this latter view, the items on the list of objective values lack any kind of unifying feature that would serve to connect them and thereby help explain why the items on the list belong there.

16. In distinguishing welfarist from perfectionist theories of intrinsic value, what can be confusing is that theories of both sorts often include some of the same values or goods on a list of items having intrinsic value. For instance, achievement is typically included among both perfectionist goods and welfarist goods. What distinguishes welfarism from perfectionism is not items on a list of intrinsic goods but the *explanation* offered for why the items on the list belong there. A welfarist will say that achievement is a constituent in a person's welfare (assuming that achievement contributes to one's happiness), while a perfectionist will say that achievement is one fundamental way in which a human being can perfect herself.

17. Brink, 1989, 231 characterizes his value pluralism as objectivist welfarist theory of value. However, the sort of value theory he describes in 2006 as perfectionistic seems essentially identical to his 1989 view. Admittedly, the use of terms like "welfarism" and "perfectionism" vary from philosopher to philosopher. So in the text I am not concerned with whether the pluralist theory of value I am ascribing to Brink is best classified as welfarist or perfectionist.

18. To be fair, Brink only attempts to sketch a theory of value in his 1989 book. In one place he remarks that in a "fully developed theory we would have to determine what priority relations, if any, obtain among various intrinsic goods, necessary conditions, and extrinsic goods" (1989, 235). If such priority relations could be established, this would help overcome the issue being raised about the theory's determinacy.

19. One might read Brandt's remark as having to do with consequentialism as a decision procedure, since he is concerned with our having evidence of (and thus our ability to be guided by) value pluralist consequentialism. But the point he is making about determinacy applies to value pluralist consequentialism as a criterion or standard of right conduct as well.

20. What about versions of rule consequentialism that feature a plurality of rules? I shall have my say about this type of theory in the concluding chapter.

21. Rawls, 1971, 22–27 develops this line of criticism.

FURTHER READING

Philosophical Literature

The entries by David O. Brink (2006), Julia Driver (2009), and Walter Sinnott-Armstrong (2011) listed in the previous chapter are also recommended further reading for this chapter.

Brandt, Richard B. 1979. *A Theory of the Good and the Right.* Oxford: Oxford University Press. Includes a systematic defense of a version of rule utilitarianism.

Brink, David O. 1989. *Moral Realism and the Foundations of Ethics.* Cambridge: Cambridge University Press. See chapter 8 for a defense of a version of utilitarianism that employs a pluralist theory of value.

Driver, Julia. 2012. *Consequentialism.* London: Routledge. Highly recommended overview of consequentialist moral theory and defense of *global consequentialism*—the view that the moral quality of anything is determined entirely by the value of that thing's consequences.

Hooker, Brad. 2000. *Ideal Code, Real World.* Oxford: Oxford University Press. A sophisticated defense of rule consequentialism.

Hooker, Brad, Elinor Mason, and Dale E. Miller, eds. 2000. *Morality, Rules, and Consequences: A Critical Reader.* Lanham, MD: Rowman & Littlefield. A collection of articles by scholars debating rule consequentialism and related issues in moral theory.

Hurley, Paul. 2009. *Beyond Consequentialism.* Oxford: Oxford University Press. A penetrating critique of forms of consequentialism.

Kagan, Shelly. 1989. *The Limits of Morality.* Oxford: Oxford University Press. An uncompromising defense of act consequentialism.

Lyons, David. 1965. *Forms and Limits of Utilitarianism.* Oxford: Oxford University Press. Critical discussion of versions of rule utilitarianism.

Mulgan, Tim. 2001. *The Demands of Consequentialism.* Oxford: Oxford University Press. Defense of a version of consequentialism developed as a response to the demandingness objection.

Portmore, Douglas W. 2011. *Commonsense Consequentialism: Wherein Morality Meets Rationality.* Oxford: Oxford University Press. Defense of a novel and sophisticated version of consequentialism.

Scheffler, Samuel. 1982. *The Rejection of Consequentialism*. Oxford: Oxford University Press. Chapter 1 includes a penetrating discussion of the demandingness and distributive justice objections to utilitarianism.

———, ed. 1988. *Consequentialism and Its Critics*. Oxford: Oxford University Press. A collection of essays by various authors critical of consequentialism generally and utilitarianism in particular.

Sidgwick, Henry. [1907] 1966. *The Methods of Ethics*. 7th ed. New York: Dover. Book 4 of this masterpiece defends a version of utilitarianism.

Smart, J. J. C., and Bernard Williams. 1973. *Utilitarianism: For and Against*. Cambridge: Cambridge University Press. An important, relatively short book with Smart defending a version of act utilitarianism and Williams objecting.

Sumner, L. W. 1996. *Welfare, Happiness, and Ethics*. Oxford: Oxford University Press. An illuminating discussion of competing theories of welfare plus a defense of welfarism.

Empirical and Empirically Focused Literature

Berker, Selim. 2009. "The Normative Insignificance of Neuroscience." *Philosophy & Public Affairs* 37: 293–329. A critique of Joshua Greene's use of neuroscientific evidence as a basis for debunking deontological moral intuitions.

Greene, Joshua. 2008. "The Secret Joke of Kant's Soul." In *Moral Psychology*, vol. 3, ed. W. Sinnott-Armstrong. Referred to in the chapter in relation to the bold denial defense of consequentialism.

Haidt, Jonathan. 2001. "The Emotional Dog and Its Rational Tail: A Social Intuitionist Approach to Moral Judgment." *Psychological Review* 108: 814–34. A much-discussed article defending what Haidt calls a social intuitionist account of psychological processes resulting in moral judgment, according to which intuitive moral judgments are the result of quick emotion-driven automatic responses. An implication of Haidt's view seems to be that many intuitive moral judgments of the sort used to object to consequentialism are untrustworthy.

7

Ethical Egoism

Most people help others from time to time. Sometimes people perform heroic, self-sacrificing deeds. Michael A. Monsoor, a Navy SEAL officer, was part of a sniper team in Iraq. He died on September 29, 2006. Here is a quote from the U.S. Navy website:

> While [Monsoor was] vigilantly watching for enemy activity, an enemy fighter hurled a hand grenade onto the roof from an unseen location. The grenade hit [Monsoor] in the chest and bounced onto the deck. He immediately leapt to his feet and yelled "grenade" to alert his teammates of impending danger, but they could not evacuate the sniper hide-sight in time to escape harm. Without hesitation and showing no regard for his own life, he threw himself onto the grenade, smothering it to protect his teammates who were lying in close proximity. The grenade detonated as he came down on top of it, mortally wounding him.[1]

What explains *why* people help others? What explains *why* Petty Officer Monsoor sacrificed his life for others?

In his 1975 presidential address to the American Psychological Association, Donald Campbell made the following remark:

> Psychology and psychiatry . . . not only describe man as selfishly motivated, but implicitly or explicitly teach that he ought to be so.[2]

Campbell makes two claims: a descriptive claim about how people are in fact motivated and a normative claim about how people ought to be motivated. Campbell's motivational claim obviously conflicts with what sometimes *seems* to be the case: on at least some occasions—the actions of Monsoor being a particularly clear example—people are not selfishly motivated. Campbell's normative claim also conflicts with what many people believe about how people ought to be and what they ought to do. Both these descriptive and normative claims are called "egoism," and this chapter examines their plausibility—though, of course we are mainly interested in a moral version of the normative claim, namely, ethical egoism.

1. WHAT IS ETHICAL EGOISM?

Ethical egoism is the view that what an individual morally ought to do is what will be in his or her self-interest. Understood as addressing the theoretical aim of a moral theory, the idea is that what *makes* an action right or wrong (obligatory, optional, or wrong) has to do with (and only with) how the action in question would affect the self-interest of the individual performing the action. This theory goes against what most people consider morality to be about. That is, it seems to be part of common sense that morality (what one morally ought to do) sometimes conflicts with one's self-interest. However, ethical egoism does recognize that individuals are separate spheres of interests with personal projects that mean a lot to those who have them. And so, unlike some forms of consequentialism, ethical egoism fully respects the separateness of persons. In order to properly understand ethical egoism, let us build up to a formulation of the theory by making some general remarks about its main characteristics.

First, the version of ethical egoism we shall consider is a *consequentialist* theory in the sense that it explains the rightness and wrongness of actions in terms of the intrinsic goodness and badness of the consequences of those actions.[3] Second, the version also embraces a *welfarist* conception of value according to which human happiness (well-being) has positive intrinsic value and unhappiness (ill-being) has negative intrinsic value, and these are the only items having intrinsic value that bear on the deontic status of actions. However, unlike utilitarianism (according to which rightness and wrongness depend on the values of the consequences for *all* who will be affected by one's action) egoism claims that the only consequences that matter are those bearing on the *agent's* personal welfare, well-being, or happiness, or what is often called one's *self-interest*. If we put all of this together we have the view that (i) one's *own* welfare is the only thing that is both intrinsically valuable *for oneself* and morally relevant when it comes to what it is right for one to do, and (ii) what makes an action right or wrong depends entirely on how the action and its consequences would affect one's own welfare. Call this *welfarist ethical egoism*.

Third, because it is the agent's welfare that matters in determining the deontic status of action, ethical egoism embraces what is called an *agent-relative* (or *agent-centered*) conception of welfare. This contrasts with the versions of consequentialism we have studied that embrace an agent-neutral conception of welfare. One way to draw the agent-relative/agent-neutral contrast is in terms of whether what has value for purposes of deontic evaluation makes essential reference to the agent. Agent-relative theories do make essential reference to the agent; agent-neutral ones do not. So while many versions of consequentialism, particularly classical utilitarianism, are strongly impartialist views—both in the sense of being agent-neutral and in the sense of being non-prioritarian (no special weight is given to the welfare of individuals who are members of some designated group), ethical egoism is a strongly *partialist* theory.

Fourth, ethical egoism shall be understood as a *maximizing* theory. It claims that what one morally ought to do is to perform that action which, if performed, would produce the *greatest amount* of personal happiness (or promote to the *greatest possible extent* one's self-interest) compared to other actions one might perform instead.

Fifth, the theory (or at least the version we are going to consider) makes the rightness or wrongness of an action depend upon both the short-term and the long-term consequences of the action, as those consequences affect self-interest. To be prudent is to carefully and wisely manage one's interests. So, since the theory concerns maximizing one's happiness over the course of one's life, let us say that the theory is *prudentialist*. If one is interested in one's own happiness over the course of one's life, it would be short-sighted to go around doing things for purposes of immediate gratification while ignoring one's future. Sometimes, I'd rather stay home, eat potato chips, and watch *American Idol* than go to the gym and work out for an hour. But in recognition of the fact that going to the gym regularly will contribute in an important way to my health and thus to my future happiness, I choose to forgo the immediate pleasures of eating and watching, and spend time doing something much less fun. I am acting to promote my long-term happiness. And if the two actions just mentioned are my only options on some occasion, then ethical egoism would imply that I morally ought to go to the gym.

Finally, let us introduce a technical term, *agent utility* of an action (performed by a particular agent), to refer to the net balance of intrinsic value the agent in question would experience were she to perform the action in question. Then we can easily present the egoist's theory of right conduct in terms of actions and their associated agent utilities as follows:

Theory of Right Conduct

An action A performed by person P is *obligatory* if and only if (and because) P's performing A would produce a higher agent utility than would any other action P could perform instead.

An action A performed by P is *wrong* if and only if (and because) P's performing A would produce a lower agent utility than would some other action P could perform instead.

An action A performed by P is *optional* if and only if (and because) P's performing A would produce at least as much agent utility as would any other action P could perform instead, but there is at least one other action P could perform that would promote at least as much agent utility as would A.

It should be clear how each of the five characteristics of this theory—that it is consequentialist, welfarist, partialist, maximizing, and prudentialist—are reflected in the above principles.

As with other theories, we can formulate a single principle that encapsulates the egoist's theory of right conduct. The following will serve nicely:

> **EE** An action A performed by person P is *right* (not wrong) if and only if (and because) P's performing A would produce at least as much agent utility as would any other action P might perform instead.

(Henceforth, I will use 'EE' to refer to any of the principles of right conduct formulated above.)

Notice what this theory says (understood as addressing the theoretical aim of moral theory): what *makes* an action right or wrong is determined entirely by facts about how much net personal happiness (or unhappiness) an action would produce were it to be performed, compared to the net personal happiness (or unhappiness) of other alternative actions one could perform instead. The insertion of "and because" in EE is meant to reflect this fact. This is worth emphasizing because sometimes one hears claims such as: "People ought to pay attention to their own well-being or happiness and not get involved in trying to make others happy." Now this may sound as if it is an expression of ethical egoism, but in many cases it really isn't. Often, people who make such claims are thinking that *everyone* would be better off if people minded their own business. But to think this is to express acceptance of a basically utilitarian perspective where the idea is that one is more likely to maximize the happiness of all people affected by what one does if one simply concentrates on one's own happiness. And even if such a thought overreaches in supposing that this is true of everything one does, it may well be true some of the time.

2. SOME FORMS OF EGOISM

In chapter 3, we distinguished different ideas and theories that are called "relativism." For purposes of clarification, we must do the same sort of thing here. There are three main types of egoism that figure in discussions of moral theory: *ethical egoism, rational egoism,* and *psychological egoism.* Furthermore, there are different species of each of these general types. In this section, let us focus on forms of ethical egoism, with a passing reference to rational egoism. Because the psychological variety will play an important role in the remainder of the chapter, we take it up in the next section.

The theory of ethical egoism just presented (EE) is but one form that this moral theory might take. Here is not the place to consider in detail the various alternative forms of this view. However, some brief mention of some of them will be useful for what follows. Let us consider two dimensions along which versions of ethical egoism may differ. First, we may distinguish *objective* from *subjective* versions of ethical egoism. EE is an objective version in the sense that it makes the rightness or wrongness of an action dependent ultimately upon which action *as a matter of objective fact* would maximize self-interest. Contrast this version with the following subjectivist version:

SEE An action A performed by person P is right (not wrong) if and only if (and because) A is the action which P *believes* would produce at least as much agent utility as would any other action P might perform instead.

This version is subjectivist because according to it, whether an action is right or wrong is entirely dependent on what the individual happens to believe will maximize her self-interest, regardless of whether (as a matter of objective fact) that action would (if performed) maximize self-interest.[4] That is, it makes right and wrong depend on the agent's own subjective perspective (her beliefs) regarding her self-interest. The importance of distinguishing between EE and SEE will come up in section 4. In the meantime, it is worth noting that SEE initially seems to be less plausible than EE as an account of right action. We are interested in what makes an action objectively right or wrong, and at best SEE only seems to tell us what makes an action subjectively right or wrong. Furthermore, most all of the objections raised against EE apply to SEE.[5] So, it is EE (and as we shall see, a rule-based alternative) that is the strongest competitor to other moral theories.

It is standard to formulate ethical egoism in terms of self-interest. And in the version we are considering, self-interest is being equated with an individual's own happiness or welfare. And, as we've noted, such versions are welfarist. But, as we know from chapters 5 and 6, there are different philosophical theories about happiness. According to a *hedonistic* theory of welfare, one's welfare or happiness is constituted by experiences of pleasure and absence of pain. A competing account of welfare is the *desire-fulfillment* view, according to which happiness is constituted by having certain of one's desires fulfilled—roughly, one's desires whose fulfillment will positively affect one's life.

But to be contrasted with welfarism is a perfectionist conception of self-interest, according to which what is in one's self-interest involves perfecting one's nature. So, for instance, knowledge and achievement are typically cited as capacities that human beings possess, the development of which contributes to an individual perfecting herself—becoming an excellent specimen of a human being. Perfectionism about value was discussed in chapter 3 in connection with natural law theory. So, in addition to objective and subjective versions of ethical egoism, we can distinguish welfarist from perfectionist versions. That gives us four possible versions: objectivist/welfarist; objectivist/perfectionist, subjectivist/welfarist, and subjectivist/perfectionist. Readers encountering these distinctions for the first time should not be distracted by them for present purposes. The point of bringing up these different forms of ethical egoism is to help make clear the version under discussion—objectivist and welfarist—and to indicate that ethical egoism is a type of moral theory that can assume different forms.[6] If, for instance, perfectionism is a better theory of personal value than welfarism, an ethical egoist would want to formulate her theory accordingly.

Rational egoism, as the label suggests, is a theory about the rationality of action. While ethical egoism addresses the question "What makes an action right or wrong?," rational egoism addresses the more general question "What makes an action rational or irrational?"

Were we to use EE as a model for a companion version of rational egoism, we would have:

RE An action A performed by person P is *rational* (in the sense of being rationally permissible) if and only if (and because) A is the action which produces at least as much agent utility as would any other action P might perform instead.

And of course, we could formulate subjectivist versions of this doctrine, and versions that embrace one or another conception of self-interest. We will not be discussing RE in this chapter. One reason for bringing it up is that some critics of EE object to the theory on grounds that it is not a *moral* theory at all. Sometimes, for instance, it is claimed that a theory of morality must include a concern for how one is to treat others for *their* sakes and not ultimately for one's own sake. But we need not examine this particular controversy because it doesn't really matter for present purposes whether ethical egoism gets to count as a moral theory. Suppose it doesn't get to. Then its main idea about what one ought to do can be captured in RE (or some version of rational egoism), and its advocates can argue that it is a competitor to all moral theories. Granted, if it is not a moral theory, it does not purport to explain what makes an action morally right or wrong; rather, it attempts to explain what makes an action rational or irrational. However, an assumption of most if not all of the moral theories being discussed in this book is that it is always rational to do what is morally right. So, by implication, a moral theory attempts to capture one kind of rational action—rational action that is also morally right action. And so viewed in this way, RE does compete with any moral theory that would deny that all morally right action (a species of rational action) is necessarily self-interested action. So, whether EE is to be considered a moral theory or not, it is still worth discussing in a book on moral theory.

Having explained the basics of ethical egoism, presented a version of the view (EE), distinguished a few of its varieties, and distinguished it from rational egoism, let us move on to psychological egoism.

3. PSYCHOLOGICAL EGOISM

Ethical egoism, as we have seen, is a *normative* theory about what one morally *ought* to do (or refrain from doing). It should not be confused with a *descriptive* claim about what does *in fact* motivate people to do what they do. According to what is called *psychological egoism*, people are psychologically "wired" in such a way that they necessarily always act out of the motive of self-interest. Joel Feinberg, in an influential essay on the topic, explains the view this way:

[P]sychological egoism is the doctrine that the only thing anyone is capable of desiring or pursuing ultimately (as an end in itself) is his *own* self-interest. . . . Universal selfishness is not just an accident or a coincidence on this view; rather, it is an unavoidable consequence of psychological laws. (Feinberg, 1968, 547)[7]

In the psychological literature, an implication of this view when it comes to interacting with others is often called *social egoism*: "We care for others only to the degree that their welfare affects ours."[8] As we shall see, one kind of argument that might be used in an attempt to defend ethical egoism has as one of its premises the thesis of psychological egoism. So, in order to understand psychological egoism (and thereby avoid confusing it with ethical egoism) and also be in a position to understand the argument in question, let us formulate the psychological egoist's thesis with some care.

We first need to distinguish egoistic from altruistic motives. What makes a motive one or the other is the *object* of the motive. Let us say that if you are motivated by a desire to benefit *yourself*, then the motive is one of self-interest. By contrast, if you are motivated by a desire to benefit others as an end in itself—just because you want to benefit *them*—then the motive is altruistic. Clear cases of egoistic motives include:

- wanting to win a competition solely for the personal glory the victory will bring *you*,
- helping someone cross the street only because someone you want to impress is watching, and you want to impress him because you think he will do *you* a favor, and
- wanting to get a massage to relieve *your* back pain.

We also need to distinguish *ultimate* or *fundamental* motives for action from *nonultimate* or *instrumental* motives. You might be motivated to study hard in your philosophy course in order to get a good grade. So, for instance, suppose the prospect of getting a good grade motivates you to go to the library on Friday evening when your friends are out having fun. When your friends ask you why you aren't coming out with them, you give your reason—that you need to study to earn a good grade, your motive being to get a good grade in the course. But of course, if you are like most people, there is some further aim or goal you have that explains *why* you are motivated to get a good grade. Perhaps it's because good grades are needed to get into a high-powered graduate program. Here, what we should say is that your aim of getting a good grade (which motivates you to study) is based on a more fundamental aim you have, namely to get into a high-powered graduate program. The latter aim is more fundamental for you than is the former aim. The dispute between psychological egoists and their opponents (who think that people can be and sometimes are altruistically motivated) is over a person's ultimate motives. What the psychological egoist claims is that everyone (whether they realize this or not) has but one ultimate, fundamental aim in life which is what really motivates them to do what they do, namely, to promote one's self-interest, to be as happy in life as possible. Moreover, this is not supposed to be true for most of the people most of the time, but it is supposed to be universally true owing, as Feinberg remarks, to a psychological law of behavior. In other words, according to psychological egoism:

PE Any action a human agent deliberately performs always has as its ultimate motivation that agent's self-interest.

In short, according to PE, you always do what you believe (or somehow sense) will be in your self-interest, and this is something you can't help: you necessarily act in ways in order to promote your own well-being.

A number of important comments about PE should be kept in mind as we go.

First, psychological egoism should be distinguished from *psychological hedonism*—a species of psychological egoism according to which human agents are always ultimately motivated by what they believe will result in one's having pleasurable experiences and/or minimizing one's having painful experiences. The first two of the above bulleted examples of egoistic motivation are not concerned with the agent's pleasure or pain. The psychological egoist (who is not committed to psychological hedonism) allows that ultimate egoistic motives can include desires for such things as power, money, and personal glory.

Second, PE does not claim that everyone always goes around thinking about how they can promote their own self-interest. Sometimes, of course, we make choices after thinking about what would be in one's self-interest, as when someone agrees to undergo surgery or stick to a diet because she thinks it will be best *for her* to do so. But on many other occasions, one will do things for oneself or for others without a thought of how it will affect one's self-interest. Still, says the psychological egoist, what has happened in cases where one is not consciously pursuing what is in one's self-interest is that self-interest is really behind what one does. For example, when it comes to doing things for others, one learns very early in life that helping actions and acts of kindness toward others tend to promote one's long-term interests. Acts of kindness tend to make people like you, and when people like you they tend to do things for you and they help make your life go better.

Third, it would be implausible to claim that people really know what would *in fact* be in their self-interest; we are often mistaken about what would make us happy. Most normal people do aim at their own personal happiness. The psychological egoist says that this aim is one's *sole* ultimate aim. However, to pursue your own happiness, you have to have some beliefs about what would make you happy. But have you ever gotten something you really wanted and that you thought would bring about much personal enjoyment, and were mistaken? People can and often do have false beliefs about what would in fact promote their self-interest. In light of this fact, what the psychological egoist is claiming is that people are always ultimately (and solely) motivated by what they *believe* will be in their self-interest.

Fourth, we need to distinguish short-term from long-term self-interested motivation. Those who smoke are presumably doing it for the pleasure they get from smoking. They are acting from self-interest. But many (hopefully most) of them know that smoking is bad for their health; they are not motivated by their long-term self-interest. So, we should distinguish PE from the much stronger claim:

PE+ Any action an agent deliberately performs always has as its ultimate motivation that agent's long-term self-interest.

Those who defend psychological egoism are only claiming that people always (and necessarily) act to promote what they take to be in their self-interest, whether it be short-term or long-term. They aren't claiming that people always act in ways that they believe will be in their long-term self-interest. So, PE and PE+ should be recognized as distinct, and it is the weaker claim—PE—that represents the thesis defended by psychological egoists.

Fifth, PE mentions a proper subset of one's actions—*deliberate* actions. People do all sorts of things accidentally. I accidentally step on a nail. Clearly, this is something I did, but it would be false to suppose that I did it out of any motive. What psychological egoism refers to are those actions we do on purpose, that we do deliberately.

Sixth, the most important thing to understand about motivation generally and psychological egoism in particular is that *it is the ultimate object or target of a motive* that determines whether it is self-interested. We've already made this point when introducing the distinction between egoistic versus altruistic motives, but it is worth repeating because it is sometimes lost sight of, as we shall see below in our discussion of PE. Suppose on some occasion one's basic motive is *to have a good time*. The italicized phrase refers to the object or target of the motive, and obviously in this example, the target is a state of oneself. Actions that have this motive are self-interested actions, or "selfish" actions.[9] If, on the other hand, one's fundamental motive is *to benefit others*, then one's motive is altruistic, and actions that flow from that motive are acts of altruism. And again, although it should be clear by now it is worth noting explicitly that actions in which someone helps someone else are not necessarily altruistic. The above example of helping someone cross the street out of self-interest makes this point clear.

Seventh, psychological egoism is opposed by *psychological altruism*:

PA Human agents can and sometimes do act from the ultimate motive of benefiting others.[10]

Those who think that human beings do sometimes act from ultimate altruistic motives are *motivational pluralists*. They think that human beings (at least by and large) have both egoistic and altruistic ultimate motives.

Finally, since these forms of egoism and altruism are descriptive claims about how people can and do act, they ought to be subject to empirical, scientific investigation and theorizing. And, as we shall see in section 5, there is scientific evidence that does bear directly on the dispute between psychological egoism and psychological altruism.

But before going further, let us pause to review some of the main points that have been made so far.

- Ethical egoism is a theory about what makes an action right or wrong (obligatory, optional, or wrong) and so, because it purports to specify how individuals morally ought to act, it is a *normative* theory.
- Rational egoism is a theory about what makes an action rational or irrational. It, too, is a *normative* theory, but not a moral theory. This kind of egoism will not be discussed in this chapter.
- Psychological egoism is a *descriptive* theory about how human beings are capable of being motivated and says that they are only capable of acting in ways that

they take to be in their self-interest. It makes no normative claims about what it is rational or irrational to do, or about what one morally ought or ought not to do. It is opposed by psychological altruism.

- Those who accept psychological altruism are *motivational pluralists*. They hold that human agents are often ultimately egoistically motivated, but that they are also sometimes ultimately altruistically motivated.[11]

Despite the fact that ethical and psychological egoism are different kinds of theory, they both make reference to self-interest, and so one might wonder how they might be connected. Can one of them be used to support the other? Since we are interested in moral theory, let us consider whether and how psychological egoism might be used to argue for ethical egoism.

4. AN ARGUMENT FROM PSYCHOLOGICAL EGOISM

Suppose that PE is true, and everyone is necessarily (as a matter of psychological law) motivated by self-interest. This (supposed) fact about motivation does not by itself imply anything about how people ought to act. But one might try to build an argumentative bridge from PE to EE by adding a premise to the effect that if one is under a moral obligation to perform some action, then the action in question must be something one is capable of performing. Arguably, if there is some action I am not *physically* able to perform (like leap over the Empire State Building in a single bound unaided by any device), then I can't be morally obligated to perform that action. Superman, of course, can be so obligated. And one can say a similar thing about actions that one is not *psychologically* able to perform. This idea here is usually called the *"ought" implies "can"* thesis. And it strikes many people as very plausible.[12] If we combine PE with this thesis, the resulting argument is this:

Argument from Psychological Egoism

1. If there are any actions that one is morally obligated to perform, then one *can* perform them (= "ought" implies "can" principle, where "can" concerns what it is psychologically possible for one to do).
2. If an action is one that one (psychologically) can perform, then it is an action whose performance is ultimately motivated by one's self-interest (from PE).

Thus (from 1 and 2),

3. If there are any actions that one is morally obligated to perform, they are actions whose performance is ultimately motivated by one's self-interest.
4. There are actions that one is morally obligated to perform.

Thus (from 3 and 4),

5. All obligatory actions are actions whose performances are ultimately motivated by one's self-interest.

Let's pause for a moment to see where we are. Notice that the conclusion of this argument is not what we were after, namely, ethical egoism—the claim that all obligatory actions are ones whose performances, *as a matter of objective fact*, promote, indeed, *maximize* one's self-interest. But what step 5 says is that obligatory actions are ones that are motivated by one's self-interest—by what the agent *believes* to be in her self-interest. But the claim that all obligatory actions are actions one believes to be in her self-interest represents a subjectivist version of ethical egoism (similar to SEE). Suppose, then, we extend the argument as follows:

6. If all obligatory actions are actions whose performances are ultimately motivated by one's self-interest, then all obligatory actions serve to maximize one's self-interest.

Thus (from 5 and 6),

7. All obligatory actions are actions whose performances serve to maximize one's self-interest. (=? EE)

There is an obvious flaw in this extended argument: step 6 is just false. As we noted earlier in explaining psychological egoism, even if one always acts from the motive of self-interest, this does not mean that as a result of acting one does in fact promote one's self-interest. People have false beliefs about what is in their self-interest. And even if people's actions did always serve to promote their self-interest, this would not show that they always act in ways that contribute to the maximization of their self-interest. Thus, because the above argument has a false premise, the argument is not sound.

Perhaps there is a sound argument that has step 7 as its conclusion. If this were true, then the following principle would be true: *An action A performed by person P is obligatory if and only if P's performing A would contribute to maximizing agent utility* (notice the lack of "and because" in this principle). But this still would not be enough to show that EE is true (hence the "?"). That is, even if there is an argument that proves that all obligatory actions (if performed) do in fact contribute to maximizing one's self-interest, it does not automatically follow that what *makes* an action obligatory is that it maximally promotes one's self-interest. To see this, suppose the divine command theory is true—that what *makes* an action right or wrong are God's commands. Now suppose that God commands that one perform actions that always turn out to be in one's self-interest—actions that maximize agent utility for each person, if not in this life, then the next. In this case EE would be false even though it is true that what one is obligated to do is to perform actions that maximally promote one's self-interest.

To sum up, even if we suppose that PE is true, it is not clear how to develop a sound argument from PE to EE. But in any case, any such argument with PE as a premise would only be a good argument if PE is true.

5. IS PSYCHOLOGICAL EGOISM TRUE?

Most people have heard of Mother Teresa (1910–1997), sometimes referred to as the Saint of Calcutta, who devoted her life to helping the poor. She devoted her life to the welfare of others. In 1975 Everett Sanderson jumped onto the subway tracks in New York in front of a rapidly approaching train in order to save a four-year-old child—a complete stranger—from certain death. After putting the child out of harm's way, Sanderson barely escaped being crushed by the train.[13] We began this chapter with a recounting of the heroic deed of Petty Officer Michael A. Monsoor.

The saintly and heroic actions of these individuals certainly *seem* to be motivated by altruism—a genuine direct concern for the welfare of another person. Of course, this explanation of why these individuals did what they did is opposed by psychological egoism.

As we've already noted, PE expresses a thesis about human motivation—about what in fact motivates people to do what they do. We have also noted that this view of motivation goes contrary to what most people seem to assume about human beings. Even if self-scrutiny and keen observation of other people makes one suspect that despite appearances, much of what people do is motivated by self-interest, it is also true that we celebrate heroes and saints—people like Mother Teresa, Everett Sanderson, and Petty Officer Michael Monsoor who seem to have been acting altruistically and not at all from self-interest. Such evidence is anecdotal. And what psychological egoists will say about such cases is that despite appearances, such people are really motivated by self-interested concerns. And as long as we remain at the level of ordinary observation, the egoism versus altruism debate is likely to persist. After all, one only observes another person's outward behavior; one can't directly inspect others' motives to find out what makes another person tick. What we need is a way of scientifically investigating the matter. Human motivation is one major area of research in the field of psychology, so we ought to look to psychology for evidence bearing on this debate. What do psychologists tell us about altruism and egoism?

The pioneering work of C. Daniel Batson is particularly important. Batson has designed experiments that attempt to overcome the difficulty of disentangling a person's motives in order to help determine whether people are sometimes genuinely altruistically motivated. In what follows I will attempt to convey the gist of Batson's experiments, the results of which favor the case for genuine altruism. Let us begin by bringing into clear focus a challenge that must be met in attempting to design experiments whose results are significant for the debate between egoistic and altruistic explanations of people's helping behavior.

The challenge in question concerns the fact that people who help others in distress are often moved to do so by feeling empathy for the person they help.[14] But, of course, this doesn't mean that such helping behavior is *ultimately* motivated by a desire to help; there are any number of possible self-interested motives that might explain why one helps another person for whom one feels some concern. Such motivation would then be ultimately egoistic, not altruistic. Among the most commonly cited pro-egoistic explanations are these:

Aversive-empathic arousal reduction: When encountering another person in distress, one is likely to experience feelings of discomfort and distress as a result—feelings that one wishes to eliminate or at least reduce. By helping the person in question, one reduces the other's distress, which is a means to reducing or eliminating one's own. Hence, people sometimes help others because it is a *means* of reducing or eliminating their own discomfort or distress.

Self-punishment avoidance: When encountering another person in distress, one anticipates the feelings of guilt and shame that one is likely to experience if one fails to help, feelings one wants to avoid. By helping the person, one avoids these feelings; one helps as a *means* to some further self-interested end.

Social esteem/self-rewards attraction: When encountering another person in distress, one anticipates feeling good about oneself and perhaps (if others are witness to one's helping) being praised and perhaps materially rewarded by others. These anticipated positive benefits to self are what motivate one to help: helping the person in need is thus a *means* to a self-interested goal.

Suppose that people who do help others are often benefited in one or more of these ways, and suppose they act in the realization that they will so benefit. It may be the case that the desire to help is only a means to one of these self-interested goals, or it may be that these self-interested goals are foreseen unintended consequences of helping. As Batson remarks:

> Social egoism claims that benefitting the person in need is an instrumental goal on the way to the ultimate goal of benefitting oneself. Altruism argues back that simply to show that self-benefits follow from benefitting the other does not prove that the self-benefits are the helper's goal. It is at least logically possible that the self-benefits are unintended consequences of the helper's reaching his or her ultimate goal of benefitting the other. If this is the case, then the motivation is altruistic, not egoistic. (Batson, 1990, 340)

So, the challenge to be met in obtaining evidence either in favor of altruism or in favor of egoism is to design experiments that somehow can ascertain a person's ultimate goal or motive in acting. Batson's strategy for meeting this challenge is to (1) determine a person's potential goals or motives for some action, and then (2) observe that person's behavior in a range of circumstances that vary in such a way that it is possible for a person with more than one goal to obtain one of those goals without obtaining the other. The basic thought here is this: If people who help others in distress also derive some benefit from such helping, then if they are given the opportunity (in situations where others are in distress and the person could help) to obtain the benefit without helping, and they nevertheless help, this supports the altruistic hypothesis that benefiting the other is the ultimate goal while the benefits to self are unintended consequences. On the other hand, if a person (confronted with someone in distress) acts to obtain the benefit without helping, this is at least compatible with the egoist's claim that such helping is merely a means to a further self-interested goal, and it is self-interest that is in the driver's seat.

Batson and colleagues designed experiments to test all three of the above-mentioned pro-egoist explanations against the competing altruistic explanations. In connection with the aversive-empathic arousal reduction explanation, Batson designed the following experiment.[15] Participants in the experiment observe a "worker" whom they believe is being caused distress by a series of uncomfortable shocks. They are given the opportunity to take the place of the worker and receive the shocks themselves. Some participants are informed that if they do not help, they will *not* have to continue observing the worker being shocked ("easy escape" from the uncomfortable situation). Other participants are told that if they do not help, they *will* continue to observe the worker being shocked ("difficult escape" from the uncomfortable situation). Egoism predicts that when people's empathy is highly aroused and they are given the easy escape option, they will likely take that option. Altruism, by contrast, predicts that in the situation just described, people will likely help. The results of this experiment have consistently favored altruism. Furthermore, Batson has also designed experiments to test the other two egoistic hypotheses mentioned above against altruism, and the results of these experiments also favor altruism over egoism. So overall the results of these various experiments provide some support for the claim that the ultimate motivation of empathy-produced helping behavior is often the welfare of the other person. And if this is so, then the very strong claim expressed by PE is false.[16]

Of course, even if PE is false, it does not mean that people are not predominantly egoistically motivated. Perhaps most people most of the time do act from the ultimate motive of self-interest. But if altruistic behavior is possible and if morality sometimes demands that one acts for the benefit of others, even in cases where doing so is not to one's own benefit, then those demands are not beyond what human beings are capable of meeting, at least so far as human motivation is concerned.

In defense of psychological altruism (PA), I have cited some carefully devised experimental evidence. There are other types of empirical evidence that are often used to support altruism. Some of it is narrative evidence. For instance, social scientists have intensively studied a group known as the Righteous Gentiles, who during World War II risked their lives and sometimes the lives of their families to save Jews from Nazi persecution. Extensive interviews of many of these people have been the basis for concluding that many of them acted not out of self-interest but out of genuine concern for the people they tried to protect.[17] In addition to experimental and narrative evidence, some appeal to evolutionary biology in support of altruism. In the Further Reading section of this chapter, I refer readers to some of this literature.

To sum up: scientific evidence together with common everyday observation ought to be enough to justifiably reject psychological egoism in favor of motivational pluralism, the view that in addition to being ultimately motivated by self-interest, human beings (by and large) can be, and sometimes are, ultimately motivated by altruistic desires. And if PE is false, the argument to ethical egoism featured in the previous section is unsound. Of course, just because a particular argument for a conclusion is a bad one does not mean the conclusion is false: ethical egoism might be true even if psychological egoism is false. So, we still have to examine the plausibility of ethical egoism, which we will address shortly. But first, one might reasonably ask what has led some people to suppose that psychological egoism is true. Remember: psychological egoism is not just the thesis that most people most of the time act out of self-interest, or even that all people all of the time happen to do so. It is the strong claim that people are necessarily always motivated by self-interest. And one answer to the question about why some people may believe PE is that there are lines of reasoning about human motivation that involve certain confusions but are nevertheless seductive. So let us conclude this section by examining some of these ways of reasoning.

The "What You Most Want" Argument

You decide to go to visit the dentist even though you know that lying there while the dentist works on your teeth will be unpleasant. As you are leaving to keep your appointment, we have the following short exchange.

> You: "I really don't want to go, but I have to, otherwise my cavity will get much worse, and the tooth will have to come out."
>
> Me: "So really what you want most of all is to avoid losing the tooth. So you're really doing what you most want. Stop complaining."

You leave after shooting me a look of exasperation, and I think to myself that what I said is true because the following argument strikes me as correct:

1. Whenever someone performs an action, that person necessarily always does whatever he or she most wants to do, given the options.
2. If someone necessarily does what he or she most wants to do, then that person is necessarily acting out of the motive of self-interest.

Thus,

3. Whenever anyone acts, that person necessarily always acts out of the motive of self-interest (= PE).

This argument is intended to be an "armchair" argument for PE. That is, its premises are supposed to be true in virtue of the very meaning of the terms that occur in them, and so one can determine their truth just by thinking about them (from one's armchair). And what is true by definition (meaning) is necessarily true—can't be false. For instance, consider the claim: all bachelors are unmarried males. You don't need to go around surveying men asking them if they are bachelors and then asking the bachelors whether they are unmarried; if you understand the meanings of the terms "bachelor," "unmarried," and "male," you have all you need to determine the truth of the claim. So, the proponent of this argument rests her case on what is meant by certain terms, in particular, what it means to "want" something. Let us take a closer look.

Consider premise 1. There is an ordinary sense of the words "want" and "desire" according to which this premise is just false. Suppose on Monday I volunteer to help with an all-day clean-up project being organized in my neighborhood scheduled for the following Saturday. But when Saturday comes along, I am exhausted by a strenuous week's work at my regular job and just don't feel like doing the volunteer work. I say to you: "I really don't *want* to help with the clean-up, but they are counting on me, so I've got to go. What I really want to do most of all is stay home and sleep." Call this the *liking* sense of "want." What one wants to do in this sense is always something that one feels some attraction toward doing, something that one believes one will *like* doing. According to the liking sense of "want," premise 1 is false. People sometimes make themselves do things they don't like doing.

Of course, someone who advocates the above argument in favor of PE will probably admit what has just been said. However, the advocate will proceed to point out that there is a sense of "want" according to which premise 1 is true. Call this the *explanatory* sense of "want." Whenever one chooses to do something, no matter how much one does not want (in the liking sense) to do it, it always makes sense to explain her behavior in terms of a combination of her beliefs, which guide one's behavior, and some motivating factor, a desire or want. If I don't feel like doing the volunteer work on Saturday but make myself go anyway, then we can say that given my options (stay home or go) I ended up doing what, in the explanatory sense, I wanted to do. On this explanatory usage, premise 1 is true; indeed, it is necessarily true because whenever one chooses to perform an action, it is appropriate, for purposes of explaining one's behavior, to attribute to the person a want or desire to do the thing she ends up doing. The point is that by making use of the explanatory sense of wanting something, we have defined a sense of "want" so that premise 1 is guaranteed to be true. So let's understand premise 1 accordingly.

But now another problem arises. If the conclusion is going to follow logically from the premises, then the term "want" must be used with the same meaning in both premises. So the second premise must be understood as claiming that whenever one does what one wants to do in the explanatory sense of "want," then one is acting from the motive of self-interest. But now this premise seems false. Just because whenever one chooses to perform some action, one can be said to be doing what one "wants," it does not follow that one's motive for acting is self-interest. What makes a motive one of self-interest is its object—what the motive is aimed at accomplishing. The trivial fact that from the perspective of explaining one's behavior, one always does what one wants to do does not have any implications for what motives one is acting from. Indeed, the same general point can be made about the liking sense of "want." Suppose on some occasion I do what I most like to do—what attracts me the most. It still does not follow that the motive behind what I do is self-interest. Some people like to help others. But that does not mean their motive is one of self-interest. It might be. But the point is that nothing in this argument shows us that it *must* be. Perhaps what initially attracts some people to the "what you most want" argument is the idea that all of one's wants are *one's own*. That's obvious. But from the fact that all of *my* wants are wants *of* me, it does not follow that they are wants *for* me.

With this caution in mind, let us move on to another argument for PE—a hedonistic version.

The Satisfaction Argument

1. The result of having one's desired goals or aims met (or getting what one wants) is that the desire is satisfied.
2. But satisfaction is an experience that involves some degree of positive feeling; if not pleasure then at least relief.

Thus,

3. Whenever one acts, one's actions are ultimately motivated by the pleasure (or relief) one gets from satisfying the desire.

This argument is clearly bad. The first premise is only plausible if what one means by an aim, goal, or desire being *satisfied* is that one knowingly obtains or acquires the object of the desire. If I desire or want to own a rifle, then that desire is met (= satisfied) if I knowingly come into possession of a rifle. In this sense of the term, to talk about a desire being satisfied does not entail anything about how I feel or what I experience in knowing that my desire has been met. In the second premise, however, "satisfaction" refers to a type of subjective feeling. So, "satisfied" (and "satisfaction") have two meanings, and in premise 1 the term means one thing, and in premise 2 it means something else. But as we learned in connection with Mill's "proof" of the principle of utility (chapter 5, section 4), arguments that trade on multiple meanings of a word or phrase commit the fallacy of equivocation and are thus at bottom invalid.

Suppose, then, we focus on the relation between action, desire, and pleasure. We act on our various desires. But doesn't one desire what one *believes* will bring one pleasure? I desire or want to go swimming on a hot summer day in Tucson because I believe that my doing so will bring me pleasure and relief from the heat. So, isn't the motive of bringing about one's own pleasure (indeed maximizing one's pleasure and minimizing pain) the fundamental motive behind all action? And doesn't this have to be the case? So isn't a hedonistic version of PE true after all?

The Pleasure Argument

1. All desires are ultimately based on the motive of bringing about as much plea-sure for oneself as possible, and *must* be so based.
2. If one's fundamental motive is necessarily a desire for one's own (maximal) pleasure, then PE is true.

Thus (from 1 and 2),

3. PE is true.

The conclusion follows logically from the premises, and the second premise is true by definition. So, any fault in the argument must lie with premise 1. What the ad-vocate of this argument needs is evidence to support this premise, and evidence that is strong enough to overturn the evidence for altruism mentioned earlier. But even if most people most of the time act from the ultimate motive of pleasure (their own), and even if some people act this way all of the time, what needs to be shown is that humans always act from the motive of pleasure and that this *must* be the case. But the work of Batson casts serious doubt on these claims.

The "what you most want" and "satisfaction" arguments attempt to prove PE based on what we mean by terms like "want," "desire," and "satisfaction," and they fail be-cause of ambiguities in and confusions about those terms. The lesson to be learned from those failures is that no armchair argument is going to settle the egoism versus altruism debate about human motivation; only empirical evidence can do that. The "pleasure" argument fails because no empirical evidence was brought forth to support its central claim, at least no evidence strong enough to undermine or override the evidence from social psychology. Conclusion: although the debate in question is a live one, there is good (if not conclusive) empirical evidence to reject PE in favor of PA.

Of course, even if psychological egoism is false, ethical egoism might still be true. Is it?

6. EVALUATION OF ETHICAL EGOISM

Perhaps the main intuitive attraction of the theory (recall from chapter 1 the crite-rion of intuitive support) is that it reflects the idea that ethical matters have to do with human well-being or welfare and that it is each individual's primary moral task in life to "look out" for himself or herself.[18] And of course, the evaluation of a moral theory is a comparative matter, and one might think that ethical egoism does not suffer from the serious maladies that beset its nonegoistic rivals.[19] It certainly avoids the separateness-of-persons objection leveled against utilitarianism. But it has come in for its share of criticisms, some that misfire, others that do not.

Consistency. Does EE imply contradictory moral evaluations? Some have argued that it does. One such argument begins with the following intuitively plausible principle of noninterference:

> **PNI** It is morally wrong for one to knowingly interfere with someone else doing his or her duty.

For instance, if you morally ought to return a borrowed book to your friend, then it would be wrong for me to interfere with your doing so (unless I have a good moral reason for doing so). Turning now to EE, suppose that there is one ticket left to the basketball finals and that it is in my self-interest to get that ticket, given how much I would enjoy the game. And suppose the same is true of you—it is in your self-interest to get that ticket. And suppose you and I both know this. According to EE, I ought to do what I can (consistent with my overall self-interest) to get that ticket and thus knowingly prevent you from doing what you ought to do. But then according to PNI, such interference is morally wrong. So (according to the argument under consideration), I both morally ought and morally ought not to do what I can to get the remaining basketball ticket—a contradiction.

Now it doesn't take much to see that this objection misfires. The inconsistency is generated not simply by applying EE to the case at hand, but by applying both EE *and* PNI. EE and PNI do yield conflicting moral verdicts about this case (and many others). But consistent with her theory, the ethical egoist will reject PNI. According to the egoist, it would be morally wrong to knowingly interfere with someone else's performance of duty if and only if such interference would not be in one's own best interest. Nothing contradictory follows from this.

The lesson to be learned here is that if one wants to show that some moral theory is *internally* inconsistent (which is what the consistency desideratum is all about), one needs to argue that the principles of the theory, when applied to particular cases, sometimes yield inconsistent deontic verdicts about the particular case. Furthermore, it should be clear from thinking about EE that it is not going to yield inconsistent verdicts.[20] The theory purports to explain what makes an action by some agent right or wrong in terms of how the action will affect that agent's self-interest. If it is not possible for an action to both maximize and not maximize (all things considered) the agent's self-interest—and it isn't—then there will not be a case in which EE yields contradictory verdicts about a particular action. What may lead to confusion about EE and the issue of consistency is that it will direct different agents on certain occasions to attempt to do something that can only be done by one of them. But this is familiar and not at all contradictory. Think of competition in sports.

Determinacy. The principles of a moral theory are highly determinate when those principles, together with the relevant facts, yield definite verdicts about the rightness or wrongness of actions in a large range of cases, if not in all cases. For ethical egoism, the relevant facts in question are facts about the effects of various actions on the agent's (overall) self-interest. If we grant that in any situation one might confront, there is an objective fact of the matter about the effects of alternative courses of action on one's self-interest, the principles of ethical egoism will satisfy the determinacy standard. Of course, in a great many circumstances one simply will not know which of one's actions really are in one's self-interest, and so it looks as if the principles in question won't be of much use in guiding one's deliberation and choice. But recall that the criterion of determinacy does not concern how *useful* the principles of a theory would be in practice; the usefulness of a theory has to do with its applicability.

Applicability. This standard concerns whether the principles of a moral theory satisfy the practical aim of specifying a decision procedure that human agents can reliably use to arrive at correct moral verdicts, given their often limited knowledge of relevant information. As just noted, individuals often lack relevant information about how actions they might perform will affect their overall self-interest. Without such information, one cannot reliably apply the egoist principles of right conduct that refer to actual consequences of actions—that is, the consequences that would in fact occur were one to perform one or another action. This same issue came up in our chapter 5 discussion of utilitarianism, and in response the utilitarian wanted to insist that her principles of right conduct—principles that make the rightness of an action depend on *actual* consequences—represent a criterion of rightness and not primarily a decision procedure. The utilitarian's proposal for moral deliberation in contexts where one is uncertain about the actual consequences of possible courses of action was to consider the likely or probable consequences—the *expected* utilities of one's alternatives. But in cases where one is also ignorant of the expected utilities of alternative courses of action, the utilitarian's proposal is to do what is subjectively right—that is, one is to perform the action that one reasonably believes will have the highest utility. The ethical egoist can offer the same sort of advice with respect to matters concerning the agent utilities associated with alternative courses of action—go with knowledge of expected agent utilities, and if that is not feasible, then make use of the subjective version of ethical egoism—SEE.

What about contexts in which there is not time to engage in egoistic deliberation? After all, in most situations in life, the process of stopping to consider various actions one might perform and their likely effects on one's long-term welfare would certainly not maximize one's self-interest. Imagine being required to deliberate on each and every occasion—whether, for example, as you are getting out of your car to put your keys in your left or right pocket. Of course, deliberating about what is in your long term self-interest is certainly appropriate in some circumstances, where, for example, one is making "life decisions" about a career, or about getting married. And in such cases where deliberation can be expected to lead one to make welfare-maximizing choices, ethical egoism requires one to deliberate. But for most everyday contexts in which egoistic calculation is out of the question, the egoist can offer the following. Through experience one hopefully learns how to guide one's behavior in ways that are likely to promote one's self-interest. One learns, for instance, that acquiring good social skills is in one's self-interest—skills that can automatically guide one's behavior without having to deliberate. In fact, it may well be the case that internalizing commonsense moral rules against lying, killing, arrogance, and so forth, and thereby allowing such rules to guide one's behavior, will best serve one's long-term self-interest. A similar point was made in our chapter 5 discussion of act utilitarianism. Mill noted that over time human beings "have acquired positive beliefs as to the effects of their actions on their happiness" (Mill, [1863] 1979, 23). The beliefs in question are represented by the rules of commonsense morality, and it is reasonable to suppose that following such "rules of thumb" will increase one's chances of maximizing one's long-term welfare.

So, in handling questions about the applicability of the principles of her moral theory, including contexts of egoistic calculation and contexts where such calculation is not feasible or is ruled out as not being in one's self-interest, the ethical egoist can take a (suitably modified) page from the utilitarian for dealing with such practical matters.

External coherence. According to this standard, a moral theory ought to be consistent with (if not be supported by) well-established theories and assumptions from other fields of inquiry. The appeal to psychological egoism in defense of ethical egoism attempts to satisfy this desideratum. But there is (as we've noted) fairly convincing scientific evidence against PE. So suppose then that psychological altruism (PA) is true. Would this refute EE? No: even if it is possible for human beings to act altruistically, it doesn't follow that they morally ought to do so. Nor does it follow that something other than agent utility makes an action obligatory, optional, or wrong. EE is compatible with PA. Of course, if people can act altruistically it leaves open the possibility that they are sometimes morally required to act for altruistic reasons. And this is something to be determined by engaging in moral theory.

Internal coherence and explanatory power. Does EE conflict with deeply held and widely shared considered moral beliefs? It would certainly seem so—that's why this theory is often considered to be a challenge to commonsense morality. In the previous chapter, we saw how cases of, for example, medical sacrifice and promising cause trouble for classical act utilitarianism. It is a fairly easy exercise to think up similar cases in which sacrificing the life of an innocent person, or breaking a promise, would be in a person's self-interest and thus be morally required according to EE. But clearly, killing innocent human beings and breaking promises, even if such acts would in certain circumstances maximize one's self-interest, are often, if not always, morally wrong. Furthermore, if EE cannot meet the internal coherence standard, then it can't represent a correct explanation of what makes right actions right and wrong actions wrong. It thereby fails the standard of explanatory power.

But recall from chapter 6 that one option for utilitarians (and for consequentialists generally) who want to avoid such counterexamples is to move from act to rule versions of their view. The idea is that concrete actions are to be evaluated according to a correct set of moral rules, and what makes a rule correct is its acceptance utility. The same general strategy is open to the ethical egoist. We first define the *agent acceptance utility* of a rule as the level of agent utility that would result for the agent were the agent to accept and thus be guided by the rule. We then define a correct rule of action governing a situation for an agent as one, the acceptance of which by the agent, that would produce at least as great a level of agent utility for that agent as would the acceptance of any alternative rule governing the situation in question. Finally, we define a version of rule ethical egoism as follows:

> **REE** An action is morally right (in the sense of not being wrong) if and only if (and because) it is permitted by a rule applying to a situation that has at least as high an associated level of agent acceptance utility as does any other alternative rule applying to the situation.

The rule ethical egoist now proceeds to point out that even if in some particular, isolated case, breaking a solemn promise would have the highest agent utility, this action is *not* mentioned in a rule with the highest agent acceptance utility, and it is thus properly classified as wrong. Note that the rule ethical egoist's use of rules is distinct from the recommendation by the act ethical egoist that one internalize and follow the rules of commonsense morality. For the act ethical egoist, such rules are mere rules of thumb—rules that provide good advice for living a life in which one aims to maximize self-interest. The right act for the act ethical egoist remains the act that, from among one's alternative courses of action in some circumstance, maximizes one's long-term self-interest. And in some cases this may require breaking one of the rules in question. By contrast, for the rule ethical egoist, what explains why some particular action is right is that it is permitted by a rule having as high an agent acceptance utility as any competing rule for the situation in question. If the relevant rule forbids, say, breaking promises, then even in particular cases where breaking a promise would best promote one's self-interest, it would be wrong according to REE to break the promise. In short, for the rule ethical egoist, rules play a role in explaining what *makes* an action right or wrong, while for the act ethical egoist they do not.

However, rule ethical egoism still seems open to counterexamples. Although in many circumstances the egoist may expect that following the rules of commonsense morality—rules against lying, stealing, killing innocent people, and so forth—will by and large promote her overall self-interest, there may be cases in which conforming to such rules will result in great personal disaster, and the agent knows this. In such cases, the rule ethical egoist will propose a disaster avoidance rule, according to which in cases where the agent knows for certain that only by breaking one or more of the other rules applying to her situation can she avoid great personal disaster, she ought to do what will avoid great personal disaster. Arguably, such a rule will have the highest agent acceptance utility in cases where it applies. And surely, if the guiding idea of ethical egoism is to maximize one's overall self-interest, such a disaster avoidance rule is well grounded. But now the rule ethical egoist is open to certain counterexamples. Consider a modified version of the brain surgeon case that was described in chapter 6. The brain surgeon knows she is on the brink of crushing financial disaster owing to reckless investments. She is to perform delicate brain surgery on a patient who just happens to be her rich uncle who she knows plans to leave his vast fortune to her when he passes on. The surgeon is highly skilled, but because the operation is so delicate, were she to intentionally botch the operation and kill her uncle, no one else would know or suspect that the surgeon had murdered him. Suppose too that she would suffer no pangs of guilt or other negative consequences as a result of killing him. Given that the disaster avoidance rule applies to this case and given that it has the highest agent acceptance utility, REE is committed to the claim that the surgeon morally ought to kill her uncle. But this implication is surely counterintuitive. The problem, then, is that there is good reason for the rule ethical egoist to allow an "avoid personal disaster" rule as among the rules that have the greatest agent acceptance utility. But in so doing, the egoist opens herself up to counterexamples.

Finally, one sort of objection often made to ethical egoism is that the theory violates the following standard of *publicity* for evaluating a moral theory:

> The principles of a moral theory should be such that they do not rule out as impermissible making public (by, for example, teaching) the moral theory and its associated moral principles. Moral theories whose principles rule out such teaching fail to satisfy this standard.

The rationale behind this standard has to do with the practical aim of a moral theory, namely to provide principles that can be used as a decision procedure in guiding people's behavior. After all, if the principles of a moral theory are to guide people's behavior, they need to be taught as part of one's moral education. However, one can easily see how ethical egoism will violate this standard. If I'm an ethical egoist, then presumably it is *not* in my interest to get others to believe in EE; *I'll* presumably be better off if other people believe in an ethic of altruism. That is, if others are taught and come to accept some sort of nonegoistic moral theory whose principles require respecting the life, liberty, and property of others, as well as a requirement to help others in need even in cases where those who help need not personally benefit, this will certainly be better for me as an ethical egoist than if others are taught and come to accept ethical egoism. And if so, then my teaching or advocating egoism is (according to EE) morally wrong. Presumably, the same will be true for others. So it is fairly clear that ethical egoism violates the publicity standard.

The publicity worry just raised concerned the effects on the welfare of individuals if ethical egoism were to be publically taught and advocated: *I* end up worse off if all others are ethical egoists. But it is worth noting that the same sort of worry can be raised in relation to situations that have the structure of what are called Prisoner's Dilemma cases. In these situations, *everyone* ends up worse off if everyone is an ethical egoist. Let me explain.

The dilemma in question illustrates the somewhat ironic point that in certain situations if all involved parties are ethical egoists and act accordingly, then each party will end up worse off than had they acted nonegoistically. David Shoemaker has a nice presentation of it:

> Suppose that you and your accomplice Fabio have managed to steal the Queen's crown jewels from Buckingham Palace. You disabled the internal security cameras, but an external surveillance camera captured you both on the grounds, so you were both arrested and locked up in separate interrogation rooms. All the police have on you now is criminal trespassing, which carries a sentence of a year, but the detective in charge wants to nail you both for the more serious charge of grand theft. A trial will be expensive, though, and you may manage to get off altogether because you'll probably hire a big shot defense attorney, so the detective wants to get a confession out of both of you to save time and money and ensure a conviction. He thus offers you the following deal (which he'll also offer to Fabio): If you confess and incriminate Fabio, you'll be released on probation, and Fabio will serve ten years in prison. If you don't confess, and Fabio instead confesses and incriminates you, he'll be released and you'll serve ten years in prison. If you both confess, then you'll both get five years (cooperation reduces the charge). And if neither of you confesses, you'll each get one year for criminal trespassing.[21]

Suppose you and Fabio are both egoists. What is in your best interest—confess or not? When Fabio considers what is in his best interest, what will he do? Here is a visual aid that summarizes the four possible combinations of choice and their outcomes.

| | | Fabio | |
		Confess	Not confess
You	Confess	5 years each	You: probation Fabio: 10 years
	Not confess	You: 10 years Fabio: probation	1 year each

Remember: you have to decide what to do without communicating with Fabio.

Here is how you will reason if you want to maximize self-interest. "Fabio will either confess or not confess. If he confesses, I'd better confess too, otherwise I get ten years. If he does not confess, I'm better off if I do confess. So, I'll confess!" But since Fabio reasons the same way, you both end up confessing and consequently land in jail for five years each. Even if you promised each other before the attempted robbery that if caught neither of you will confess, it is nevertheless in your self-interest to ignore the promise and confess, and the same is true of Fabio. The dilemma is that when everyone acts according to the principles of EE, then in situations that have the structure of a Prisoner's Dilemma, each will be worse off than he or she would have been had each not acted according to EE. Had Fabio not been an ethical egoist, and had he falsely believed that you were not an egoist, then he might have kept silent and you would have merely ended up on probation. That would be the best outcome for you.

The above two-person Prisoner's Dilemma was of course contrived. But the point it is used to illustrate does have real-world application in many-person versions of the dilemma—cases in which if each individual does what is in her or his greatest self-interest, the result will make everyone worse off. Consider, for instance, the situation of fishermen who make their living by catching and selling fish. If there are enough fishermen fishing in the same vicinity, then they are likely to be in a situation where if each fishes without restricting how much he catches, the total number of fish in that vicinity will be drastically reduced. And with much fewer fish to catch, everyone is worse off. However, regardless of how much fish the other fishermen catch, from the perspective of EE, each fisherman ought to catch as much as he can. The reasoning behind this ought-claim is much the same as featured in the two-person Prisoner's Dilemma. But, of course, if all of the fishermen are egoists, their collective action will eventually make them all individually worse off. What is best for an egoist, then, is to be in a world in which others accept an altruistic moral theory. Since the act of promulgating ethical egoism is likely to reduce the number of those who accept an altruistic moral theory, ethical egoism implies that it is typically (if not always) morally wrong to promulgate that theory.

Is this publicity objection damaging to egoism? Here are two points in response. First, as noted above in section 2, if EE is not to be taken as moral theory, but as a theory of rational action that competes with moral theories in prescribing what it is best for one to do or what one "ought" to do, then, arguably, the publicity standard does not apply. Second, if EE is best understood as a moral theory, then like the utilitarian, the egoist can claim that his theory is only meant to address the theoretical aim of moral theory. The fact that according to EE it is morally wrong to teach and promulgate this theory does not show that the theory fails to *explain* what *makes* an action right or wrong. The issue associated with publicity has to do with matters of practice rather than explanation. Perhaps the implication about the morality of promulgating egoism is something a clear-headed ethical egoist must live with.[22]

7. CONCLUSION

A major complaint against utilitarianism is that it fails to respect the separateness of persons—that each person is a separate center of care and concern. It is a strongly impartialist moral theory. With ethical egoism, the pendulum swings far in the other direction: it is a strongly partialist moral theory. If these two types of consequentialism swing too far in opposite directions, then what we want is a moral theory that lies somewhere between these extremes—a theory that respects the separateness of persons while at the same time accommodating the idea that in some sense moral requirements are impartial. The moral theory of Immanuel Kant, featured in the next chapter, promises to satisfy these demands.[23]

NOTES

1. http://www.navy.mil/moh/monsoor/SOA.html.

2. Quoted by Monroe, 1996, 179 and by Batson, 1990, 337.

3. Not all theories that claim to be a form of ethical egoism are versions of consequentialism. Lester Hunt, 1999, for instance, defends what he calls "flourishing egoism," which he contrasts with consequentialist versions of ethical egoism. Because of the emphasis Hunt puts on virtue and self-interest, his view is perhaps best understood as a version of virtue ethics, which is sometimes construed as a kind of ethical egoism. For an illuminating examination of the claim that virtue ethics is a form of egoism, see Annas, 2008.

4. Another, related distinction is between actual consequence versions of ethical egoism (which are equivalent to what are here being called objectivist versions) and probable consequence versions of the view. For more on the actual/probable consequence distinction, see chapter 5.

5. *Most* all, because when it comes to applying an egoistic principle to one's conduct, one has no choice but to use SEE. Hence, SEE satisfies the standard of applicability introduced in chapter 5, section 5.

6. Another important distinction is between act and rule versions of ethical egoism that will come up later in this chapter.

7. Some authors formulate psychological egoism without claiming that such motivation is governed by a psychological law. On this more modest version, psychological egoism claims that human agents always as a matter of fact act out of the motive of self-interest. The objections raised against psychological egoism in section 5 are equally effective against both ways of understanding this thesis. My reason for going with Feinberg's formulation has to do with the argument discussed in section 4 that makes use of the "ought" implies "can" thesis.

8. Batson, 1990, 336–46.

9. I prefer not using the term "selfish," in discussing egoism, since this term *suggests* a complete disregard for the interests or well-being of others. But a person who is motivated entirely by self-interest will not disregard the well-being of others in cases where attending to the welfare of others is in his or her self-interest.

10. Since PE is formulated as a claim about how people are motivated as a matter of psychological law, and so how they are (by such law) necessarily motivated, a thesis of altruism that is the strict denial of PE would only claim that such genuinely altruistic motivation is psychologically possible. Because those who defend genuine altruism are interested in defending the claim that some human behavior really is genuinely altruistic and not just possibly so, I have formulated PA accordingly.

11. Such pluralists also allow that some deliberate actions can be ultimately motivated by both types of motives. For discussion of motivational pluralism, see Sober and Wilson, 1998, especially chapters 3 and 10. It is worth noting that psychological altruism is compatible with what Gregory Kavka calls *predominant psychological egoism*, the view that self-interested mo-

tives "tend to take precedence over non-self-interested motives in determining human action" (Kavka, 1986, 64).

12. This is not to say that the thesis is completely uncontroversial. But here is not the place to examine its plausibility.

13. The case is discussed in Flescher and Worthen, 2007, 148–49.

14. I shall adopt Batson's use of the term "empathy," by which he means "an other-oriented emotional response congruent with the perceived welfare of another. If the other is in a state of benefit—having achieved a goal or won a prize, or is playing gleefully—empathic feelings are likely to include pleasure, delight, satisfaction, and joy. If the other is in a state of need—having failed at a task or suffered a loss, or is enduring pain—empathic feelings are likely to include sympathy, compassion, sorrow, and pity" (Batson, 1990, 339 n.1). Readers should be aware that Batson's usage is quite broad (as he indicated in this quote) and includes what some other philosophers and social scientists call sympathy. An illuminating discussion of empathy, sympathy, and related notions of care and compassion can be found in Darwall, 1998.

15. For present purposes I have simplified my description of Batson's design. Interested readers are referred to his 1990 article and 1991 book for further detail.

16. For a critical evaluation of Batson's work, see Sober and Wilson, 1998, chapter 8.

17. One can find a number of books about the Righteous Gentiles. I have benefitted in particular from Monroe, 1996, and from Flescher and Worthen, 2007.

18. This "looking out for oneself" idea is reflected in certain religious ethical doctrines according to which one's most basic duty is to save one's own soul.

19. Ayn Rand, 1964, for instance, argued that (1) one's happiness is the primary moral aim of each person, (2) an ethic of *self-denying altruism*, according to which one ought always act to promote the well-being of others (one's own well-being is not to be considered) is incompatible with this moral aim, and since (3) EE is compatible with this aim, EE must be the correct moral theory. But the obvious problem with this argument (granting that one accepts the first premise) is that it commits the fallacy of false dilemma—the fallacy of assuming that there are fewer options among which one must choose than there really are. None of the other moral theories in this book—all of them alternatives to ethical egoism—require this implausible form of altruism—not even a strongly impartialist theory such as utilitarianism. Even if Rand's argument is more charitably understood as claiming that the only options are egoism (a strongly partialist theory) and utilitarianism (a strongly impartialist theory), it still commits the fallacy in question. Versions of ethical pluralism featured in the later chapters of this book are not committed to either strong partialism or strong impartialism.

20. And so other versions of the inconsistency argument, including those that work only from principles within EE, are bound to fail. See, for instance, Shaver, 2002.

21. Shoemaker, 2012, 33.

22. Shoemaker, 2012, 34–35, suggests that the egoist might avoid the publicity objection by embracing REE. As he notes, the success of this ploy will depend on whether, for an agent, a rule that permits the promulgation of ethical egoism would have at least as high an agent acceptance utility as would any other alternative rule governing the situation in question.

23. It is worth noting that there are non-egoistic versions of *agent-relative consequentialism* that are put forth as alternatives to strict impartialist and strict partialist moral theories. See Portmore, 2001, 2007. However, as noted in chapter 5, note 5, space does not permit a discussion of this interesting species of consequentialism.

FURTHER READING

Philosophical Literature

Butler, J. 1726. *Fifteen Sermons on Human Nature Preached at Rolls Chapel.* New York: Robert Carter & Bros., 1860, reprinted as *Fifteen Sermons*, Charlottesville, VA: Lincoln-Rembrandt, 1993. A classic and influential critique of psychological egoism. See in particular, Sermon 11, "On the Love of Our Neighbor."

Feinberg, J. [1968] 2008. "Psychological Egoism." In *Reason and Responsibility*, 14th ed., ed. J. Feinberg and R. Shafer-Landau. Belmont, CA: Thomson Wadsworth. An excellent critical discussion of PE.

Hunt, Lester. 1999. "Flourishing Egoism." *Social Philosophy & Policy* 16: 72–95. Defense of a non-consequentialist form of ethical egoism inspired by the work of Ayn Rand.

McConnell, T. C. 1978. "The Argument from Psychological Egoism to Ethical Egoism." *Australasian Journal of Philosophy* 56: 41–47. Critical examination of the argument in question.

Paul, E. F., F. D. Miller, and J. Paul, eds. 1993. *Altruism*. Cambridge: Cambridge University Press. Ten essays by leading philosophers on the topic of altruism.

Shaver, Rob. 2002. "Egoism." *The Stanford Encyclopedia of Philosophy*, ed. E. N. Zalta. http://plato.stanford.edu. A clear, concise presentation and discussion of ethical, rational, and psychological egoisms.

Shoemaker, D. 2012. "Egoisms." In *Conduct and Character: Readings in Moral Theory*, 6th ed., ed. M. Timmons. Belmont, CA: Thomson-Wadsworth. A clear and engaging treatment of psychological and ethical egoisms.

Empirical Literature

Batson, C. D. 1990. "How Social an Animal? The Human Capacity for Caring." *American Psychologist* 45: 336–46. A presentation of experimental evidence in favor of altruism.

———. 1991. *The Altruism Question*. Hillsdale, NJ: Lawrence Erlbaum. An extensive examination of the evidence bearing on altruism.

Dawkins, R. [1976] 1989. *The Selfish Gene*, 2nd ed. Oxford: Oxford University Press. Explains from a Darwinian perspective (and for a nonspecialist audience) how altruistic *behavior* can arise among human beings given what Dawkins describes as the "selfish" nature of genes.

Flescher, M. A., and D. L. Worthen. 2007. *The Altruistic Species*. West Conshohocken, PA: Templeton Foundation Press. An illuminating defense of altruism with discussion of approaches to the egoism versus altruism debate from the fields of psychology, evolutionary biology, philosophy, and religion.

Monroe, Kristin R. 1996. *The Heart of Altruism*. Princeton, NJ: Princeton University Press. A defense of altruism based on an examination of interviews in which subjects describe their helping experiences.

Sober, E., and D. S. Wilson. 1998. *Unto Others: The Evolution and Psychology of Unselfish Behavior*. Cambridge, MA: Harvard University Press. Collaboration between a philosopher (Sober) and an evolutionary biologist (Wilson) who develop an evolutionary-based case for psychological altruism.

Stich, S., J. M. Doris, and E. Roedder. 2010. "Altruism." In *The Moral Psychology Handbook*, ed. J. M. Doris. Oxford: Oxford University Press. An overview of the evolutionary and social psychology debates over the issue of altruism.

8

Kant's Moral Theory

Immanuel Kant (1724–1804) made important contributions to all of the major fields of philosophy and ranks as one of history's most influential philosophers. He wrote three important books in moral philosophy: *Groundwork of the Metaphysics of Morals* (1785), *Critique of Practical Reason* (1788), and *The Metaphysics of Morals* (1797). His work in philosophy generally and in ethics in particular is marked by its originality, subtlety, and difficulty. This chapter will provide an overview of some of the main ideas in Kant's theories of right conduct and value.

A leading idea of Kant's moral theory is that moral requirements are requirements of reason. To act immorally is thus to act in a way that is contrary to reason. In Kant's terminology, moral requirements can be expressed as "categorical imperatives"—imperatives grounded in reason and which can be derived from a supreme moral principle—the Categorical Imperative.[1] The place to begin in coming to understand Kant's moral theory is with his conception of duty.

1. KANT ON THE IDEA OF DUTY

Kant's moral theory attempts to make sense of what Kant takes to be the ordinary, commonsense idea of duty. He expresses this idea in the following passage from the preface of the *Groundwork*:

> Everyone must grant that a law, if it is to hold morally, that is, as a ground of an obligation, must carry with it absolute necessity; that, for example, the command "thou shalt not lie" does not hold only for human beings, as if other rational beings did not have to heed it, and so with all other moral laws properly so called; that, therefore, the ground

of obligation here must not be sought in the nature of the human being . . . [but] simply in the concepts of pure reason. (*G*, 4:389/44–5)[2]

A main point that Kant is making here concerns the scope of moral obligation: such obligations, like the duty not to lie, hold not just for human beings but for all rational agents. Although at this time in our history, we are only acquainted with human rational agents, there may be nonhuman species of intelligent life whose members are rational agents, and Kant is claiming that those rational nonhumans (assuming there are some) are subject to moral requirements just as we are. Why does Kant say this?

The answer is that he thinks that moral requirements are requirements of reason, specifically practical reason. Practical reason has to do with one's capacity to deliberate and make free choices. Principles of practical reason set forth requirements for deliberating and choosing rationally, and Kant holds that some of these principles are moral principles specifying moral requirements. If Kant is right about this, then moral requirements, as requirements of reason, would have to be valid for every rational agent, regardless of whether such agents are *Homo sapiens*.

A comparison may help make the point. What is called theoretical reason concerns that use of reason involved in coming to rational beliefs about how things really are.[3] The use of theoretical reason is involved in, for example, scientific and mathematical reasoning where there are principles expressing requirements that govern rational thinking in these areas. Consider the following principle governing rational inferences about some object of study (called a population) based on a sample:

> If x percent of a sample taken from some population has a certain characteristic, then one may infer (assuming the sample is representative of the population) that approximately x percent of the entire population has the characteristic in question.

Now this principle may need some refinement, but the point is that it does not hold just for human beings; rather, it represents a universally valid standard for rationally drawing conclusions about a population on the basis of a sample and thus holds for all rational beings. Kant's idea about moral principles is the same: they purport to express rational requirements on choice and action that apply to all rational agents.

Notice that Kant's idea that moral obligations represent requirements of reason concerning choice and action contrasts with how other moral theories we have examined understand such requirements. Mill's utilitarian moral theory attempts to base the principle of utility (and hence moral obligation) on facts about what human beings desire. Aquinas's natural law theory attempts to base moral obligation on facts about natural human tendencies. In the passage quoted above, Kant claims that the basis, or ground, of obligation cannot be discovered by appealing to facts that pertain specifically to human beings since in attempting to do so, one misses the idea that moral requirements hold for all rational agents, human and nonhuman.

Let us explore in more detail Kant's views about the demands of practical reason.

2. KANT AND THE DEMANDS OF PRACTICAL REASON

According to Kant, moral requirements represent demands on rational agents that are, in a sense to be explained below, "unconditional." The unconditional demands are properly expressed by what Kant calls categorical imperatives. Furthermore, he claims that underlying all particular moral requirements is a supreme principle of morality that he calls the Categorical Imperative.

In order to appreciate and explain these points, it will help to begin with a discussion of some of the kinds of rational requirements on choice and action that are nonmoral in character, requirements that Kant expresses by what he calls hypothetical imperatives.

Let us begin by noting that we sometimes evaluate the choices and actions of individuals as being either rational or irrational (even though we may not use these terms in expressing our evaluation). For example, suppose that I very much want to earn a degree in mathematics at a particular university, so I make earning it one of my ends. Now suppose further that taking a particular calculus course, say, Calculus 500, is a requirement for earning a mathematics degree at the university in question and that I am aware of this requirement. Then it seems clear that I ought to take the calculus course in question. If I refused to do so yet persist in my goal of earning the degree in math, I would be acting irrationally. Here we have a case of what philosophers call means-end rationality: given some end or goal that one intends to achieve, one ought to perform those actions that are necessary (perform the necessary means) for achieving that end, or else give up the end. In the particular case under discussion we can express the main idea in terms of this principle:

> **H** If you intend to earn a mathematics degree and taking Calculus 500 is necessary for earning the degree, then you ought to take Calculus 500 (or give up the goal of earning a mathematics degree).

It should be clear that for any goal or end someone might attempt to achieve, relative to which there are actions that must be performed to realize the goal, there will be principles like H that tell the agent to either perform the necessary actions or give up the goal. Since failing to conform to such a principle would be manifestly irrational, it should be clear that H and principles like it are principles of rationality pertaining to choice and action—that is, they represent principles of practical rationality.

It is particularly important to grasp here that principles like H specify what it is rational to do given certain goals that one has. People vary widely in the goals they have. Thus, whether or not a specific principle like H applies to an individual depends on whether she has the particular goal featured in the principle. If you don't intend to earn a mathematics degree, then it is not true of you that you ought to take Calculus 500 or give up your end (unless, of course, the achievement of another of your goals requires taking this course).

We can express the idea that principles like H only apply to, and have binding force for, persons relative to their goals by saying that such principles are conditionally valid for agents: a principle of the sort in question imposes rational constraints on one's behavior only on the condition that one has the goal or end specified in the principle. As we shall see, Kant thinks that principles of practical rationality expressing moral requirements are unconditionally valid.

Kant calls practical principles like H hypothetical imperatives. Calling them hypothetical is another way of indicating that for Kant they are conditionally valid—they apply to, and have binding force on, an agent only on the condition (hypothesis) that the agent has the end in question. He calls them imperatives because although H and other such principles are expressed in terms of what an agent ought to do, given certain ends she has, we can also express such requirements in a way that more clearly brings out their action-guiding force by replacing talk of what an agent ought to do with an imperative directing her to do it. Thus, according to Kant, H can alternatively be expressed this way:

H* If you intend to earn a mathematics degree and taking Calculus 500 is necessary for earning the degree, then take Calculus 500 (or give up the goal of earning a mathematics degree).

Given the pattern exemplified by H and H*, it should be clear that underlying all specific hypothetical imperatives is the following formal principle:

HI If one intends E and recognizes that doing A is necessary for bringing about E, then do A (or give up E).

Clearly H and other principles of the same form are instances of HI, and so if HI is a correct principle of practical rationality, then so are all of its specific instances.[4]

One might ask how it is that we come to recognize principles like H to be principles of practical rationality. One way to approach this question is to think about the very concept of rational choice and action and imagine an ideally rational agent—an agent who necessarily reasons and acts in a perfectly rational manner—and then ask what principles would in fact govern the behavior of such an ideal agent. Upon reflection, it seems intuitively clear that a fully rational agent who sets for herself a certain end E and who recognizes that doing action A is necessary for her bringing about E would (insofar as she is fully rational in her deliberation and choice) do A.[5]

Of course, we are not fully rational agents. For one thing, even in cases where we know what reason requires of us when it comes to choice and action, we can fail to take the rational course of action. Sometimes, for instance, we act irrationally under the influence of some desire. So, for human beings who are not by nature always and unfailingly rational, principles that describe how in fact a completely rational agent would behave are presented as principles that prescribe how we ought to behave (if we are to be rational in our choices and actions).

3. MORALITY IS NOT A SYSTEM OF HYPOTHETICAL IMPERATIVES

Because requirements flowing from hypothetical imperatives are only conditionally binding on an agent, they cannot express genuine moral requirements since, according to Kant, the very idea of a moral requirement or duty involves there being some action (or omission) that one must do (or omit) regardless of what ends one might happen to adopt based on one's desires.

In making this claim about the concept of duty, Kant takes himself to be saying something true about our ordinary, commonsense idea of duty. Is Kant right about this? Consider a couple of cases. Suppose first that you come into my office for advice about what courses to take next semester and I say to you that you really ought to take Logic 101. When you ask me why, I point out that this course is a requirement for getting a degree in philosophy, to which you respond that you have no intention of earning a philosophy degree. Upon hearing this, I would naturally retract my claim about your having to take logic; it does not truly apply to you.

But now think for a moment about your reaction to someone who, in response to a claim that she has a duty of gratitude to care for her sick relative, responds by saying, "You know, caring for my sick relative just does not serve any of the personal goals I happen to have." I think a common (and proper) reaction would be to say that this kind of response is irrelevant: whether or not someone morally ought to do something does not depend on how the required action fits with the goals and ends the person happens to desire. So in striking contrast to the previous case, we would not retract the claim about what one morally ought to do just because of what that person may happen to desire. The kind of requirement expressed by a moral duty is, in Kant's terminology, unconditionally valid, and part of what this means is that its validity is not dependent on those desire-based ends that one might or might not happen to have.

To summarize this discussion: Our desires for various ends are the basis for conditionally valid requirements on choice and action that can be expressed as hypothetical imperatives. But for Kant, such imperatives, because they are only conditionally valid, cannot express genuine moral requirements. Morality is not a system of hypothetical imperatives governing the rational pursuit of our desire-based chosen ends.

A related point concerns the pursuit of our own happiness. Kant claims that as human beings we necessarily have our own happiness as an end. (See *G*, 4:415/68.) But happiness, on Kant's view, results from the fulfillment of certain ends or goals, which, again, we form on the basis of our desires.[6] As we have just explained, the ends or goals we adopt on the basis of desire cannot be the ground of moral requirements. Furthermore, it is obvious that moral requirements often conflict with what would contribute to our personal happiness. So, even though all human beings necessarily have their own happiness as an end, this fact about us cannot be the basis for moral requirements: morality is not a doctrine of personal happiness.

These conclusions about the basis of moral requirements are negative. We need a positive account of their basis, to which we now turn.

4. THE SUPREME PRINCIPLE OF MORALITY: THE CATEGORICAL IMPERATIVE

If moral requirements are unconditionally valid for all rational agents, then there must be requirements that are, in Kant's terminology, categorical. But how can there be such categorical imperatives? What could be the basis for such requirements? Answering this question takes us to the heart of Kant's theory of right conduct.

A leading idea in Kant's thought about the basis of moral requirements is that there must be something of unconditional worth or value, some end of action, which can be a source of the unconditionally valid requirements of morality. Kant distinguishes two sorts of ends. First, there are ends that can be brought about through action. Individuals make plans that involve the aim of accomplishing some goal or obtaining some object. Such goals are adopted ends that guide deliberation and subsequent action. The ends one adopts (as least the morally permissible ones) can be said to have a kind of worth or value. But those ends that we adopt on the basis of our desires only acquire worth or value for us as a result of being objects of our choice. Their worth or value is conditional—conditional on being the objects of desire that one aims to fulfill. In searching for an end (or ends) that can ground categorical requirement, we are looking for some end (or ends) whose worth is not acquired in this way but is valid for all rational agents independently of their various desires.[7] The second sort of end that Kant recognizes is what he calls "existent" ends—things such as persons that already exist. It is this sort of end that Kant thinks can ground categorical requirements. Such an end would be "an end in itself"—something possessing unconditional, intrinsic worth and thereby deserving of certain sorts of treatment. And, according to Kant, there is such an end: "Rational nature exists as an end in itself" (*G*, 4:428–9/79). Rational nature as an end in itself possesses a kind of unconditional, intrinsic value—what Kant sometimes calls "dignity"—that can be the basis of a supreme principle of morality and thus a basis of moral requirements derivable from such a principle.

But what is it about rational nature in virtue of which it has this kind of dignity? In response, Kant claims that "Autonomy is . . . the ground of the dignity of human nature and of every rational nature" (*G*, 4:436/85). Autonomy, for Kant, refers to a capacity, inherent in all rational agents, to act freely on the basis of reason and independently of our desires. Autonomy, or freedom of choice, is thus the basis of moral requirements that can be expressed as categorical imperatives. As Kant remarks:

> The ground of the possibility of categorical imperatives is this: that they refer to no other property of choice (by which some purpose can be ascribed to it) than simply to its freedom. (*MM*, 6:222/377)

Unfortunately, Kant's conception of autonomy and its relation to categorical imperatives are difficult topics and the subject of much controversy among ethics scholars. Here is not the place to examine these topics. Rather, let us make do with a summary of some of the main connections Kant is making among the concepts just introduced.

These connections can be summarized by the following chain of reasoning: Since (1) our rational natures make us ends in ourselves, and (2) we have this status because we possess autonomy, it follows that (3) our nature as autonomous agents makes us ends in ourselves. (4) Anything with the status of an end in itself has unconditional value, and so (5) our autonomous rational natures have unconditional value. (6) If something has unconditional value, then there is an unconditional requirement to *respect* it—the kind of response that something with such worth calls for. (7) Thus, there is a basic unconditional requirement to respect the autonomy of agents. This basic requirement is expressed in Kant's supreme moral principle, the Categorical Imperative.

Kant uses the term "humanity" to refer to the sort of autonomy that is part of our natures as rational creatures. Here, then, is one formulation of his supreme moral principle that we may call the Humanity as an End in Itself formulation (HEI, for short).

> **HEI** So act that you use humanity, whether in your own person or in the person of any other, always at the same time as an end, never merely as a means. (*G*, 4:429/80)

As we shall see, Kant offers more than one formulation of his supreme principle of morality. But the main idea expressed by the HEI formulation is that a person's autonomy (humanity) serves as a supremely authoritative constraint on the pursuit of her desire-based ends. Let us consider this principle in a bit more detail.

HEI really incorporates a negative requirement and a positive requirement. Begin with the negative which concerns never treating humanity merely as a means. I treat someone as a means to my own ends when, for example, I gain their cooperation in helping me achieve what I want. If I ask you to drop me off at the airport and you willingly agree, I am using you as a means to help me achieve one of my ends. There is nothing morally wrong in using you in this way. However, treating people *merely* as means to one's own ends involves treating them in ways that fail to respect their humanity. So, for instance, a mugger who demands that his victim hand over his wallet or else be shot to death is engaged in an act of coercion which improperly interferes with the victim's unfettered use of his autonomy. An unscrupulous scientist who lies to potential subjects about the dangers of participating in some experiment in order to gain their cooperation is another clear instance of what Kant would refer to as using persons merely as means to help accomplish one of her ends.

So, for Kant, there is a morally important difference between treating someone as a means in order to help you achieve one or more of your adopted ends, and treating someone *merely* as a means to your own ends. The difficult interpretive task is to articulate exactly what counts in Kant's view as treating someone merely as a means to one's own ends. Digging into this issue would require more space than can be allowed in covering the basics of Kant's moral theory, despite the obvious importance of this issue. However, a few remarks are in order.

First, it is useful to keep in mind the difference between *regarding* someone merely as a means and *acting* in ways that constitute wronging someone. The above examples of coercion and lying are intended to be examples of the latter. But consider this example from Derek Parfit, which involves a gangster

> who . . . regards most other people as mere means, and who would injure them whenever that would benefit him. When this man buys a cup of coffee, he treats the coffee seller just as he would treat a vending machine. He would steal from the coffee seller if that was worth the trouble, just as he would smash the machine. But though this gangster treats the coffee seller as a means, what is wrong is only his attitude toward this person. In buying his cup of coffee, he does not act wrongly. (2011, 216).

The point of the example, as Parfit makes clear, is that not all instances of what one may properly call treating (regarding) someone merely as a means—instances having to do with one's attitude towards that person—constitutes wrongful treatment by means of outward action. As we shall see in the next section, Kant does condemn arrogance in one's attitude toward others as violating a duty toward others. So Kant's moral theory is not just about wrongful actions, it is also concerned with proper and improper attitudes towards oneself and others. *Schadenfreude*, the German word for taking malicious joy in another's misfortune, is another example of a kind of attitude toward others, which qua attitude, Kant thinks is a violation of duty.

The difficult interpretive task lately mentioned is to define what it means to outwardly act in ways that treat persons merely as means to one's own ends so that such treatment is plausibly interpreted as morally wrong behavior. A common strategy by those who work on this problem is to appeal to the idea of consent in attempting to spell out Kant's conception of treatment merely as means.[8] One very plausible thing to say is that treating others in ways to which they could not *rationally consent* in pursuit of one's ends is central in understanding treating others merely as means. But then, one wants to know what types of treatment are such that one cannot consent to them on pain of failing to be rational. So appeal to rational consent doesn't get us very far unless we clarify that idea. Instead of taking this on which would require getting into some complicated issues, my plan is to illustrate in the next section the kinds of actions that Kant thought are instances of such wrongful behavior.

While the negative, prohibitive part of HEI forbids treating persons merely as means to one's own ends, what I am calling the positive part requires that one adopt certain ends of action that one is to promote. The two most basic such ends are self-perfection and the happiness of others. In other words, in fully respecting the dignity of one's own humanity, "it is not enough that the action does not conflict with humanity in our person as an end in itself; it must also *harmonize with it*" (*G*, 4:430/80–1). The same point applies to one's treatment of others. It is not enough to simply avoid treating them merely as means, which one could do by simply ignoring them; one is also morally required to help promote their humanity as end-setting individuals concerned with their own well-being.

To get a clearer understanding of the negative and positive implications of Kant's supreme moral principle, let us briefly consider his system of duties, which will help readers gain at least an intuitive understanding of Kant's HEI formula.

5. KANT'S SYSTEM OF DUTIES

According to Kant, then, moral requirements are properly expressed as categorical imperatives. Kant claims that from his fundamental moral principle, the Categorical Imperative, we can derive all other duties and that they can be organized into a system. First, using the Categorical Imperative, we can derive two very general duties, and then from these derived duties, we can derive further, more specific duties.

The two most general duties are (1) the duty of self-perfection and (2) the duty to promote the happiness of others. Two things need explanation here: first, how Kant arrives at the claim that perfection and happiness are duties; and second, why we do not have a duty to promote our own happiness and why we do not have a duty to bring about the perfection of others. Let us take these one at a time.

The guiding idea contained in the Categorical Imperative is the requirement to treat oneself and others in ways that protect and promote one's own humanity and the humanity of others. Kant claims that "The capacity to set oneself an end—any end whatsoever—is what characterizes humanity" (*MM*, 6:392/522); this capacity, as we have noted, refers to our autonomy. In order, then, to fully protect and promote our capacity to set ends, we obviously need to develop certain powers that would enable us to effectively set and pursue ends of our choosing. Developing such powers is a matter of perfecting oneself. Hence, from the Categorical Imperative we can derive a general duty to perfect ourselves.

Furthermore, our nature as autonomous agents essentially involves using our end-setting capacities to pursue various projects in life that are aimed at achieving our own happiness. Just as we recognize our own happiness as a legitimate end, consistency demands that we recognize the happiness of all other individuals as having a similar legitimacy. Hence, from the Categorical Imperative we can derive the general duty of promoting the happiness of others. This does not mean that we must help others in their goals no matter what those goals happen to be. Rather, according to Kant, we have a general duty to promote the morally legitimate goals of others.

Now the reason we do not have an obligation to promote our own happiness is that, as already noted, by nature we necessarily have our own happiness as an end and so we are strongly naturally inclined to act in ways that promote our happiness. But the idea of a moral duty involves the idea of being morally constrained to act in ways that we are not naturally inclined to act. Hence, we do not have a moral duty to promote our own happiness.

Furthermore, since our own perfection is something that must be achieved by our own efforts (I can't do it for you), I don't have a duty to develop your various natural and moral powers (though my actions can help or hinder you in your efforts at self-perfection).

Thus, for Kant, once we bring into view what would, in general terms, be involved in respecting our own humanity and in respecting the humanity of others, we can arrive at two general duties: duties to adopt as guiding aims one's own perfection and the happiness of others. Kant calls them ends that are at the same time duties. Let us refer to them simply as *obligatory ends*. And notice something about such ends. Earlier we noted that Kant does not think that moral requirements can be based on any *desire-based* ends of action. Now like a desire-based end, an obligatory end is the kind of end that can be brought about through action, in contrast to what Kant calls "existent" ends. But unlike desire-based ends, an obligatory end is one whose adoption is grounded in one's rational recognition that the end in question is one that one morally ought to adopt. And the reason one morally ought to adopt such ends is because only by doing so does one fully respect the unconditional worth (and hence dignity) of rational beings.

These obligatory ends provide, respectively, the basis for deriving more specific duties to oneself and to others. Consider, first, duties to oneself regarding self-perfection. This obligatory end of action is the basis for duties of omission (negative duties) and also for duties of commission (positive duties). After all, there are actions we should avoid in order to maintain and not destroy or otherwise degrade our autonomy, but there are also actions the performance of which would positively promote our autonomy, thus increasing its powers. Furthermore, it is part of Kant's view of human beings that for purposes of moral theory, we can distinguish between humans considered as natural creatures (and thus part of the animal world) and humans considered as rational agents capable of autonomous choice. He thus divides duties to oneself into duties one has considered as a natural being and duties one has considered as a moral being. Figure 8.1 summarizes Kant's duties to oneself as presented in *The Metaphysics of Morals*.

In defending each of these duties, Kant appeals to considerations of respecting one's own humanity. For instance, he argues that suicide is wrong because it involves "disposing of oneself as a mere means to some discretionary end [which] is debasing humanity in one's own person" (*MM*, 6:423/547). With regard to lying, the central claim is that "By a lie a human being throws himself away and, as it were, annihilates his dignity as a human being" (*MM*, 6:429/552–3). Suicide, lying, and other duties of omission involve actions whose performance would destroy or at least degrade humanity in the person.

As figure 8.1 indicates, Kant (following tradition) distinguishes "perfect" from "imperfect" duties. Perfect, or "narrow," duties are so called because the kinds of actions forbidden are fairly precisely specified and presumably we are to refrain from such types of action in all or most circumstances.

	Duties of Omission Perfect (narrow) duties	Duties of Commission Imperfect (wide) duties
	To avoid:	To develop:
As a Natural Being	Suicide (and self-mutilation) Carnal self-defilement Gluttony and drunkenness	One's own natural powers of Spirit Soul Body
As a Moral Being	Lying Avarice Servility	One's moral nature by striving to become virtuous

Figure 8.1.   Duties to Oneself Regarding Self-Perfection

By contrast, duties of commission, listed on the right in the chart, are imperfect or "wide" duties because, although they require that agents adopt certain ends as general guiding objectives in life, agents have a great deal of leeway in deciding how and when to act on those ends. Compared to the narrow, perfect duties, imperfect duties are wider in terms of what agents can do to fulfill them. For instance, powers of the spirit involve those capacities having to do with the exercise of one's reason; powers of soul have to do with those capacities involving memory and imagination; while powers of the body are those physical capacities that must be developed for all sorts of purposes. Now it is up to the individual to decide which specific powers of spirit, soul, and body to develop and how much time she will devote to their development. Presumably such decisions will be partly based on what one plans to do in life. Obviously, someone who aspires to be a mathematician is going to concentrate mainly (but not exclusively) on developing certain powers of spirit. An athlete will no doubt concentrate instead on developing certain powers of body.

Finally, perfecting our moral natures has to do with striving to make the thought of duty the sole motive in dutiful action—in other words it has to do with progressing toward a state of moral virtue. (The topic of moral virtue is taken up in section 9 below.) This duty seems much more specific than duties connected with our natural powers, but Kant claims that nevertheless working on becoming morally virtuous (something we need not be doing at all times) involves a kind of latitude or leeway and so counts as an imperfect duty.

Regarding the other main obligatory end—the happiness of others—Kant distinguishes duties of love, which are not strictly speaking owed to another person, from duties of respect, which are. And, as before, he distinguishes negative duties of omission from positive duties of commission. Figure 8.2 summarizes duties regarding the happiness of others. Kant argues that duties of omission involve actions the

	Duties of Omission Perfect (narrow) duties	*Duties of Commission* Imperfect (wide) duties
	To avoid the vices of:	To cultivate the virtues of:
Of Love	Envy Ingratitude Malice	Beneficence Gratitude Sympathetic feelings
Of Respect	Arrogance Defamation Ridicule	Respect for others as ends in themselves

Figure 8.2.   Duties to Others Regarding Their Happiness

performance of which fails to respect humanity as an end in itself, while promoting humanity as an end in itself requires that we develop attitudes of beneficence, gratitude, sympathy, and respect for others.

To bring before us clearly the different levels of duty in Kant's system, the visual aid in figure 8.3 may help. Level 1 represents the most general moral principle of the system; level 4 represents duties in concrete situations. In between are levels of varying generality, which we have been summarizing (level 3 is summarized in figures 8.1 and 8.2). There are two important things to keep in mind about the relations between these levels.

First, going from level 1 to 2 and from 2 to 3 requires that we appeal to facts about the specific nature of human beings. Kant makes this clear when he writes:

> [A] metaphysics of morals cannot dispense with principles of application, and we shall often have to take as our object the particular nature of human beings, which is cognized only by experience, in order to show in it what can be inferred from universal moral principles. (*MM*, 4:217/372)

As explained earlier, because the Categorical Imperative is a principle of practical rationality, it is valid for all rational creatures, human and nonhuman. Kant's point is that its implications for human morality require that we take into account various facts about the nature of human beings. For instance, it is because as human beings we have powers of body, mind, and spirit that need development that we have a duty to perfect ourselves.

A second, related point is that going from level 3 to level 4, in which rules are applied to particular circumstances, is not a mechanical procedure. Kant fully recognizes that the application of rules requires the use of good judgment, including being sensitive to the details of individual cases. This point is made especially clear in Kant's casuistical remarks that he appends to his presentation of the various duties in his system.

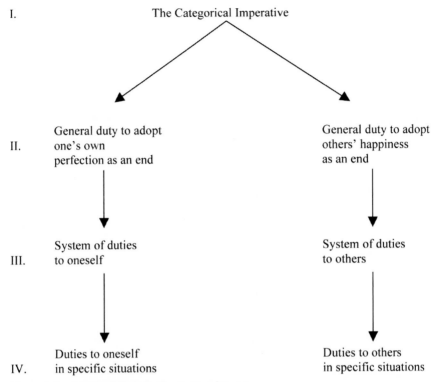

Figure 8.3.   Levels of Duty in Kant's Moral System

Casuistry is the art of applying principles to specific cases to reach justified moral conclusions about those cases. In doing so, the details of one's situation are important. For instance, in connection with the duty not to commit suicide, Kant asks whether it would be morally wrong "to hurl oneself to certain death (like Curtius[9]) in order to save one's country" (*MM*, 6:423/548), or whether it would be right for someone suffering from a form of madness (that makes him a danger to others) to commit suicide (*MM*, 6:423–24/548). Obviously, here and elsewhere in his remarks on casuistry, Kant is considering how particular facts pertaining to situations might affect the rightness or wrongness of various actions. So we should avoid supposing that because the basis of Kantian duties is an abstract moral principle that supposedly holds for all rational agents, it therefore must ignore the important particularities of human beings and the particular circumstances in which they find themselves.

Considering the various duties featured in his ethical system, it should be clear that Kant thought that the Categorical Imperative is supposed to be rich in its implications. Moreover, its application in our world requires knowledge both about human nature and about the morally relevant details of particular cases. Unfortunately, Kant's theory has sometimes been misunderstood on these points.

A final point worth stressing is this. As I interpret Kant, there can be cases in which two or more of the duties apply to a person's circumstances, but because they favor doing different and incompatible actions, only one of them can turn out to be what one is morally obligated to do. Here is an example inspired by one of Kant's own examples.[10]

> *Lizbeth's lie.* Lizbeth is hiding an acquaintance, Tom, who is wrongly believed by some murderous gang members to have ratted out one of their gang to the police. A gang member shows up at Lizbeth's front door asking her for the whereabouts of Tom. To tell the truth would surely lead to the murder of Tom, and so would (let us suppose) just refusing to answer. So Lizbeth lies, saying that she doesn't know where Tom is.

Given the circumstances it was not possible for Lizbeth to both protect Tom and avoid lying. That Tom was being targeted for murder provides grounds for doing what one can to prevent the murder, which in this case is to lie. But that one's act would be a lie provides grounds for not engaging in that act. What I believe Kant should say about this case is that Lizbeth's circumstances are such that there are two grounds of obligation, "one or the other of which is not sufficient to put [her] under obligation. When two such grounds conflict with each other, practical philosophy says, not that the stronger obligation takes precedence . . . but that the stronger *ground of obligation* prevails" (*MM* 6:224/379). In this case, it seems clear that the stronger ground of obligation is the fact that one is able to prevent a murder which requires lying. So although in most cases lying is wrong, arguably in this case it is morally obligatory.

6. KANT'S THEORY OF RIGHT CONDUCT

Now that we have examined some of the detail of Kant's system of duties, let us summarize his theory of right action, using the HEI formulation of the Categorical Imperative. The main idea is that morality requires that we treat all human beings, including ourselves, as ends in themselves and never merely as means to one's own ends. We can shorten this by saying that morality requires that we respect humanity. We have just noted that Kant allows that there can be conflicting "grounds of obligation," which we have interpreted as the claim that there can be circumstances in which two or more such grounds can conflict and one must decide which ground of obligation is superior in strength. In cases where there are competing grounds of obligation, let us say that the act (or omission) favored by the stronger ground respects humanity to a greater degree than the act (or omission) favored by the comparatively weaker ground. With this in mind, we can set out Kant's theory as a set of principles:

Theory of Right Conduct: Humanity Formulation

An action A in circumstance C is *obligatory* if and only if (and because) failing to perform A in C would (from among the alternative actions open to one in C) fail to respect humanity to a greater degree than would any alternative action.

An action A in C is *wrong* if and only if (and because) performing A would fail to respect someone's humanity to a greater degree than would any other alternative action open to one in C.

An action A in C is *optional* if and only if (and because) either (i) performing A would not fail to respect someone's humanity to a greater degree than would any other alternative action open to the agent in C, or (ii) neither performing A nor failing to perform A in C would involve failing to respect humanity.

We can fill out Kant's theory by adding principles of perfect and imperfect duty.

Actions whose performance would wrongly interfere with or in some way count as disrespecting someone's humanity violate perfect duty. (Similar remarks apply to one's attitudes including, for example, arrogance toward others and servility toward oneself.)

Failing to adopt certain ends, or having adopted them, failing on suitable occasions to act on them, counts as failing to positively promote or respect humanity and thus constitutes a violation of imperfect duty.[11]

It is important to note that as I am interpreting Kant's moral theory, it is the HEI formulation of the Categorical Imperative that functions as a moral criterion, telling us what makes an action right or wrong. Thus, facts about the action as it bears on treating persons as ends in themselves or, equivalently, respecting their humanity represent the most fundamental right- and wrong-making properties of all choice and action according to Kant's theory.

7. THE UNIVERSAL LAW FORMULATION OF THE CATEGORICAL IMPERATIVE

As mentioned above, Kant expresses his supreme principle of morality in various ways. According to the Universal Law (UL) formulation of that principle featured in Kant's sample applications, one is to:

UL *Act as if the maxim of your action were to become by your will a universal law of nature.* (*G*, 4:421/73)

Those familiar with Kant's ethics might be surprised that I have said nothing so far in this chapter about the UL formulation. Typically, ethics texts focus mainly on this formulation in expounding Kant's moral theory, since in the *Groundwork* it seems to be featured over the others and since Kant seems to recommend it over the others when he says that "one does better always to proceed in moral appraisal by the strict method and put at its basis the universal [law] formula of the categorical imperative" (*G*, 4:436–37/86).

I have said that I take the HEI formulation to represent Kant's fundamental criterion of right action, and thus I have featured it in my presentation of his moral theory. The UL formulation, as I understand it, provides a decision procedure to guide moral deliberation rather than a moral criterion.[12] (Notice that in the passage just quoted, Kant recommends the UL formulation for use in contexts of moral appraisal, when we are deliberating about what to do.) With this in mind, let us proceed to consider the UL formulation.

Since the UL formulation mentions an agent's maxims and employs the idea of consistent willing, we first need to say something about these notions.

Maxims

Kant defines a maxim as "a subjective principle of volition" (*G*, 4:402n/56) on which an agent acts whenever she acts intentionally. When one acts, one represents to oneself the action one is proposing to do (or has done) and the circumstances in which the action is to take place. Furthermore, one acts for some purpose or end. To take a simple case, suppose I am having trouble with the spelling of a word and I finally decide to look it up in a dictionary to get the spelling straight. My act of looking up the word flowed from my intention to perform this action in certain circumstances in order to achieve a certain purpose. My intention is what Kant means in talking about one's maxim associated with the actions one performs. A maxim is thus a psychological state expressing one's intention to perform (or omit) some action and thereby represents the agent's view of what she is doing. Maxims can be expressed in thought and language by sentences having this form:

I will _____, if/when _____ in order to _____.

where the first blank is filled by a description of the action, the second blank with a description of the circumstances in which the agent is contemplating doing (or has done) the action, and the last blank with a description of the agent's purpose or end to be achieved by the action. We will consider some sample maxims below.

Notice three points about maxims. First, Kant is not committed to the idea that we all go around mentally rehearsing maxims and then acting on them. One need not be consciously attending to the maxim on which one acts, though one could presumably, upon reflection, become aware of the maxim. While driving my car I am acting on a maxim, but normally when I drive, I'm thinking about where I'm going, the road conditions, the traffic, and so forth; I am not thinking about or rehearsing the maxim or intention from which my driving actions flow. Second, since maxims represent the agent's view of the circumstances and action, they may involve mistaken beliefs. I might falsely believe that I have a bad heart and act accordingly and thus be acting on a maxim that does not correctly represent my circumstances. Finally, a maxim, as a principle of volition, expresses what one wills to do; adopting a maxim involves setting oneself to do (or omit) some action or pursue some end.

Consistent Willing

We can distinguish between direct and indirect willing. Direct willing involves setting oneself to do some action (or to refrain from doing one) that is within one's direct voluntary control—like willing your arm to move. But one can also will in the sense of setting for oneself some end or goal that is not immediately under one's control—like earning a college degree. This latter is an example of indirect willing.

There are at least two ways in which one might be inconsistent in what one wills. First, if one wills to perform some action or bring about some end where the very idea of the action or the end is self-contradictory, one is guilty of inconsistent willing. Thus, to set out to draw a four-sided triangle involves an inconsistency in willing since one is aiming at bringing about something that in its very conception is self-contradictory. We can refer to this as the first pattern of inconsistent willing. As we shall see below, the lying promise example that Kant uses to illustrate the application of the UL formulation of the Categorical Imperative involves this sort of inconsistency.

One might also be guilty of inconsistent willing when there is a conflict between different actions or ends that one wills. Suppose, for example, one intends to donate money to all charitable organizations that help the poor. Suppose also that one refuses to help any organization that contributes to global warming. Now if we suppose that there is some organization, O, that both helps the poor and contributes to global warming, we have an inconsistency in the will. One both wills to contribute money to O (since it is a charitable organization) and does not will to contribute money to O (since it contributes to global warming). Call this the second pattern of inconsistent willing. Again, as we shall see, Kant's example involving refusing to help others in need involves this kind of inconsistency in willing.

Let us now turn to Kant's UL formulation of the Categorical Imperative (and the two tests associated with it), where we will encounter both types of inconsistent willing.

Kant's Tests

Kant claims that the UL formulation of the Categorical Imperative can be used to test the morality of one's actions by determining whether one can consistently will that the maxim of one's action could become a universal law of nature. Kant's test employs the idea that for a proposed course of action to be morally permissible, it must be such that, as a rational agent, one could consistently will that everyone act in the way one is proposing to act. And this amounts to determining whether one could consistently will that everyone adopt and act on the maxim associated with the action in question. This will be made clearer when we turn in a moment to some of Kant's examples.

Let us introduce a bit of terminology. To say that a maxim is universalizable is to say that it can be consistently willed as a law of nature. Let us distinguish between maxims of commission and maxims of omission associated with some action. If, for example, the action is one of keeping a promise, then the action of commission would be described by:

I will keep my promise whenever _____.

The corresponding maxim of omission, then, would be:

I will omit to keep my promise whenever _____.

Making use of this distinction, we can formulate principles for determining the conditions under which an action is obligatory, optional, or forbidden.

Principles of Right Conduct: Universal Law Formulation

An action A is *obligatory* if and only if one cannot universalize the maxim of omission associated with A.

An action A is *wrong* if and only if one cannot universalize the maxim of commission associated with A.

An action A is *optional* if and only if one can universalize the maxims of commission and omission associated with A.

Let us now examine some of the details of Kant's test.

In the *Groundwork*, Kant illustrates how his test works by considering four examples: committing suicide, making false promises, letting one's talents rust, and refraining from helping others. He also claims that the UL formulation really embodies two tests that can be used to distinguish perfect from imperfect duties. Rather than work through all four illustrations, it will be enough for our purposes if we just consider the false-promising case (which is supposed to violate a perfect duty) and the case of refusing help to others (which is supposed to violate an imperfect duty).

The False-Promising Example

Regarding the case of false promising, Kant has us imagine someone who

> finds himself urged by need to borrow money. He well knows that he will not be able to repay it but sees also that nothing will be lent him unless he promises to repay it within a determinate time. He would like to make such a promise, but he still has enough conscience to ask himself: is it not forbidden and contrary to duty to help oneself out of need in such a way? (*G*, 4:422/74)

The maxim associated with this contemplated action is:

> **M1** I will get money on a false promise whenever I am in need of money and I have no other way of getting it.[13]

Kant's test has agents consider whether they could consistently will that everyone perform the type of action mentioned in the maxim under the circumstances. The idea is to ask yourself whether you could, without contradicting yourself, will that it be a law of nature that everyone do what you are proposing to do. In asking yourself this question, you are, in effect, asking yourself whether you could consistently will as a universal law of nature the following generalized version of your maxim, in this case, M1:

GM1 Everyone will get money on a false promise whenever they are in need of money and have no other way of getting it.

Kant then argues:

> I then see at once that it [one's maxim, M1] could never hold as a universal law of nature and be consistent with itself, but must necessarily contradict itself. For, the universality of a law that everyone, when he believes himself to be in need, could promise whatever he pleases with the intention of not keeping it would make the promise and the end one might have in it itself impossible, since no one would believe what was promised him but would laugh at all such expressions as vain pretenses. (*G*, 4:422/74, bracketed remark inserted)

Kant's claim is that we cannot conceive of the maxim as a universal law (we cannot conceive of GM1 as a law of nature without falling into contradiction) and so we cannot consistently will the maxim as universal law. And so, concludes Kant, the action mentioned in the maxim is forbidden—a violation of duty.

Unfortunately, Kant's reasoning in this passage is compressed, and it isn't clear exactly how the false-promising maxim, were it to be a universal law of nature, "must necessarily contradict itself." Scholars of Kant's ethics disagree over how (if at all) there is a contradiction here. But assuming there is some sort of contradiction, the main idea seems to be this.

Kant's test has us consider whether we can imagine, without contradicting ourselves, a world in which the maxim in question functions as a universal law of nature. To imagine the lying-promise maxim as a universal law of nature apparently requires that we imagine a world like ours except that it is a law of nature that everyone who believes he or she is in need of money will get the money by making a false promise. In attempting to conceive of such a world, we end up in contradiction. After all, if everyone who thinks that he or she needs money makes a lying promise to get the money, eventually this will be found out, with the result that those who believe themselves to need money will not be able to get the money on promise, "since no one would believe what was promised him." Thus, in attempting to conceive of a world in which the false-promising maxim is a universal law governing the behavior of those who think they need money, we are attempting to do the following:

1. Imagine a world in which there is a law according to which everyone who thinks he is in need gets the money on a promise, but also
2. Imagine a world in which (because of the results of widespread false promising) it is not the case that everyone who thinks he is in need gets money on a promise.

Putting (1) and (2) together, we are attempting to:

3. Imagine a world in which everyone believing himself to be in need of money both (by law) gets the money on a promise, but where it is not the case that everyone in those circumstances gets the money on a promise.

By this line of reasoning we have thus uncovered a contradiction in attempting to conceive of the maxim as a universal law of nature. Hence, the maxim in question is not universalizable, and the action mentioned in the maxim is wrong.

The false-promising maxim presumably cannot even be conceived without contradiction as a universal law of nature, and maxims that fail this test—the contradiction in conception test (CC test)—feature actions that are violations of perfect duty.

This case, where the state of affairs one is attempting to will cannot even be consistently conceived, fits the first pattern of inconsistent willing that was presented above. However, some maxims corresponding to actions that violate one's duties can be conceived as universal law without contradiction but are such that they still cannot be consistently willed as a universal law of nature, thus fitting the second pattern of inconsistent willing. Such actions are violations of imperfect duty.

The Example of Refraining from Helping Others

The example of refraining from helping others illustrates Kant's second test, the contradiction in the will test (CW test). Kant considers a person whose life is going well and who realizes that he is in a position to help others but refuses to do so, thus adopting and acting on the maxim:

M2 I will refrain from helping those in need whenever I am in a position to help and despite the fact that I am well off.

The associated generalized version of M2 is:

GM2 Everyone will refrain from helping those in need whenever they are in a position to help and despite the fact that they are well off.

Here is what Kant says about such a person and the associated maxim:

> [A]lthough it is possible that a universal law of nature could very well subsist in accordance with such a maxim, it is still impossible to will that such a principle hold everywhere as a law of nature. For, a will that decided this would conflict with itself, since many cases could occur in which one would need the love and sympathy of others and in which, by such a law of nature arisen from his will, he would rob himself of all hope of the assistance he wishes for himself. (*G*, 4:423/75)

According to Kant, the nonhelping maxim passes the CC test—one can consistently conceive of a world in which (by law) those who are well off refuse to help those in need. However, one is still involved in an inconsistency in attempting to will the maxim in question as a universal law of nature. Kant's idea here seems to be this. First, if one wills GM2, then by implication one is committed to willing the following:

I Everyone will refrain from helping me whenever they are in a position to help and despite the fact that they are well off.

But, according to Kant, as a rational agent, one necessarily wills that one be helped whenever one is in need. That is, it is a constraint on being a rational agent that one adopt the following maxim:

RM I will that I be helped whenever I am in need and others are in a position to help me.

But RM is inconsistent with I: RM involves willing that you be helped in certain circumstances, while I (which one necessarily wills in willing GM2) involves willing that you not be helped in those same circumstances—a contradiction. Thus the maxim in question is not universalizable; attempting to will the original nonhelping maxim as a universal law exemplifies the second pattern of inconsistent willing. Since the nonhelping maxim passes the CC test but fails the CW test, the action mentioned in the maxim violates an imperfect duty to help others.

Are these arguments about false promising and helping others convincing? Perhaps the false-promising case is persuasive, but I suspect that many readers will be suspicious of Kant's insertion of what I have labeled a maxim of rationality (RM) into the helping-others example. After all, consider the diehard individualist who would rather die than accept any form of charity from others. This individual may be acting imprudently, but in failing to adopt RM is he guilty of being irrational? It is perhaps difficult to say without saying much more about what is involved in being rational. I will let the reader mull this over.

Before we consider the plausibility of Kant's tests, I wish to make two remarks about them. First, Kant's tests should be distinguished from rule utilitarianism, which was briefly discussed in chapter 6. Although some versions of rule utilitarianism, like Kant's tests, involve considering what would happen if everyone were to act in a certain way, they are very different. The rule utilitarian is interested in the values of the consequences of everyone acting in some way or accepting a certain rule, while Kant's tests focus on whether, in willing one's maxim as universal law, one is caught in some sort of inconsistency. As I have been interpreting Kant's tests, the projected consequences (results) of willing one's maxim as a universal law play a role in determining whether the maxim passes the tests, but it is not the goodness or badness of the consequences that is of concern. Kant does not argue that because the consequences of everyone (in need of money) making a lying promise would be bad or undesirable, acting on the false-promising maxim is wrong.

The second remark I wish to make concerns the difficult issue of how the UL formulation of the Categorical Imperative is related to the HEI formulation. Kant claims that they are equivalent in that they represent different ways of expressing the same supreme law of morality, but it is by no means obvious that they are equivalent. I am proposing that the HEI formulation expresses a moral criterion and thus that it expresses what it is that most fundamentally makes an action right or wrong. But I am also proposing that we think of the UL formulation, not as a moral criterion telling us what makes actions right or wrong, but rather as a decision procedure for use in arriving at justified conclusions about the rightness or wrongness of actions. The HEI formulation, then, addresses the main theoretical aim of a moral theory, while the UL formulation addresses the main practical aim of a moral theory.

If this interpretation of the two formulations is plausible, then the UL formulation must be somehow deeply related to the HEI formulation if it can be used as a decision procedure. The idea would have to be that the universalizability of one's maxim is a reliable indicator of whether or not the action featured in the maxim treats humanity as an end in itself. But this idea needs to be defended and would take us beyond the aims of this chapter.

8. OBJECTIONS TO KANT'S TESTS

Kant thought that his universalization tests would yield results that are consistent with commonsense views about the rightness and wrongness of various actions. But critics have argued that Kant's tests yield the wrong moral conclusions over a range of cases where commonsense notions about right and wrong seem fairly clear and accurate. In some cases a maxim will fail one of Kant's tests (yielding a negative verdict about the corresponding action) but the action is not morally wrong (false negatives), and in other cases a maxim that features a wrong action will pass Kant's tests, yielding a mistaken positive verdict about the act (false positives).

As an example of the first kind of case, consider the investor who intends to withdraw all of her money from the bank once the stock market index climbs another two hundred points.[14] One cannot consistently conceive of this maxim being a universal law of nature, for reasons similar to those presented in connection with the case of false promising. If one attempts to imagine a world in which this maxim functions as a law, one ends up attempting to imagine a world in which everyone withdraws their money under the conditions specified. But since banks do not have the necessary funds on hand to support massive withdrawals, one is also attempting to imagine a world in which it is not the case that everyone in the circumstances in question withdraws their money from a bank. Thus, because the maxim cannot be universalized, the action in the maxim is morally wrong. But surely adopting and acting on this maxim is not morally wrong, so Kant's CC test yields a false negative.

Here is an example of a false positive. Suppose that I plan to make a false promise in order to get money from someone named Igor Cycz on March 8 so that I can make a down payment on a metal detector. I thus formulate my maxim as:

M3 I will get money on a false promise whenever it is March 8 and I can get it from someone named Igor Cycz in order to buy a metal detector.

Now if I consider whether this maxim can be universalized, I ask whether I could consistently conceive of a world in which everyone in the circumstances in question obtains money on a false promise. Since the circumstances mentioned in my maxim are extremely rare, this maxim will pass the CC test, and so we must conclude that the action mentioned in the maxim is morally permissible (at least in the circumstances so specified), but surely it isn't.[15]

The problem of false negatives and false positives is related to a more general problem for Kant's universalization tests, namely, the problem of relevant maxims.[16] A maxim represents an agent's conception of what she is doing or proposes to do, and for every action there are innumerable possible maxims on the basis of which the action in question might be performed. To make this point more clearly, suppose that I am hiding an innocent person who is being hunted by some killers. The killers come to my door and ask me whether I know where the hunted person might be hiding. Suppose I lie and deny that I know anything of the whereabouts of their intended victim. Here are a couple of the possible maxims on which I might act:

M4 I will tell a lie whenever I am asked a question and don't want to give the correct answer.

M5 I will tell a lie whenever I am asked a question whose truthful answer will likely lead to the death of an innocent person.

Both maxims fit my circumstances in the sense that they both contain correct (or what I believe to be correct) information about my circumstances.

Now presumably, if I test the first maxim by Kant's tests, it will fail to be universalizable, thus implying that an act of lying in this case would be wrong. (I leave the details as an exercise for the reader.) However, if I test M5 by Kant's tests, it will (arguably) pass with the implication that the action in question is not morally wrong. Intuitively, we judge that the second maxim is (of these two) the one that should be used in testing the morality of lying in this case. What we need from Kant is a principled reason for selecting one possible maxim for purposes of testing the morality of an action over the many others that also apply to the same action. This is the problem of relevant maxims.

Critics often allege that Kant's UL version of the Categorical Imperative is useless without a solution to the problem of relevant maxims. It is useless and hence fails to satisfy the main practical aim of a moral theory—the aim of providing a useful decision procedure—because, given the multiplicity of maxims associated with any action, one can use Kant's tests to derive inconsistent moral verdicts about the same action. We just noted this in connection with maxims M4 and M5. Without a solution to the problem of relevant maxims, that part of Kant's moral theory having to do with providing a correct decision procedure fails the consistency standard for evaluating a moral theory.

Here is how the problem of relevant maxims is related to the problem of false negatives/false positives. For instance, the maxim of making a false promise to someone named Igor Cycz on March 8 includes morally irrelevant information of a detailed sort that has the effect of ensuring that the maxim will pass Kant's tests. After all, there will be very few occasions on which anyone could act on this particular maxim. If everyone who planned to borrow money on March 8 from someone named Igor Cycz in order to buy a metal detector made a false promise, this would not (as in Kant's original example) result in the collapse of the practice of promising. No contradiction in conception would result. Formulating maxims with a lot of true but irrelevant detail will allow almost any maxim to pass Kant's tests. Intuitively, such maxims are not relevant for purposes of morally evaluating the actions they mention.

A maxim like M4 suffers from the opposite problem: it fails to include morally relevant information. If we could supply a theory of relevant maxims on Kant's behalf, we would have a principled basis for determining just what information about one's circumstances and action is morally relevant and should be included in one's maxim and what information should not be included. We would then presumably have a way of eliminating the false negatives/false positives problem.

I hope what I am about to say about the problem of relevant maxims is obvious. A moral theory is in the business of specifying what features of an action and circumstances are the most fundamental morally relevant features—features that make an action right or wrong. If we examine Kant's moral philosophy asking ourselves what features of actions and one's circumstances are the most basic morally relevant features, the answer seems to be provided by the HEI formulation: facts about how one's action (in the circumstances) would bear on humanity in the person—on our capacities as autonomous agents—are the most fundamental morally relevant features in determining the moral status of actions.

So, for instance, the reason the second of the two maxims featured in the example about lying to the would-be killers (M5) is to be favored for use in Kant's tests over the first one (M4) is that it contains some morally relevant information that is not present in M4. The fact that one's telling the truth or even being otherwise evasive might well lead to the death of an innocent person, thus annihilating that person's autonomy, is a morally relevant feature of the circumstances in question.

In general terms, I am suggesting that we look to the HEI formulation of the Categorical Imperative and, in particular, to the derived duties that make up Kant's system of ethical duties (to oneself and to others) as a basis for deciding which features of actions and circumstances are morally relevant and thus should be included in a specification of one's maxim. In other words, the duties featured in Kant's system specify the main ways in which actions and omissions bear on respecting the humanity of persons. Whether an action would be an instance of suicide, or an instance of a lie, or an instance of defamation, or an instance of nonbeneficence, and so forth for the other duties, has to do with respecting humanity in oneself and others. In circumstances where one can save an innocent life only by telling a lie, the fact that by lying one would be saving someone has to do with protecting humanity and so is obviously morally relevant. But facts about the proposed time of some action and the names of individuals involved in the circumstances are not relevant; such facts are not reflected in any of the types of actions featured in Kant's ethical system.[17]

If, following my earlier suggestion, we view the HEI formulation of the Categorical Imperative as a moral criterion specifying what makes an action right or wrong, and if we think of the various duties that Kant attempts to derive from this formulation as specifying the main ways in which actions can affect respect for humanity, then we might ask of what use the UL formulation is. After all, it appears as if we can simply appeal to the HEI formulation to figure out what we ought to do, and thus the rather complicated testing procedure associated with the UL formulation is unnecessary.

Those interpreters of Kant's ethics who think that there are serious problems with the UL formulation would be glad to ignore it and simply concentrate on the HEI formulation. However, following my suggestion, one might also view the UL formulation as primarily a decision procedure that looks to the HEI formulation as a basis for properly formulating maxims to be tested. The idea would be that the UL formulation involves thinking about a course of action from the point of view of morality. In particular, it provides a method for agents to follow when they are considering whether certain facts about their circumstances can justify performing an action that, in other contexts, would be wrong. Ordinarily, acts of lying are wrong, but what about lying to save a would-be murder victim? Does this fact about the action justify lying? Determining whether one could universalize the relevant maxim is perhaps a way of deciding the issue from the moral point of view.

9. KANT'S THEORY OF VALUE

To complete our presentation of Kant's moral theory, let us turn briefly to Kant's theory of value. You may recall that Kant contrasts ends of the sort that can be brought about through action, and already existent ends including people. Certain instances of both kinds of end have a kind of elevated value that Kant refers to using such terms as "unconditional," "supreme," and "unqualified" to signify their comparative importance.

Human Dignity and the Value of Autonomy

In presenting his theory of right conduct, we have already touched on the idea that for Kant, autonomy, or the capacity for free choice, has intrinsic unconditional value; it is what confers on human beings (and rational agents generally) the kind of status that Kant refers to as dignity. One's capacity for autonomous choice, including especially the capacity to act for moral reasons—reasons other than those that are grounded in one's desires—is, as noted earlier, the basis for categorical requirements on choice and action. Kant refers to this particular capacity for autonomous choice as one's "predisposition to good in us, which makes the human being worthy of respect" (*MM* 6:441/562–63). Of course, one may misuse this capacity by acting immorally, and when one does, one's *use* of autonomy is bad or evil. Still, *as a capacity for good*, our autonomy and thus our dignity has, according to Kant, "unconditional, incomparable worth" (*G*, 4:436/85). So, it is an important feature of Kant's moral theory that because all persons are ends in themselves and thus deserving of a kind of respect, any person "can measure himself with every other being of this kind and value himself on a footing of equality with them" (*MM* 6:435/557). This sort of equality implies that one "cannot deny all respect to even a vicious man as a human being . . . even though by his deeds he makes himself unworthy of it" (*MM* 6: 463/580).

If it is one's predisposition to good associated with one's autonomy that is the basis of one's dignity and worthy of respect, what is this good to which Kant is referring?

Moral Worth

The good in question has to do with those sorts of ends that one can choose to produce, namely, a good will and being a person of moral virtue. These two ends are closely related and to understand what they are and how they are related, it is important to start with Kant's distinction between actions that merely fulfill one's obligations, actions *in accordance with* duty, and actions that are not only in accordance with duty but also are *done from the motive of duty*. The shopkeeper who gives correct change to young and inexperienced customers because he is interested in guarding his good business reputation fulfills a moral obligation and so acts in accordance with duty, but since his motive is one of self-interest, his dutiful action does not possess what Kant calls moral worth. Only when the act of giving correct change is motivated solely by the thought that the action is a duty does the shopkeeper's action possess moral worth.

But a single action done from the sole motive of duty does not mean that the agent is a morally virtuous person in general. For Kant, the kind of moral worth that concerns one's whole person—being a virtuous person—involves "the moral strength of a *human being's* will in fulfilling his duty" (*MM*, 6:405/533). The idea is that being a morally good person involves two basis elements. First, it involves being disposed to act from the sole motive of duty whenever duty calls, which Kant refers to as a *good will*. And, second, it involves being able to act consistently from a good will, which requires an inner strength that enables one to resist the temptation to transgress the requirements of duty. Together, a good will plus the strength to overcome temptation and act from a good will is what makes one a virtuous person.[18]

Moral worth possessed by persons, that is, moral virtue, plays a key role in Kant's conception of the highest good for human beings.

The Highest Good

Kant's view about the *highest (complete) good* for human beings is not only intrinsically interesting but also leads Kant to certain "practical postulates" concerning human immortality and God. While virtuous character is the supreme good for Kant, it is not the highest good, by which Kant seems to mean goodness in its most complete form.

> [F]or this [the highest good], happiness is also required. . . . For to need happiness, to be also worthy of it, and yet not to participate in it cannot be consistent with the perfect volition of a rational being that would at the same time have all power, even if we think of such a being only for the sake of experiment. (*CPR*, 5:110/228–29)

Kant's point seems to be that human beings are (in part) essentially creatures with needs and desires whose satisfaction constitutes each such being's happiness. If we reflect on a situation in which an individual who possesses virtue is also happy and compare it with a situation in which that same virtuous person lacks happiness, we see that the former situation is better than the latter. Thus, according to Kant, the highest good for human beings involves two components: the possession of virtuous character (which, as the supreme good, represents a limiting condition on other components of the highest good) together with happiness (understood as a reward for one's virtuous character). The reason that virtue is "supreme" is because it's worth or goodness does not depend on (is not "conditional on") anything else. It's worth is owing to its intrinsic nature. But an individual's happiness as something good—good in the sense of its being worthy of approval—does depend on the character of the individual whose happiness it is. As Kant remarks: "an impartial rational spectator can take no delight in seeing the uninterrupted prosperity of a being graced with no feature of a pure and good will (*G*, 4:393/49). And because the goodness of happiness is dependent in this way on having a good will (and, we might add, on being virtuous), being in a state of virtue is the limiting condition on happiness as a component of the highest, complete good.

However, for Kant, as we have seen, the demands of duty and the pursuit of one's own happiness are often in conflict. Certainly, coming to have a morally virtuous character is no guarantee that in this life one will be happy. After all, the self-sacrificing son who sadly puts aside his dream of becoming a lawyer in order to carry on the family farming business may not be particularly happy, despite acting on his sense of filial duty. But since Kant insists (for reasons we shall not go into here) that the highest good must be attainable, he is led to two postulates, *postulates of practical reason*. Since, according to Kant, coming to have a truly virtuous character, understood as a state of *complete* moral perfection (what Kant refers to as *holiness*), is something that one cannot achieve during this lifetime—it is always in progress—we must recognize that

> [t]his endless progress is, however, possible only on the presupposition of the existence and personality of the same rational being continuing endlessly (which is called immortality of the soul). Hence the highest good is practically possible only on the presupposition of the immortality of the soul, so that this, as inseparably connected with the moral law, is a postulate of pure practical reason. (*CPR*, 5:122/236)

This postulate takes care of the possibility of the first element of the highest good. But as already noted there is no necessary connection (at least in this life) between being virtuous and being happy. And this point leads to

> the supposition of the existence of a cause adequate to this effect [happiness as a reward for virtue], that is, it must postulate the existence of God as belonging necessarily to the possibility of the highest good. (*CPR*, 5:124/240)

Thus, the highest good—virtue rewarded with happiness—is only possible on the assumption that we are immortal and that there is a God. Those who are familiar with the epistemological doctrines of Kant's *Critique of Pure Reason* (1781) will recall that in that work, Kant argues that human knowledge about the world is limited to what can be based on experience (where experience includes introspection, as well as experience had through the five senses). In particular, Kant claims that although we can consistently conceive of such metaphysical things as freedom of the will, immortality of the soul, and God, nevertheless, human beings cannot have knowledge of such things; they are not possible objects of experience. In his moral writings, Kant still insists that humans cannot have knowledge of freedom, immortality, and God. However, freedom (autonomy) is a presupposition of the possibility of moral requirements as categorical imperatives, and immortality and God must be postulated in order to allow for the possibility of the highest good.[19]

10. BRIEF RECAP

This completes my presentation of Kant's moral theory, including his theory of right conduct and of value. As I mentioned at the outset of this chapter, Kant's views in ethics are complex, and I have only attempted to go over some of the basic elements of his theory. Since we have covered a good deal of territory, it might be useful, before turning to evaluation, to recall the major ideas in Kant's overall moral theory.

- *Kant's conception of moral requirements.* For Kant, moral requirements are categorical and apply to us in virtue of our powers of practical reason (our autonomy) and independently of our desires. They are expressed as categorical imperatives.

- *The supreme principle of morality.* Kant's Categorical Imperative understood as a moral criterion specifying what makes an action right or wrong is expressed by the Humanity as an End in Itself (HEI) formulation of Kant's supreme principle. Basically, it requires that we always treat humanity as an end in itself and never merely as a means to our own ends. The system of duties implied by this principle involves both duties to ourselves and to others.
- *The universality tests.* Kant's theory includes a decision procedure for coming to justified conclusions about the rightness and wrongness of actions. This procedure is expressed by Kant's Universal Law (UL) formulation of the Categorical Imperative.
- *The theory of value.* Kant's theory of value is based on the idea that our capacity for free choice (autonomy) and in particular our capacity for moral behavior has the sort of unconditional value that can ground unconditional, categorical moral requirements. According to Kant's account of moral worth, virtue is a matter of possessing a certain kind of strength—the strength required to do one's duty from the sole motive of duty (on occasions where duty calls). Finally, Kant's notion of the highest, most complete good is that of an individual being happy in proportion to her being virtuous. The possibility of the existence of this highest good requires that we postulate our own immortality and the existence of God.

11. EVALUATION OF KANT'S MORAL THEORY

Some advantages of Kant's theory are mentioned in the next, concluding section. In this section, I mainly focus on objections to this theory, partly because doing so helps deepen our understanding of Kant's complex views in ethics. The objections I wish to consider concern (1) Kant's conception of duty, (2) his account of moral virtue, and (3) his theory of right conduct. Let us take these up in order.

Moral Requirements (Duties) as Requirements of Reason

Kant, as we have seen, believes that moral requirements are requirements of reason on choice and action. In particular, he thinks that there are certain ends of action that reason, apart from any of our desires, prescribes for us as rational agents. The ends of self-perfection and the happiness of others are the two most basic obligatory ends in Kant's ethical system. But are there really any ends that it would be intrinsically irrational to fail to adopt? Whether there are such rationally required ends is a difficult and complex issue over which contemporary philosophers disagree.

Many philosophers interested in questions about practical rationality are in basic agreement with the Scottish philosopher David Hume (1711–1776), who argued that when it comes to what it is rational and irrational to do, reason can only function to help us discover ways to best satisfy our desires. As Hume dramatically put it: "Reason is, and ought only to be the slave of the passions, and can never pretend to any other office than to serve and obey them" (Hume, [1739] 1978, 415). On Hume's instrumentalist view of practical reason, there cannot be any truly valid categorical imperatives since they purport to set forth requirements on choice and action not based on desire. But if all reasons for action are based on desire, then the only sorts of requirements possible are those expressed by mere hypothetical imperatives.[20]

Suppose that Hume and his followers are right and there are no intrinsically rational requirements of reason on choice and action, that all reasons for action are based on our desires. What then?

In that case, there are options in relation to Kant's moral theory. The first is that we can agree with Kant that our ordinary notion of duty is based on the assumption that there are categorical requirements of reason; then, if Hume is right, we have to conclude that the ordinary conception of duty rests on a false assumption. And if our ordinary conception rests on a false assumption, we would have to conclude that there really are no moral duties (given what we mean by a moral duty). Consider a parallel. Ordinary religious claims of Christians presuppose that there is a God of a certain sort. Suppose there is no such God, what then? Clearly, we would have to conclude that religious claims about God are false—there is no such being about which such claims are true.

The other option in response to Hume on this matter is to question whether the ordinary conception of duty really does presuppose that there are categorical requirements of reason on choice and action. Some philosophers have claimed that we should understand ordinary moral claims about duty as involving a system of hypothetical imperatives.[21] One way to make sense of this suggestion is to suppose that insofar as we value and desire human flourishing, certain kinds of actions should be avoided and other sorts of actions should be encouraged. Moral requirements, on this conception, get their binding force from the desire for personal flourishing and the recognition that one's chances of flourishing are greater if individuals accept a code of behavior that protects the interests of individuals in certain ways and positively promotes everyone's interests.

I have not rehearsed any of the specific criticisms that Hume and his followers might press against the Kantian view of practical reason; I have simply noted that this issue deeply affects the overall plausibility of Kant's moral theory and is an issue of ongoing philosophical concern.[22]

Kant on Virtue

According to Kant's account of moral virtue, the virtuous person—the person with a good will—(1) is someone who possesses moral strength of will in being able to overcome temptation and (2) is someone who acts from the sole motive of duty (when duty calls).

According to critics, Kant's account of moral virtue is problematic on both counts. First, Kant seems to portray the truly virtuous person as someone who is in a state of conflict in having to overcome temptation in the face of duty. But this conflict model of the virtuous agent is contrasted by the critics with the picture of someone whose desires and feelings are in complete harmony with her moral obligations, someone who does not suffer from the kind of conflict that is characteristic of the Kantian virtuous person. Critics making this point often look to the work of Aristotle, who distinguishes the person of mere continence from the truly virtuous person. Someone is continent if he is able to muster the moral strength of will to overcome temptation, while the truly virtuous person for Aristotle does not (in general) suffer from such conflict. If we reflect on which of these two sorts of persons seems morally preferable, it is clear that we think the latter more desirable than the former. The person who has to resist the temptation to steal is in a less morally desirable state than someone who does not consider stealing as a serious option. If this is correct, then Kant's account of the virtuous person seems defective as a moral ideal.

The second objection to Kant's account of virtue has to do with his claim that only the motive of duty has moral value and hence that motives like love and benevolence lack such value. Suppose that you are convalescing in a hospital and one of your friends, Asha, comes to visit. Compare two cases.[23] In the first, Asha comes to see you because of her genuine care and concern for you—you are someone she very much likes. In the second, she comes to see you only because she thinks it is her duty to do so. Now even if we think that acting from the sole motive of duty is of moral value, it seems clear (from the case I've described) that we place value on motives other than the motive of duty. Reflection upon such cases has led many philosophers to claim that altruistic motives and emotions like care, compassion, and direct concern for others possess moral value.

I will not attempt to evaluate these criticisms. However, it is worth noting that in recent years scholars of Kant's ethics have increasingly turned their attention to Kant's later moral writings, especially *The Metaphysics of Morals*, where his developed views on moral virtue are arguably closer to the Aristotelian harmony conception of the morally virtuous person.[24] Also, the austere Kantian doctrine that only the motive of duty confers moral worth on actions has been defended against those who would claim that other motives and emotions have moral worth.[25] At this time, it seems to me that our understanding of Kant's account of virtue is in transition, so it would be premature to either endorse or dismiss this aspect of Kant's overall moral theory.

Theory of Right Conduct

Let us now turn to Kant's theory of right conduct and, in particular, his supreme moral principle, the Categorical Imperative. I wish to raise questions about its justification and about its role in moral theory.

On justifying the Categorical Imperative. In the *Groundwork*, Kant tells his readers that the twofold aim of the book is to set forth and establish the supreme principle of morality. Kant attempts to establish his supreme principle by arguing that (1) human beings must presuppose that they possess autonomy (freedom of the will) and that (2) the principle governing autonomy is the Categorical Imperative. In presenting the HEI formulation of the Categorical Imperative, we noted the deep connection between morality and autonomy in Kant's thinking. However, we did not explore Kant's difficult and controversial argument connecting autonomy and the Categorical Imperative, and this is not the place to take it up.

Instead, let me suggest that even if Kant's attempt to establish the Categorical Imperative fails, one might attempt to justify it by showing that it fits well with, and helps explain our considered moral judgments. In other words, one might appeal to the standards of internal support and explanatory power in attempting to justify this principle. An exploration of these matters would take us well beyond our survey of Kant's moral theory and so cannot be pursued here.

On the role of the Categorical Imperative in moral theory. Kant's Categorical Imperative is supposed to function as the supreme principle of morality, serving both as a moral criterion and as a decision procedure. Can it plausibly do so?

Some critics complain that the Categorical Imperative, because it is so abstract, is necessarily insensitive to morally relevant details of concrete particular situations calling for moral decision. The idea is that the Categorical Imperative seems to yield a kind of moral absolutism according to which certain general types of action are always morally wrong.[26] But such absolutism, because it is insensitive to morally relevant details of particular situations, overlooks exceptional cases, cases in which suicide, lying, and other such actions are not wrong. If this charge can be made to stick, then Kant's theory would violate the standard of internal support.

I do not think this sort of objection, based on an appeal to the standard of internal support, has much force against Kant's theory. In presenting his system of duties, I made a point of explaining how particular facts about concrete situations calling for a moral decision play a role in Kant's considered view. This point emerges clearly from Kant's various casuistical questions which we noted at the end of section 6. Since we have already dealt with this issue, we need not revisit it here.

Also, my formulation of Kant's theory of right conduct associated with the HEI formula allows for the idea that there can be cases where more than one duty from Kant's system applies to a particular situation, each duty favoring an action incompatible with performing the action favored by the other, and where it is the duty that most respects humanity as an end in itself that one is morally obligated to perform. This way of formulating Kant's theory presupposes that there can be some instances in which, say, the duty not to lie is overridden by a duty (based on beneficence) to save an innocent life. This way of thinking about conflicting duties anticipates the moral theory of W. D. Ross which we take up in the next chapter.

A second objection has to do with indeterminacy. According to my interpretation, the HEI formulation of the Categorical Imperative represents Kant's fundamental moral criterion of right action. But critics have expressed skepticism about the possibility of basing a system of duties on a moral principle that features the concept of respecting humanity. The problem is that this concept is quite vague and there will be many actions where it is doubtful that there is a determinate fact of the matter about whether it respects humanity. Kant's theory thus fails to satisfy the determinacy standard for evaluating moral theories.

To take just one example, consider the action of killing a human being. A pacifist might claim that any instance of intentionally killing a human being (even in war and self-defense) is wrong because all such killing involves a violation of respect for humanity. Kant and many others would no doubt disagree. But is the concept of respecting humanity clear enough in what it involves to decide on the basis of the concept of respecting humanity whether or not the pacifist is right about killing humans? This is but one example, but it illustrates the worry about determinacy stemming from the fact that the notion of respecting humanity is so vague.

This worry is nicely expressed by James Griffin:

> Every moral theory has the notion of equal respect at its heart: regarding each person as, in some sense, on an equal footing with every other one. Different moral theories parlay this vague notion into different conceptions. . . . [M]oral theories are not simply derivations from these vague notions, because the notions are too vague to allow anything as tight as a derivation. (Griffin, 1986, 208)

Griffin's talk of "equal respect for persons" is equivalent to talk about respecting humanity. We can illustrate Griffin's point by noting that in developing and defending a version of utilitarianism, Bentham claimed that on his theory, every person counts equally in determining the morality of an action. In short, many, if not all, of the moral theories we have already considered can fairly claim to capture the idea that persons are to be treated with equal respect.

The upshot is that although the idea of respecting humanity, or, equivalently, treating persons as ends in themselves, is an intuitively attractive moral ideal, it is too vague to be the basis for a supreme moral principle that one can use to derive a system of moral duties. To be fair, we have not spent time examining various proposals for understanding Kant's notion of treating persons merely as means, and arguably Kant's conception of dignity, when spelled out, together with a particular conception of treating persons merely as means, may serve to add content to the HEI formulation enough to be the basis for deriving (by argument) the various duties that compose Kant's system.[27] But suppose this cannot be made to work. What then?

What this implies for Kant's ethical system is that when it comes to understanding what it is that makes actions right or wrong, the real work is done at the level of the various duties to oneself and duties to others that were summarized in figures 8.1 and 8.2. That is, instead of thinking of Kant's moral theory in terms of a very general moral principle that can be used to derive more specific duties, think of his system as involving a plurality of moral rules—rules that forbid suicide, lying, defamation, and other duties of omission, as well as rules that require self-development, beneficence, and other duties of commission. We end up with a theory of right conduct that is properly described as a version of moral pluralism—there is a plurality of basic morally relevant features of actions and circumstances whose presence bears on the deontic status of actions.

But moral pluralism of this sort leads to questions about conflict of duty situations. Conflict of duty situations are ones in which one must choose between satisfying two or more duties, because they can't all be satisfied. In the example of the would-be killers who are inquiring into the whereabouts of someone you are hiding, you must choose between observing the duty not to lie and observing the duty of beneficence to help those in need (in this case the innocent would-be victim). Conflict of duty situations are particularly important since moral quandaries about such issues as abortion, euthanasia, capital punishment, treatment of animals, and others involve conflicting values and obligations. How can Kant's theory deal with such cases?

One suggestion (mentioned earlier) would be to use the UL formulation of the Categorical Imperative where the maxim to be tested mentions all of the morally relevant information pertaining to the situation. Perhaps testing such maxims will determine how one is to act, and thus determine which of the competing duties should be observed. This possibility needs to be explored, but we cannot pause here to do so.[28]

Another suggestion is that we make use of Kant's distinction between perfect and imperfect duties. Kant indicates that perfect, narrow duties are strict while imperfect, wide duties are not. Applied to conflict of duty cases, the idea would be that when we must choose between fulfilling a perfect duty and fulfilling an imperfect duty, the former, stricter duty is to be observed. After all, imperfect, wide duties allow latitude as to the time and manner of fulfillment. So when any such duty conflicts with a perfect duty, doesn't it make sense to comply with the strict duty?

This proposal has two rather obvious difficulties. First, we have already described a case in which, arguably, the duty to render aid to someone (a duty of beneficence) outweighs one's duty not to lie. Again, if I have made a promise to meet someone at a specific time to help with some project of theirs, wouldn't I be doing the right thing if, on my way to keep my appointment, I break my promise in order to help an accident victim? Here, an imperfect duty seems to outweigh a perfect duty.

A second obvious problem arises in cases where a perfect duty conflicts with a perfect duty or an imperfect duty conflicts with another imperfect duty. The proposal under consideration says nothing about such cases. I have an imperfect duty to develop my moral powers and, in particular, a duty to strive to have a good will. But what if I am a budding young artist and recognize that the only way to ascend to the top of my field is to become the protégé of a great artist of dubious character? I judge that being under the direction of this great artist will no doubt lead me to adopt a way of life that will conflict with developing my moral powers. In short, my imperfect duty to develop my natural talents conflicts with my imperfect duty to develop my moral character. Now it seems pretty clear what Kant would say about this matter, but in claiming that the duty to develop one's moral self outweighs the other duty, we have gone beyond the proposal under consideration.

What, then, should we say about conflict of duty situations in relation to Kant's moral theory? Here, again, I think the most plausible route is to admit that any moral theory, including Kant's, is limited in its power to resolve such conflicts. I thus propose that we interpret Kant's theory as a limited pluralistic moral theory.

It is a version of pluralism because (as explained earlier) when it comes to specifying those features of actions that make them right or wrong, the real work is done (so I claim) by the moral rules featured in Kant's system of duties. On my proposal what we have is a set of moral rules—rules featuring the various duties to oneself and to others—and when they conflict, there is no super principle or rule that can adjudicate the conflict. In short, I propose that if we are skeptical of the idea that Kant's Categorical Imperative can function, as he seems to have thought, as a very general moral criterion with determinate implications for the deontic status of actions, what we are left with is a limited, pluralistic moral theory.

12. CONCLUSION

Let us conclude with a brief overall assessment of Kant's moral theory, bringing together some of the critical remarks made in the previous section.

In criticizing Kant's theory of moral virtue, we have raised some standard objections that question the austerity of Kant's picture of the virtuous agent. However, we have also noted that in recent years Kant's ethics scholars have been paying more attention to his later, somewhat neglected moral writings, which seem to indicate a less austere and thus more plausible conception of virtue.

Intuitive appeal. Regarding Kant's theory of right conduct, I think we can agree that his guiding idea that morality has to do with treating humanity as an end in itself has a great deal of intuitive appeal. It also has some comparative advantages over some of its main rivals. Unlike the natural law theory, it is not embroiled in sticky questions about intending versus merely foreseeing; and unlike utilitarianism, it is not guilty of being overly demanding in its requirements. Moreover, because Kant's theory features both duties of self-perfection and duties concerning the happiness of others, it combines the best of natural law and utilitarian traditions.

Consistency and applicability. Against Kant's tests, we noted that unless there is a solution to the problem of relevant maxims, the UL formulation of the Categorical Imperative will lead to inconsistent verdicts about the morality of specific actions. My suggestion for dealing with this problem is to recognize that the HEI formulation of the Categorical Imperative is supposed to specify fundamental morally relevant features of actions—features that should be reflected in maxims appropriate for moral testing.

Internal support, explanatory power, and determinacy. We also raised questions about how Kant's theory of right conduct is to be justified. We did not explore Kant's notoriously difficult attempt to justify the Categorical Imperative. We did note, however, that if this principle can be shown to fit with our considered moral beliefs and can plausibly explain what makes actions right or wrong, then in satisfying the standards of internal support and explanatory power, it will be strongly justified.

Rather than pursue such matters, I suggested that the central idea of respecting humanity that is featured in the HEI formulation of the Categorical Imperative is too vague to yield determinate moral verdicts about a wide range of cases. I furthermore suggested that Kant's theory of right conduct might best be viewed as a system of moral rules—some rules specifying duties to oneself, others specifying duties to others—without there being a super principle from which these various rules might be rigorously derived. This means that in cases in which the moral rules conflict, Kant's theory (that is, my proposed reworking of the theory) is limited in its power to resolve such conflicts and generate determinate moral verdicts.

I have not argued at length for this way of viewing Kant's ethics and will not be able to do so here. But since my proposal in relation to Kant's moral theory is greatly influenced by the pluralist moral theory of W. D. Ross, let us now turn to Ross's theory.

NOTES

1. I will continue to refer to Kant's supreme moral principle using capital letters.

2. I have used the Mary Gregor translations of Kant's moral writings that are included in *Practical Philosophy* (see references section), and I will cite Kant's works using the following abbreviations: *G* for *Groundwork of the Metaphysics of Morals*; *CPR* for *Critique of Practical Reason*; and *MM* for *The Metaphysics of Morals*. References include the volume and page number from the Akademie edition of Kant's works (so that readers using translations other than Gregor will be able to locate quoted passages by referring to the Akademie page numbers included in most translations), followed by the page number from *Practical Philosophy*.

3. In chapter 4, section 4, we encountered the distinction between practical and theoretical reason in connection with Aquinas's moral theory.

4. That is, all of its instances that correctly specify the necessary means to some end.

5. As we shall see in connection with categorical imperatives, Kant imposes constraints on the sorts of ends a fully rational agent would adopt.

6. Kant denies that we can determine with any degree of reliability which ends will, if achieved, contribute to our own happiness. He thus denies that we can formulate hypothetical imperatives that specify the means we must take in order to achieve our own happiness. Instead, he says we must make do with "counsels of prudence," which recommend certain courses of action with no guarantee that following them will in fact result in happiness. See *G*, 4:418–9/71.

7. Among the category of ends that can be brought about through action, Kant distinguishes desire-based ends from obligatory ends. This distinction will be explained below in section 5.

8. For illuminating work on this issue, see the work of Samuel J. Kerstein, 2007, 2009, and 2011.

9. Kant is presumably referring to Marcus Curtius, an ancient Roman figure who (according to legend) rode his horse into a great chasm which (again according to legend) could only be closed if something precious (in this case, the courage and strength of a Roman warrior) were sacrificed.

10. See below, note 26.

11. It would be incorrect to say that all actions whose performance or nonperformance would fail to promote humanity violate imperfect duty since, normally, actions that count as fulfilling imperfect duties are not morally required (owing to the latitude in fulfilling them), and so failing to perform them is not necessarily a violation of such duties. However, there are cases in which failing to promote humanity constitutes a violation of imperfect duty. Arguably, in cases where some stranger is in desperate need of one's help (no one else is around) and one can help him or her at little or no cost to oneself, it would be a violation of the duty of beneficence to refrain (for no good reason) from helping. Kant's doctrine of imperfect duty is complex, and I have not discussed it in any detail. For a useful discussion of such duties, see Baron, 1995, chapter 3.

12. I defend this interpretation of the different roles of the HEI and UL formulations in Timmons, 1997.

13. I am following Kant in not making explicit what further end this person might have, since the argument Kant uses to show that this maxim would fail one of his tests does not depend on such information.

14. This is a version of an example by Feldman, 1978, 116.

15. I am assuming that the maxim would also pass the CW test. But even if it does not, it is a defect in Kant's universalization test if this maxim does not fail the CC test.

16. This problem is often called the problem of relevant descriptions because maxims contain descriptions of one's action and circumstances.

17. This is not to say that such facts could never be relevant; facts of this sort might be relevant, but only if they have a bearing on treating humanity as an end in itself. In the false-promising case I am imagining, such facts have no such bearing and so are morally irrelevant.

18. In chapter 10 on virtue ethics, the topic of virtue and vice will be discussed in some detail.

19. In *The Critique of Practical Reason* (at 5:114/231), Kant claims that if the highest good is not possible then the moral law (the Categorical Imperative) is false, which for Kant would mean that moral requirements are not genuine. However, Kant's reasons for this claim are obscure and the subject of scholarly debate.

20. A more radical critique of Kant's ethics involves the claim that the kinds of moral judgments that are distinctively deontological, including for instance the judgment in the trolley footbridge scenario that it would be wrong to push the large man onto the track in order to save five innocent workers (for a brief presentation of the trolley cases, see chapter 4, section 12), are driven by emotion and are not the products of a rational process. Greene, 2008 defends this view on the basis of results from empirical science, including evolutionary theory. For a reply to Greene, see Timmons, 2008.

21. A well-known contemporary defense of this view is Foot, 1972.

22. For a recent and advanced discussion of this matter, see the papers in Cullity and Gaut, 1997.

23. This example is like the one featured in Stocker, 1976.

24. See, for example, Johnson, 1997 and Engstrom, 2002.

25. See Marcia Baron's essay in Baron, Pettit, and Slote, 1997.

26. Moral absolutism was discussed in chapter 4 in connection with the natural law theory. Kant himself encourages this interpretation of his theory in a short essay he published toward the end of his life, "On the Right to Lie from Beneficent Motives," in which he claims that lying, even to save an innocent life, is always morally wrong. However, as I hope my presentation

of Kant's moral theory makes clear, moral absolutism of this sort is not implied by either of the formulations of the Categorical Imperative we have examined. Hence, I reject absolutist interpretations of Kant's moral theory.

27. For a discussion of Kant's attempt to derive a system of duties from the Categorical Imperative, see Smit and Timmons, 2013.

28. For more on this issue, see Timmons, 2006.

FURTHER READING

Philosophical Literature

Aune, Bruce. 1979. *Kant's Theory of Morals*. Princeton, NJ: Princeton University Press. An accessible presentation of the main doctrines of Kant's *Groundwork* and *The Metaphysics of Morals*.

Baron, Marcia W. 1995. *Kantian Ethics Almost without Apology*. Ithaca, NY: Cornell University Press. Part 1 considers issues connected with supererogation and imperfect duty in Kant's system, while part 2 deals with matters concerning Kant's conception of virtuous disposition and acting from duty.

———. 1997. "Kantian Ethics." In *Three Methods of Ethics*, by Marcia W. Baron, Philip Pettit, and Michael Slote. Oxford: Blackwell. A relatively short and useful overview of Kant's moral theory in which it is contrasted with, and defended in relation to, consequentialism and virtue ethics.

Betzler, Monika, ed. 2008. *Kant's Ethics of Virtue*, Berlin & New York: Walter de Gruyter GmbH. Eleven essays by top scholars on various aspects of Kant's theory of virtue.

Denis, Lara, ed. 2010. *Kant's Metaphysics of Morals: A Critical Guide*. Twelve newly written essays on major topics in Kant's final main work in practical philosophy.

Guyer, Paul, ed. 1998. *Kant's Groundwork of the Metaphysics of Morals: Critical Essays*. Lanham, MD: Rowman & Littlefield. Essays by leading Kant's ethics scholars covering the main doctrines in Kant's *Groundwork*. Also included is a useful bibliography.

———. 2000. *Kant on Freedom, Law, and Happiness*. Cambridge: Cambridge University Press. Twelve essays on central topics in Kant's moral and political philosophy.

———. 2007. *Kant's Groundwork of the Metaphysics of Morals: A Reader's Guide*. New York: Continuum Press. A useful guide to Kant's *Groundwork*.

Herman, Barbara. 1993. *The Practice of Moral Judgment*. Cambridge, MA: Harvard University Press. A collection of Herman's essays that are particularly suggestive in relation to Kant's views on moral worth and the application of the Categorical Imperative.

Hill, Thomas E., Jr. 1992. *Dignity and Practical Reason*. Ithaca, NY: Cornell University Press. A collection of some of Hill's essays on Kant's ethics. Of particular interest is his attempt to make sense of and defend the Kingdom of Ends formulation of the Categorical Imperative, which was not discussed in this chapter.

———. 2000. *Respect, Pluralism, and Justice*. Oxford: Oxford University Press. Ten essays by Hill on topics relating to the book's title.

———. 2002. *Human Welfare and Moral Worth*. Oxford: Oxford University Press. Twelve of Hill's essays on various themes in Kant's ethics.

———, ed. 2009. *The Blackwell Guide to Kant's Ethics*. Oxford: Wiley-Blackwell. A useful collection of twelve essays by various scholars covering basic themes in Kant's ethical and political philosophy.

Horn, Christof, and Dieter Schönecker, eds. 2006. *Groundwork for the Metaphysics of Morals*. Berlin: Walter de Gruyter GmbH. A collection of thirteen essays that collectively comprise a cooperative commentary on the *Groundwork*.

Johnson, Robert. 2008. "Kant's Moral Philosophy." *The Stanford Encyclopedia of Philosophy*, ed. E. N. Zalta. http://plato.stanford.edu. A very accessible overview of key elements in Kant's moral philosophy.

Korsgaard, Christine. 1996. *Creating the Kingdom of Ends*. Cambridge: Cambridge University Press. Essays that deal with themes from both the *Groundwork* and *The Metaphysics of Morals*.

O'Neill, Onora. 1989. *Constructions of Reason*. Cambridge: Cambridge University Press. Essays on Kant's ethics including important work on maxims and the tests associated with Kant's UL formulation.

Reath, Andrews, and Jens Timmermann, eds. 2010. *Kant's Critique of Practical Reason: A Critical Guide*. Cambridge: Cambridge University Press. Nine newly written essays that collectively explore main themes in Kant's second major work in moral philosophy.

Sedgwick, Sally. 2008. *Kant's Groundwork of the Metaphysics of Morals: An Introduction*. Cambridge: Cambridge University Press. A useful commentary and exegesis of Kant's *Groundwork*.

Timmermann, Jens, ed. 2010. *Kant's Groundwork of the Metaphysics of Morals: A Critical Guide*. Cambridge: Cambridge University Press. Eleven newly written essays that collectively explore main themes in Kant's *Groundwork*.

Timmons, Mark, ed. 2002. *Kant's Metaphysics of Morals: Interpretative Essays*. Oxford: Oxford University Press. Essays by different scholars on various aspects of Kant's more mature moral philosophy.

Trampota, Andreas, Oliver Sensen, and Jens Timmermann, eds. 2012. *Kant's Tugendlehre* (Doctrine of Virtue). Berlin and New York: Walter de Gruyter GmbH. A collection of essays by various scholars that collectively represent a cooperative commentary on part 2 of *The Metaphysics of Morals*, The Doctrine of Virtue.

Wood, Allen. 1999. *Kant's Ethical Thought*. Cambridge: Cambridge University Press. A detailed interpretation of Kant's moral theory.

Empirical Literature

Greene, Joshua. 2008. "The Secret Joke of Kant's Soul." In *Moral Psychology*, vol. 3, ed. W. Sinnott-Armstrong. Cambridge, MA: MIT Press. Uses results from empirical psychology and brain science in an effort to show that classic versions of deontology, including Kant's, represent mere attempts to rationalize what are really spontaneous emotional reactions that prompt distinctively deontological judgments about particular cases.

9

Moral Pluralism

Jean-Paul Sartre, a twentieth-century French existentialist philosopher, describes the case of a young man who is torn between staying with his mother and joining the French Free Forces in resisting Germany during World War II.[1] On one hand, he has a great deal of concern for his mother, who will be alone if he leaves, and feels he ought to stay with her. But, on the other hand, he feels an obligation to his country in this time of war. He can't satisfy both obligations. What should he do?

This is a conflict of duty situation. In the last chapter, the case involving someone hiding an intended murder victim and lying to the would-be killers is another instance of this type of situation. Moral theories featuring a supreme moral principle, such as classical utilitarianism, imply a resolution of such conflicts. For the utilitarian, the young man's true obligation is to perform whichever action would maximize utility. Granted, deciding on the basis of utilitarian calculation what he ought to do will involve educated guesswork, and there is no assurance that the young man (or anyone else) would come to the correct (utilitarian) moral conclusion about what should be done. Nevertheless, the utilitarian can claim that there is a correct answer to the young man's quandary. It is the answer dictated by the principle of utility.

But suppose there is no single moral principle expressing some single general feature upon which the deontic status of all actions depends? This is what Sartre thought. He was skeptical of there being any such principle that one could apply to the case of the young man that would determine which of the courses of action open to him is morally right. Nor did Sartre think that there was some other rigorous method by which the man's dilemma could be resolved. Suppose Sartre is right about this matter. What then for moral theory?

One reaction is to give up on certain pretensions of moral theory, particularly those associated with monistic moral theories, and embrace some form of moral pluralism. To see what this involves, let us consider the contrast between monism and pluralism in ethics.

1. MORAL PLURALISM

Regarding the morality of actions, *moral monism* is the view that there is a single basic feature of actions that determines their deontic status. Hedonistic utilitarianism represents a version of monism since, on this view, an action is morally right if and only if it would produce at least as much overall utility (measured in terms of increase of pleasure and reduction of pain) as any other alternative action one might perform instead.

One criticism of hedonistic utilitarianism and other forms of moral monism is that they are overly reductive: they attempt to boil all morally relevant considerations down to a single, fundamental feature possessed of moral relevance. The result, according to the critics, is that such views distort moral reality, making it appear much more unified and simpler than it really is.

Instead, one might hold that there is a plurality of equally basic morally relevant features and thus a plurality of moral principles or rules.[2] The idea would be that each such rule expresses a basic morally relevant feature that, when present, bears on the overall deontic status of actions. So, for example, suppose that being an instance of lying is a basic morally relevant feature an action might possess, and suppose the same is true of being an instance of giving aid to someone in need. If so, we would have at least two basic moral rules, and, being basic, they could not be derived from some further, even more basic moral principle. Morality might be too complex to be captured in a single principle specifying some single underlying feature that determines the deontic status of any action.

One can be a pluralist about the nature of right action, about the nature of intrinsic value, about moral worth, or any combination. If we focus for the time being on the nature of right action, *moral pluralism* involves two main claims:

1. There is a plurality of basic moral rules.
2. There is no underlying moral principle from which these rules can be derived and which thus serves to justify them.

Although there are various ways in which moral pluralism might be developed, the version we find in the writings of twentieth-century philosopher W. D. Ross (1877–1971) is one of the most influential versions in current moral theorizing. This chapter will focus on the rudiments of Ross's moral theory.

2. MORAL PLURALISM AND
CONFLICT OF DUTY SITUATIONS

In recognizing a plurality of basic moral rules, moral pluralism must come to grips with conflict of duty situations. Suppose that the list of basic moral rules recognized by the pluralist includes:

P1 One has a duty to keep one's promises.
P2 One has a duty to render aid to those in need.

Now consider the following case.

> *Important promise.* John has promised Jill to pick her up at her house at noon on Friday in order to get her to an important job interview. Jill's car is in the shop and so she is depending on John who, in the past, has always been reliable. However, while driving to Jill's house, John sees a stopped vehicle, hood up, and the motorist inspecting the engine, likely in need of help given the frustrated look on his face. John is mechanically inclined and knows a lot about car engines. Unfortunately, no one else is currently in sight who might help the motorist. But John can't stop to help and also get Jill to her job interview on time; he has to choose between helping someone in need and keeping his promise to his friend.

In this particular situation, John can't fulfill both obligations expressed by P1 and P2. Moreover, application of these two rules yields contradictory moral verdicts. P1 implies that he ought to keep his promise and thus that it would be wrong to stop and help. P2 implies the reverse: he ought to stop and help out and thus it would be wrong to keep his promise.

How might the moral pluralist handle such cases? One way would be to come up with some strict lexical ranking of the rules according to their relative importance. Rules higher up on the list would outrank, and hence take precedence over, those lower on the list. Call this brand of pluralism *lexical moral pluralism.*

Lexical moral pluralism can neatly handle cases of moral conflict. If, for example, we rank the rule about promise keeping higher than the rule about rendering aid, then in the sort of case envisioned, we have a way to resolve the moral quandary in which P1 and P2 come into conflict.

The obvious problem with this prioritizing strategy is simply that it does not seem possible to rank order the moral rules featured in the pluralist's theory and do so in a way that will yield plausible moral verdicts in all cases of conflict. For example, it is pretty clear that in *Important promise*, John ought to get Jill to her interview on time and so comply with P1. However, there are going to be cases in which the obligation to render aid to others outweighs in moral importance the obligation to keep one's promise, when it is not possible to do both. Consider a variation on the previous example.

Car accident. John has promised Jill to come over to her house mid-day to help her with a term paper due that afternoon. On his way over, he comes upon a serious one-car accident, the driver thrown from the car and in need of immediate help. No one else is around who might help. He won't be able to help the accident victim and make it to Jill's in time to help with her paper before it is due.

In this situation, unlike the previous one, the importance of rendering aid is greater than the importance of keeping one's promise. Of course, we may be able to form some generalizations about the relative importance of various types of obligations. Perhaps by and large the obligation to keep one's promises outweighs the obligation to help others. But the point is that it is not possible to come up with a fixed, once-and-for-all ranking that would tell us how, in every possible circumstance, we are to decide between competing moral obligations.

Then it might seem that the moral pluralist is in a serious bind. There are conflict of duty situations in which we have competing obligations, yet there does not seem to be a way to adjudicate the conflict. There are actually two problems facing the pluralist. First, if the pluralist is going to avoid having rules that yield contradictory moral verdicts, she must somehow formulate her rules or otherwise organize them so that contradiction is avoided. This is a matter of satisfying the consistency standard for evaluating moral theories, so call this the *consistency problem* for the pluralist. Second, the pluralist needs to explain how we can adjudicate conflicts among moral rules in circumstances where they conflict and thereby arrive at justified verdicts about the rightness and wrongness of actions. Call this the *adjudication problem.*[3]

3. PRIMA FACIE DUTIES

Ross's theory of right conduct involves a solution to this conflict problem. But to understand it, we must examine his particular version of moral pluralism, which features the notion of a *prima facie duty.*

To explain this notion, let us consider a very familiar sort of situation that does not involve having to make a moral decision. Suppose that you very much want to spend this evening with a certain friend, someone you are quite fond of. Your friend is dead set on going to see a particular film this evening and, in fact, has invited you to go. So, given your desire to spend time with her, you have a reason for going to the film in question. Moreover, if there are no other considerations that affect your choice, then not only do you have a reason to go to the film with your friend, you have a sufficient, all-things-considered reason to go.

However, suppose things are more complicated and it turns out that the film is one that you have recently seen and did not like, and you are quite sure that you would dislike having to sit through it again. So, you clearly have some reason for not going to the film with your friend. Since you have some reason for going and some reason for not going, you have to decide what to do by balancing your competing reasons. In balancing these competing reasons, you are trying to decide which of them is, in this situation at least, most important. Suppose you decide that spending time with your friend is more important in this situation than avoiding the film. All things considered, you decide that you should go.

Let us turn now to Ross. He distinguishes between what he calls a prima facie duty and a "duty proper" (which he also refers to as one's actual duty). His distinction here is basically the same as the one we just noted between what you have some reason to do and what you should do all things considered, only here we are concerned with what you have moral reasons to do. So one's *all-things-considered duty* is another name for what Ross sometimes calls one's duty proper and sometimes one's actual duty.

Here is how Ross explains the idea of a prima facie duty:

> I suggest "prima facie duty" or "conditional duty" as a brief way of referring to the characteristic (quite distinct from that of being a duty proper) which an act has, in virtue of being of a certain kind (e.g., the keeping of a promise), of being an act which would be a duty proper were it not at the same time of another kind which is morally significant. (Ross, 1930, 19–20)

Let us illustrate the idea of a prima facie duty using Ross's own example of keeping a promise. Suppose that I have promised to meet you at a specific time and place in order to help you with a writing assignment. My act of meeting you at the specific time and place has a certain feature or characteristic; namely, it is an instance of keeping a promise. This fact about my act is morally relevant (significant) and provides a moral reason in favor of my doing the act. Ross would say that because of this fact about my act, the act is a prima facie duty. To say that the action in question is a prima facie duty is to say that (1) it possesses some morally relevant feature that counts in favor of my doing the act and (2) this feature is such that were it the only morally relevant feature of my situation, then the act in question would be my duty proper.

Unfortunately, Ross's term *prima facie* is misleading, as he himself points out. It suggests that what he has in mind is some action that at first glance seems to be one's duty but which, upon closer inspection, is not. But this isn't what he means. Some action one might perform on some occasion is a prima facie duty if on the occasion in question one has a moral reason to perform the action. Perhaps a way of seeing what Ross has in mind is to notice that calling an action a prima facie duty is to consider it under a single description—a description that picks out a morally relevant feature of the action that constitutes a moral reason to either perform the action or refrain from performing the action (depending on whether the reason favors the action or disfavors it). Thus, to classify an action as a prima facie duty is to zero in on one aspect or feature of the action that has a bearing on its rightness or wrongness. As we shall see below in section 5, whether an action is what Ross calls a duty proper (and thus something that we are morally required to do) depends on all of its morally relevant features. But first, let us focus on Ross's list of basic prima facie duties.

4. BASIC PRIMA FACIE DUTIES

According to Ross, there are seven basic prima facie duties, each of which is featured in a moral rule. Here is a brief characterization of each.

- *Duties of fidelity.* Some duties of fidelity depend on one's having made an explicit promise to some party, which grounds a prima facie duty to keep one's promise. But Ross also recognizes an implicit promise to be truthful that one can normally be assumed to make when one engages in conversation with others. So this type of duty includes the duty to avoid lying and deception. So, for instance, the fact that an action would be an instance of lying is a moral reason that counts against performing that action—it is among the basic wrong-making features in morality.
- *Duties of reparation.* These duties depend on one's having in the past performed a wrongful act in regard to others. So the fact that an action would make up for a past wrong is a morally relevant feature of the act and counts as a basic moral reason in favor of performing the action.
- *Duties of gratitude.* This category of duty concerns one's having been benefited by others. The fact that an action of mine would constitute paying back one of my beneficiaries is a fundamentally morally relevant feature—a basic moral reason—that counts in favor of my performing the action in question.
- *Duties of justice.* Duties of justice here concern distribution of benefits among persons according to merit. So, for example, if someone is getting more or less than that person deserves, then (assuming one can do something about it) this fact constitutes a moral reason to rectify the situation.
- *Duties of beneficence.* One is often in a position to help others improve their character or their intelligence, or increase their pleasure and reduce their pain. That some action one could perform in a certain set of circumstances would result in such benefits to others is a fundamental morally relevant feature of one's situation and grounds a prima facie duty of beneficence. Expressing the same idea using the terminology of moral reasons, we can say that if one is in a situation in which one could benefit others in one or more of the ways mentioned above, then this fact about one's circumstances constitutes a moral reason in favor of performing the act of beneficence.
- *Duties of self-improvement.* Actions through which one would improve one's own character or intelligence are actions one has a prima facie duty to perform. The fact that some action I could perform on some occasion would promote the development of my own character or intelligence is a moral reason that favors performing the action in question.
- *Duties of nonmaleficence.* In addition to duties of beneficence, Ross recognizes a prima facie duty to avoid injuring others. The fact that an action of mine would in some way injure another person is a feature of an action that counts against doing it—this fact counts as a moral reason to avoid performing the action in

question. Thus, in addition to one's prima facie duty of beneficence, one also has a prima facie duty of nonmaleficence.

Ross recognizes additional prima facie duties, but he claims that they can be understood as arising from a combination of the basic ones on his list. Such prima facie duties are nonbasic. For instance, according to Ross, the prime facie duty to obey the laws of one's country results from the three basic prima facie duties of gratitude, fidelity, and beneficence:

> The duty of obeying the laws of one's country arises partly . . . from the duty of gratitude for the benefits one has received from it; partly from the implicit promise to obey [those laws]; and partly (if we are fortunate in our country) from the fact that its laws are potent instruments for the general good. (Ross, 1930, 27–28)

How does Ross attempt to justify this list of basic prima facie duties? In striking contrast to those moral philosophers who would attempt to prove moral principles or rules, Ross claims that because his seven basic rules of right conduct are self-evident, they need no proof:

> That an act, qua fulfilling a promise, or qua effecting a just distribution of goods, or qua returning services rendered, or qua promoting the good of others, or qua promoting the virtue or insight of the agent, is prima facie right, is self-evident; not in the sense that it is evident from the beginning of our lives, or as soon as we attend to the proposition for the first time, but in the sense that when we have reached sufficient mental maturity and have given sufficient attention to the proposition it is evident without any need of proof, or of evidence beyond itself. It is self-evident just as a mathematical axiom, or the validity of a form of inference, is evident. . . . In both cases we are dealing with propositions that cannot be proved, but that just as certainly need no proof. (Ross, 1930, 29–30)

Intuitionism in epistemology is the view that there are propositions expressing truths that can be understood and seen to be true (or at least justifiably held) without relying on independent evidence; their truth can be grasped by an exercise of intuition.[4] Ross's own brand of intuitionism involves some important complexity that we cannot pause to consider here, though we will return to it briefly in section 11. Let us turn instead to a statement of his theory of right conduct.

5. ROSS'S THEORY OF RIGHT CONDUCT

Just as there are features of certain actions that morally favor the doing of them, there are features of certain actions that count morally against the doing of them. Duties of nonmaleficence represent clear examples involving features that count against a course of action. Ross thus distinguishes between *right-making features*—moral reasons that count in favor of some action—and *wrong-making features*—moral reasons that count against some action. But here it is important to emphasize that the presence of a right-making feature does not automatically mean that the action is a right action (in the sense of being a duty). There might be other opposing features—opposing moral reasons—that outweigh the right-making feature that favors performing the action. And thus despite there being a moral reason in favor of performing the act, the act might still be morally wrong. Saying this is just a way of reminding ourselves that the kind of right- and wrong-making reasons featured in Ross's various prima facie duties simply refer to features which, taken alone, serve to make an action or omission a prima facie duty. We have already noted that, according to Ross's view, one's actual duty (duty proper) depends upon all the morally relevant features present in the situation. Furthermore, in the following passage, he makes it clear that one's actual duty depends on a comparison of various alternative actions open to one in a given situation.

> [R]ight acts can be distinguished from wrong acts only as being those which, of all those possible for the agent in the circumstances, have the greatest balance of prima facie rightness, in those respects in which they are prima facie right, over their prima facie wrongness, in those respects in which they are prima facie wrong. . . . For the estimation of the comparative stringency of these prima facie obligations no general rules can, so far as I can see, be laid down. (Ross, 1930, 41)

The idea is that in circumstances in which there is but one prima facie duty that applies, one's actual duty is solely determined by that lone prima facie duty. Suppose, for example, there is someone who needs help and I am in a position to help her. As already noted, this fact about my situation grounds a prima facie duty of beneficence to help. Now if, in the circumstances at hand, there are no other morally relevant features grounding any other prima facie duties, then my prima facie duty of beneficence turns out to be my actual, all-things-considered duty. However, Ross thinks that most situations in life calling for a moral response are not this simple. Rather, he thinks that in most situations we will be confronted with conflicting prima facie duties, and what he refers to as the "most stringent" of these duties is one's actual duty. To say that one prima facie duty is more stringent than another, competing prima facie duty is not, however, to say that the latter prima facie duty is somehow canceled out or "silenced." Rather, the idea is that in such situations, one prima facie duty overrides other, competing prima facie duties. Consequently, in cases where one has a prima facie duty that is overridden, this fact about the situation may generate a further prima facie duty. For instance, in the case where I ought to break my promise to you in order to help an accident victim, the fact that my prima facie duty to keep my promise is overridden (but not canceled) means that I now have a new prima facie duty of reparation—to do what is necessary to make it up to you.

Making use of the idea that in particular contexts some prima facie duties are more stringent than others, we can set forth the theory of right conduct associated with Ross's view as follows.

Theory of Right Conduct

An action A in some circumstance C is *obligatory* (one's actual duty) if and only if (and because) one has a prima facie duty to do A in C that is more stringent than any other conflicting prima facie duty that would favor performing some action other than A in C. That is, in Ross's terms, the comparative stringency of the prima facie duties relevant in circumstances C favor doing A over all other alternative courses of action open to one in C.

An action A is *wrong* in C if and only if (and because) one has a prima facie duty to refrain from performing A in C that is more stringent than any other conflicting prima facie duty that would favor performing A in C.

An action A in C is *optional* if and only if (and because) either (i) one has no prima facie duties in C, or (ii) if one is subject to conflicting prima facie duties in C—one or more favoring A and one or more favoring some alternative action—then these conflicting prima facie duties are equal in their stringency, neither one overrides the other.

According to Ross's theory of right action, then, what makes some particular action all-things-considered right or wrong depends on the presence of basic right-making and/or wrong-making features that figure in Ross's list of prima facie duties and their comparative stringency.[5]

Now that we have the rudiments of Ross's theory of right conduct before us, let us return to conflict of duty situations, which seem to pose a problem for pluralists.

6. CONFLICT OF DUTY SITUATIONS REVISITED

In section 2, we noted that any plausible version of moral pluralism must avoid both the consistency and the adjudication problems that concern conflict of duty situations. This section and the next explain how Ross handles them.

The consistency problem, recall, is that in cases of moral conflict, where two or more rules apply and together they yield inconsistent moral verdicts, nonlexical pluralism apparently fails to avoid contradiction. In the example we were using to illustrate this problem, the two moral rules

P1 One has a duty to keep one's promises.
P2 One has a duty to render aid to those in need.

both apply and lead to contradictory moral verdicts about what one ought to do.

The problem obviously stems from the fact that, as stated, both rules express absolute, exceptionless requirements. Since the moral rules expressing prima facie duties are clearly not exceptionless—the fact that they allow exceptions is built right into them—Ross avoids the problem. So, on behalf of Ross, we can replace the original rules with these:

RP1 One has a prima facie duty to keep one's promises.
RP2 One has a prima facie duty to render aid to those in need.

Obviously, softening the two original rules in this way allows that when a situation arises in which they both apply, but in which the agent cannot both keep a promise and render aid, one of the two prima facie duties is overridden and so gives way to the other. We don't end up with contradictory moral verdicts. Ross's theory, with its rules of prima facie duty, thus avoids the consistency problem.

But notice that resolving the consistency problem in this way does not tell us how we are to resolve moral conflicts. We are still left with the adjudication problem. Ross tells us (in the last passage quoted above) that there seem to be no rules that govern questions of comparative stringency in particular contexts, so how are we to make reasonable judgments about our all-things-considered duties?

7. THE ROLE OF MORAL JUDGMENT

It is Ross's view that coming to all-things-considered moral verdicts about a particular action in contexts where there are conflicting prima facie duties requires moral judgment. Such judgment is to be understood as a capacity for balancing and weighing competing moral considerations and determining which of them (if any) is most stringent—a capacity that is not simply a matter of following principles or rules. Moral judgment takes us beyond moral rules and involves a kind of "creative insight" into the situation under consideration in determining what ought or ought not to be done.[6] Ross points out that

> In this respect the judgment as to the rightness of a particular act is just like the judgment as to the beauty of a particular natural object or work of art. A poem is, for instance, in respect of certain qualities beautiful and in respect of certain others not beautiful; and our judgment as to the degree of beauty it possesses on the whole is never reached by logical reasoning from the apprehension of its particular beauties or particular defects. (Ross, 1930, 31)

In making aesthetic judgments about the beauty of some particular object, there are no precise principles or rules whose application yields a determinate aesthetic verdict; rather, in arriving at an overall aesthetic assessment, one must rely on aesthetic judgment. Similarly, in judging the rightness of some particular concrete action, all one can do is to examine carefully the various morally relevant facts of the case, determine which prima facie duties one has in the situation, and use one's capacity for moral judgment in coming to a conclusion about one's all-things-considered duty. If one's capacity for moral judgment is sufficiently developed, one will be able to arrive at a correct judgment about one's actual, all-things-considered duty. Of course, many situations involve a good deal of moral complexity, and Ross cautions that we should not expect to be able to judge our all-things-considered duties with certainty. The role of moral judgment, then, in coming to all-things-considered moral verdicts in particular cases is Ross's way of handling the adjudication problem.

Let us now continue our survey of Ross's pluralism by turning to his theory of value.

8. ROSS'S THEORY OF VALUE

Just as Ross is a pluralist about right and wrong, he is also a pluralist about value. According to Ross, there are four basic kinds of intrinsic good: virtue, knowledge, the state consisting of pleasure in proportion to virtue (justice), and pleasure. Moreover, what makes such states of affairs good and the degree of goodness they possess varies depending on the type of good in question. For instance, what makes instances of experiencing pleasure intrinsically good is their pleasant nature, while the intensity and duration of the pleasure affect its degree of intrinsic value. The intrinsic value of knowing something and its degree of value depends on such factors as one's knowledge being the apprehension of some fact, the degree of certainty and thus absence of doubt about what is known, and the degree of generality of the known fact. Considerations of space do not allow a full discussion of the various aspects of Ross's nuanced discussion of these goods, the degree of goodness instances of them possess, or how they can be compared.[7] But we should keep in mind that specifying a list of intrinsic goods is one thing, explaining what makes them good is another. It is the latter explanatory task that addresses the theoretical aim of a theory of intrinsic value.

Ross's manner of arguing for these goods involves having his readers engage in thought experiments comparing two states of the universe, one that lacks some good under scrutiny and another state identical to the first but containing the good in question. For instance, in arguing that virtue is intrinsically good, Ross remarks:

> It seems clear that we regard all such [virtuous] actions and dispositions as having value in themselves apart from any consequence. And if one is inclined to doubt this and to think that, say, pleasure alone is intrinsically good, it seems to me enough to ask the question whether, of two states of the universe holding equal amounts of pleasure, we should really think no better of one in which the actions and dispositions of all persons in it were thoroughly virtuous than of one in which they were highly vicious. To this there can be but one answer. (Ross, 1930, 134)

With regard to the completeness of his list, Ross makes two observations. First, he reports that he is not able to think of some other item that is intrinsically good and not merely either a species of one or other of the four intrinsic goods on his list or reducible to some combination of them. Aesthetic enjoyment, for instance, seems to be a combination of pleasure and insight into (and hence a kind of knowledge about) the object of enjoyment. Hence, such enjoyment is reducible to a combination of pleasure and knowledge—no need to add it to the list of basic intrinsic goods.

The second observation in defense of his list is that it fits with a widely recognized classification of basic elements of the mind or soul into the faculties of cognition, feeling, and conation. Knowledge is an ideal state of cognition, pleasure is an ideal state of feeling, virtue (which has primarily to do with desire) is an ideal state of conation, and pleasure in proportion to virtue represents an ideal relation between the feeling and conative parts of the mind.

Moral Worth

Moral worth (or what Ross and many philosophers refer to as *moral* goodness) has to do with one's overall character, as well as with feelings, desires, and actions that "spring" from one's character. Ross illustrates his view by focusing on actions that have moral worth which, he explains, derive their worth from the desires which produce them.

Like Kant, Ross holds that acting from a sense of duty has intrinsic moral worth, though unlike Kant, Ross understands such motivation to be a matter of having a desire to do what is right. He also recognizes two other desires possessing such worth. First, there is the direct desire to produce good, which includes the desire to improve the character of persons (ourselves included) and the desire to improve the intellectual condition of persons (again, ourselves included). Second, Ross recognizes the desire to produce some pleasure or prevent some pain for other beings as having intrinsic moral worth. Actions resulting from such desires are basic types of virtuous action. And so, corresponding to these types of virtuous action, there are three corresponding types of vicious action motivated by one or more of the following vicious desires: the desire to do what is wrong, the desire to bring about evil, and the desire to cause another person pain.

In recognizing three irreducibly basic types of morally valuable desire, Ross again proceeds by inviting his readers to consider "what we really think" about matters of moral worth (which can be facilitated through the use of thought experiments) in coming to reasonable conclusions about the kinds of desires and actions proceeding from them have such value.

Now that we have Ross's pluralist theories of right conduct and value before us, how are they related?

9. THE STRUCTURE OF ROSS'S MORAL THEORY

It turns out that Ross's theory exhibits an interesting and complex structure. Some of Ross's prima facie duties have to do with the effects of our actions on others and ourselves. The duty of justice concerns bringing about a proper proportion of pleasure (or happiness) in relation to virtue—one of the four basic intrinsic

Value-Based Prima Facie Duties	Duties of Special Obligation
Beneficence Self-Improvement Justice Nonmaleficence	Fidelity Gratitude Reparation

Figure 9.1. Types of Prima Facie Duty in Ross's Moral System

goods. The duties of beneficence and self-improvement concern production of the goods of pleasure, knowledge, and virtue in others and of virtue and knowledge in ourselves. Thus, commenting on the prima facie duty of justice, Ross says that it, along "with beneficence and self-improvement, comes under the general principle that we should produce as much good as possible" (Ross, 1930, 27; 1939, 252).

The prima facie duty of nonmaleficence requires that we refrain from harming others in various ways and that we thus refrain, as much as possible, from producing bad consequences. So these four prima facie duties, resting on a conception of good and bad consequences, may be called "value-based" prima facie duties.

By contrast, duties of "special obligation" are related by the fact that they concern past actions of ourselves or others and include the prima facie duties of fidelity, gratitude, and reparation. So, on Ross's view, there are two main types of duty, some based on considerations of value, others not. Figure 9.1 summarizes these two groups. Thus, part of Ross's theory of right conduct depends on his theory of value; part of it does not.

10. SUMMARY OF ROSS'S MORAL PLURALISM

In section 1, we noted that pluralist theories of right make two central claims. Let us restate them to allow for pluralist theories of value and then add some items to the list to capture some distinctive aspects of Ross's pluralism.[8]

1. There is a plurality of basic moral rules and a plurality of basic intrinsic goods.
2. There is no underlying moral principle that serves to justify these moral rules, nor is there some basic or fundamental intrinsic good underlying the plurality of basic intrinsic goods.
3. These different moral rules may conflict.
4. There is no fixed priority of moral rules that resolves such conflicts.
5. Moral judgment—a capacity for adjudicating conflicts that cannot be fully captured by moral principles or rules—is needed to reach determinate moral verdicts in certain cases.

Ross's theory is a prime example of a limited, pluralistic moral theory. The theory—composed of various rules and values—is limited in its power to yield determinate all-things-considered verdicts about the deontic status of actions.

11. EVALUATION OF ROSS'S THEORY

Let us move on to an evaluation of Ross's theory.

Intuitive appeal and consistency. Ross's theory of right conduct has some notable advantages in being able to accommodate certain deep-seated features of common-sense morality. (Here, we are employing the standard of intuitive appeal.) First, it fits nicely with how ordinary folks reason about matters of morality. In contexts calling for moral deliberation one is normally confronted with competing moral demands and has to judge which demand, from among the competitors, has the greatest moral weight in the case at hand. Ross's view fairly accurately describes this very common feature of moral experience and associated manner of moral deliberation.[9] A related point is that Ross's theory nicely captures the significant role that multiple moral rules play in people's moral thinking.

Second, Ross's view deals plausibly with conflict of duty situations. As we have seen, on his view, rules of prima facie duty can, in cases of conflict, be overridden, and thus his theory avoids the kind of inconsistency that threatens whenever supposedly exceptionless moral rules come into conflict. Ross's theory apparently satisfies the standard of consistency.

Determinacy. I turn now to the charge of indeterminacy. A moral theory is indeterminate when, with respect to some moral issue or range of issues, it fails to yield moral verdicts about such cases—it fails to imply any unambiguous conclusion about the deontic status of the actions in question. Moral theories whose basic principles or rules rely on concepts that are excessively vague typically manifest indeterminacy. All moral theories can be expected to be somewhat indeterminate, owing to the fact that all concepts likely to be featured in the principles or rules of the theory will be somewhat vague. However, the more determinate the theory the better the theory is, according to the standard of determinacy for evaluating moral theories.

Ross's theory is guilty of being indeterminate when it comes to verdicts about one's actual duty since the rules of the theory, together with relevant factual information about one's situation, fail to imply any determinate conclusions about such duties.[10] But this is not because of excessive vagueness with respect to the various concepts that pick out right-making and wrong-making features that serve as moral reasons either for or against various courses of action. Concepts like promising, reparation, self-improvement, and the others featured in the rules of prima facie duty are reasonably clear. Indeed, at the level of judgments about one's prima facie duties, Ross's theory does not suffer from indeterminacy: in a wide range of cases it yields determinate verdicts about one's prima facie duties.

Moreover, the indeterminacy at the level of judgments of one's actual duties is perhaps not so worrisome since such indeterminacy is explicable as part of the very type of moral theory that Ross is defending. After all, Ross stresses the need for a moral theory that fits the complexity of moral phenomena, and such complexity (so he might plead) imposes a limit on how determinate a set of moral principles or rules that compose a moral theory can be. So, in the end, I would argue that the fact that Ross's theory is indeterminate when it comes to judgments about our actual duties is not a troublesome objection to his theory.

Internal support and explanatory power. Ross's theory accommodates the intuitively appealing idea that personal relationships have moral significance. The fact that one has made a promise to someone, and thus entered into a kind of relationship with some specific individual, counts, and counts directly in determining what one ought to do in response. Most forms of consequentialism do not attribute any direct significance to such facts. Rather, for a consequentialist view, a moral obligation to keep a promise directly depends on the values of the consequences of keeping it; the fact that one promised has no intrinsic moral significance as it does for Ross. So, not only does Ross's view fit with moral judgments having to do with personal relationships, it seems to be able to more plausibly explain their significance, at least compared to some forms of consequentialism. Here is how Ross puts this point:

> The essential defect of the "ideal utilitarian" theory[11] is that it ignores, or at least does not do full justice to, the highly personal character of duty. If the only duty is to produce the maximum of good, the question who is to have the good—whether it is myself, or my benefactor, or a person to whom I have made a promise to confer that good on him, or a mere fellow man to whom I stand in no special relation—should make no difference to my having a duty to produce that good. But we are all sure that it makes a vast difference (1930, 22).

Ross's theory of right conduct and his theory of value seem to fit well, and thus receive some support from, our considered moral beliefs. We have just noted that Ross's theory of right conduct nicely accommodates certain of our beliefs about the moral importance of personal relationships. This belief about morality is reflected in some of our considered moral beliefs as when, for example, we judge that even if a sum of money that I have reserved for my daughter's education could be given to a more promising and needy student, my prima facie obligation to support my daughter, because she is my daughter, is of greater stringency than any prima facie obligation I have toward the education of some other individual.

Again, Ross's pluralism about what sorts of things have intrinsic value and what sorts of motives have moral value arguably fits better with commonsense views on these matters than does, for example, hedonism about intrinsic value and a rigoristic view of moral goodness that, following Kant, only recognizes the motive of duty as having genuine moral worth.

However, a worry can be raised concerning the seeming demandingness of Ross's theory. Ross claims that the value-based prima facie duties oblige us to "produce as much good as possible," or, in the case of nonmaleficence, to minimize the bad effects of our actions on others. So, he concludes that in almost all situations, we are confronted with some actual duty to discharge.

> It is obvious that any of the acts that we do has countless effects, directly or indirectly on countless people, and the probability is that any act, however right it may be, will have adverse effects (though these may be very trivial) on some innocent people. Similarly, any wrong act will probably have beneficial effects on some deserving people. Every act therefore, viewed in some aspects, will be prima facie right, and viewed in others prima facie wrong. (Ross, 1930, 41)

So, on Ross's theory, we are obligated to maximize the good unless there is some prima facie duty, representing a special obligation like fidelity, that is, in the situation, more stringent. But if I am just lying around on some Sunday afternoon taking it easy, it seems implausible to suppose what I am doing is morally wrong (given that I could go help someone). Ross's moral theory seems excessively demanding in its claim that on all or most occasions we have some duty or other to discharge. In this way, it suffers from the same sort of problem typically raised against maximizing versions of utilitarianism that we considered in section 2 of chapter 6; that is, it fails to fit with certain of our considered moral beliefs.

One response on behalf of Ross would be to distinguish between something's being a moral consideration that favors performing some action and something's counting as a ground for a prima facie duty. The sort of distinction at work here is described by David McNaughton:

> The view that moral requirements provide reasons for acting which override other kinds of reason must be distinguished from the view that moral considerations always override other reasons for acting. The latter view would commit us to saying that any moral reason, however weak, always outweighs any other reason, however strong. But there are situations where, although there are moral reasons in favour of a certain action they are not decisive; they do not constitute a requirement that one acts in that way. (McNaughton, 1988, 115)

Following McNaughton's proposal (modified to apply to Ross's view), we could say that the fact that in a situation there is some action I could perform that would benefit others is a moral consideration that favors acting accordingly, but this kind of consideration does not ground a prima facie requirement. On the other hand, the fact that some specific person has been injured and I am the only one around who can help her (and I realize this fact) is an example where such facts do ground a prima facie duty of beneficence. The upshot would be that only in some circumstances do facts about helping others ground a prima facie duty; in most other contexts, the fact that I could do something or other to help someone or other only gives me some moral reason to act accordingly but does not ground a prima facie duty to so act. This would allow room for acts of supererogation in which one does more to help others than one is even prima facie required to do. Of course, one would have to say something about when one is in a context involving a prima facie obligation of beneficence and when one is only confronted with a moral consideration of beneficence. However, if this could be done, then this is one way Ross's theory would avoid the demandingness problem.

All in all, then, Ross's moral theory seems to satisfy the standard of internal support. However, before turning to some objections to Ross's theory, we ought to take notice of something that was mentioned very briefly in chapter 1 (note 6) concerning the standard of internal support. As explained in chapter 1, the principles or rules of a moral theory are said to enjoy internal support when they (together with any relevant nonmoral factual information) entail our considered moral beliefs. By contrast, if a moral theory features principles or rules whose implications conflict with a good many of our considered moral beliefs, this counts against those particular principles or rules. In this way, our considered moral beliefs are taken to be a basis for testing moral principles and rules.[12] However, the principles or rules of a moral theory may be consistent with our considered moral beliefs but fail to entail them. This is the case with the rules of prima facie duty featured in Ross's theory, and it is worth pausing to explain this point in a bit more detail.

As we have seen, the rules of prima facie duty featured in Ross's theory of right conduct do not (together with relevant nonmoral factual information) entail determinate moral verdicts in a wide range of cases. Thus, they do not enjoy the kind of strong internal support that a principle or rule enjoys when it does entail our considered moral beliefs. But although the rules of prima facie duty do not entail determinate moral verdicts, they do seem to be at least largely consistent with our considered moral beliefs. Let us say that when the principles or rules of a moral theory are consistent with our considered moral beliefs, this fact provides weak internal support for those principles or rules. And when the principles or rules of some theory (together with relevant nonmoral factual information) entail our considered moral beliefs (or a wide range of them), then let us say that this fact provides strong internal support for those principles or rules.

Given the distinction between strong and weak internal support, we must conclude that Ross's theory of right conduct enjoys only weak internal support from our considered moral beliefs.

I want to continue our discussion of Ross's theory by briefly considering three challenges often brought against his theory: (1) the apparent unconnectedness of the various prima facie duties, (2) the apparent arbitrariness of moral judgment, and (3) its intuitionist epistemology.

The Unconnected-Heap Problem

Ross's seven basic prima facie duties seem unconnected—a heap of duties with nothing that ties them together so that they can be clearly understood as representing moral requirements. Call this the unconnected-heap problem.

One plausible response to this problem has been proposed by Robert Audi. His idea is that we can make use of Kant's notion of treating humanity as an end in itself (and never merely as a means), or, more simply, the notion of respect for persons, and view Ross's basic prima facie duties as interconnected by this basic moral notion. Here is how Audi explains his proposal:

> Is it not plausible to hold that in lying, breaking promises, subjugating, torturing, and the like one is using people merely as a means? And in keeping faith with people, acting benevolently toward them, and extending them justice, is one not treating them as ends, roughly in the sense of beings with intrinsic value (or whose experiences have intrinsic value)? The point is not that Ross's principles can be deduced from the categorical imperative . . . rather, the intrinsic end formulation of the imperative expresses an ideal that renders the principles of duty intelligible or even expectable. (Audi, 1997, 48)

In discussing critically Kant's Humanity formulation of the Categorical Imperative, I pointed out that the notion of treating persons as ends in themselves (respecting persons) is vague and there is reason to be dubious of Kant's attempt to use this formulation of his supreme principle for purposes of deriving a system of duties. One way to put Audi's proposal is that we can view Ross's moral rules as an interpretation of the vague notion of respect for persons and, in doing so, be able to view them as having a kind of interconnection and thus unity that makes sense of the idea that they express moral requirements. One way for a moral theory to be unified is for it to feature a single moral principle that specifies one underlying feature that can be used to derive moral rules and specific obligations. This is what versions of moral monism aspire to do. But we now see that unity of the sort indicated by Audi can be enjoyed by a pluralist moral theory.

But aside from this way of answering the unconnected-heap complaint, Ross would no doubt remind us that in doing moral theory "it is more important that our theory fit the facts than that it be simple" (Ross, 1930, 19). Given Audi's proposal and Ross's reminder, I don't think that this objection has much force against Ross's theory.

Moral Judgment and the Problem of Arbitrariness

Moral judgment of the sort involved in balancing and weighing competing prima facie duties and coming to a conclusion about one's all-things-considered duty has struck some philosophers as suspect. By definition, such judgment is not simply a matter of applying principles or rules that then yield a correct moral conclusion about some particular case. But then, why suppose the deliverances of moral judgment are anything but arbitrary from the point of view of rationality? To sharpen the objection, let us work with an example.

Consider a case in which the issue is whether it is morally permissible for a physician to engage in euthanasia in a particular case. Suppose that the physician's patient is experiencing very severe pain (about which little can be done), is going to die in a matter of days, and is asking to be given a life-ending drug. In such a case, consideration of the patient's medical situation arguably grounds a prima facie duty to honor the request. On the other hand, the fact that bringing about the patient's death in this way would be a matter of knowingly and intentionally bringing about the death of an innocent person arguably grounds a prima facie duty to refrain from administering the drug. Now consider a thoughtful, well-educated individual contemplating this case whose moral sensibility (when it comes to matters of life and death) involves a deep feeling for the sanctity of human life. Such a person might, upon due consideration, conclude that the prima facie duty not to intentionally take an innocent human life is more stringent than the duty to alleviate the patient's pain. But no doubt there are thoughtful, well-educated individuals who, upon considering the case carefully, would judge that the prima facie duty to alleviate pain, at least in this case, overrides the opposing prima facie duty. People seem to vary quite a lot in their moral sensibilities, and thus one can expect quite a bit of variation in the all-things-considered judgments that thoughtful people will make in contemplating the very same cases. Thus, isn't the overall Rossian account of moral decision making unacceptably arbitrary?

Notice that this complaint is not saying that Ross's theory allows people to judge their actual duties without having any reasons to back up their judgments. Quite the contrary: thoughtful, well-educated people will be able to advance reasons (at least in principle) for the moral conclusions they draw in cases involving conflicts of duties. Rather, the complaint here is that the conclusion about actual duties that one arrives at will depend on one's moral sensibility, and since thoughtful people's moral sensibilities often differ, and since Ross gives us no clue for determining which from among conflicting sensibilities might be correct, there is a kind of arbitrariness in coming to conclusions about actual duties on the basis of moral judgment.

Although a full response to this objection is not possible here, three points are worth stressing. First, philosophers who are suspicious of moral judgment often point to natural science as a model of rational inquiry, assume that such inquiry is completely rule governed, and draw the conclusion that a view like Ross's that relies on moral judgment is defective. But recently some philosophers of science have argued that scientific rationality must make room for scientific judgment—a capacity for evaluating evidence and coming to reasonable scientific conclusions that goes beyond following rules.[13] If judgment is involved in scientific inquiry and if scientific inquiry is our very model of nonarbitrary, rational inquiry, then reaching moral verdicts by the use of moral judgment need not be an arbitrary matter.

Second, we have been focusing on judgment that is involved in adjudicating conflicts among prima facie duties. But even moral theories that do not explicitly recognize a role for this adjudicative kind of moral judgment must admit that judgment is involved in the application of principles or rules to particular cases. In order to apply a rule against lying to a particular case, one must be able to determine that the act in question is an instance of lying. Now suppose that such a determination involves applying some rule—a rule for applying moral rules. Then won't there have to be some further rule for applying the rule for applying moral rules? And then won't there have to be yet another rule for applying this further rule? Clearly, to avoid an infinite series of rules and rules for applying rules, we must recognize that applying a rule involves a capacity for what we are calling judgment. And if judgment is involved in the application of rules and principles, and if the process is not unacceptably arbitrary, then why suppose that judgment involved in adjudicating moral conflicts is unacceptably arbitrary?

Finally, in response to the arbitrariness objection we should allow that "moral ties" are possible. Perhaps in some cases, like the euthanasia case described above, the correct moral conclusion to draw is that both refraining from the act of euthanasia and engaging in it are morally permissible. This possibility is allowed for, given how the deontic category of the morally optional was defined for Ross's theory. One situation in which an action is morally optional for Ross is when there are competing prima facie duties that are equally stringent.

These brief remarks are by no means enough to answer fully the arbitrariness charge that has been raised against moral judgment.[14] But investigating the matter further would take us well beyond our survey of moral theories.[15]

Intuitionism

Recall that intuitionism in ethics is the view that some moral claims are self-evident and can be known through an appropriate grasp of those claims. Throughout the last half of the twentieth century, intuitionism (as an account of the justification of moral claims) was largely dismissed by most moral philosophers. Recently, the situation has changed, and this view has been revived and ably defended.[16] Space does not permit us to examine the various philosophical issues raised by intuitionism. Instead, it should be noted that even if one rejects an intuitionist moral epistemology, this does not mean that one is thereby entitled to reject Ross's moral pluralism. Far from it. If it turns out that Ross's theory does a better job than any of its competitors in explaining the nature of right and wrong action—if, that is, it more adequately satisfies the standard of explanatory power than does its competitors—his theory would enjoy a strong measure of justification.

12. CONCLUSION

I believe that Ross's limited, pluralistic moral theory can plausibly deal with the unconnected-heap and arbitrariness challenges. The theory itself is significantly indeterminate, but fidelity to the complex nature of morality is important, and, arguably, we cannot get more determinacy from theory than we find in a theory like Ross's. Finally, I have noted that even if one rejects epistemological intuitionism, there are other ways to justify a moral theory. In particular, in evaluating Ross's theory in relation to the main theoretical aim of a moral theory, we ought to take seriously the idea that a plurality of basic moral features is needed to adequately explain what makes right actions right and wrong actions wrong. Although I have not mounted a philosophical defense of this kind of pluralism, I do think that some version of limited, pluralistic moral theory (Ross's theory being a clear example) ought to be a default position in ethics—a position that monist theories must unseat.[17]

In the next chapter, we examine some varieties of virtue ethics—a type of moral theory that makes considerations of virtue central in providing an account of right action. As we shall see, what I take to be the most plausible shape this kind of view will take will be an instance of a limited, pluralistic moral theory.

NOTES

1. See Sartre, 1965.

2. Recall from chapter 1 the distinction between moral principles and moral rules regarding right conduct. We are taking a moral principle as a general moral statement that purports to specify conditions under which any action is right or wrong. A moral rule is less general than a principle and states that some specific type of action is right or wrong.

3. As we shall see later, solving the first problem does not automatically yield a solution to the second.

4. This term is also used to refer to moral pluralism. But pluralism and epistemological intuitionism are independent of one another; commitment to one does not entail commitment to the other. To avoid confusion, I will only use the term in the epistemological sense explained here.

5. For the sake of simplicity, I have expressed Ross's theory of right conduct in terms of principles that make reference to prima facie duties without referring in the principles to the underlying right- and wrong-making features that Ross would use to explain what makes an action all-things-considered obligatory, optional, or wrong. But, of course, it would not be hard, though very tedious, to reformulate the principles to make such information explicit. For example, in specifying what makes an action A in C wrong, one would have to formulate the principle to claim that A has one or more of the basic Rossian wrong-making features by listing them all (e.g., A is either an instance of infidelity, or failure of reparation, etc., for each of the prima facie duties), and then the principle would have to go on to say that if any right-making features (again, listing them) favor one's doing A, then the strength of the relevant wrong-making features outweighs the right-making features.

6. I borrow the term "creative insight" from Larmore, 1987, 19.

7. Three things about Ross's theory of intrinsic value are worth noting. First, on Ross's view, experiences of pleasure (and pain) are properly understood to be aspects or parts of a more complex state of affairs having to do with the context in which such experiences occur. The significance of this idea is that as part of a complex the pleasure is only a prima facie good-making feature of the complex; it may be overridden by other factors, thus making the complex something that is all things considered intrinsically bad. Ross's examples of this are cases in which the pleasure is either underserved or is taken in, say, an act of cruelty. In such cases, these additional elements outweigh the positive value that pleasure contributes to the whole. This interesting point does not seem to apply to the other items on Ross's list of intrinsic goods. Second, Ross holds that these intrinsic values

can be ranked in order of importance with virtue at the top and (innocent) pleasure at the bottom. Arguably, justice is ranked between knowledge and pleasure. Third, Ross's theory of intrinsic value underwent some changes between his 1930 *The Right and the Good* and his 1939 *Foundations of Ethics*. For an overview, see Skelton, 2010. My presentation is based on the earlier book.

8. Here, I am following Hooker's, 2000a, 105 useful summary of Ross-style pluralism.

9. See Gill and Nichols, 2008 for some empirical evidence that supports this observation.

10. One exception would be a case in which, given the facts, only one prima facie duty is applicable to one's circumstances, in which case it is also one's actual duty.

11. Here, Ross is referring to the moral theory of G. E. Moore, 1903. The label "ideal" refers to Moore's nonhedonistic theory of intrinsic value.

12. Though, as pointed out in chapter 1 and discussed further in chapter 5, some philosophers dispute testing moral principles and rules in this way.

13. See, for example, Brown, 1988, chapter 4 and Putnam, 1981, chapter 8.

14. Here is an appropriate place to mention what Henry Richardson, 1990 calls the method of specification, which (roughly speaking) involves taking very general moral principles such as Ross's principles of prima facie duty and in light of particular cases in which two or more principles apply to a case but favor different actions, one reflects on various factors concerning the principles in question and the case at hand with the aim of making more specific one of the principles whose application to the case yields a determinate verdict. Richardson's specificationist model is presented as an alternative to the Rossian account as a method that avoids worries about arbitrariness. Unfortunately, space does not allow discussion of the specificationist method. Richardson's excellent paper is highly recommended for those interested in the issue of using moral principles to reach determinate verdicts about hard cases.

15. See Larmore, 1987, chapter 1 for a defense of moral judgment.

16. The work of Robert Audi, 1997, 2004 has been particularly influential in reviving intuitionism in ethics. See also Huemer, 2005 and the essays in Hernandez, 2011.

17. For an attempt to do just this, see Hooker's, 2000a defense of rule consequentialism.

FURTHER READING

Philosophical Literature

Audi, Robert. 1997. "Intuitionism, Pluralism, and the Foundations of Ethics." In *Moral Knowledge and Ethical Character*. New York: Oxford University Press. A defense of ethical intuitionism making use of Ross's moral theory.

———. 2004. *The Good in the Right*. Princeton, NJ: Princeton University Press. An illuminating defense of epistemological intuitionism and a pluralist moral theory.

Dancy, Jonathan. 1991. "An Ethic of Prima Facie Duties." In *A Companion to Ethics*, ed. Peter Singer. Oxford: Blackwell. A useful presentation and critique of Ross's theory of right conduct.

Gaut, Berys. 2002. "Justifying Moral Pluralism." In *Ethical Intuitionism: Re-evaluations*, ed. P. Stratton-Lake. Oxford: Oxford University Press. A defense of moral pluralism on epistemological grounds other than intuitionism.

Gill, Michael B. 2012. "Agonizing Decisions and Moral Pluralism." In *Conduct and Character: Readings in Moral Theory*, 6th ed., ed. M. Timmons. Belmont, CA: Wadsworth-Cengage. An engaging defense of moral pluralism as the best explanation of the responses of regret and remorse that are typically experienced by individuals forced to make agonizing moral decisions.

———. 2012. "The Non-consequentialist Moral Force of Promises: A Response to Sinnott-Armstrong." *Analysis* 73: 506–13. A defense of the Rossian view against the objections by W. Sinnott-Armstrong in his article listed below.

———, and Shaun Nichols. 2008. "Sentimental Pluralism: Moral Psychological and Philosophical Ethics." *Philosophical Issues* 18: 143–63. This essay includes a defense of descriptive moral pluralism—the view that ordinary commonsense moral judgments are guided by a plurality of moral rules—as well as prescriptive moral pluralism of the sort featured in this chapter. Their defense appeals to relevant empirical literature.

Mason, Elinor. 2011. "Value Pluralism." *The Stanford Encyclopedia of Philosophy*, ed. E. N. Zalta. http://plato.stanford.edu. An excellent overview of the varieties of and debates about value pluralism in ethics.

McNaughton, David. 1996. "An Unconnected Heap of Duties?" *Philosophical Quarterly* 46: 433–47. A defense of Ross's moral pluralism against the unconnected-heap and indeterminacy objections.

Rawls, John. 1971. *A Theory of Justice*. Cambridge, MA: Harvard University Press. Section 7, pages 34–40, includes a brief critique of moral pluralism (which Rawls calls intuitionism).

Ross, W. D. 1930. *The Right and the Good*. Oxford: Oxford University Press. A classic defense of moral pluralism.

———. 1939. *Foundations of Ethics*. Oxford: Oxford University Press. Contains chapters that further elaborate and defend the moral theory presented in his 1930 book.

Sinnott-Armstrong, Walter. 2009. "How Strong Is This Obligation: A Consequentialist Argument from Concomitant Variation." *Analysis* 69: 438–42. Reprinted in *Conduct and Character: Readings in Moral Theory*, 6th ed., ed. M. Timmons. Belmont, CA: Wadsworth-Cengage, 2012. Focusing on conflict of duty cases of the sort featured in Ross's theory, Sinnott-Armstrong defends a thoroughly consequentialist approach to both the resolution of such conflicts and the grounds of obligation.

Skelton, Anthony. 2010. "William David Ross." *The Stanford Encyclopedia of Philosophy*, ed. E. N. Zalta. http://plato.stanford.edu. Very helpful overview of Ross's moral philosophy.

Stratton-Lake, Philip, ed. 2002. *Ethical Intuitionism: Re-evaluations*. Oxford: Oxford University Press. Wide-ranging collection of twelve essays on the topic of epistemological intuitionism. Includes the Gaut and McNaughton articles mentioned above.

Empirical Literature

Moral pluralism as a normative (or prescriptive) theory about right and wrong is to be distinguished from what may be called *descriptive moral pluralism*, a psychological thesis according to which a plurality of moral rules typically figure causally in ordinary people's moral deliberation and in the processes that result in people coming to have all-things-considered moral beliefs. The following entries are all concerned with the descriptive thesis. For a discussion of the bearing of the descriptive psychological thesis on normative moral pluralism, see Gill and Nichols, 2008. It should be noted that the following authors defend "sentimentalist" versions of descriptive moral pluralism according to which (roughly) moral rules are based on emotion.

Haidt, Jonathan. 2012. *The Righteous Mind: Why Good People are Divided by Politics and Religion.* New York: Pantheon Books. Part II defends descriptive moral pluralism.

———, and Craig Joseph. 2004. "Intuitive Ethics: How Innately Prepared Intuitions Generate Culturally Variable Virtues." *Daedalus* (Fall): 56–66. Authors hypothesize a variety of distinct psychological explanatory grounds for different moral rules.

Nichols, Shaun. 2004. *Sentimental Rules.* Oxford: Oxford University Press. Includes a defense of the view that emotionally based moral rules are essential to ordinary moral judgment.

Rozin, P., L. Lowry, S. Imada, and J. Haidt. 1999. "The CAD Triad Hypothesis." *Journal of Personality and Social Psychology* 76: 574–86. Postulates that different emotions—contempt, anger, and disgust—align with different moral codes and thus different kinds of moral rules.

Schweder, R., N. Much, M. Mahapatra, and L. Park. 1999. "The 'Big Three' of Morality (Autonomy, Community, Divinity) and the 'Big Three' Explanations of Suffering." In *Morality and Health*, ed. A. Brandt and P. Rozin. New York: Routledge. Builds on the work of Rozin et al.

10

Virtue Ethics

We often look to others as models for the type of person we would like to be because we think they possess certain admirable character traits. Suppose Miriam has just begun her career as a finance director for a large company. She relies on directors from other branches within the company for information that she needs to be able to do her job. But she has a problem with the director from marketing, who is rather difficult to get along with and who has not been responsive to Miriam's requests for timely information. The matter is delicate because for Miriam to do her job well, she needs to have a good working relation with her peers from other departments. During a meeting she sees how skillfully a company director, Agnes, is able to interact with combative associates in a manner that is respectful and friendly while at the same time she is able to stand her ground and make her views known. Over a period of months it becomes clear to Miriam that Agnes is quite skilled at handling difficult interpersonal interactions, and she comes to admire Agnes for having an admirable character trait (call it interpersonal diplomacy) that she would like to develop.

Just as Miriam looks to Agnes as someone to be like in certain business dealings, so in moral thought generally we might look to individuals as models of the types of persons we would like to be. Jesus, Buddha, Socrates, and Martin Luther King are among the individuals who have been thought to exemplify certain traits of character and who therefore serve as models of what sort of person to be.

The main focus of the moral theories we have examined so far has been on moral questions about what to do. Questions about what sort of person to be and, in particular, questions about the morality of character have remained in the background. However, there is a tradition in ethics, going back to Plato and Aristotle, in which the primary focus of moral inquiry is on questions of what sort of person to be: excellence of character rather than right conduct is of primary concern here. Questions about what sort of person to be concern the sorts of qualities of character it is morally praiseworthy to acquire and maintain. Such qualities are called virtues. In recent times moral theories that take virtue to be central for understanding morality have been called virtue ethics. These theories will be the focus of this chapter.

Our study of virtue ethics will begin with some remarks about the nature of virtue, and then we will turn to the moral philosophy of Aristotle, whose work on virtue and morality continues to influence contemporary work in virtue ethics. We will then be in a position to present and critically examine some representative examples of contemporary virtue ethics.

1. WHAT IS A VIRTUE?

Let us begin with a general characterization of the concept of a virtue and then proceed to illustrate with an example.

A *virtue* can be roughly described as (1) a relatively fixed trait of character or mind (2) typically involving dispositions to think, feel, and act in certain ways across a range of different circumstances, and which furthermore (3) is central in the *positive* evaluation of the moral worth of persons. And so a *vice* is (1) a relatively fixed trait of character or mind (2) typically involving dispositions to think, feel, and act in certain ways across a range of different circumstances, and which furthermore (3) is central in the *negative* evaluation of the moral worth of persons.

Focusing on virtues, consider, for example, honesty.[1] To call someone honest is (in part) to attribute to that person a relatively fixed character trait that we can describe in terms of the person's thinking (an intellectual component); feeling (an affective component); and motivation and action (a motivational-behavioral component). Let us focus on each of these elements in turn.

- *Intellectual component.* First, an honest person is someone who has correct beliefs about when it is appropriate to tell the truth, how much of the truth it is appropriate to reveal, and so forth.
- *Affective component.* Second, an honest person is disposed to feel and express approval toward those who tell the truth and feel and express disapproval toward those who lie. An honest person is also disposed to feel guilty, or in some way badly, about her own acts of dishonesty and is likewise disposed to feel good about acts that express her honesty.
- *Motivational-behavioral component.* Finally, the virtue of honesty involves being disposed to tell the truth and avoid telling lies across a range of different circumstances, where one is motivated to do so by a direct concern for honesty. Moreover, a person with this virtue typically, if not always, succeeds in telling the truth on appropriate occasions and avoids lying.

This brief profile of honesty is not intended to express a fully adequate account of this complex trait; far from it. For instance, there is more to the motivational-behavioral component of honesty than truth-telling and the avoidance of lying to others; honesty has partly to do with how one views oneself. Avoiding self-deception is a form of honesty. Moreover, it may be possible to have and exemplify the virtue of honesty without all three components holding true of the honest person. That is, while I have described honesty partly in terms of having a direct concern for the truth, it is arguable whether honesty strictly requires this specific kind of concern and associated motivation. Henry Sidgwick (1838–1900), for instance, claimed that the virtue of veracity (roughly, honesty) centrally involves "a settled resolve to produce in the minds of others impressions exactly correspondent to the facts, whatever his motive may be for doing so" (Sidgwick, [1907] 1966, 224). So he would disagree that the veracious person is necessarily motivated by a direct concern for the truth.

However, even if such motivation is not a strict requirement for being an honest or veracious person, it is still true that the honest person who is so motivated can be said to possess the virtue in a most desirable way. After all, such a person enjoys a kind of harmony among her feelings, motives, and behavior that is lacking in someone who, for example, is grudgingly, but nevertheless steadfastly, honest. The point to keep in mind is that virtues may differ among themselves with regard to whether possession of the trait requires some specific motive (or range of motives) and also with regard to how central certain emotional elements are in possessing this or that virtue.

Another important feature of a trait like honesty is that normally it is acquired as a result of confronting over time a number of situations that call on us to be honest. By performing acts of honesty (in those circumstances calling for such actions) one comes to have the relevant set of intellectual, emotional, and motivational components characteristic of this trait. Thus, honesty and, in general, many (if not all) virtues are to be distinguished from excellences that one might have by nature—like a perfect sense of musical pitch, or natural beauty, or good eyesight. We are responsible for the virtues we have, and thus their possession is worthy of praise.

Philosophers often sort virtues into different groups. Most important for our concerns are the moral virtues, a partial list of which would most likely include benevolence, conscientiousness, courage, generosity, gratitude, justice, honesty, loyalty, and temperance. In addition to moral virtues, there are also intellectual virtues, including such acquired traits as open-mindedness, intellectual courage, and perseverance. Other widely recognized virtues like wit, obedience, and thrift, to name just a few, do not clearly belong in either of these categories. I doubt that it is possible to distinguish sharply between the moral and the nonmoral virtues. However, all that is required for our purposes is that we keep in mind clear cases of moral virtues like the ones mentioned above.

Virtue theorists are also interested in hierarchical relationships among the virtues, where the assumption is that some virtues are more basic than others. What are called cardinal virtues are most basic in the sense that (1) their being virtues does not depend on their being forms of, or otherwise subordinate to, any other virtue; and (2) all other moral virtues are either forms of, or are subordinate to, them. For example, many ancient Greek philosophers thought there were four cardinal virtues:

wisdom, courage, temperance, and justice. Having wisdom—roughly, the disposition to judge correctly about which ends to choose and the best means for obtaining them—requires (or at least is aided by) such virtues as carefulness (in deliberating about means and ends) and ingenuity (in figuring out how to best satisfy a number of ends). These latter two virtues are thus subordinate to wisdom. Christian thinkers like Aquinas identified seven cardinal virtues: the three theological virtues, faith, hope, and love; and the four human virtues of prudence, fortitude, temperance, and justice. William Frankena (1908–1994) argued that justice and benevolence are the two cardinal moral virtues.[2] This issue of hierarchy will come up again when we turn to contemporary versions of virtue ethics.

What I have said about the nature of virtue is but the tip of a rather large iceberg. To further our understanding of virtue ethics, let us now consider some of the leading ideas about the role of virtue in the good life that we find in Aristotle's writings.

2. ARISTOTLE ON VIRTUE AND THE GOOD LIFE

Aristotle's *Nicomachean Ethics*, one of the great works of moral philosophy, treats many topics in ethics with insight and subtlety. Most relevant for our purposes is Aristotle's conception of the highest good for human beings and the role that virtue plays in a good life, the rudiments of which are presented in books 1 and 2.

The Highest Good and Eudaimonia

Aristotle begins book 1 by claiming that human activities, including crafts and various forms of investigation, all seem to aim at some end, or good, and hence the good for human beings is apparently some end (or set of ends) at which human activities aim. The highest good, then, would be that end (or set of ends) that is most choiceworthy among the various ends pursued by humans. Aristotle's idea here is that we pursue all sorts of ends, some of them because we think they are a means to, or will contribute to, our obtaining further ends. One aims to do well in, say, a history course one is taking partly because one aims to complete a history major. And one aims to complete the major in order to earn a university degree, which in turn one wants in order to pursue graduate study in that discipline, and so on. In this way, ends can be organized into a hierarchy where the ends lower in the system are pursued for how they contribute to those ends higher up in the system.

The highest good, then, would be some end (or set of ends) that meets the following conditions: it is an end (1) for which all other ends are ultimately pursued, (2) which is pursued for itself, and (3) which is never pursued as a means to any other end. Any such end, in Aristotle's terminology, is *unconditionally complete*. Being unconditionally complete is one mark of the highest good being sought. Another mark is *self-sufficiency*, which an end possesses when having it makes life choiceworthy and lacking in nothing.

If the highest good must be unconditionally complete and self-sufficient, then ends like wealth are obviously eliminated from consideration, and so are the ends of pleasure and honor. We may choose pleasure and honor for themselves, but they lack unconditional completeness because there is something further for which we choose such ends, namely, *eudaimonia* or, as the Greek is usually translated, happiness (though sometimes it is translated as flourishing). Happiness is unconditionally complete since we pursue happiness as an end for its own sake, never for some further end, and all other ends are pursued for the sake of happiness. Thus, it is supreme among ends. Moreover, a happy life is self-sufficient, since achieving it makes life worth living and lacking in nothing. Thus, for Aristotle, the highest good for humans is a life of eudaimonia, or happiness.

The Function Argument

Of course, equating the highest good for humans with happiness (or flourishing) is not particularly informative; we need to specify further just what a happy human life consists of. Certainly, if we are interested in human happiness, we need to consider the essential nature of human beings, since what will make for a happy life depends crucially on the sort of beings human beings are. What, then, is the essential nature of human beings?

Aristotle answers this question with his so-called function argument, the guiding ideas of which can be set forth in four main steps.

First, we understand the nature of something when we understand its proper function or purpose (its *telos*).[3] Consider an artifact like a paint brush. To understand the nature of a paint brush (what it is), one must understand its purpose or function, which is to apply paint. A similar point can be made with regard to the roles human beings may occupy and the occupations they may have. To occupy the role of a parent involves having and raising children, and if one's occupation is farming, one engages in those activities proper to farming (or a particular kind of farming). Of course, roles and occupations vary from one individual to another. But Aristotle's main idea is that apart from the various roles and occupations one may have, all human beings share a certain common nature in virtue of being human. Furthermore, this common nature can be specified in terms of the function of human beings—a function they have simply in virtue of being human. Step 1 of the argument, then, can be put this way:

1. The highest good of human beings concerns their purpose or function.

The second step in the function argument is the claim that if we are interested in the highest good of human beings—which we have identified with eudaimonia— then we need to focus on those features of humans that are distinctive of humanity (at least compared to other terrestrial creatures with which we are familiar). Thus, step 2:

2. The purpose or function of human beings concerns what is distinctive of such beings.

All terrestrial living things participate in life, and plants are capable of nutrition and reproduction, so such capacities are not the focus of human eudaimonia. Furthermore, lower animals are capable of sense perception and locomotion, so these capacities as well cannot be central to human eudaimonia. What is comparatively unique to humans is their rational capacity. In particular, human beings possess both theoretical reason, through which we are able to grasp truths, and practical reason, by means of which we are able to determine which ends to pursue and how best to pursue them. Thus, the third step of the function argument:

3. Rationality (or the exercise of our rational mental capacities) is what is distinctive of humans and hence its exercise is central in understanding the function of human beings.

From these three steps, then, we can derive the intermediate conclusion:

4. The highest good of human beings involves the rational exercise of the soul (mind).

Now certainly something having a function can fulfill that function better or worse. There is a difference between a paint brush that can be used to apply paint and one that not only can do this but also applies paint well or in an excellent manner. We distinguish as well between a parent and a truly good parent, a farmer and a good farmer. A similar point applies to humans and the use of their rationality. We can distinguish between someone's merely using their reason and someone's using it well. Now as we know from our previous discussion, a virtue is an acquired disposition whose exercise promotes excellence in feeling and action. Aristotle thus writes, "[T]he virtue of a human being will likewise be the state that makes a human being good and makes him perform his function well" (NE, 42/1106a).[4] So the next main step in the argument is:

5. The good of a thing is its performing its function well, which, for humans, involves rational activity in accordance with, or guided by, virtue.

Putting this point together with the intermediate conclusion, we can draw the final conclusion of the function argument:

6. The highest good (and hence eudaimonia) of human beings is a life of rational activity of the soul in accordance with virtue.

So Aristotle's function argument attempts to derive a conclusion about the highest good for humans on the basis of facts about the function of such creatures. This argument, as you might expect, is very controversial. But let us not pause here to consider the objections to the argument. Rather, it should be noted that some contemporary virtue ethicists attempt to follow Aristotle in basing a moral theory on claims about eudaimonia, even if they disagree with Aristotle about what constitutes eudaimonia for humans. Later in the chapter, we will return to this issue.

Aristotle's function argument concludes that virtue is central to leading a happy, or *eudaimon*, life; this conclusion leads him to discuss in some detail the nature of virtue and vice. Among the most interesting doctrines concerning virtue and vice in Aristotle's work are the doctrine of the mean and the reciprocity of the virtues. Let us briefly examine them.

The Doctrine of the Mean

The conclusion of the function argument gives us a somewhat clearer idea of human eudaimonia, but obviously more must be said about the nature of virtue and the specific virtues that are involved in the highest good for humans. Although Aristotle would agree with much of what we said earlier in characterizing virtue, an important ingredient in his definition of virtue is the idea that a moral virtue is a mean—"an intermediate condition"—between two extremes. Aristotle writes:

> 7. [V]irtue is concerned with feelings and action, in which excess and deficiency are in error and incur blame, while the intermediate condition is correct and wins praise, which are both proper features of virtue. Virtue, then, is a mean in so far as it aims at what is intermediate. (NE, 44/1106b)

This is Aristotle's famous doctrine of the mean. The easiest way to understand it is to work with some examples.

According to Aristotle, courage is a virtue concerned in particular with proper feelings of fear and confidence. Focusing on the emotion of fear, we can say that a person who possesses the virtue of courage is disposed to react to dangerous situations with a proper amount of fear. On appropriate occasions, then, the courageous person avoids the excess of reacting with too much fear, which is typical of the vice of cowardliness, but such a person also avoids the opposite defect of reacting with too little fear, which is typical of the overconfident, rash person. Both cowardly and overconfident individuals fail to respond in the right way to situations of danger, whereas the courageous person experiences the proper amount of fear given the circumstances.

Generosity is a virtue that, for Aristotle, primarily concerns the giving and taking of money. While the generous person gives the right amount to the right people or causes, the ungenerous person fails to give enough or to the right people or causes, while the extravagant person either gives too much or gives to the wrong people or causes. Again, the idea is that between these vices lies the intermediate state of generosity. The truly generous person, then, gives the right amount to the right people and causes. Figure 10.1 lists some of the virtues and associated vices of character recognized by Aristotle.

Vice (defect)	Virtue (mean)	Vice (excess)
cowardliness	*courage*	rashness
stinginess	*generosity*	extravagance
insensibility	*temperance* (in relation to bodily pleasures)	intemperance
self-deprecation	*truthfulness* (about oneself in social contexts)	boastfulness
boorishness	*wittiness*	buffoonery
quarrelsomeness	*friendliness*	flattery

Figure 10.1.   Some Virtues and Associated Vices in Aristotle

A further important aspect of Aristotle's conception of the virtues is that in order to possess them, one needs practical intelligence (phronesis).[5] Having the virtue of practical intelligence (intelligence, for short) involves having sound judgment about practical matters. In particular, it involves the capacity to determine the right manner of feeling and action in contexts that call for some sort of virtuous response. Such judgment cannot be captured by any system of rules; rather it represents a capacity to come to correct judgments about practical matters that cannot be fully captured or reduced simply to the application of rules to particular cases. Intelligence, then, is a higher-order, overarching virtue involved in having the more specific virtues such as generosity, honesty, and benevolence. The role of intelligence in the possession and exercise of the virtues brings us to another interesting thesis about the virtues.

The Reciprocity of the Virtues

Aristotle apparently embraced the idea that having any one virtue requires that one have them all. Although this thesis is often referred to as the unity of the virtues, let us call it the *reciprocity of the virtues thesis* in order to distinguish it from another unity thesis to be introduced below.

Although at first the reciprocity thesis may seem clearly mistaken—after all, can't one be a just person and yet fail to be temperate?—there is a line of reasoning that

leads naturally to the thesis. Suppose, for instance, that a person is on a military campaign where food and water must be rationed.[6] Justice requires that he take only his
fair share of supplies. But unless this person is also temperate, he will not be disposed
to take just his fair share. If he is intemperate, he will be disposed to take more than
his fair share, thus disposing him to injustice. Thus, being a truly just person requires
that one also be temperate.

Now we can engage in a similar line of reasoning beginning with possession of
the virtue of temperance that will lead us to conclude that full possession of this
virtue requires being a just person as well. Thus, the virtues of justice and temperance are reciprocal: having one requires having the other. If systematic examination
of the conditions required for possession of the other moral virtues leads to the same
result, we arrive at the reciprocity thesis. I will leave it to the reader to ponder the
plausibility of this thesis.

There is another, even more controversial unity thesis associated with the virtues
according to which there really is not a plurality of virtues, but a single virtue.
According to this *single-virtue thesis*, when we talk about honesty, courage, temperance, justice, and the rest, we are really referring to a single psychological state.
Although Aristotle rejects the single-virtue view, Socrates is often cited as one of
its proponents. Specifically, the Socratic view is that all virtue is knowledge about
what is good and bad for human beings. Thus, to speak of courage is to speak of
that part of knowledge of good and bad that concerns proper actions and emotional reactions in circumstances of danger, while to speak of justice is to speak
of that part of knowledge of good and bad that concerns such things as proper
distribution of goods in society.

In light of what was just said about practical intelligence and the reciprocity of
the virtues, one can see how one might be led to embrace this single-virtue thesis.
We noted that, according to Aristotle, possession of a virtue requires possession
of intelligence, which, in turn, requires possession of all other virtues. But then
if intelligence is operative in all cases of virtuous action, shouldn't we conclude
that there is just one virtue—intelligence? If so, then what appear to be different
character traits are really just aspects of a single complex state of the virtuous
individual. Thus, what we call bravery, generosity, honesty, and the rest involve
the operation of the all-encompassing virtue of intelligence applied in different
circumstances.

While the single-virtue thesis entails the reciprocity thesis (if all virtues are at
bottom one, then having one requires having them all), one can hold the latter but
reject the former, which seems to have been Aristotle's considered view.[7] Again, I will
let the reader ponder the plausibility of the single-virtue thesis and not comment on
it here.[8]

We have only scratched the surface of the rich and subtle thought of Aristotle
on the virtues and their relation to human eudaimonia. But as I mentioned at the
outset, Aristotle's moral views, and his views about practical matters in general,

significantly inform contemporary discussions of virtue ethics. So having glanced at some of the main elements in Aristotle's treatment of the virtues and the good life for humans, let us now turn to developments in contemporary virtue ethics, beginning with some general remarks aimed at situating this general type of moral theory with respect to the views featured in the previous chapters.

3. VIRTUE ETHICS: SOME GENERAL REMARKS

Virtue ethics is often distinguished from other moral theories by citing a number of related points of contrast. Thus it is claimed that virtue ethics is "agent-centered" rather than "act-centered," that it is concerned with "being rather than doing," and that it attempts to answer the question "What sort of person should I be?" rather than "What should I do?"

Such contrasts can be misleading because they suggest that virtue ethics is simply not concerned with questions about right and wrong action and thus is not a rival to the moral theories we have been studying. However, as we shall see, virtue ethics does provide an account of right action that does rival the accounts featured in other moral theories. To see this more clearly, it will help to contrast the overall structure of virtue ethics with the structures characteristic of other, competing views.

As explained in chapter 1, a moral theory has two main components: a theory of right conduct and a theory of value. And within a theory of value, we distinguish accounts of intrinsic value and of moral worth. A moral theory is in the business of explaining the connections among the various batches of concepts. If one makes the deontic concepts (and associated categories to which they refer) featured in a theory of right conduct most basic in one's moral theory and then defines the value concepts in terms of the deontic concepts, one's overall moral theory is duty based. If, by contrast, one makes one of the two groups of value concepts most basic and defines the remaining two groups of concepts in terms of the most basic group, one's overall moral theory is value based. For instance, utilitarianism is a value-based theory featuring a welfarist conception of intrinsic value as most basic. *Virtue ethics* represents the other route for a value-based theory to go: make the concepts of virtue and vice—aretaic concepts—basic and then use them to define right and wrong action (and perhaps nonaretaic value).

I have been putting the basic contrasts between types of moral theory in terms of concepts and how they are definitionally related. However, one can also express the main differences between types of moral theory in terms of talk about various sorts of facts. So, we can express the basic idea behind virtue ethics as follows:

> **VE** Facts about virtuous agents and, in particular, facts about virtuous character traits possessed by such agents (1) are more basic than facts about right conduct and (2) are what explain why an action is right or wrong.

Notice that virtue ethics does not merely claim that focusing on what the virtuous agent would do can function as a decision procedure in helping us come to conclusions about the morality of actions. This point is worth stressing.

It might be the case that one way of coming to know whether an action is right or wrong in some circumstance is by appealing to what a virtuous agent would do. If, in the circumstance in question, a virtuous agent would refrain from doing A, then that is a reliable sign that A is wrong. But this way of *coming to know* whether an action is right or wrong is compatible with various possible explanations of what *makes* an action right or wrong. Even if one way (perhaps the best way) of coming to know what is right and wrong is by appealing to the choices of a virtuous agent, it might still be the case that what makes an action right or wrong is that it maximizes welfare, and if so, then a utilitarian moral theory provides a correct moral criterion of right conduct. Or, again granting that the best way to determine what one ought to do is by consulting a virtuous agent, it might nevertheless be the case that what makes an action right or wrong is to be explained in terms of how such actions bear on respecting persons, in which case a Kantian moral theory provides a correct moral criterion of right conduct.

What makes virtue ethics distinctive as a moral theory and thus a competitor to utilitarianism, Kant's moral theory, and other theories is the fact that it specifies a moral criterion that differs from these other views. It thus offers us an explanation of right and wrong action in terms of facts about a virtuous agent: an act is right *because* it is what a virtuous person does or would do. This claim about explanatory priority is expressed in VE.

Now in setting forth a theory of right conduct, any version of virtue ethics must accomplish two main tasks. First, it must begin with an account of a virtuous agent since, according to this type of theory, it is facts about the virtuous agent that make an action right or wrong. Accomplishing this first task involves in turn giving an account of a virtuous agent, by (1) specifying those character traits possessed by the agent that are virtues and (2) explaining what makes some character trait a virtue.

Suppose, then, that we are given an account of a virtuous agent, including an account of those character traits that are the virtues. With an account of a virtuous agent in hand, the second main task for virtue ethics is to characterize or define right and wrong action in terms of facts about a virtuous agent. In some circumstances, there are actions that a virtuous agent, guided by her virtuous character traits, would not fail to do. Such actions are obligatory. In other circumstances, there are actions that a virtuous agent would not do because they would express a vice. Such actions are wrong. So, for example, a wrongful act of telling a lie in some circumstance is wrong, according to virtue ethics, because a virtuous person would avoid telling the lie. And a virtuous person would avoid the lie because doing so would be dishonest, and dishonesty is a vice. And again, in still other circumstances, there are actions that a virtuous agent might (or might not) do, and this fact about them is what makes them optional. Here, then, are the principles of right conduct according to virtue ethics.

Theory of Right Conduct

An action A (performed in certain circumstances) is *obligatory* if and only if (and because) A is an action that a virtuous person (acting in character) would not fail to perform in the circumstances in question.

An action A (performed in certain circumstances) is *wrong* if and only if (and because) A is an action that a virtuous person (acting in character) would avoid performing in the circumstances in question.

An action A (performed in certain circumstances) is *optional* if and only if (and because) A is an action a virtuous person (acting in character) might perform in the circumstances.

Notice that there is an element of idealization built into these definitions.[9] Since we are defining the notions of objective rightness and wrongness, we are to suppose that a model hypothetical virtuous agent (whose choices and actions are the basis of right and wrong action) is aware of all of the morally relevant features of the circumstances pertaining to the act under evaluation and that the virtuous person (in the circumstances) acts (or refrains from acting) in ways that express the relevant set of virtues. This is why our model virtuous agent is described as "acting in character." We make these stipulations because we recognize that actual virtuous individuals may fail on occasion to exercise some virtue and so may, for example, fail to do the act that is obligatory. The virtuous agent featured in our definitions, then, is free from the kinds of defects that might interfere with an actual virtuous person's acting from virtue.

Much of the focus in the recent literature on virtue ethics concerns the relation between right conduct and virtue. A moral theory counts as a version of virtue ethics if right and wrong action is explained in terms of what a virtuous agent would or would not do. This is expressed above in VE. But VE says nothing about how the category of virtue or goodness of character generally (moral worth) is related to the category of intrinsic value. There are two main possibilities here.

One might take the notion of intrinsic positive value (intrinsic goodness) as basic and use it to define or explain the virtues. In this case the concept of virtue is derivative or at least not fundamental in one's overall moral theory. For instance, one might take the notion of a happy or flourishing life as fundamental and characterize the virtues as traits that contribute to living a happy life. The resulting moral theory will have the following structure: (1) a notion of value such as eudaimonia is fundamental, (2) virtue is understood in terms of eudaimonia, and (3) right action is in turn characterized in terms of virtue.

The second possibility is to treat virtue as morally fundamental and use it to define or explain both rightness and intrinsic goodness. The idea would be that certain character traits (or aspects of them) are intrinsically valuable—their goodness does not derive from being related to some other good. Moreover, facts about virtue and the life of a virtuous agent can be used to explain what makes a life an intrinsically good one—a life worth living—and what makes right actions right.

Figure 10.2 shows these two possible structures a virtue ethic might take. Any version of what we are calling virtue ethics features a virtue-based account of right action, although those versions conforming to the first structure are not (as a whole) virtue-based moral theories.

Finally, it is useful to pause for a moment to distinguish what we are calling virtue ethics from what Adams, (2006, 4–6) refers to indifferently as an "ethics of character" and an "ethics of virtue," and what others call "virtue theory." To minimize confusion, let us stick with the first of these labels. An ethics of character represents an attempt to address the questions: "What makes a person a person of moral worth, a person of good character?" "What makes a character trait a virtue or a vice?" These are questions any complete moral theory addresses as part of giving a theory of moral worth. But presumably an ethics of character also prescribes that one become a virtuous person, or at least makes prescriptions for moral education regarding the teaching or inculcation of virtues. Thus, one might propose a utilitarian or consequentialist account of the moral worth of persons and traits, or a Kantian account, or an account that fits with natural law theory, and so on, and then go on to propose that one acquire and maintain such traits of character. The point (to repeat) is that what is being called "virtue ethics" not only provides answers to these questions, but goes further in attempting to explain right conduct in terms of virtue, vice, and character generally. (This distinction between virtue ethics and ethics of character will come up again in section 6 in connection with empirical challenges to a particular conception of character and character traits that is often associated with virtue ethics.)

Let us now consider some examples of contemporary virtue ethics.

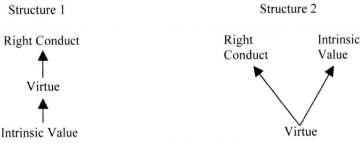

Figure 10.2. Two Main Structures for Virtue Ethics[1]

4. AN ETHICS OF CARE

One of the most important developments in recent moral theory has been the emergence of what has come to be called care ethics, which, as the label indicates, treats care as central for understanding the nature of morality. The development of care ethics was largely sparked by the psychologist Carol Gilligan's 1982 book, *In a Different Voice.* Gilligan's book is concerned to describe a "different moral voice" that she detected in various studies in which women subjects were asked to describe and react to various moral dilemmas. For instance, one study involved twenty-nine pregnant women, ranging in age from fifteen to twenty-three, who were facing the decision of whether to have an abortion. The moral voice of many of these women represents a moral perspective that Gilligan calls a care perspective, which she contrasts with a familiar justice perspective.[10] Here is how Gilligan explains some basic points of contrast between these perspectives:

> From a justice perspective, the self as moral agent stands as the figure against a ground of social relationships, judging the conflicting claims of self and others against a standard of equality or equal respect (the Categorical Imperative, the Golden Rule). From a care perspective, the relationship becomes the figure, defining self and others. Within the context of relationship, the self as moral agent perceives and responds to the perception of need. The shift in moral perspective is manifest by a change in the moral question from "What is just?" to "How to respond?" (Gilligan, 1987, 23)

Both moral perspectives, then, involve contrasting conceptions of (1) the image of self and its relation to other members of the moral community, (2) the nature of moral problems that arise for members of this community, and (3) how such problems can be rationally resolved. Figure 10.3 summarizes the differences between the justice and care perspectives with respect to these three points of contrast.

In her book, Gilligan argues that although many of her subjects were able to organize and think about a moral issue from either perspective, females tended to approach moral issues from the care perspective, while males tended to employ the justice perspective. Because psychological studies of moral development as well as moral theories have traditionally focused almost exclusively on the justice perspective, part of the importance of Gilligan's work is to bring into focus a moral orientation centered around care.

Inspired by Gilligan's work, some moral philosophers have attempted to develop and defend an ethic of care. The basic idea is that care is fundamental for understanding moral phenomena. Focusing on care as a virtue allows one to develop care ethics as a version of virtue ethics.[11] Let us begin by clarifying the notion of care, and then we will be in a position to present and evaluate an ethic of care understood as a version of virtue ethics.

Points of Contrast	Justice	Care
Conception of Self	The self as an individual, one among other individuals. Individuality is primary.	The self as a member of various Relationships. Relatedness to others is primary.
Nature of Moral Problems	To protect individual interests in a manner that preserves equal respect for all. Moral problems in need of resolution center around questions of inequality.	To maintain and foster connections with others. Moral problems in need of resolution center around questions of disconnection and abandonment.
Moral Reasoning	Proper moral reasoning involves viewing matters impartially and appealing to order to resolve moral conflicts.	Proper moral reasoning involves a sensitivity to the particularities of a moral issue. Principles may be of some use but cannot always be used to resolve moral conflicts.

Figure 10.3.   Justice and Care Perspectives Contrasted

5. WHAT IS CARE?

It is important to distinguish three senses of the term "care" in English, and hence three types of care.[12] Here is a brief description of each type.

- *Caring for.* To care for something (like ice cream) or some person involves liking and being attracted to the thing or person in question. You might not care for Thai cuisine; I do. I might not care for someone (perhaps because he makes me feel uncomfortable) whereas you do care for him.
- *Having care of.* If something or someone is entrusted to me, I have care of the thing or person in question. Someone may have care of her sick daughter, in the sense of having the responsibility for her well-being. I may have care of your plants and cats while you are away; they are in my charge. Clearly, one may have care of without liking or being attracted to what one has care of, and so one may have care of something without caring for it.
- *Caring about.* To care about something or someone involves "being invested" in that thing or person; it involves regarding that thing or person as important to oneself.[13] Caring about something differs from caring for that thing. A father may not care for his teenage son but care about him. In caring about him, the father's own well-being is tied to his son's. He is delighted when his son excels in sports, is unhappy when he finds that his son has taken up smoking. One can also care for someone in that one likes and is attracted to the person in question, but one may not care about that person because one is rather indifferent toward her well-being.

It is this notion of caring about that is featured in care ethics, and so let us focus on it.

Some Dimensions of Caring About

The notion of caring about is complex, and it will help in our understanding of care ethics if we make explicit some of its dimensions.

First, one can care about all sorts of things: persons, ideas, material objects, cultures, and so on. We are particularly interested in caring about persons—both ourselves and others—and in regard to such caring, it is important to distinguish *personal* and *impersonal* care, particularly in relation to caring about others. My caring about someone is personal when it is the particular person in question who is cared about. I care about my daughter because Emily is the person she is. By contrast, I care about someone impersonally when, for example, in a context of helping them, it is not the particular person in question who sparks my care, but the fact that this person is someone who needs my help. The identity of the person I help through my impersonal care is irrelevant to my caring; I care about them because they satisfy the description "someone in need" and I care about helping those in need (whoever they are). This distinction will be important later on.

Some other dimensions of caring about involve *breadth* and *degree*. Regarding breadth, one may only care about a small number of people and be indifferent to the rest of humanity; or, at the limit, one may care about all of humanity. But even if one's care extends to everyone, it is likely that there will be differences in one's degrees of caring about. Loving one's family members and friends involves caring about them very deeply. Normally, one's level of care directed toward casual acquaintances is of a lower degree than the sort one has for loved ones, though higher in degree than the level of care one has toward strangers.

We are particularly interested in care as a virtue, where the relevant notion of care is caring about and where, in particular, we are interested in caring about persons. Here, then, is a partial profile of caring about as a virtue:

- *Intellectual component.* Caring about persons (including oneself) involves the capacity to recognize when those cared about are in need, as well as knowing in general what is good for individuals in certain circumstances.
- *Affective component.* Caring about other persons involves being disposed to feel pleasure in response to their successes, pain in response to their failures. The intensity of such pleasures and pains will normally vary in relation to the closeness of the other. In caring about oneself, one is disposed to feel joy at one's successes, unhappiness and perhaps depression over one's failures.
- *Motivational-behavioral component.* Caring about others typically involves a non-self-interested desire to help them—one is disposed to act on someone's

behalf out of a direct regard for that person's welfare. Caring about oneself involves wanting to do those things that will best promote one's well-being and wanting to avoid what will be detrimental to one's well-being.

Being a caring person—having the virtue of caring about—is far more complex than is indicated in the above profile. But I trust that enough has been said about the concept of caring about so that we can proceed to examine a version of virtue ethics that takes this concept as central.

A Version of Virtue Ethics Featuring Care

If we let care be the fundamental or cardinal moral virtue, then we can reformulate our generic statement of the principles of right conduct to capture the idea that the virtue of care is central in determining the rightness and wrongness of actions. In doing so, we simply specify that our hypothetical virtuous agent is one with the virtue of caring about—a caring agent.

Theory of Right Conduct: Ethics of Care

An action A (performed in some circumstance) is *obligatory* if and only if (and because) A is an action that a caring agent (acting in character) would not fail to perform in the circumstances in question.

An action A (performed in some circumstance) is *wrong* if and only if (and because) A is an action that a caring agent (acting in character) would avoid performing in the circumstances in question.

An action A (performed in some circumstance) is *optional* if and only if (and because) A is an action that a caring agent (acting in character) might perform in the circumstances in question.

We shall consider the advantages of virtue ethics, as a general type of moral theory, later on in the chapter. What many find especially attractive about an ethics of care is the fact that it can accommodate our sense that special moral significance attaches to those closest to us. This is not, of course, to say that considerations of caring for strangers cannot be more important in some situations than caring for loved ones and friends. But in general we suppose that relationships one has with family and friends have a special moral significance that is not plausibly captured by impartialist views like utilitarianism. Granted, the utilitarian can claim that we are more likely to maximize utility by giving special attention to family and friends, but this sort of indirect explanation of the moral significance of such relations seems less plausible than the account on offer by an ethics of care.

Objections to the Ethics of Care

One objection to the ethics of care is that not all instances of caring about are morally good. This point is developed by Jeffrey Blustein:

> One might care about another person in such a way that one does not leave the other sufficient scope for the expression and development of an independent personality. One might also care too much about x in the sense that x occupies too much of one's attention. My appraisal of x itself might be sound enough and x might not be something or someone that I wish I did not care about, but I might be so preoccupied or obsessed with x that I am prevented from leading a happy and productive life. (Blustein, 1991, 40)

Other problematic cases include caring about someone in a way that involves injustice. To help someone in their plan to rob a bank simply to help them accomplish their goals is clearly wrong. Certainly, caring about someone or something is not morally admirable unless such caring is tempered by other moral considerations. The point of these observations is that in developing a care ethic, it is not enough to appeal to the notion of caring about since, as the examples illustrate, there can be bad forms of such care.

Now in response to this worry, the defender of care ethics has a ready reply. Regarding the case Blustein describes, one can say that *genuine* care—the sort of care that exemplifies the virtue of caring about—does not, for example, stifle the development of the person who is cared about, because having this virtue normally involves knowing what is in the genuine interests of self and others and being disposed to act accordingly. Since the virtue of caring about normally involves knowledge of what is genuinely good for objects of one's care, and since stifling someone's individuality and autonomy is not good for them, a person who acts as a caring person will care in ways that allow for the expression and development of an independent personality. Furthermore, genuine caring not only involves caring for others but caring for oneself. An individual who is so obsessed with caring for another person that it stifles his own life fails to care enough about himself.

Again, in caring, one must understand the impact of one's caring efforts on the immediate recipient of the care and on others who may be affected. Blindly helping the would-be robber carry out her plan—even if one is motivated by the desire to help—obviously ignores the impact on others and society generally of giving such help. So having the virtue of caring about involves having the sort of understanding that guides one's caring activities in ways that avoid bad forms of "care."

This kind of response seems entirely appropriate, but notice what is happening. The virtuous caring person who would avoid helping a criminal carry out some devious plan because of how it would affect the welfare of others is someone whose care is tempered by justice.[14] It would be an act of injustice to help the would-be robber. In other words, the sort of caring about that is good and worthy of admiration is tempered by other virtues like justice. And this observation leads us to the next objection.

Critics of care ethics have argued that the virtue of care (even if the theory features the broad notion of caring about) is not an adequate basis for understanding the entirety of morality.[15] As we have just noticed, justice is required if we are to properly understand certain duties and obligations, and a case can be made for the importance of other virtues as well.

There are two ways in which a care ethicist might attempt to accommodate justice and other virtues. First, she might appeal to the reciprocity thesis and claim that to properly and fully possess a virtue like care requires that one possess certain other virtues. Perhaps one need not suppose that in having one virtue, one must possess all the rest. It might be that there is a core set of moral virtues whose possession is a package deal. But then what began as a monistic virtue ethic based on the sole virtue of caring about is now transformed into a pluralist version of virtue ethics featuring a number of basic virtues along with care. But this is to give up a care-based virtue ethic.

The second way in which a defender of a care-based virtue ethic might deal with the objection under discussion is to argue that the virtue of care is the most fundamental virtue and all other moral virtues are forms of, or subordinate to, care. Consider, for example, the virtue of honesty. One might argue that honesty is a form of caring about oneself and others. In caring about oneself and others, one cares about a person's capacity for making rational decisions—one cares about their autonomy. And in so caring, one must possess the virtue of honesty since deceiving oneself and others hinders autonomy. In a similar manner, one might claim that temperance is involved in properly caring about oneself.

Now if the care ethicist can incorporate a range of moral virtues in the way just explained, then one seemingly has a way of accommodating our duties and obligations that involves being just, honest, brave, and so forth while retaining a monistic virtue ethic based on care.

But now notice this. If honesty, temperance, justice, courage, and the other moral virtues are understood to be forms of care, then one suspects the notion of care being invoked is so abstract and "thin" that we might as well admit that there is a handful of specific virtues, none of which is more basic than the others. And once we admit this, we end up with a moral theory involving a very abstract moral ideal—the agent who cares about others—and instead of thinking that this ideal can be used to derive more specific virtues, it is more plausible to suppose that it functions as a way of connecting all of the more specific virtues that are the basis of moral evaluation. Let me explain this point a bit further by relating it to some observations we made in connection with Kant's concept of respecting humanity and in connection with Ross's moral pluralism.

In chapter 8 we noted that the idea of respecting humanity (treating someone as an end in themselves) is best understood as a very abstract moral ideal. It is too abstract (so it was suggested) to be the basis of a moral principle that one could use to derive a system of specific moral duties. Rather, as was suggested in chapter 9 in connection with Ross's theory, this ideal serves to connect the various rules of prima facie duty and help us understand why those rules having to do with fidelity, reparation, gratitude, justice, beneficence, self-improvement, and nonmaleficence express moral requirements. I am making a similar suggestion about the notion of care.

Once we notice that the broad notion of care featured in care ethics involves other virtues as forms of caring about, then the role of care in a moral theory is analogous to the role of respecting humanity in the theories of Kant and Ross. This means that like Ross's theory (as well as my interpretation of Kant's theory) an ethic of care is best understood as embracing a kind of pluralism, in this case, virtue pluralism. The suggestion, then, is that there is a plurality of equally basic moral virtues that determine moral goodness of persons as well as the basis of the rightness and wrongness of actions. What makes them *moral* virtues is that they can be seen as forms of care.

I am not suggesting that there are no essential differences between, for example, Kant's moral theory and an ethic of care. A care ethic recognizes the moral importance of the sort of care present in relationships of love and friendship—what I have been calling personal care—and this may be missing (and certainly is not emphasized) in Kant's theory. According to Kant's moral theory, one of the two major categories of duties of virtue concerns the happiness and well-being of others. Kant does allow that we can show differential concern and care for those who are close to us: "If one is closer to me than another (in the duty of benevolence) . . . I am therefore under an obligation to greater benevolence to one than to the other."[16] However, this sort of caring about—an impersonal form of caring—involves caring about loved ones and friends as persons possessing dignity and not as persons with the particular identities involved in personal care. (You may recall that we noted a similar point about how a utilitarian might account for the value of caring about particular others.)

Even if a care-*based* version of virtue ethics is problematic for the reasons mentioned, we can nevertheless incorporate into a pluralistic version of virtue ethics the idea that moral significance attaches to personal caring. So let us now consider a pluralist version of virtue ethics.

6. PLURALIST VIRTUE ETHICS

Pluralist versions of virtue ethics recognize a plurality of basic or cardinal virtues (at least two) that are central in characterizing the notion of a virtuous agent. And for the virtue ethicist, as we have seen, the notion of a virtuous agent is central in explaining the nature of right action. To illustrate, let us work with a version of virtue ethics that recognizes benevolence, courage, generosity, gratitude, justice, honesty, loyalty, and temperance as basic moral virtues. Thus, recalling the principle concerning obligatory actions featured in the virtue ethics theory of right conduct:

An action A (performed in certain circumstances) is *obligatory* if and only if (and because) A is an action that a virtuous person (acting in character) would not fail to perform in the circumstances in question.

If we now define a virtuous agent as one who possesses the set of virtues just mentioned, we end up with a more precise principle of obligation:

An action A (performed in certain circumstances) is *obligatory* if and only if (and because) A is an action that a person having the virtues of benevolence, courage, generosity, gratitude, justice, honesty, loyalty, and temperance would not fail to perform in the circumstances.

The principles for the categories of the optional and the wrong are specified in a similar manner.

A pluralistic virtue ethic must involve some account of how conflicts among the virtues are to be resolved. Suppose, for example, one of your family members is wanted by the police, and since you know of his whereabouts, you are torn between being truthful and being loyal.[17] In cases where two or more virtue considerations are relevant and indicate incompatible courses of action, what should one do?

I am sympathetic to those virtue ethicists who propose that conflicts among the virtues be understood in a way analogous to how Ross understands conflicts of duty.[18] Ross, you may recall, denies that there is any fixed rank ordering of the basic prima facie duties to which one can appeal in adjudicating conflicts among them. Nor, according to Ross, is there any moral super principle or rule that determines how such conflicts are to be adjudicated. Rather, coming to correct moral verdicts in these cases of conflict is a matter of having and using good moral judgment, or phronesis.

I believe the most plausible form of pluralist virtue ethics will be similar to Ross's theory in denying that there is any fixed rank ordering of basic virtues to which one can appeal in adjudicating cases where the virtues conflict. That is, in circumstances where considerations involving one virtue favor the performance of an action while considerations involving another virtue favor refraining from that same action, a virtuous agent must use sound moral judgment in coming to a correct verdict about what ought to be done. Of course, this means that the most plausible version of virtue ethics is going to be a limited, pluralistic moral theory.

Let us now turn from presentation to evaluation of virtue ethics.

7. EVALUATION OF VIRTUE ETHICS

The recent revival of virtue ethics has been spurred largely by dissatisfaction with other moral theories, particularly Kantian and consequentialist theories. The dissatisfaction centers around the accounts of right action and virtue offered by rivals to virtue ethics.

The main complaint about non-virtue-based accounts of right action is that they attempt to identify abstract moral principles and rules that are then supposed to be applied to particular cases in order to arrive at justified moral judgments about the particular case at hand. Three related criticisms are often raised here. Let us examine them.

First, critics contend that the sorts of principles and rules featured in Kantian and utilitarian moral theories are too abstract to be very helpful in particular cases. This seems particularly true in connection with the Humanity formulation of Kant's Categorical Imperative, which requires that we treat ourselves and others never as mere means but always as ends in ourselves. Because this principle is so abstract, it seems to be useless for purposes of deciding what one ought to do in a wide range of particular cases. Does the practice of capital punishment involve using the one executed as a mere means? One finds advocates of this practice claiming that it respects the dignity of those executed and so does not amount to treating them as mere means, but one also finds opponents of capital punishment who claim that the dignity of the executed is violated and so the practice does treat some persons as mere means.

Virtue ethics avoids this problem because, although its account of right action does involve an appeal to abstract principles that make reference to what an ideal virtuous agent would do in certain circumstances, the principles are made more concrete when a specification of the virtues is added to the account.

A second related complaint is that non-virtue-based accounts of right conduct tend to be too reductive, in the sense that they attempt to account for our obligations in terms of a single fundamental morally relevant feature. Kant's theory attempts to account for obligation in terms of whether an action treats someone as a mere means, while utilitarianism attempts to account for obligation in terms of whether an action maximizes utility. The problem with such accounts of right action, according to the critics, is that they cannot plausibly account for various areas of moral life. In particular, a utilitarian moral theory is not able to account plausibly for special relationships involving family and friends. A pluralist version of virtue ethics, which can and should allow for considerations of caring about particular others, obviously avoids this problem and, in general, does not suffer from trying to account for right and wrong in terms of utility maximization or in terms of any single feature of actions.

Finally, critics often contend that non-virtue-based accounts of right action are unacceptably algorithmic in the way they attempt to deal with concrete moral problems. That is, such accounts seem to involve the idea that anyone who understands the principle of utility or the Universal Law formulation of the Categorical Imperative can mechanically apply it to some concrete situation calling for a moral response and derive a correct moral verdict about what one ought or ought not do. But, according to the critics, such a mechanical approach to moral decision making ignores the important role of moral judgment or phronesis in proper moral judgment and decision making. And, as we have seen, moral judgment plays a crucial role in a virtue-based account of right action.

I hope that it is fairly obvious to the reader that these objections to non-virtue-based approaches to accounts of right action do not favor a virtue-based account over certain non-virtue-based approaches. For example, Ross's non-virtue-based account of right action (1) does not involve overly abstract moral principles that determine the deontic status of individual actions; (2) is not overly reductive; and (3) rejects any algorithmic approach in the process of reaching correct moral verdicts about particular cases by recognizing an important role for moral judgment in this process. I have also argued that other moral theories, including natural law theory, utilitarianism, and Kant's moral theory, when suitably refined, are much like Ross's view in these respects.

So although the features of virtue ethics just mentioned are advantages of the theory over theories that lack them, they do not single out this type of moral theory as superior to all rival moral theories.

Turning from accounts of right action to accounts of virtue, defenders of virtue ethics make a dual complaint about how the virtues are treated by utilitarianism (and consequentialism generally) and Kantian approaches. First, the very notion of a virtue is often defined by such theories in terms of motivation, that is, as a matter of simply being disposed to do what is right. Thus, for example, the virtue of honesty is defined simply as the character trait that disposes one to tell the truth and avoid lies on appropriate occasions. One problem with such definitions, according to the critics, is that a virtue-based account of right action is obviously ruled out from the start. Clearly, an account of right action cannot be truly virtue based unless right and wrong action can be explained in terms of virtue or the activities of the virtuous agent without appealing to the concept of a right action in understanding what a virtue is. And defenders of virtue ethics think that the virtues can be understood independently of the notion of right action (and related deontic notions).

The second complaint is that defining a virtue merely as a disposition to do what is right does not do justice to the rich complexity of virtuous character traits. As we have seen, a virtue is a complex state involving not only a motivational-behavioral component but also intellectual and affective components.

Again, these complaints do not show that a virtue ethic is necessarily superior to rival moral theories, since it is open to a non-virtue-based theory to reject definitions of the virtues in terms of right action and recognize the complexity of virtuous character traits.

So far, then, we have not found any reasons for preferring a virtue ethic to at least some of its rivals. If a virtue-based ethic is superior to its non-virtue-based rivals, it will have to be because grounding a theory of right conduct on considerations of virtue provides a more plausible account of right action than does any competing view. But there are reasons for doubt about this matter, as we shall see.

Objections to Virtue Ethics

Let us consider five main objections to virtue ethics. The first has to do with the fact that the theory fails to provide real guidance in concrete situations calling for a moral decision; the second raises a skeptical worry about the conception of character traits in general and the virtues in particular; the third and fourth have to do with how the theory explains right action; and the fifth concerns the threat of relativism. Let us take these up in order.

Indeterminacy. The standard of right conduct set forth by virtue ethics tells us that an action's rightness or wrongness depends on what a virtuous agent (acting in character) would (or would not) do in some specific situation. A virtuous agent possesses a range of virtues, and in cases where the relevant virtues conflict, there is no super rule or rank ordering of the virtues that determines what the virtuous agent would do. Rather, as we have explained, in such cases, the virtuous agent, who, we assume, has practical intelligence, is able to discern which virtue consideration in the situation at hand is most important and acts accordingly. Such intelligence or phronesis is not something that can be fully characterized in terms of rules or principles. Thus, according to the objection, the theory fails to yield real guidance in a great many cases.

Earlier, the fact that the principles of virtue ethics (at least the kind of pluralist version presented in section 6) do not represent a moral algorithm for making moral decisions and are thus significantly indeterminate was put forth as an advantage of the theory—an advantage because it looks as if we cannot plausibly expect more determinacy from the principles of a plausible moral theory. Here, this very same fact about the theory is being used to criticize it.

The best response to this objection is simply to admit that virtue ethics is limited in this way and then go on to explain that such limits are to be expected given the complexity of moral phenomena. Since we have already encountered this theme of limited determinacy and will briefly return to it again in the concluding chapter, let us move on to other objections.

External support. One apparent challenge to virtue ethics comes from experimental social psychology, specifically from a research program known as "situationism," and so has to do with the standard of external support. The basis of the challenge is skepticism about character traits generally and virtues in particular ("virtue skepticism")—understood as attributes of one's personality that are "robust" in the sense that they dispose one to display trait-consistent behavior across a range of different situations. A host of experimental data supposedly casts doubt on people's behavior being explained by such traits; rather, according to the situationist paradigm, people's behavior is far more sensitive to variable factors of situations they confront than is compatible with possession of robust traits. From the perspective of the situationist, traits (including virtues) are rare if not non-existent. If we should not (in general) believe that people's behavior is explained (and predicted) by psychological character traits, if character traits (including virtues) are non-existent or extremely rare, then presumably this is bad news for approaches to ethics that make virtue central. As Gilbert Harman, a leading defender of situationist-inspired virtue-skepticism, puts it: "if we know that there is no such thing as a character trait, and we know that virtue would require having character traits, there is nothing one can do to acquire character traits that are more like those possessed by a virtuous agent" (2000, 224).

If Harman is correct, then *any* normative moral theory (and so not just versions of virtue ethics) prescribing that one ought to acquire those robust character traits that count as virtues is guilty not only of being psychologically unrealistic, but (more seriously) in violation of the "ought" implies "can" doctrine—roughly, the thesis that for it to be true that one ought to perform some action or, as in the present case, bring about some state of affairs (having a virtue), it must be an action or state of affairs one can in fact perform or bring about.

Unfortunately, space does not permit more than a few passing remarks at what turns out to be a complicated debate in empirical psychology.[19] So rather than plunge into these deep waters, I wish to make two related comments about the bearing of virtue skepticism on moral theories that feature the virtues. My claim is going to be that even if skepticism about the virtues is correct, this fact alone does not show that VE is false. Nor does it show that moral theories that develop an ethics of character are completely misguided.

To be clear, the kind of virtue skepticism under consideration is a claim about people's *actual* psychology. So, for example, the view implies that at least for the most part, people's pro-social "moral" behavior is not to be explained (or predicted) by their possession of the virtue of compassion or some other pro-social trait. Assume (just for the sake of argument) that this psychological claim is true. What implications would this have for our version of virtue ethics, for VE? VE makes the deontic status of action depend on what a hypothetical virtuous agent (acting in character) would do or not do. As explained earlier, it does not make right and wrong depend on an agent's actual character traits; it does not say, for instance, that the rightness of an act of helping a stranger in need depends on (and is explained by) the act being a product of the agent's virtue of compassion. An agent lacking the virtue of compassion, but who, on some occasion, is engaged in helping behavior does the right act so long as it is what a hypothetically virtuous agent would do in the circumstances in question. This shows that even if very few human agents, if any, possess virtues, the version of virtue ethics featured in this chapter may still be true. Compare: suppose first that someone holds the view that one morally ought to do what Jesus would do because Jesus has certain virtues which are the basis of explaining right and wrong action for humans. And now suppose that Jesus (as God) has virtuous character traits that are beyond the reach of human beings. And, finally, suppose that were Jesus in the situation in which you now find yourself, he would tell the truth. Then, on the basis on these suppositions, one morally ought to tell the truth. One's telling the truth will not flow from the sort of virtuous character trait possessed by Jesus, but for purposes of doing what one ought to do this does not matter. The truth of (empirical) virtue skepticism does not entail that VE is a mistaken theory of right conduct.

Now consider how virtue skepticism bears on ethical theories of character. You may recall from our earlier discussion in section 3 that an ethics of character attempts to answer questions about the nature of the virtues and about what makes a person overall virtuous with the additional aim of prescribing that we try to cultivate such traits and thereby strive to become virtuous overall. If Harman is right and there is nothing one can do to acquire such traits, then success in acquiring them cannot be required. Granted. But this does not (strictly speaking) rule out an ethic of character that would only prescribe that one strive as best one can toward such ideal traits of character. An ethics of character, so understood, is not undermined by the situationist critique of the virtues. Kant, you may recall, held that the duty of self-perfection is the duty to strive toward an ideal of complete virtue; he denied that humans (at least in this life) can achieve perfection.[20] Besides, Harman's claim is far stronger, it seems, than one is permitted to infer from the relevant experiments: at most they show that the virtues are rare; they do not show that as psychological attributes no one has any of them. And if one embraces either the unity or the reciprocity thesis described earlier in section 2 (which put high standards on having any one virtue), then one can concede without worry the alleged skeptical results of the experiments and then go on to insist that genuine possession of a virtue is a difficult achievement.

Two final comments. First, despite my remarks about the bearing of virtue skepticism on VE and the ethics of character, it is still true that if Harman is right and people do not have character traits, or (more modestly) we lack good reason for thinking they do, then thinking of ethics in terms of virtue is arguably less attractive than it would be otherwise.[21] But second, although we have not discussed the relevant literature, one finds powerful defenses of the reality of robust traits generally and virtues in particular in opposition to trait and virtue skepticism. (See, for example, Snow, 2010.) I venture to say (with some caution) that virtue ethics and the ethics of character are safe from virtue skepticism.

Internal support and explanatory power. Even if the first two objections to virtue ethics can be met in the ways just described, the remaining three objections are more problematic. Although I do not think they count decisively against this type of theory, they do present serious challenges to any virtue-based account of right conduct and at least call for the advocate of virtue ethics to work out certain details of the theory. The first of these has to do with the question of whether what one morally ought to do in various situations is just what the virtuous agent, acting in character, would not fail to do—it has to do with the criterion of internal support. Critics have come up with examples that suggest VE's account of right action does not square with our considered moral beliefs in particular cases. One such example concerns self-improvement. Robert Johnson (2003) imagines a mendacious person who is a compulsive liar, even about trivial matters that cause little or no harm to others. He has the vice of dishonesty. At some point in life he becomes convinced that he ought to change because he comes to see mendacity as a vice and honesty as a trait one ought to have. But in order to bring about this personal change, he cannot simply say to himself with conviction, "ok, from now on I won't tell lies"; he knows better. What he must do is engage in a regimen that involves taking concrete steps such as writing down lies that he tells and reflecting on their true significance, rewarding himself at the end of those days in which he tells no lies, and other such tactics. The point is that he morally ought to engage in some such activities for purposes of moral self-improvement, but none of these concrete activities are characteristic of what an ideally virtuous agent would engage in. An ideally virtuous agent has the virtue of honesty, so such actions are not characteristic of a fully virtuous agent. So, here we have a counterexample to the claim that the act one morally ought to do (in any circumstance) is an act that a fully virtuous agent, acting in character, would not fail to do.

Perhaps there is a way to amend VE so that it avoids this counterexample and others. One challenge in doing so would be to avoid appealing to deontic concepts in characterizing a fully virtuous agent, for otherwise the account of right action on offer would be circular.[22] Even if this challenge can be overcome, I think something more seriously worrisome for VE looms and concerns the criterion of explanatory power. The worry I have in mind can be posed in the form of a dilemma. Let me explain.

According to the theory of right conduct in question, an action's rightness or wrongness depends on what a virtuous agent (acting in character) would do in some situation. The idea is that facts about our hypothetical virtuous agent—facts about her character traits—are what explain why certain actions are right and others are wrong. Let us take an example.

Suppose that in a situation in which some particular individual needs help, our hypothetical virtuous agent would not fail to perform an act of beneficence. According to the theory of right conduct, such an action is right (indeed, obligatory). What on this account makes it right? Presumably, the fact that such an action would flow from, and hence express the character trait of, benevolence. But, we may ask, why does this character trait bestow upon actions flowing from it the property of rightness? The obvious thing to say is that this character trait is good. The goodness of the character trait, then, bestows upon the action flowing from it the property of rightness.

Of course, we can now ask why this character trait is good. There would seem to be two possible responses. First, one might claim that its goodness cannot be explained but rather is just an unexplained fact about the trait in question. But this response seems unsatisfying since there does seem to be a way of plausibly explaining why a trait like benevolence is good. Here is one such explanation. The goodness of benevolence is due to the fact that it involves certain attitudes and motives directed toward the well-being of others—others who have a dignity and worth. It is thus the fact that others have a dignity and worth that explains why certain attitudes and motivation characteristic of benevolence are good.

But notice what has happened. If we explain the goodness of benevolence in the way just proposed, then it seems we can explain the rightness of an act of beneficence directly in terms of how such an act affects creatures having dignity and worth. In other words, when we follow through and try to understand what it is, according to virtue ethics, that makes right actions right and wrong actions wrong, we are led by a series of plausible steps to a view that makes rightness and wrongness depend on facts about whether the action treats others in a manner that respects their dignity and worth.[23]

So the dilemma is this. In explaining right conduct in terms of character traits, we can ask what it is about those traits that confer rightness or wrongness on an action. Traits that confer rightness do so in virtue of their being good. Now, either the goodness of such traits is an unexplained brute fact or it isn't. On one hand, to claim that it is an unexplained brute fact seems implausible in light of the fact that we can offer explanations of the goodness of such traits. On the other hand, the sorts of explanations we are inclined to offer allow us to explain the rightness of an action without appealing to character traits themselves.

There are two possible responses to this dilemma. First, an advocate of virtue ethics might claim that certain character traits just are intrinsically good and that their goodness need not be further explained. In coming to know which character traits are good and hence count as virtues, one might claim that there are self-evident truths about the virtues that, given sufficient maturity, one can come to grasp through intuition.[24] Or, if one rejects intuitionism, one can perhaps appeal to the standard of internal support and argue that because claims about the goodness of certain traits are supported by the body of our considered moral beliefs, we have good reason to suppose that the traits in question are intrinsically good.

Another response to the dilemma is to attempt to explain the goodness of certain character traits in terms of their contribution to human eudaimonia or flourishing.[25] The prospects for accomplishing this Aristotelian project are featured in the fourth challenge, to be taken up shortly. However, for the time being, let us suppose that the goodness of a character trait (and hence its status as a virtue) is to be explained by appeal to some notion of human flourishing. In particular, one can attempt to show that possession of certain traits contributes to the flourishing of the individual who possesses them or that they contribute to the flourishing of people in general. And, of course, one might attempt to show both claims. But if one can explain the goodness of a character trait in terms of its contribution to human flourishing, why can't one explain the rightness of an action (or perhaps a type of action) directly in terms of its contribution to human flourishing? If we can, then we don't need to first explain the goodness of traits in terms of flourishing and then explain the rightness of actions in terms of the goodness of traits; we can explain both the goodness of traits and the rightness of actions directly in terms of flourishing.

These worries go to the heart of virtue ethics because if virtue considerations do not serve to properly explain the deontic status of actions, then the principles of virtue ethics fail to satisfy the standard of explanatory power, which means that they do not express correct moral criteria for right action. But instead of pursuing this further, let us turn to questions about the attempt to account for the virtues in terms of human flourishing.

Virtues and human flourishing. A final challenge to virtue ethics has to do with a skeptical worry about the virtues. There has been some dispute among philosophers about what character traits are virtues. Is compassion a virtue? The nineteenth-century German philosopher Friedrich Nietzsche denied it. What about modesty? The seventeenth-century Scottish philosopher David Hume did not think so. Humility? Not according to Aristotle.[26] So how can we determine which character traits really are the virtues and which ones really are the vices? We need some account of why a character trait is a virtue.[27] One might claim that what counts as a virtue fully depends on the values of one's culture and that, consequently, there is no objective backing to what is and is not a virtue; rather it is all relative to culture. But it has been the aim of those advocating virtue ethics to avoid this kind of relativism.

So the challenge to the virtue ethicist is to provide an account of the virtues that explains why certain character traits are virtues and others are vices, and to do so in a way that avoids relativism.

Some contemporary virtue ethicists have taken on this challenge by attempting to follow Aristotle's lead and ground the virtues in an account of eudaimonia (happiness, flourishing). As we have seen, the basic idea behind this sort of neo-Aristotelian approach is to argue that certain character traits are virtues because they contribute to eudaimonia (either of the individual who possesses them or of people generally). The two-part strategy associated with this idea is, first, to provide an account of human flourishing and, second, to show that certain character traits, because they importantly contribute to such flourishing, are for that reason good and hence count as virtues.

What account, then, can be given of human flourishing? Presumably, we base an account of the flourishing of something on that thing's internal nature; in particular, we base it on the characteristic activities of the thing in question. Were there a single, relatively specific characteristic human activity—such as contemplation—then one could go on to specify those character traits that contribute importantly to this activity, and they would be the virtues. Human beings are capable of intellectual contemplation, but it seems arbitrary to pick this specific form of human activity and claim that a contemplative life alone is what true human flourishing is all about. The problem is that humans, unlike other animals, are quite diverse in their goals and activities. We thus recognize human lives given over to projects other than contemplation as flourishing lives. Can one specify which projects are truly characteristic of human beings in order to come up with some specific form of characteristic activity that constitutes human flourishing?

Certainly, it won't help the project of grounding some set of virtues to appeal to the *actual* goals and projects of individuals in giving an account of flourishing, because doing so will lead very quickly to relativism. Some individuals place a high premium on competitive activity where certain character traits serve the person well. Others shun competition and aim to lead a simple, conflict-free life; for them a different set of character traits contributes to their flourishing. And so on. If we appeal to the actual goals and projects of individuals, we end up making what counts as a virtue relative to a person's value system. As we have noted, the virtue ethicist hopes to avoid relativism.[28]

The hope is to find some characteristic feature of human beings that such beings have quite apart from their specific goals and projects and whose realization in humans could plausibly be understood to constitute human flourishing. One suggestion is that flourishing for humans consists in the development of a cohesive sense of self and the activities that express one's self.[29] To develop such a sense of one's self will require, for instance, that one form a coherent, integrated plan for living so that one's goals and projects can be achieved. Certain character traits like prudence will be needed for success in pursuing the development of a unified sense of self. However, the problem with appealing to a very general notion of flourishing like the one in question is that it is not specific enough to be of use in determining which from among a great many character traits are virtues and which are vices.

A nice illustration of this point can be found in an article by Sarah Conly where she persuasively argues that traits like courage and justice cannot be shown to be virtues by appealing to this very general conception of flourishing. Here is her example of how one might flourish (in the sense of having a developed and unified sense of self) without being a just person.

> Take Lorenzo the Magnificent. If Florence in the Renaissance was great it is largely Lorenzo who made it so. Astute and ambitious, he navigated the labyrinthine difficulties of fifteenth-century Italian politics with dexterity, establishing himself securely as tyrant. Under his rule, industry, commerce, and public works made enormous progress, leading Florence to unequaled prosperity. At the same time, Lorenzo was not only a great patron and appreciator of the arts, but extremely creative himself. . . . He seems, indeed, to have done everything well. And while we are not privy to Lorenzo's personal experience, there seems to be good reason to believe that, successful in all he undertook, he was happy. Yet there is no doubt that Lorenzo was an extremely unjust person. He trampled the liberty of Florence underfoot, he lied, he spied, and he assassinated his enemies with abandon. Yet, while incontrovertibly unjust, he seems to have flourished. (Conly, 1988, 92)

A similar point can be made about the other character traits that typically show up on lists of virtues. Conly concludes that no account of flourishing is going to be able to serve as a plausible justification of what we ordinarily take to be virtues. And while I would not draw such a strong conclusion on the basis of the problems we have just considered, the challenge to the virtue ethicist to provide an account of the virtues remains.[30]

The challenge now under consideration, like the previous one, can be expressed as a dilemma. On one hand, if an account of eudaimonia is going to be of some use in specifying some traits as virtues and others as vices, it will likely be too narrow in its conception of flourishing, thus implausibly restricting the kinds of lives that can count as flourishing. On the other hand, if one attempts to work with some conception of flourishing that is wide enough to allow for various recognizable types of human flourishing, the conception in question will be too vague and general to be of use in specifying certain traits as virtues and others as vices and do so in a way that captures what we normally think about virtue and vice.

One apparent way out of this dilemma is to grant that one can flourish through a variety of types of lives. This pluralistic conception of human flourishing is nicely described by Hilary Putnam.

If today we differ with Aristotle it is in being much more pluralistic than Aristotle was. Aristotle recognized that different ideas of Eudaimonia, different conceptions of human flourishing, might be appropriate for different individuals on account of the difference in their constitution. But he seemed to think that ideally there was some sort of constitution that every one ought to have; that in an ideal world (overlooking the mundane question of who would grow the crops and who would bake the bread) everyone would be a philosopher. We agree with Aristotle that different ideas of human flourishing are appropriate for individuals with different constitutions, but we go further and believe that even in the ideal world there would be different constitutions, that diversity is part of the ideal. And we see some degree of tragic tension between ideals, that the fulfillment of some ideals always excludes the fulfillment of others. But to emphasize the point again, belief in a pluralistic ideal is not the same thing as belief that every ideal of human flourishing is as good as every other. We reject ideals of human flourishing as wrong, as infantile, as sick, as one-sided. (Putnam, 1981, 148)

Being a pluralist about human flourishing would avoid the narrowness that results if we try to claim that only one way of life constitutes genuine flourishing. This form of pluralism would presumably allow us to derive sets of virtues pertaining to each of the types of human flourishing. And, as Putnam points out, this sort of pluralism about human flourishing avoids a kind of "anything goes" relativism.[31]

It seems to me that the kind of pluralism about flourishing Putnam advocates is the most promising route for the virtue ethicist to take. But pursuing this project in detail is not something we can tackle here.

8. CONCLUSION

Virtue ethics represents an alternative to the other moral theories surveyed in this book. Because of its recent emergence as a contender, philosophers sympathetic to virtue ethics are in the process of working out what such a theory is all about, particularly with respect to right action. I have suggested that the most plausible version of virtue ethics will take the shape of a limited, pluralistic moral theory.

The various challenges I have raised for virtue ethics are just that—challenges—and as the virtue ethics approach develops, we may find that there are convincing ways of dealing with them. In the meantime, the recent flurry of interest in virtue ethics has sparked the development of an important rival to Kantian, utilitarian, and other moral theories and has served to bring matters of character, virtue, and vice into clearer focus in moral theory.

NOTES

1. Some might prefer to call the trait I am about to describe "truthfulness."
2. See Frankena, 1973, 63–65.

3. The ideas that follow are familiar from our chapter 4 study of Aquinas's natural law moral theory, which, as we noted, was influenced by the work of Aristotle.

4. All references are to Terence Irwin's 1985 translation of Aristotle's *Nicomachean Ethics*, hereafter abbreviated NE; the first page number refers to the Irwin translation, the second to the standard form of reference (Bekker page and column) to Aristotle's works.

5. In chapter 9, we saw that an important element in W. D. Ross's moral theory is the role played by what he calls "moral judgment," which I understand to be identical to what Aristotle calls "phronesis."

6. This example was suggested to me by Tim Roche.

7. See NE, 169–71/1144b–45a.

8. For an illuminating discussion of these theses in Aristotle and the works of other ancient philosophers, see Annas, 1993, chapter 2.

9. It is worth noting that some contemporary versions of virtue ethics—so-called "agent-based" versions—make the rightness or wrongness of an action depend on the *actual* motives on which the agent acts (more precisely, on the character traits that move the person to perform the action). See, for example, Slote, 2001, a leading defender of the view. Such views do not involve idealization of the sort featured in the principles just presented. Considerations of space do not permit a discussion of agent-based theories. For a critical assessment of Slote's view, see Das, 2003, Copp and Sobel, 2004.

10. The justice perspective is to be understood broadly and so is meant to include the moral points of view expressed not only in Kant's moral theory (which the following quote makes clear) but also in utilitarianism, natural law theory, and Ross's moral pluralism.

11. Although one need not develop the view as a version of virtue ethics.

12. The following distinctions are drawn in Blustein, 1991, chapter 2. See also Tronto, 1989 for a discussion of the distinction between caring for and caring about.

13. This is how Frankfurt, 1999 describes caring about.

14. One might respond by saying that helping the robber would be a failure to care enough about others who will likely be negatively affected by the robbery. But if we think of care as something one should have for all others, including strangers, and if this involves respecting their rights, then it looks as if at least a part of the care perspective collapses into the justice perspective. (Thanks to Michael Bukoski for this observation.)

15. See Friedman, 1987 for a discussion of this point.

16. Kant, [1797] 1997. *MM*: 6451/571.

17. You may recall the case of Ted Kaczynski, the Unabomber, whose brother eventually notified authorities with information leading to the arrest of Kaczynski.

18. Pincoffs, 1986, chapter 6, especially 103–4 advances this sort of view. But another approach to such cases is to say that, when properly understood, the virtues often do not conflict. See Hursthouse, 1999, 52. Space does not permit considering this approach.

19. Some of the complications have to do with the experiments in question, including especially their interpretation. A particularly significant issue concerns how to understand the very idea of behavioral consistency that is a hallmark of a trait as robust. I refer interested readers to Russell, 2009, chapters 8–10, and Snow, 2010 for overviews and extended critical discussions of situationist-driven virtue skepticism, including a review of the various often-cited experiments that are supposed to cast doubt on the virtues. See also Adams, 2006, chapters 8 and 9 for critical discussion of empirically based virtue skepticism.

20. Of course, if the situationist is right about character traits generally—character trait skepticism—then, since an ethics of character seems to assume that some such traits do ex-

plain much human behavior, this sort of skepticism would seriously undermine interest in an ethics of character. Why even strive toward acquisition of a virtue if traits in general lack psychological reality?

21. As Daniel C. Russell puts it: "Some philosophical psychologists have argued that since there is little evidence for psychological dispositions [robust traits], and since virtue theory as such is a normative theory about such dispositions, therefore virtue theory as such is empirically misguided . . . and therefore of little practical value to creatures like us" (2009, 239).

22. Das, 2003 raises the circularity worry for the virtue ethical views of Slote, Hursthouse, and Swanton.

23. I am not claiming that all other virtues can be explained in just this way—by appealing to dignity and worth. The example of beneficence is meant to challenge the claim that we can best explain moral rightness and wrongness in all cases by appealing to character traits.

24. This kind of epistemological intuitionism was explained in chapter 8.

25. I mentioned earlier that Aristotle's use of *eudaimonia* is often translated as "happiness." However, contemporary philosophers working out moral theories inspired by Aristotle prefer talking about human flourishing, perhaps because talk of happiness in ethics is associated with hedonistic theories of the good featured in classical utilitarianism.

26. This particular list I take from Hursthouse, 1999, 32.

27. In section 3 of this chapter, we noted that one main task for virtue ethics is to give an account of the virtuous agent, which in turn requires an explanation of what makes a character trait a virtue.

28. Harman, 1983 makes this point.

29. Attributed by Conly, 1988, 89 to Alasdair MacIntyre, 1981.

30. For an intriguing attempt to carry out the neo-Aristotelian project, see Hursthouse, 1999, part 3.

31. Conly, 1988, 88–89 briefly considers, and finds reasons to reject, a pluralist approach—what she calls "collective notions of flourishing." She suspects that appealing to a plurality of ideals of flourishing involves a kind of circularity that undermines the project of justifying a set of virtues by appealing to a conception (or conceptions) of flourishing.

FURTHER READING

Philosophical Literature

Annas, Julia. 2006. "Virtue Ethics." In *The Oxford Handbook of Ethical Theory*, ed. D. Copp. New York: Oxford University Press. Excellent overview of both classical and contemporary versions of virtue ethics.

———. 2011. *Intelligent Virtue*. Oxford: Oxford University Press. A defense of a conception of virtue as reason-guided, skill-like activity and response that is partly constitutive of happiness.

Anscombe, Elizabeth. 1958. "Modern Moral Philosophy." *Philosophy* 33: 1–19. Reprinted in *Collected Philosophical Papers*. Minneapolis: University of Minnesota Press, 1981. An important paper challenging the notion of duty featured in moral theory and advocating a revival of interest in the virtues for doing moral philosophy. Reprinted in Crisp and Slote, 1997.

Copp, David, and David Sobel. 2004. "Morality and Virtue: An Assessment of Some Recent Work in Virtue Ethics." *Ethics* 114: 514–54. An overview of virtue ethics with particular focus on the works by Foot, Hursthouse, and Slote cited here.

Crisp, Roger, ed. 1996. *How Should One Live? Essays on the Virtues*. New York: Oxford University Press. Contains essays on virtue ethics written for this volume by various scholars.

——, and Michael Slote, eds. 1997. *Virtue Ethics*. New York: Oxford University Press. Contains classic essays on virtue ethics.

Foot, Philippa. 2001. *Natural Goodness*. Oxford: Clarendon Press. A novel defense of a virtue-oriented approach to ethics.

Gilligan, Carol. 1982. *In a Different Voice*. Cambridge, MA: Harvard University Press. Groundbreaking work in moral psychology that has inspired the development of care ethics.

Held, Virginia, ed. 1995. *Justice and Care: Essential Readings in Feminist Ethics*. Boulder, CO: Westview Press. A collection of essays by various authors exploring the relations between justice and care.

Hurka, Thomas. 2001. *Virtue, Vice, and Value*. New York: Oxford University Press. An exploration of the nature of virtue and vice. Chapter 8 raises objections to recent versions of virtue ethics.

Hursthouse, Rosalind. 1999. *On Virtue Ethics*. Oxford: Oxford University Press. A defense of a neo-Aristotelian version of virtue ethics.

——. 2010. "Virtue Ethics." *The Stanford Encyclopedia of Philosophy*, ed. E. N. Zalta. http://plato.stanford.edu. Recommended overview of work in and about virtue ethics.

MacIntyre, Alasdair. 1981. *After Virtue*. Notre Dame, IN: University of Notre Dame Press. An important book in helping to revive interest among philosophers in the virtues and virtue ethics.

Noddings, Nel. 1984. *Caring: A Feminine Approach to Ethics and Moral Education*. Berkeley and Los Angeles: University of California Press. A defense of a care ethic with particular attention paid to moral education.

Paul, Ellen F., Fred D. Miller, and Jeffrey Paul, eds. 1998. *Virtue and Vice*. Cambridge: Cambridge University Press. A wide-ranging collection of essays by leading scholars.

Pincoffs, Edmund. 1986. *Quandaries and Virtues: Against Reductivism in Ethics*. Lawrence: University of Kansas Press. A defense of a pluralistic version of virtue ethics.

Russell, Daniel C. 2009. *Practical Intelligence and the Virtues*. Oxford: Oxford University Press. A defense of an essentially Aristotelian conception of virtue ethics involving practical intelligence as a necessary part of the virtues and thus a commitment to the unity of the virtues.

Slote, Michael. 2001. *Morals from Motives*. Oxford: Oxford University Press. A defense of so-called agent-based virtue ethics.

Statman, Daniel, ed. 1997. *Virtue Ethics: A Critical Reader*. Washington, DC: Georgetown University Press. Contains important essays on virtue ethics and includes a useful introductory essay by the editor.

Swanton, Christine. 2003. *Virtue Ethics: A Pluralist View*. Oxford: Oxford University Press. A defense of a "target centered" virtue account of right action.

Zagzebski, Linda. 1996. *Virtues of the Mind*. Cambridge: Cambridge University Press. Part 2 contains an extended account of the virtues as well as a version of virtue ethics.

Empirical and Empirically Focused Literature

The following list is necessarily very selective, given the extensive literature on situationism, character, and the virtues. I refer those interested to the bibliography in Snow, 2010 listed below.

Doris, John M. 2002. *Lack of Character: Personality and Moral Behavior.* Cambridge: Cambridge University Press. A fully developed situationist-based defense of virtue skepticism and the related idea of character fragmentation. See especially chapters 3–5.

Harman, Gilbert. 1999. "Moral Philosophy Meets Moral Psychology." *Proceedings of the Aristotelian Society* 99: 315–31. Often-cited defense of virtue skepticism.

Kamtekar, Rachana. 2004. "Situationism and Virtue Ethics on the Content of Our Character." *Ethics* 114: 458–91. An influential defense of the virtues against situationist-based skepticism.

Miller, Christian. 2003. "Social Psychology and Virtue Ethics," *Journal of Ethics* 7: 365–92. Highly recommended article that provides an overview of and response to the situationist-based virtue skepticism of Harman and Doris.

Mischel, W. 1968. *Personality and Assessment.* New York: Wiley. Landmark book critical of trait-based conceptions of personality, helping spearhead the situationist research program in psychology.

Ross, L., and R. E. Nisbett. 1991. *The Person and Situation.* Philadelphia: Temple University Press. Influential discussion of the situationist research program.

Russell, Daniel C. 2009. *Practical Intelligence and the Virtues.* Oxford: Oxford University Press. See chapters 8–10.

Snow, Nancy E. 2010. *Virtue as Social Intelligence: An Empirically Grounded Theory.* New York and Oxford: Routledge. An overview and critique of situationist-based virtue skepticism and defense of an empirically grounded conception of the virtues.

11

Moral Particularism

The moral theories surveyed in the previous chapters feature moral principles and rules that purport to specify those features of actions in virtue of which they are right or wrong. They are all versions of what is called "moral generalism"—the idea that general moral principles play an ineliminable role in understanding morality, particularly when it comes to explaining why particular actions have the deontic status they do. These theories all agree that in correctly applying moral principles of right conduct to concrete circumstances, one must attend to the morally relevant details of each context or circumstance. In the third chapter, devoted to moral relativism, we expressed this widely shared assumption as the context sensitivity thesis: the rightness or wrongness of a concrete action, performed in some context, depends in part on morally relevant facts that hold in the context—facts concerning agents and their circumstances.

Moral particularism, like traditional moral theories, emphasizes the importance of the details of concrete situations in determining the morality of actions. But this view is far more radical in its claims about how the morality of an action often depends on such details. The moral particularist challenges the idea that it is possible to specify once and for all those features that are always going to be relevant in determining the rightness or wrongness of an action. Indeed, the particularist goes further and challenges what is perhaps the deepest assumption of traditional moral theory, namely that to properly explain the deontic status of particular actions requires an appeal to moral principles or rules. If this assumption is mistaken, then the project of traditional moral theory is itself deeply mistaken.[1] And if, as we have been assuming, moral *theory* is all about articulating and defending explanatory moral principles, then moral particularism is aptly described as antitheory.

Its antiprinciple stance represents the negative side of particularism. But its advocates are not moral skeptics, and so the view also has a positive side. So, let us begin with a characterization of moral particularism, after which we will explore some of the main lines of controversy between this view and its generalist opponents.

1. WHAT IS PARTICULARISM?

We begin with the negative side of moral particularism, the side that is opposed to moral principles. There is a variety of such negative claims, and particularists can differ over which ones they do and do not accept. Space does not permit a discussion of them all, so let us focus for the time being on the following two prominent particularist theses.

> *Principle eliminativism*: There are no correct or true moral principles that represent moral criteria and are needed to explain the deontic status of particular actions.

This very strong claim obviously represents a challenge to traditional moral theory, which, as we have made clear in previous chapters, has the theoretical aim of setting forth principles that purport to explain the underlying nature of right and wrong. And here it is worth reminding ourselves of two fundamental kinds of moral principles encountered in previous chapters.

What we may call "decisive" principles include such all-encompassing generalizations as the principle of utility and Kant's Categorical Imperative. They are decisive because they set forth conditions that provide considerations which, when present, decide the deontic status of an action. They are all-encompassing because they refer to actions generally and purport to explain what makes any action right or wrong. But what we may call act-specifying principles—including so-called "absolutist" principles of the sort encountered in the chapter on natural law theory—are also a species of decisive principle (or rule). The principle *It is wrong to intentionally bring about the death of an innocent human being, regardless of the good consequences that may result from doing so* specifies an action type (intentionally killing an innocent human being) and in effect says that the fact than an action is of this type (has the feature in question) provides a decisive reason against performing acts of this sort—they are always wrong. Decisive principles are contrasted with defeasible principles of the sort featured in Ross's moral theory. Ross's principles (or rules) of prima facie duty specify some action type (or, equivalently, some feature of an action) that provides a moral reason either for or against a course of action, but one that may be overridden by competing moral reasons. Principles of both sorts are intended to be explanatory. What is worth noticing is that a moral generalization such as *Murder is wrong* is not a candidate explanatory principle because part of the meaning of "murder" is wrongful killing, and so this generalization is fundamentally trivial. So, a principle eliminativist has her sights set on what are put forth as nontrivial explanatory generalizations about the deontic status of actions.

If principle eliminativism is true, then the project of traditional moral theory and its search for such principles, whether decisive or defeasible, is like searching for a fountain of youth—completely hopeless. Of course, moral principles are often cast in the practical role of providing a decision procedure for engaging in reflective moral deliberation in which one is mulling over some moral question, as well as for reliably guiding individuals to make correct spontaneous moral judgments and associated choices in contexts where there is no time for reflection and deliberation. Against the use of such principles, the particularist defends the following thesis:

> *Principle abstinence*: A morally committed agent who wants to come to correct verdicts about particular cases and act accordingly should not rely on moral principles for guidance.

Particularists defend this thesis by arguing that relying on moral principles is liable to distort one's thinking about the details of particular cases and thus mislead us in our efforts to arrive at correct moral verdicts about right and wrong, good and bad.

Before going further, notice that these two theses are independent; one may coherently accept one and deny the other. One might hold that there are no correct or true moral principles but still think that it is better to rely on moral principles in our moral deliberation even if they aren't true, because doing so will lead to better moral decision-making overall than trying to make moral decisions without any guidance from principles. Again, one might deny principle eliminativism and hold that there are true or correct moral principles that express criteria of, say, right action, but deny that such principles should guide ordinary moral thinking. You may recall from the chapter 5 discussion of utilitarianism that some utilitarians hold that the principle of utility is *not* to be understood as providing a decision procedure. But as also noted, utilitarians who take this line often recommend that when it comes to practical moral decision making, one should rely on moral rules for practical guidance. So (using "principle" in this context to refer also to moral rules) these utilitarians are not committed to the above thesis of principle abstinence.[2] The particularist who does embrace this thesis is against the reliance on principles in moral decision making.

The positive side of moral particularism is that there is a genuine difference between right and wrong, good and bad. So, for example, the particularist holds that a concrete action is morally wrong when there are moral reasons for not performing the action that count decisively against performing that action in question. The crucial point is that, for the particularist, explaining the deontic status of a particular action does not require subsuming the action under a moral principle. Furthermore, the moral particularist claims that not relying on moral principles in our moral thinking is no bar to good moral thinking and coming to have genuine moral knowledge; indeed (as lately noted), the particularist who embraces principle abstinence warns against relying on moral principles and rules. When it comes to moral knowledge, particularists are fond of stressing the importance of possessing a kind of moral sensitivity—a developed capacity for "discernment" that allows one to respond to morally relevant details of particular cases without reliance on moral principles or rules. More will be said about this notion of discernment later in the chapter.

In order to gain some understanding of what is at issue between generalists and their particularist opponents, let us start with the thesis of principle eliminativism—the thesis that there are no true or correct moral principles of the sort featured in traditional moral theory. And a way to begin this discussion is by calling attention to three important assumptions which, arguably, are shared by generalists who engage in moral theorizing with the aim of articulating and defending moral principles that would serve the theoretical role of explaining the nature of right and wrong, good and bad. The three assumptions in question, which are challenged by particularists, are (1) the generic generalist thesis, (2) the universal relevance thesis, and (3) the polarity thesis. Let us examine them in order.

2. THE PROJECT OF TRADITIONAL MORAL THEORY

In illustrating these three assumptions, let us, for the sake of simplicity, focus on principles of right conduct that purport to set forth those underlying features of actions and practices that explain why such actions and practices have the deontic status they do in fact have.

The Generic Generalist Thesis

Moral theories represent moral phenomena as more or less strongly unified—as exhibiting some underlying pattern. Think of it this way. There are many types of action that we commonly recognize as being wrong: lying, theft, killing, rape, malicious gossip, and so on. One natural question to ask about these types of wrong action is whether there is any underlying feature that they all share in virtue of which they are wrong—a single wrong-making reason. We might discover that there is one underlying feature of wrong actions that makes them all wrong. If so, then the wrongness of these actions would be strongly unified by the feature in question. However, we might discover that there is no one underlying feature in virtue of which actions are right or wrong. As we have seen in the case of Ross's moral theory, there may be a plurality of such underlying features. Nevertheless, for Ross, the number of such features is relatively small.

But in addition to this idea of underlying unity, generalists maintain that basic moral reasons, if they are to do their explanatory work, must figure in explanatory generalizations—moral principles. Putting together these ideas about underlying unity and principles, we have what is arguably a deeply embedded generalist assumption of traditional moral theories:

> **G** (a) There is a small fixed set of morally relevant features of actions that are fundamental in explaining the deontic status of any action. We may call them basic or primary "moral" reasons, if we keep in mind that we are referring to underlying right- and wrong-making features that figure in explaining the morality of actions. (b) Such reasons are featured in generalizations—moral principles or rules—which are essential in providing explanations of the deontic status of actions.

This thesis is intended to be common ground among all of the moral theories featured in previous chapters. The reference in this thesis to features that are "fundamental" is worth pausing to illustrate.[3] There are a great many features of actions, persons, and their situations that may or may not be morally relevant depending on context. Suppose for the moment that the classical version of utilitarianism is true. Then the fact that some action is a lie is not of fundamental moral relevance. What is fundamentally morally relevant regarding actions for the classical utilitarian—what counts as basic moral reasons for or against some action—are facts about the production of pleasure and pain. So the fact that an action is a lie might or might not be relevant, depending on whether this fact about the action has any bearing on the production of either pleasure or pain. In contexts where this fact about an action would have no bearing on the production of pleasure or pain, it is not a morally relevant feature. So, if one is a classical utilitarian, the relevance of the fact that an action is a lie is to be explained by fundamental morally relevant facts about the production of pleasure and pain.

The point being illustrated here is simply that for any moral theory many features of a situation or facts about an action or a person might or might not be morally relevant, depending on context. But a moral theory attempts to discover those features whose explanatory relevance is fundamental. Such features represent facts about an action that are supposed to explain, at a most basic level, why the action has some particular deontic status. What makes such fundamental morally relevant features—basic moral reasons—especially interesting is the fact that they are understood by traditional moral theory to have two important characteristics: universal relevance and polarity.

The Universal Relevance Thesis

According to the universal relevance thesis,

UR If a feature is a (basic) moral reason in one case, then it must be a moral reason in any context in which it is present.

Thus, for the classical utilitarian, the fact that an action would produce some amount of pleasure (or pain) is *always* a morally relevant fact—a basic moral reason bearing on the deontic status of an action. By contrast, for a moral pluralist like Ross the fact that an action is an instance of lying is a feature that is always morally relevant—a basic moral reason that necessarily bears on the deontic status of the action in question, even though this reason may not be decisive in determining the deontic status of some particular instance of telling a lie.

The Polarity Thesis

Again, a traditional pluralist who holds that lying is a basic moral reason maintains that this feature of an action is a wrong-making feature: it *always* counts against performing the act, even if (again) in some contexts it is not decisive because overridden by other features. Lying is thus said to have a negative polarity. By contrast, other features that may be taken as fundamental in explaining right and wrong action are taken to have a positive polarity. For instance, the fact that an action would help someone in need is (arguably) a prima facie right-making feature of the action and so has a positive polarity—it *always* counts as a moral reason in favor of performing the action. In addition to assuming that basic moral reasons must be universally relevant, traditional moral theory assumes that all such reasons, whenever present, must have the same polarity. Here, then, is the polarity thesis:

> **P** A (basic) moral reason must always possess the same polarity in any context in which it is present.

For the classical utilitarian, the fact that an action would bring about some episodes of pleasure always has a positive polarity and counts in favor of performing the act—a favoring moral reason. The fact that an action would produce some episodes of pain has a negative polarity and counts against performing the act—a disfavoring moral reason. Of course, for the classical utilitarian, whether an action morally ought or ought not to be done depends on the net balance of pleasure and pain the action would bring about if performed compared to other alternative actions. But the point here is that considerations of pleasure and pain must always count, and count in the same way, in determining the morality of actions.

We can summarize the universal relevance and polarity theses by saying that there are some features of actions that are (and must be) universally relevant and relevant in the same way (have the same polarity) whenever they are present. This is how basic moral reasons work, and in doing their job they are supposed to be the features or considerations that explain and unify morality. This particular view of moral reasons and how they work is referred to as "reasons atomism":

> **RA** If a feature counts as a (basic) moral reason (and thus represents a morally relevant right- or wrong-making consideration) with a certain positive or negative polarity in one case, then it *must* be relevant and have the same polarity in all contexts in which it is present. That is, the relevance and polarity of a (basic) moral reason in a context is unaffected by other features that may be present in that context. Such features thus possess their relevance and polarity atomistically; they "carry" it with them from context to context.

Let us return for a moment to the generic generality thesis (G)—the thesis according to which (a) there is a relatively small set of features that are fundamental in explaining the deontic status of actions, and (b) such reasons are featured in moral principles that are essential in such explanations. Notice that G does not commit one to reasons atomism, RA. However, traditional moral theory is often interpreted as committed to the combination of G and RA, and thus interpreted as guided by the search for fundamental morally relevant features—(basic) moral reasons—that have their relevance and polarity fixed once and for all. And this means that the principles featured in such theories purport to set forth such atomistic reasons as explaining what makes actions right or wrong, and what makes something good or bad. Call them *atomistic moral principles*.

Particularists challenge this atomistic conception of practical reasons, and instead accept what is called "reasons holism." In doing so, they attempt to undermine the form of generalism that is characteristic of traditional moral theory. If they are right and there are no such atomistic moral principles, and if atomistic principles are the only kind suitable for purposes of moral theory, then principle eliminativism is true. Let us take a closer look.

3. HOLISM ABOUT REASONS AND PRINCIPLE ELIMINATIVISM

Against the polarity and universal relevance theses, particularists have argued by example.[4] That is, for any feature that allegedly is both universally relevant and always has the same polarity, the particularist describes situations in which the feature either fails to be relevant at all or reverses its polarity. In short, the particularist denies that there are any (or at least very many) features that are fundamental in the way that at least some traditional moral theories take for granted—that moral reasons function atomistically. And if there are no such features, then the generalist thesis, interpreted in light of RA, is false. Since a central part of the particularist's attack on moral theory concerns doubts about the theses of polarity and universal relevance, let us consider their reasons for doing so.

Reversal

The fact that an action would bring about pleasurable consequences is taken by classical utilitarians as a feature that is always morally relevant (whenever present) and relevant in the same way in that it counts in favor of the action's rightness. But consider this case as described by David McNaughton:

> A government is considering reintroducing hanging, drawing, and quartering in public for terrorist murders. If reactions to public hangings in the past are anything to go by a lot of people may enjoy the spectacle. Does that constitute a reason in favor of reintroduction? Is the fact that people would enjoy it here a reason for its being right? It would be perfectly possible to take just the opposite view. The fact that spectators might get a sadistic thrill from the brutal spectacle could be thought to constitute an objection to reintroduction. Whether the fact that an action causes pleasure is a reason for or against doing it is not something that can be settled in isolation from other features of the action. It is only when we know the context in which the pleasure will occur that we are in a position to judge. (McNaughton, 1988, 193)

Perhaps in most contexts the fact that an action would bring about pleasure has a positive polarity and thus counts in favor of the action being right. However, as the example illustrates, in other contexts the pleasure brought about by some action arguably reverses its polarity and counts against the action being right and in favor of the action being morally wrong.

Here is another example of reversal, offered by Jonathan Dancy, who has us consider a family game called "Contraband," in which players are smugglers trying to get contraband material past a customs officer. The game requires them to lie; if one doesn't do plenty of lying, it spoils the game. That an action is a lie is commonly a reason not to do it; here it is a reason in favor (Dancy, 1993, 61).

Of course, a few examples like these do not suffice to disprove the polarity thesis. Even if the particularist is correct in claiming that such features as causing pleasure and being a lie can reverse polarity, there may be other features whose polarity remains constant from context to context. But such examples serve as the basis of a challenge to the generalist: the particularist challenges the generalist to come up with features whose polarity cannot be reversed, and come up with enough such features and associated moral principles to, as it were, "cover the entire field" when it comes to explaining the deontic status of actions. The particularist doubts that there are such features, or suspects that if there are some, there are too few of them to completely unify morality.

Silencing

Even if the polarity thesis is false, the universal relevance thesis might still be true. But, again, particularists offer examples that call this thesis into question. For instance, the fact that I borrowed a book from you and promised to return it would appear to be a morally relevant consideration and gives me a reason for returning it to you. But suppose that I find out that you stole the book. One way to look at the case is to suppose that my promising to return the book to you is morally relevant and gives me some reason to return it, although the fact that you stole the book is also relevant and gives me an even stronger reason not to give it back to you. But another way to look at the case is to deny that in the context in question my having promised gives me any reason at all to return the book to you. According to this second way of looking at the case, my having borrowed the book from you is simply not morally relevant in this particular context; its relevance has been "silenced" given the context. The particularist claims that this latter way of viewing the matter is more plausible than the former way, and illustrates how features that are typically morally relevant may have their relevance silenced in certain contexts.

The phenomena of reversal and silencing are supposed to help demonstrate that moral reasons work holistically rather than atomistically. Thus, opposed to reasons atomism is the thesis of "reasons holism":

> **RH** A feature that counts as a moral reason with a particular positive or negative polarity in one context, may not count as a reason at all in another context, or it may have an opposite polarity in another context.

Again, working from examples is not enough to decisively disprove the universal relevance thesis, but examples do ground a challenge to the generalist: the particularist challenges the generalist to identify any (or very many) features that maintain their moral relevance in all contexts. The particularist thinks that the prospects for succeeding at this task are dim.

Rejection of the Aspirations of Traditional Moral Theory

Let us sum up. According to the generic generality thesis (G), there is a small set of morally relevant features that are fundamental in explaining the rightness and wrongness of actions—features that figure in moral principles which are essential in explaining the deontic status of particular actions. And, as noted earlier, traditional moral theory arguably takes such fundamental features to be atomistic—their relevance and polarity are fixed independently of particular contexts. This is the thesis of reasons atomism, RA. Thus, as earlier noted, traditional moral theory is typically understood as the search for atomistic moral principles—principles presumed to be necessary for explaining the deontic status of particular actions. But if traditional moral theory is committed to the combination of G and RA, and if (as particularists maintain) RA is false, then there are no explanatory moral principles of the sort sought by traditional moral theory. The apparent upshot of such skepticism is the thesis of principle eliminativism.

4. GENERALIST REPLIES

The particularist attack on moral principles has led to a variety of replies on the part of generalists. The issues involved in the ongoing debate between these two camps become very complicated very quickly, pursuit of which takes one into difficult metaphysical and epistemological questions that are far beyond the scope of this book. So with this caveat in mind, let us briefly consider two main strategies generalists have taken in combating principle eliminativism.

Atomistic Specification

The first strategy may be called *atomistic specification*—the strategy of refining, by making more specific, those considerations or features that serve as basic moral reasons and figure in moral principles. Consider, for instance, a moral theory (like Ross's) according to which promise breaking is always relevant and always has a negative polarity. As noted in the previous section, it seems that there are contexts in which the fact that I made a promise is silenced, and so breaking the promise does not count in a moral assessment of such refraining. In response, what the generalist can say is that the moral significance of a promise, its counting against some action or omission, depends on the obtaining of certain conditions such that if they do not all obtain then the fact that one has performed the speech act of promising is not at all morally binding. Here, for example, is how Brad Hooker (2008b, 19) proposes to fill out the conditions in question:

- The promise was not extracted by a threat to infringe on someone's moral rights.
- The promise was not made while one was literally insane.
- The promise was not the result of someone's having misrepresented or withheld facts from the promisor that she or he had a right to know.
- Keeping the promise would not require one to infringe on anyone's moral rights.
- The person to whom the promise was made has not cancelled it.

The idea is that each of these conditions represents an aspect or part of a *complete specification* of the reason provided by the fact that one has made a promise. Assuming that these conditions fully capture the conditions under which making a promise does have moral significance, one could formulate a Rossian defeasible moral principle as follows:

> *Promise*: If one has made a promise to someone to do something, and (a) that promise was not extracted by a threat to infringe on someone's moral rights, (b) it was not made while one was literally insane, (c) nor was it the result of someone's having misrepresented or withheld facts from the promisor that she or he had a right to know, (d) keeping it would not require one to infringe on anyone's moral rights, and (e) the person to whom the promise was made has not cancelled it, *then* one has a prima facie duty to do what one promised.

Working with Ross's prima facie duties, let us consider another example of how atomistic specification works. Consider the prima facie duty of gratitude. One might initially suppose that if someone has conferred a benefit upon you that was not strictly owed, then you have a duty of gratitude to repay that person, even if doing so only requires thanking the benefactor. But clearly in order for one to have a genuine prima facie duty of gratitude, certain conditions must obtain. Most obviously, no gratitude is owed if the "benefactor" did not intend to benefit you. Again, no gratitude is owed if the benefactor unjustifiably violated the rights of someone else (perhaps by stealing whatever was given to you) in order to confer the benefit. By spelling out the various conditions that must obtain in order for gratitude to be owed to a benefactor, one could compose a complex characterization of the duty like the one for promising with the aim of specifying a basic moral reason that is not subject to silencing or reversal.

The examples of sadistic pleasure and lying featured in the previous section can be handled in similar manner. For instance, instead of holding that production of pleasure—any pleasure—always counts as a favoring reason for engaging in some action, one may hold that it is the more specific feature of being an instance of nonsadistic pleasure that always counts as a moral plus. If this refinement strategy of preserving atomism can be made to work for a wide enough range of basic moral reasons, then the generalist will have a sufficient stock of corresponding principles for use in explaining the deontic status of actions. Pursuing the strategy of atomistic specification is a way of preserving both reasons atomism (RA) and the generic generality thesis (G)—the two pillars of traditional moral theory. If the strategy works, then principle eliminativism is defeated.

What do particularists say in response to this pro-atomist specificationist strategy? Dancy (2004, chapter 3) argues that it fails to respect two importantly different ways in which a consideration (feature) can be morally relevant and thus come to bear on the overall deontic status of actions. He draws a distinction between what counts as a genuine moral reason on one hand, and so-called *enablers* and *disablers* on the other hand.[5] An enabler is a relevant feature of a situation that enables a certain consideration to function as a reason in a particular context. So, for example, such facts as that a promise was not made under duress or while insane function to enable the fact that one has made a promise to count in favor of performing the relevant promise-keeping act. Disablers serve to undermine the moral force of some feature that in other, more favorable contexts, functions as a reason. The fact that one did make the promise under serious unjustified duress can serve to disable the moral significance of the promise. Given this distinction between reasons and enablers/disablers, Dancy argues that the specificationist gambit of the atomist does not work; it is insensitive to the different roles that morally relevant considerations can play in specific contexts.

Returning to Hooker's principle of promising, Dancy would say that what makes some doing or refraining that involves breaking a promise wrong—the reason that really explains its wrongness—is just the fact that one is breaking a promise. The other considerations (a)–(e) are enabling conditions, not part of the reason. And, of course, viewed in this manner the particularist's point about promising still holds: the fact that one made a promise need not always count morally, and may even reverse its typical polarity in certain contexts.

One way in which a generalist might respond to Dancy's claim about what counts as a reason is to "dig in" and hold that the so-called enabling conditions really are part of a more complex reason. Granted, it is perhaps initially odd to think of the fact that one did not make a promise under duress as part of the reason why one is morally required to, say, keep one's promise to return a borrowed book. But this may be due to the fact that we normally take such facts for granted in ordinary thought and conversation. After all, we don't normally bother to make explicit all of the morally relevant factors that bear on some action—factors that the atomist views as part of the reason. So, who is right about this? Does the specificationist gambit save reasons atomism against the holist's challenge?

Pursuing this issue about the so-called scope of moral reasons is not possible here. But suppose one is inclined to accept Dancy's distinction between reasons and enabling/disabling conditions as well as the reasons holism that goes along with drawing this distinction. (I myself lean in this direction.) Taking this path brings us to the second generalist strategy for defending against principle eliminativism. Let us call it "holistic accommodation."

Holistic Accommodation

Some generalists—that is, some who embrace the generic generalist thesis—do indeed embrace reasons holism, granting the significance of the distinction between reasons and enablers/disablers. What they go on to argue is that holism does not entail the rejection of moral principles and, further, that holist moral principles provide a better understanding of morality than does particularism. That is, these philosophers combine G with RH.

That reasons holism does not entail the rejection of principles is fairly easy to see. Consider this example offered by Sean McKeever and Michael Ridge in their 2006 book-length defense of generalism. They have readers consider a case in which someone has killed a rational agent, no other features of the circumstances seem relevant, and one concludes that the action was wrong because it was an instance of such killing. Commenting on this case, they write:

> Given holism, our judgment's soundness depends on two theses. First, it relies on the thesis that the fact that the action is the killing of a rational agent is a moral reason not to do it in this context. Secondly, it depends on the thesis that any reasons in favor of the action do not (when taken collectively) outweigh this reason. Finally, our judgment's soundness also depends on the thesis that the moral reason in question is stringent enough to make the action morally wrong.

The authors then formulate the following principle that respects the holism of reasons:

> (K) For all actions (x): If (*a*) x is an instance of killing a rational agent and (*b*) no other feature of the situation explains why the fact that x is the killing of a rational agent is not a moral reason not to perform the action and (*c*) any reasons to do x do not (when taken collectively) outweigh the fact that x is the killing of a rational agent, then x is wrong in virtue of being an instance of killing a rational agent. (McKeever and Ridge, 2006, 118)[6]

Clause *c* allows that even if killing a rational agent counts against the act, it might be overridden by competing moral reasons—something that Ross's principles allow. Clause *b* builds in the holism; it allows that there could be contexts (however unlikely) in which killing a rational agent is reversed or silenced. In discussing Ross's version of moral pluralism, we noted that the principles associated with his prima facie duties are defeasible—they allow that the moral reasons referred to in the principles can be overridden; they allow exceptions, even though for Ross, those reasons, when present, always count and always have the same polarity. Principle K is, we might say, doubly defeasible—defeasible in the way Ross's view allows, and defeasible owing to the fact that the typical relevance and polarity of the moral reason featured in the principle is also subject to defeat.

Principle K is fairly abstract; it does not specify the sorts of features that might explain why killing a rational agent might fail to be a moral reason against performing the action in certain contexts. Nor does it specify the kinds of reasons that could outweigh the fact that an action would be such a killing (in cases where this fact does count against the act). I will let readers ponder how such details might be filled in to make this principle more specific.[7] In the meantime, we already have a principle, namely, Promising, as a model for how this process of filling out a principle can be pursued. A generalist who embraces reasons holism will simply follow Dancy and view clauses (*a*)–(*e*) in Promising as enabling conditions.

The upshot of holistic accommodation is simply that the holism of reasons does not entail principle eliminativism: explanatory moral principles, says the generalist, may feature basic moral reasons that work holistically. If we now return to the three theses associated with traditional generalism, we see that the accommodation strategy embraces what we have called the thesis of generic generalism, but rejects reasons atomism in favor of reasons holism.

Victory for Generalists?

It may now appear that a generalist who is willing to embrace reasons holism has won the battle over principle eliminativism. But drawing this conclusion from what has been presented so far would fail to understand what seems to really lie at the bottom of the generalist/particularist dispute. A particularist like Dancy need not, and does not, deny that holism is compatible with the sorts of moral generalizations represented by K and by Promise. The crucial issue dividing generalists and particularists concerns the proper account of explanation in morals. For the generalist, reasons that serve to explain the deontic status of action necessarily and essentially involve moral generalizations; such generalizations provide the *basis* for explaining the deontic status of actions. Explanation for the moral generalist is a matter of subsumption; of bringing a particular case under a moral principle. Of course, application of defeasible moral principles such as Promise (interpreted holistically) will (arguably) have to be supplemented by moral judgment for purposes of determining whether the moral reason featured in the principle has been silenced or reversed and whether, if not, other moral reasons override the reason in question. Nevertheless, such principles play an important role in explaining the deontic status of actions and in the process of justifying particular moral judgments.

By contrast, for the particularist, there is no essential connection between something being an explanatory moral reason and its being associated with a moral generalization. Rather, explaining why a particular action, performed in a particular set of circumstances, is right or wrong is a matter of determining which features present in the circumstances under consideration are morally relevant, and how they bear on the overall deontic status of the action *in the particular case at hand*. Explaining the deontic status of actions as well as justifying judgments about their deontic status is thus a matter of providing a *narrative* of the morally relevant details of a particular case and how they behave in that case, rather than subsuming the case under a principle. As Dancy aptly puts it, for the particularist, "Reasons do not function in virtue of generalizations; they are about the ways things add up *here*" (1993, 106, emphasis added). Commenting on the contrasting accounts of explanation at the heart of the debate, Mark Lance and Margaret Little sum it up nicely by saying that for the particularist,

> The account of explanation is, broadly put, not one of subsumption but one of narrative. As with describing a building, we characterize the situation in ways that will get others to interpret and see it as we do. . . . To be sure, moral Principles familiar from moral theory are helpful devices to remind us of what moral import various considerations *can* have, but they serve no independent justificatory function. Adducing Principles can thus be useful pedagogy or in helping others to see things as they ought; but they carry no more justificatory weight than that. (2006, 585)[8]

If we reserve the term "principle" for those moral generalizations, understood as the generalist does, that is, as *essential* to the very working of moral reasons and thus as providing the proper basis for *explaining* the deontic status of actions, then Dancy is a principle eliminativist. So from the particularist's perspective, generalizations like Promise are mere statistical generalizations—at most what they represent are mere summaries of how various features usually function. Consider the nonmoral generalization that by and large male spouses are taller than their wives. If Juan is taller than his wife Mary, then this fact is not explained by the aforementioned generalization. Rather, the generalization is based on (and explained by) the many particular instances of male spouses being taller than their wives. Similarly, it is perhaps typically the case that promising works as a right-making reason. But according to the particularist, generalizations like Promise do not, as it were, wear the explanatory pants when it comes to particular cases; rather, as Lance and Little observe, for the particularist they can be "helpful devices" in moral thought and discussion, but nothing more. One might put the contrast being highlighted here in terms of the "direction" of explanation: for the generalist, the explanatory direction goes from principle to particular action, while for the particularist, it goes the other way.

5. BRIEF SUMMARY OF THE DEBATE OVER PRINCIPLE ELIMINATIVISM

We have covered some of the twists and turns in the debate between generalists and particularists over the theoretical role of principles in moral theorizing, but pursuing this debate any further would require that we consider the nature of explanation—a general philosophical topic at the intersection of epistemology and metaphysics that is beyond the scope of this book. However, before moving on, let us sum up the key ideas we have just encountered.

- The enterprise of traditional moral theory is typically understood as the search for moral principles that are taken to be essential in explaining the deontic status of particular actions. The idea is that there is a small set of fundamental features that figure in explanatory moral principles. Such principles express moral criteria of right and wrong action. Because of the explanatory role of general moral principles, traditional moral theories are versions of generalism.

- Particularists doubt that there are (or need to be) moral principles that play the kind of explanatory role just mentioned. They defend what we have called principle eliminativism.
- One interesting facet of the generalist/particularist debate is over the question of whether there are morally relevant features—moral reasons—that are always relevant and relevant in the same way. Reasons atomists are committed to such reasons, while reasons holists deny there are any (or very many) such reasons. Reasons atomism is arguably characteristic of traditional moral theory.
- However, as we have seen, one can be a generalist and also allow that the reasons featured in explanatory moral principles work holistically.

Let us now turn to the debate between generalists and particularists over the practical role of moral principles in guiding action and moral deliberation.

6. JUDGING CASES AND PRINCIPLE ABSTINENCE

Principle abstinence (PA), you may recall, is the thesis that a morally committed agent who wants to arrive at correct moral verdicts and act accordingly should not rely on moral principles when engaging in moral deliberation about particular cases, or in general rely on them for guiding one's behavior. The particularist is thus opposed to what we may call *principle guidance* as a method of moral deliberation, choice, and action. But what is the basis of this opposition? The answer is fairly obvious if one is thinking of simple absolutist moral principles (rules) of the following sort:

- Lying is always wrong, regardless of any good effects that may result.
- Breaking a promise is always wrong, regardless of any good effects that may result.
- Killing a human being is always wrong, regardless of any good effects that may result.

Such principles are arguably false. Since there are, for example, cases of morally justified lying, to rely on the first of these principles would lead to mistaken verdicts and decisions about a range of particular cases in which lying is not wrong. So, let us put such principles aside and consider defeasible moral principles characteristic of Ross's moral theory:

- Lying is prima facie wrong.
- Breaking a promise is prima facie wrong.
- Killing a human being is prima facie wrong.

As we know from the chapter on moral pluralism, these principles allow for exceptions. However, the particularist's complaint about relying on such principles to
guide moral thinking and decision making is that if they are understood as committed to reasons atomism, then relying on them will sometimes lead a committed
moral agent to mistaken beliefs about the relevance and polarity of such features
as being a lie, breaking a promise, and perhaps even the killing of a human being.
David McNaughton writes:

> Moral particularism takes the view that moral principles are at best useless, and at worst
> a hindrance, in trying to find out what is the right action. What is required is the correct
> conception of the particular case at hand, with its unique set of properties. There is no
> substitute for a sensitive and detailed examination of each individual case. (1988, 190)

Regarding the use of principles, the particularist allows that they may serve to
remind one of features that *may* be morally relevant, but determining the moral relevance (and polarity) of any feature in a particular context cannot be read off from a
moral principle.[9] What the particularist proposes as superior to principle guidance is
case-by-case *moral discernment.* Such discernment involves learning to become sensitive to the details of particular cases in a way that enables one to reliably determine
which considerations pertaining to a case are morally relevant and to reliably evaluate their normative weight in coming to an all-things-considered moral judgment
about the particular case under consideration. This all may sound rather mysterious,
as if moral discernment is just a matter of looking hard at some case (or imagining
it in detail) and just somehow coming to a moral verdict, and nothing more. But
this impression is mistaken. With respect to moral deliberation in which an agent is
trying to work out how to act, Dancy describes the particularist conception this way:

> There is no attempt to bring principles to bear on the situation, but there is an attempt
> to work out what matters here and how it matters, in ways that may involve an indirect
> appeal to the way things were or might be elsewhere. And when two particularists are
> engaged in dispute, it is not as if they are reduced to saying "I see it this way." There are
> ways of supporting or defending the way one takes the situation to be. A particularist
> can perfectly well point to how things are in another perhaps simpler case, and suggest
> that this reveals something about how they are in the present more difficult one. There
> need be no generalist suggestion that since this feature made a certain difference there,
> it must make the same difference here. (Dancy, 2009)[10]

He continues by remarking that in making such comparisons among cases, "what
we learn is not how things *must* be here, but how they might very well be." So the
claim by the particularist is that developed moral discernment is superior to principle guidance in leading morally committed agents to correct moral verdicts about
particular cases. This is supposed to hold for contexts of deliberation in which an
agent is mulling over some moral issue, and for cases in which one is called upon to
respond immediately in some circumstance without time for moral deliberation. The

alleged superiority of discernment over principle guidance is the particularist's basis for advocating principle abstinence.

Of course, this controversy over the practical role of moral principles is somewhat blunted if one accepts reasons holism and allows that moral principles can refer to features whose relevance and polarity can vary across contexts. In section 4, principle K, which proscribes acts of killing rational agents, was presented as an example of one such principle. But then if generalists are not committed to atomistic moral principles of the sort McNaughton and Dancy are objecting to, one wonders whether there is anything left to the dispute between generalists and particularists over the significance of principles playing a guiding role in the lives of individuals. Let us pursue this.

The debate over principle abstinence, as already noted, is one of comparative reliability in reaching moral verdicts, and it may usefully be clarified as follows. First, we focus on mature individuals of average intelligence who are both mentally stable and morally conscientious—who sincerely want to come to correct moral verdicts about the morality of actions and who (we are supposing) will typically choose and act accordingly.[11] Second, one can make moral judgments about the actions of others, one's own past actions, and about prospective actions one might perform. A principle could guide one's thinking about any of these sorts of evaluation, but our focus will be on the issue of principles and how they might guide individuals to make correct moral judgments and subsequent choices, either about situations they are now confronting or about future situations (actual or possible) they are contemplating.

Third, it is important to note that there are at least two ways in which a principle can guide one's thinking and subsequent choice. One way is where the individual consciously brings a moral principle to mind and proceeds to reason about the morality of some action using that principle as a guide—cases of moral deliberation. Another way is where the individual who accepts a particular moral principle is guided by the principle without consciously bringing the principle to mind. Cases of the latter sort are characteristic of spontaneous principle guidance; they are a very familiar type of experience and not restricted to moral guidance. For example, competent drivers have internalized various rules of the road, including, for instance, stopping at red lights. Having internalized this particular rule, drivers are guided by it without having to explicitly rehearse the rule and then apply it as they drive. Rather, the relevant perceptual cue (seeing the red light as they approach the intersection) prompts the spontaneous response of applying the brakes. Even though competent drivers do not consciously call the relevant rule to mind, it nevertheless plays a role in explaining why they stop at red lights—it is something they have internalized that "automatically" guides their driving behavior. In a similar manner, internalized moral principles can guide one's thought and behavior without one needing to bring the principles consciously to mind. For example, one might see a small child face down in the water at the edge of a lake and rush to her aid. Arguably, one's action here is unconsciously guided by having internalized a moral principle of helping those in danger of being harmed.[12]

Fourth, if moral principles play a guiding role in the lives of ordinary, morally committed individuals, they cannot be too complex; they have to be principles that ordinary individuals with limited cognitive abilities can learn and apply. Recall from section 4 the moral principle Promise. In purporting to set forth what a reasons holist would call enabling conditions and an atomist would call aspects of a complex moral reason, Promise involved some complexity. Promise expresses a defeasible moral principle—it purports to express those conditions, the obtaining of which, ground a prima facie obligation to keep one's promises. Suppose one tried to list all the conditions under which keeping one's promise is overridden. No doubt there are very many such cases. Now suppose one built those conditions into what would no doubt turn out to be a very complicated moral principle. Call it Promise*. Even if Promise* represents a correct criterion of right action regarding the morality of promising, it may very well be so complex that individuals of ordinary intelligence might not be able to properly remember the principle or even learn it. The point being stressed here is that moral principles that can play a guiding role in people's lives must be usable, given various cognitive limitations of ordinary agents and given certain contexts in which guidance is needed.

A fifth (and final point) has just been made in connection with the example of Promise*, but it is worth stressing. It may turn out that usable moral principles do not represent fully correct criteria of right action. This point was mentioned earlier in section 2, when the theses of principle eliminativism and principle abstinence were first introduced, and as there noted, was explored in our chapter 5 discussion of utilitarianism. Utilitarians take the principle of utility to be a correct criterion or standard of right and wrong action. But in light of the difficulties of reliably applying this principle to particular cases, utilitarians typically advocate the use of rather simple moral rules that (they maintain) can reliably guide committed moral agents to correct moral verdicts and decisions, particularly in contexts demanding an immediate moral response. The idea is that actions such as telling lies, breaking promises, killing human beings, and so forth tend to have a negative effect on overall utility, and so being guided by rules that prohibit such actions (exceptional cases aside)—rules that are easily learned and applied—will normally result in maximizing overall utility. In general, then, the idea is that as long as usable moral principles can help committed moral agents make correct moral judgments and choices by guiding them to focus on features of actions and circumstances that are morally relevant (or at least tend to be relevant), then one can ask whether there is any reason to suppose that such principle guidance is superior to non-principle discernment.

With these points of clarification in mind, the question, then, is whether there is any reason to think that principle guidance is any more or less reliable than particularist discernment in its ability to lead the average, morally conscientious person to correct moral judgments and choices in various contexts. Of course, because there are various sorts of moral principles, among them absolutist principles, defeasible atomistic principles, and defeasible holistic principles, we have to decide which sorts of principle to consider when comparing the reliability of a morally committed person who is guided by principles with the morally committed person who relies entirely on non-principle discernment. We have already put simple absolutist principles to the side. We could compare agents who accept defeasible atomistic principles with agents whose moral judgments and choices rely on non-principle discernment. But, since the challenge by the particularist has to do with sensitivity to morally relevant detail, it would seem that the most apt comparison would be between individuals who make use of defeasible holistic moral principles and otherwise similar individuals who do not rely on principles for coming to moral verdicts in contexts of deliberation, choice, and action. But, to return to an earlier point, this makes the comparison a delicate matter, since one might wonder whether there is (or could be) much of a difference between morally committed persons of these two sorts when it comes to the issue of the overall reliability in moral judgment, choice, and action. Even so, some considerations have been marshaled in defense of principle guidance and thus against the thesis of principle abstinence. Here I will confine the discussion to just a few points.[13]

Consider instances of special pleading—cases in which an individual avoids complying with general moral requirements that he recognizes as correct by thinking of himself as being in a situation that exempts him from whatever requirement he is trying to evade. What makes the case one of special pleading is that typically the agent's personal interests distort his thinking, and without realizing it, he thinks (though falsely) that his case is a legitimate exceptional case. Here is an example.

> *Rob's request.* Rob is a very generous donor to his Ivy League university alma mater; his daughter does not satisfy the entrance requirements of this particular university, which strictly limits the number of applicants that it admits each year. Rob thinks that his generosity toward his alma mater justifies him in intervening to make sure that his daughter is admitted, and he thinks that anyone in his position would likewise be morally justified in intervening on behalf of his or her children. So he goes to the university's administration and requests that his daughter be admitted to the freshman class. Of course, given the limits on the number of those admitted, his daughter's admission will mean that someone else is not admitted. But he thinks that his case (and cases like his) is an exception to a principle of fairness that applies to others not similarly situated.

Such cases of special pleading lead a person to mistaken moral judgments and consequent decisions. Is there any reason to suppose that a person guided by moral principles is less susceptible to such errors than the person relying on discernment? McKeever and Ridge (2006, chapter 9) make a case for an affirmative answer. Their case is based on the so-called symbolic value of seriously internalizing moral principles and the psychological resistance this creates in a morally committed individual. To seriously adopt a principle of procedural fairness, for example, as opposed to treating it as a mere "rule of thumb," arguably involves coming to appreciate the significance of such fairness so that being personally involved in unfair treatment of another person will signify an abandonment of an ideal of fairness. In being so involved, a morally committed agent compromises this ideal and with it one's ideal of being a moral person. In developing this point, McKeever and Ridge point out that someone who adopts moral principles presumably knows about the risks of special pleading, which, in adopting such principles, she wants to avoid. Commenting on this sort of motivation for adopting moral principles, they write:

> Someone who adopts a principle for this reason will attach disvalue to being the sort of person who engages in special pleading. This, in turn, will make the agent reluctant to abandon her principle in favor of another one when faced with a concrete situation which calls for decision. For such shifts in a person's principles can be associated with special pleading, and *this* symbolic value can increase the stakes and make it less likely that the agent will shift principles (2006, 206).

So the case in favor of principle guidance, and thus against the particularist thesis of principle abstinence, is that a principled person is more likely to resist engaging in special pleading compared to a person who recognizes that procedural fairness *may* be morally relevant and count against some course of action as a mere rule of thumb. Their respective psychologies differ, given the symbolic value of internalizing and being guided by moral principles.[14]

Of course, the particularist will warn that such individuals risk being too rigid in their moral thinking and so will tend to miss morally relevant details of particular cases that ought to prompt one to revise one's moral principles in light of such details. So it is important for the case being made on behalf of principle guidance (as McKeever and Ridge note) that the extra motivation for resisting special pleading that results from principle guidance not be so strong that it in effect prevents one from modifying (or even abandoning) one's principles in light of being confronted with good reasons for doing so.

Whether principle guidance is superior to non-principle discernment in guarding against special pleading is controversial.[15] And it is but one example of the kind of consideration that might be brought to bear on the debate between generalists and particularists over the practical role of moral principles in people's lives. Another, somewhat related consideration concerns the role principles might play in helping individuals to overcome moral weakness of will—cases in which one knowingly fails to resist the temptation to violate a moral requirement. And there are other considerations besides these two that can be brought to bear on the debate over principle abstinence, but I hope that enough has been said to indicate to readers what the debate is about.[16]

Here is a final remark about this dispute over the practical role of moral principles. As I have already noted, making a case for or against the thesis of principle abstinence—which is largely a question of human psychology—is going to be fairly speculative unless and until empirical evidence is brought to bear on the issue.[17] However, one might hope to find experimental research that has been conducted about the role of principles and rules in guiding people's nonmoral decision making that may be usefully brought to bear on the issue.[18] And we do find some evidence of this sort. For example, there is experimental evidence indicating that individuals who are taught to use certain cost-benefit principles for making practical decisions in everyday life tend to fare better than those who do not.[19] Of course, for present purposes most relevant are studies that compare principle guidance to non-principle expertise. Arguably, there is some experimental evidence that perhaps favors principle guidance. For example, William Grove and Paul Meehl (1996) compared 136 studies that had been conducted between 1920 and the mid-1990s in which mechanical, rule-based methods of predicting a range of human behavior were compared to the more informal judgments of a relevant group of experts. What they found indicates that highly trained experts in a particular field engaged in certain field-related tasks typically do not outperform simple rule-based methods applied to those same tasks, even though the experts often had access to more information about particular cases than was represented in the rule-based methods. Indeed, Grove and Meehl conclude from their study that mechanical rule-based methods for making such predictions about a wide range of human behaviors are almost "invariably equal to or superior to" the more informal methods employed by experts.

It is hard to know whether any conclusion may be confidently drawn from these experimental results about the controversy over principle abstinence in ethics. Many questions arise, including these: How much expertise in their field did the judges in these studies have? Were the judges perhaps partly guided by rules of prediction that were less reliable than the rules featured in the mechanical rule-based methods? Perhaps the interplay of morally relevant factors tends to be of greater complexity in morals than in these other areas of decision making, and so even if principle or rule-based decision making in, for example, predicting rates of recidivism among parolees is superior to the judgments of prison psychiatrists,[20] this may not be true in the case of moral decision making. Answering such questions is beyond the scope of this book. Rather, the point being stressed here is that one might look to experimental evidence about the role of rules and principles in nonmoral decision making for any bearing such evidence may have on the controversy between generalists and particularists over the question of principle guidance in ethics.

7. CONCLUSION

Moral particularism, often thought of as an antitheory position in ethics, helps bring into focus some of the deeply embedded assumptions of traditional moral theory, thereby aiding reflection on the project of moral theorizing. Concerning the theoretical aim of moral theory, the tradition has been to suppose that a proper explanation of the deontic status of actions crucially involves appealing to law-like generalizations (moral principles or rules) that provide a basis for explaining the particular case. (A similar point can be made about the project of explaining particular cases of items having intrinsic value, though this chapter has focused exclusively on explaining the deontic status of particular actions.) This way of understanding how moral explanation should proceed is challenged by the particularist. With regard to moral theory's practical aim of providing moral principles or rules for purposes of reliable guidance, again, particularists have argued that cultivating a moral sensibility in which moral principles and rules do not (or at least need not) play a central guiding role is preferable to one that does.

I have not so much tried to defend generalism against particularism as to make clear some of the main lines of debate between these two camps. But even if generalism does prevail over particularism with regard to matters both theoretical and practical, particularism does succeed in bringing into focus the significance of questions of how reasons work (I tend to favor holism about reasons) as well as the perils of a kind of overly rigid principle-guidance that can blind one to the subtleties of our moral lives.

NOTES

1. This is perhaps the prevailing view. But see Little, 2001 who rejects the traditional quest for exceptionless moral principles that would systematize morality, but nevertheless thinks that moral theory reconceived as acknowledging an ineliminable explanatory role for moral generalizations survives many of the particularist objections to traditional moral theory. Although Little describes herself as a particularist, her view is compatible with how I am going to characterize generalism.

2. They are not committed because what they often refer to as "rules of thumb" can be understood as mere reminders of what kinds of considerations may be morally relevant rather than as playing an important guiding role in a person's moral psychology. For more on this, see section 6.

3. This is an appropriate place to mention a dispute among generalists over whether the explanatory features referred to in moral principles that represent explanatory moral reasons must be purely descriptive, non-normative features or whether they may refer to features that are morally loaded. That is, there are really two ways in which a moral theory might attempt to satisfy G, depending on the nature of the morally relevant features that are to do the explaining. First, one might aspire to "capture" the underlying nature of right conduct entirely in terms of descriptive, *nonmoral* features of actions—features that "lie beneath" the moral features or properties of an action and serve to provide an explanation of the action's deontic status in nonmoral terms. A descriptive nonmoral feature of an action is one that can be understood without reference to a moral concept. Such features, then, are supposed to figure in moral principles that are at least implicitly invoked in explaining an action's deontic status. Some moral theories do aspire to defend moral principles that connect moral concepts (and properties) with descriptive, nonmoral concepts (and properties). Such theories would thus provide an underlying purely nonmoral, descriptive unity to morality. Consider, for example, classical utilitarianism, according to which the rightness of an action depends on how much intrinsic value it would bring about (if performed) compared to how much intrinsic value would be brought about by performing various alternative actions. On this theory, the rightness of an action depends on considerations of intrinsic value. However, according to classical versions of utilitarianism, episodes of pleasure and pain are the only bearers of intrinsic value (that are relevant to moral evaluation). So, according to classical utilitarianism, facts about how much overall pleasure and pain would be brought about by an action are what make an

action right or wrong. Alternatively (and as already noted), one might discover that although there is no one such underlying feature, there is a small set of nonmoral descriptive features that together can be used to explain the wrongness of a wide range of actions. If so, then some form of moral pluralism would be true. In either case, if there are such purely descriptive underlying features—wrong-making moral reasons—then the moral phenomenon of wrong action is unified, and unified at the level of nonmoral descriptive features of actions that serve to explain the deontic statuses of wrong actions. Sometimes the claim made by this thesis is expressed by saying that morality has fixed and definite nonmoral contours—that there is a fixed pattern of descriptive features underlying right- and wrong-making features of actions—that shape the moral status of actions.

However, not all moral theories aspire to unify morality at the level of nonmoral descriptive features of actions; some theories maintain that we find fully adequate explanations of right and wrong in terms of features that are properly characterized partly in moral terms—terms that express "thick" moral concepts. This is true of Ross's moral theory. The concepts featured in many if not all of his principles of prima facie duty are morally thick concepts. For instance, the concept of reparation includes the concept of a wrongful act. In order to keep the complexity of the generalist/particularist dispute under control, I propose to put this particular dispute over the sorts of features that provide an appropriate explanation of the deontic status of actions and thus properly figure in explanatory moral principles to one side. For a discussion of the importance of this matter, see for example, Crisp, 2000 and McNaughton and Rawling, 2000, as well as McKeever and Ridge, 2006, chapters 6 and 7.

4. But Dancy does not argue only by example. He also argues, 2004, 73–78 that because theoretical reasons—reasons for belief—work holistically, one should expect that practical reasons, including moral reasons, work holistically as well.

5. In addition to enablers and disablers, Dancy, 2004, 41–42 introduces intensifiers and attenuators that affect the strength of reasons in a context. For instance, the fact that I am in a position to help an accident victim in need of help, provides a reason for me to help. If, in addition, I am the only one around who can come to the person's aid, this consideration is not an additional reason to help, rather it serves to strengthen the reason I already have.

6. Notice that McKeever and Ridge build into the antecedent of K (the "if" clause) that there are no competing reasons that either alone or together outweigh the strength of the reason against killing a rational agent. What this illustrates is that Ross's defeasible principles (rules) of prima facie duty of the form *If F, then prima facie one has a moral obligation to M* can alternatively be expressed as exceptionless principles by doing what McKeever and Ridge do with K. That is, one can reformulate Rossian principles by building into the antecedent a clause to the effect that the reason that favors performing (or omitting) a certain act in some circumstance is not overridden by some competing moral reason. The difference, then, between a reformulated Rossian principle and K is clause *b* in K, which reflects reasons holism.

7. Of course, it is possible to hold the view that generalist principles featuring holistic reasons cannot be made fully specific owing to the fact that one could not capture all of the many ways in which a feature like promising that is normally relevant and favors acts of promise keeping can be overridden, silenced, or reversed.

8. What these authors refer to as Principles (capital 'p') are exceptionless moral principles—principles that purport to specify some feature (or set of them) that is either sufficient or necessary and sufficient for an action having some particular all-things-considered deontic status.

But the point of contrast they are drawing between particularism and generalism holds even if, as a generalist, one embraces defeasible moral principles.

9. Particularists can readily allow that moral principles and rules are of value in early moral education when children are in the process of moral learning. Their critical focus is on the moral sensibility of mature adults.

10. For more detail about particularist discernment and coming to have moral knowledge of particular cases, see Dancy, 2004, chapter 8.

11. It may be that some individuals will fare better if guided by moral principles, and some will fare better relying on nonprinciple discernment. To keep matters from becoming too complicated, we restrict interest to generalizations about ordinary, average individuals, vague as this description is.

12. Horgan and Timmons, 2007 argue that moral principles are capable of guiding one's spontaneous morally appropriate behavior on some particular occasion without having to be explicitly represented either consciously or unconsciously by the agent on the occasion in question. In their terminology, principles can guide in this way by being "proceduralized."

13. For a defense against principle abstinence, I refer readers to chapter 9 of McKeever and Ridge, 2006 and to Väyrynen, 2008.

14. As Michael Bukoski pointed out to me, first, it is likely that absolutist moral principles or atomistic defeasible principles (like Ross's) would do a better job at combating special pleading than holistic defeasible principles. And second, given the complexity of the issue about principle guidance, in all likelihood different sorts of principles will be best *in certain domains* of moral concern while nonprincipled discernment better in others. See also note 11 about differences among individuals with respect to the efficacy of principle guidance vs. discernment.

15. Dancy, 2009 gives a brief pro-particularist reply to the worry about special pleading.

16. McKeever and Ridge also argue that principle guidance may help guard against so-called framing effects (see 2006, 211–215), and Hooker, 2000b, 2008b has argued that principle guidance, compared to discernment, enhances the prospects for mutually beneficial cooperation among individuals.

17. Besides the prescriptive question of whether principle guidance is superior to non-principle discernment, there is also the descriptive question of the extent to which people as a matter of fact do make use of moral principles and rules for practical purposes. Psychologist Jonathan Haidt, 2001 has argued that despite people's tendency to justify their particular moral judgments by appealing to moral principles and rules that they sincerely believe to have guided their judgments, their judgments are very often simply based on gut reactions and not in fact principle-guided. In offering justifications for their moral judgments by appeal to principles, people are very often, and without realizing it, subject to confabulation. For a reply to Haidt, see Horgan and Timmons, 2007.

18. Here I am relying on illuminating work by Jennifer Zamzow, "Rules and Principles in Moral Decision-Making: A Practical Objection to Moral Particularism" (unpublished manuscript).

19. See for example, Larrick, Morgan, and Nisbett, 1990 and Larrick, Nisbett, and Morgan, 1993.

20. A result featured in Burgess, 1928 and one of the studies referred to in Grove and Meehl, 1996.

FURTHER READING

Philosophical Literature

Dancy, Jonathan. 1983. "Ethical Particularism and Morally Relevant Properties." *Mind* 92: 530–47. An analysis and criticism of Ross's moral generalism and an initial statement of particularism.

———. 1993. *Moral Reasons*. Oxford: Blackwell. Chapters 4–7 present a sustained defense of particularism against various versions of generalism.

———. 2004. *Ethics without Principles*. Oxford: Oxford University Press. Dancy refines and extends his 1993 defense of moral particularism.

———. 2009. "Moral Particularism." In *The Stanford Encyclopedia of Philosophy*, ed. E. N. Zalta. http://plato.stanford.edu. Excellent overview of generalism/particularism debate.

Hooker, Brad. 2000. "Moral Particularism—Wrong and Bad." In *Moral Particularism*, ed. Brad Hooker and Margaret Little. Oxford: Oxford University Press. An attempt to argue just what the title indicates.

———, and Margaret Little, eds. 2000. *Moral Particularism*. Oxford: Oxford University Press. A collection of essays written for this volume debating moral particularism.

Lance, Mark, and Margaret Little. 2006. "Particularism and Antitheory." In *The Oxford Handbook of Ethical Theory*, ed. D. Copp. Oxford: Oxford University Press. A very helpful overview of the generalism/particularism debate. Highly recommended.

Lance, Mark, Matjaz Potrc, and Vojko Strahovnik, eds. 2008. *Challenging Moral Particularism*. New York: Routledge. As the title indicates, a collection of articles (both pro and con) debating moral particularism.

Little, Margaret Oliva. 2001. "On Knowing the 'Why': Particularism and Moral Theory." *Hastings Center Report* 31: 32–40. A defense of moral theory (tempered by particularist worries about traditional moral theory) according to which holistic moral generalizations can and do play an important explanatory role in moral inquiry. A very enlightening discussion of particularism and its relation to moral theory.

McKeever, Sean, and Michael Ridge. 2006. *Principled Ethics: Generalism as a Regulative Ideal*. Oxford: Oxford University Press. A state-of-the-art critical discussion of particularism and defense of generalism.

McNaughton, David. 1988. *Moral Vision*. Oxford: Blackwell. Chapter 13 is a very readable presentation and defense of particularism, comparing particularism to Rossian pluralism.

Väyrynen, Pekka. 2008. "Usable Moral Principles." In *Challenging Moral Particularism*, ed. Mark Lance, Matjaz Potrc, and Vojko Strahovnik. New York: Routledge. An illuminating defense of moral principles as useful guides.

Empirical Literature

Fantino, E., B. A. Jaworski, D. A. Case, and S. Stolarz-Fantino. 2003. "Rules and Problem Solving: Another Look." *American Journal of Psychology* 116: 613–32. A study of the possible rigidity effects of using rules in decision making.

Grove, William M., and Paul E. Meehl. 1996. "Comparative Efficiency of Informal (Subjective, Impressionistic) and Formal (Mechanical, Algorithmic) Prediction Procedures: The Clinical-Statistical Controversy." *Psychology, Public Policy, and Law* 2: 293–323. A meta-analysis, referred to in the text, of experimental studies comparing the predictive accuracy of informal to formal methods.

Larrick, R. P., J. N. Morgan, and R. E. Nisbett. 1990. "Teaching the Use of Cost-Benefit Reasoning in Everyday Life." *Psychological Science* 1: 362–70. Experimental evidence supporting the claim that subjects trained in the use of cost-benefit rules outperform untrained subjects.

12

Conclusion

In the previous chapters, we have surveyed a variety of moral theories, including the divine command theory, moral relativism, the natural law theory, versions of consequentialism, Kant's moral theory, moral pluralism, virtue ethics, and moral particularism. My primary aim has been to explain and then critically evaluate these theories. I have not attempted to defend any one theory as ultimately correct or superior to all of its rivals. But I have tried to defend the claim that a plausible moral theory is likely going to be a limited, pluralistic theory.[1] In concluding, I want to reinforce this claim by explaining why this should not be surprising. I will then close with a few observations about the project of moral theory.

1. WHY A LIMITED, PLURALISTIC MORAL THEORY?

I want to begin with some clarificatory remarks about what I have been calling a limited, pluralistic moral theory. In chapter 9, moral pluralism was introduced in connection with W. D. Ross's theory of right conduct and characterized by the following two theses:

1. There is a plurality of basic moral rules.
2. There is no underlying moral principle from which these rules can be derived that serves to justify them.

The moral rules in question were rules of prima facie duty, each of which specified a basic or fundamental right- or wrong-making feature of actions. But as we have noted in previous chapters, one can be a pluralist about intrinsic value and about the virtues. So strictly speaking, we would need to slightly amend the above two theses

331

so that they mention values and virtues in order to have a fully general definition of moral pluralism. But aside from this rather minor point, more is needed to clarify what I have in mind by moral pluralism.

First, the kind of pluralism in question is what may be called *foundational pluralism* because at the very foundation of a pluralist moral theory is some sort of plurality, whether of prima facie duties, intrinsic values, or virtues.[2] This point is captured by the second thesis which denies that there is some single underlying principle from which the plurality could be derived. Hooker's rule consequentialism is a kind of pluralism—there is a plurality of moral rules that figure in explaining the deontic status of actions—but those rules are derived from a single consequentialist principle and so his view counts as a version of *foundational monism*.

Second, it is important to be clear about the "level" at which a moral theory counts as a form of pluralism. Ross's theory will help us here. As we know, for Ross there is no single *underlying feature* in virtue of which actions have whatever deontic status they have. His view is pluralist at the level of those most basic explanatory right- and wrong-making features of actions. But notice, Ross held that all of one's actual duties had the same *moral* property of being obligatory. At the level of moral properties themselves—the properties of obligatoriness and wrongness—he was not a pluralist. For Ross, all obligatory actions share the same property of being obligatory. All instances of knowledge, virtue, pleasure, and pleasure in relation to virtue share the same property of being intrinsically valuable.[3] But I think the most interesting debate between moral pluralists and their monist opponents is at the level of the underlying features of actions, persons, and circumstances that purports to explain what makes an action right or wrong, something intrinsically good or bad. After all, one of the aims of traditional moral theory is to examine the extent to which morality can be understood as a unified system.

To say that a moral theory is *limited* is to say that the moral principles, rules, or other elements of the theory (such as a lexical ranking of a plurality of duties) do not (together with relevant factual information) yield determinate moral verdicts about a large range of specific cases.[4]

I have claimed that any plausible moral theory is likely to be a limited, pluralistic moral theory. *But why pluralist?* The most obvious response (and one suggested throughout the book) concerns the complexity of ordinary moral thought and discourse. Here is how Bernard Williams makes the point:

> [O]ur ethical ideas consist of a very complex historical deposit. When we consider this fact, and the relations that this deposit has to our public discourse and our private lives, there seems no reason at all to expect it to take, in any considerable measure, the shape of a [strongly unified] theory. (Williams, 1995, 189)

As Williams goes on to point out, if one thinks that a proper starting place in developing a moral theory is with the various moral convictions with which we find ourselves, then in attempting to capture moral considerations that are part of a "complex historical deposit," we are going to be driven toward moral pluralism.

But why limited? This same complexity also supports the idea that no plausible moral theory is going to be able to produce some principle or method which, together with relevant nonmoral information, entails determinate verdicts about a large range of cases. So the complexity of the various moral considerations that play an important role in our thinking helps explain why any plausible moral theory is likely to be limited.

We come to the same conclusion about the likely shape of any plausible moral theory by reflecting on the importance of moral judgment (phronesis) in practical thinking in general and moral reflection in particular. Again, the point is made by Williams in connection with making judgments about what is morally important:

> Judgments of importance are ubiquitous, and are central to practical life and to reflection at a more general level about the considerations that go into practical decision. Moreover, judgments of importance indeed require judgment. There are certainly reasons why some considerations are more important than others . . . but judgment is still needed to determine how far those reasons can take you. It may be obvious that one kind of consideration is more important than another (for instance, one kind of ethical consideration is more important than another), but it is a matter of judgment whether in a particular set of circumstances that priority is preserved: other factors alter the balance, or it may be a very weak example of the consideration that generally wins. (Williams, 1995, 190)

The idea that judgment is required to decide which moral considerations in certain contexts are overriding (most important) is an idea we have seen in Ross. What Williams goes on to point out about judgment is that there is no reason to suppose that there is some one measure or fixed principle by which one can decide matters of relative importance. In other words, the sort of judgment in question that is so crucial to moral thinking cannot be fully captured in some set of principles or rules—a claim emphasized by Ross, virtue ethicists, and other moral pluralists.

Thus, the complexity of ordinary moral thought and the urge to have one's moral theory cohere with our considered moral beliefs push moral theory in the direction of being a limited, pluralistic moral theory. The importance of moral judgment reinforces this verdict. We have seen how the natural law theory, Kant's moral theory, consequentialism, and virtue ethics can take this form. Of course, Ross's theory is a prime example of a limited, pluralistic moral theory. What I am here pointing out is simply that some form of this type of moral theory is to be expected given the complexity of moral life and the apparent ineliminable role of moral judgment.[5]

Let me now make a final observation about limited (foundational) moral pluralism, focusing for a moment on theories of right conduct. One way in which a theory of right conduct can unify the seemingly diverse moral phenomena that such theories are about, namely instances of right and wrong conduct, is by featuring a single most basic right-making feature of actions that can then be expressed in a single moral principle and from which (together with relevant factual information) entail verdicts about the deontic status of action. Any such theory counts as a form of foundational moral monism. Such views promise to deliver a strongly unified moral theory.

But versions of foundational moral pluralism can also enjoy a kind of unity—admittedly weaker than what a monistic theory has to offer. Recall from the chapter on moral pluralism Audi's suggestion for dealing with the unconnected-heap objection to Ross's theory. Ross's theory of right conduct features seven basic prima facie duties, but they have struck many interpreters as an unconnected heap and hence lacking a rationale for being considered together as pertaining to morally right and wrong conduct. Audi's suggestion is that one can view the prima facie duties through the lens of Kant's Humanity formulation of the Categorical Imperative. As Audi says in the passage quoted in chapter 9, the point is not that Ross's duties can be derived from Kant's principle. Rather, the idea is that one can view the idea of respect for persons (including not treating them merely as means to one's own ends) as an ideal "that renders the principles of duty intelligible or even expectable" (Audi, 1997, 48). The sort of connectedness Ross's plurality of prima facie duties can enjoy by viewing them as all relating to respect for persons represents a kind of unity.

One could make a similar suggestion in relation to the plurality of intrinsic goods associated with Aquinas's moral theory. One could view them as having to do with the ideal of achieving or at least striving for the kind of perfection that human beings are capable of. Again, the same sort of point can be made about Brink's value pluralist version of utilitarianism. In fact he seems to make the point when he writes: that "unified theories [of value] need not be monistic. OU, for example, contains a pluralist theory of the good, but its intrinsic goods are all represented as components of human welfare" (1989, 251). I don't read Brink as merely claiming that on any pluralist view of intrinsic value, there will be a multiplicity of *bearers* of such value that can somehow be unified. Saying this much is compatible with being a foundational monist about value, because one might hold that one can derive the claim that such and so plurality of items possess intrinsic value from some single ur-value. Rather, I take his remark about viewing the fundamental items having intrinsic value enjoying a kind of unity by being components of human welfare as analogous to how Audi proposes to view Ross's plurality of duties as connected and thus unified by the ideal of treating humanity with respect.

Of course, one might embrace a more radical kind of foundational moral pluralism and hold, for example, that some bearers of intrinsic value can be understood as components of human welfare, while others are best viewed as components of human perfection. Such a view would not enjoy the kind of unity I've just been describing. Speaking for myself, I tend to favor this more radical kind of pluralism, but defense of this view would require the ambitious project of defending some particular moral theory.

2. THE PROJECT OF MORAL THEORY ONCE AGAIN

Suppose I am right and any plausible moral theory is going to be a form of moral pluralism that is also limited in the manner explained. Now (1) if versions of many of the moral theories we have studied (if not all of them) can take this form, and (2) if, because they are limited in power, they are likely to be consistent with our considered moral beliefs, then they are going to have pretty much the same (limited) implications about which actions are right and what sorts of things (including people) are good. And if they do, then do they all collapse into a single theory? What is left of the differences between, and conflicts among, such theories, assuming that they basically agree in what they imply about right, wrong, good, and bad?

The answer is that these theories still differ in two important ways. First, they differ in overall structure. Recall the remark by John Rawls at the beginning of chapter 1: "Moral theory is the study of substantive moral conceptions, that is, the study of how the basic notions of the right, the good, and moral worth [the morally good] may be arranged to form different structures" (Rawls, 1975, 286). Given that there are three kinds of basic moral notions, there would seem to be the following kinds of possible structures that a moral theory might take. (1) One kind of notion is most basic and can be used to characterize the other two. (2) Of the three types of basic notions, two are equally basic, while the third is to be understood in terms of one or both of the others. (3) All three types of notions are equally basic—each can be understood without appeal to the other two. (4) None of the three types of notions is basic—to understand any one of them, we must appeal to the other two.

The moral theories we have examined differ in structure.[6] For instance, consequentialism and virtue ethics are value-based theories, but while consequentialism takes the idea of the overall value of outcomes to be basic in explaining right action, many versions of virtue ethics take the concept of moral worth (moral goodness) and thus considerations pertaining to character to be most basic. Thus one important difference among the moral theories concerns matters of structure, which is significant for at least two reasons.

First, for purposes of understanding morality, philosophers are interested in relations among concepts. Questions about structure expressed by Rawls have to do with relations among the basic concepts in ethics and the categories they signify.

Second, the issue of structure has implications for theoretical questions about what makes something right or wrong, good or bad, as well as for practical questions about how to proceed in coming to have justified moral beliefs. If some type of value-based moral theory is correct—say, a theory that makes the rightness and wrongness of actions depend on some relation between actions and what is of intrinsic value—then this fact would give us insight into the nature of rightness and wrongness. Again, knowing what makes an action right or wrong should be useful in our practices of justifying moral beliefs. If, for example, we knew that some version of consequentialism were true, then we would know that to justify a moral belief about the rightness of an action would require that we bring considerations of welfare to bear on the matter.

In addition to differences over structure, moral theories differ in content. For instance, both the natural law theory and consequentialism are value-based theories that make considerations of value basic in morality. However, natural law theorists typically embrace a perfectionistic account of intrinsic value; many versions of consequentialism reject perfectionism in favor of a welfarist account of intrinsic value.

So, even if we should expect a correct moral theory to be both limited and pluralistic, this does not settle questions about the structure or content of the theory. There is still much interesting work to be done in arriving at a philosophically justified view about which form of limited, pluralistic theory is best. Indeed, given my remarks about judging the plausibility of a moral theory, there is work to be done in metaethics on the issue of how (if at all) it is possible to arrive at a philosophically justified moral theory. Such issues are matters of lively contemporary debate in ethics.

NOTES

1. If we allow moral particularism to count as a nongeneralist version of moral pluralism, then my remarks apply to this nontraditional type of moral theory as well.

2. Mason, 2011 usefully distinguishes foundational from so-called *normative pluralism*. The latter, less radical form is the view that there is a plurality of bearers of intrinsic value, which most any moral theory can accept without also accepting foundational pluralism.

3. One can be a pluralist about moral properties. See Mason, 2011 for discussion.

4. We can be more specific by distinguishing theoretical limits and practical limits. I have been most interested in the former. But the moral principles featured in a theory might be difficult or impossible to use as a decision procedure and thus be practically limited without also being theoretically limited. This point is reflected in the fact that moral principles might not satisfy the standard of applicability but might nevertheless have determinate implications and thus satisfy the standard of determinacy.

5. There are other reasons to favor foundational moral pluralism, including the claim that there are so-called discontinuities among values that prevent them from being put on a single scale of comparison, thus suggesting that there is an irreducible plurality of intrinsic values that cannot be derived from some single super intrinsic value. Again, see Mason, 2011 for discussion of such points and for an overview of the debate between monists and pluralists.

6. Here is a place to mention the project of *consequentializing* moral theories that present themselves as non-consequentialist. As explained by James Dreier, the project is fairly straightforward: "We merely take the features of an action that the [non-consequentialist] theory considers to be relevant, and build them into the consequences. For example, if a theory says that promises are not to be broken, then we restate this requirement: that a promise has been broken is a bad consequence" (1993, 23). The upshot of this project is supposed to be that all plausible competing moral theories can be expressed as one or another form of consequentialism and so the standard divide between consequential and non-consequentialist theories is not a particularly deep or useful way to classify them. For an overview of this project see Portmore, 2009. However, it is also possible to *deontologize* competing moral theories and express them as versions of deontology as explained by Portmore using Kant's moral theory as one example (2007, section 5) and by Hurley (forthcoming). Against those who have claimed that the possibility of consequentializing competing moral theories means that all moral theorists are really consequentialists, Portmore argues that, for example, act utilitarianism and Kant's moral theory still differ in what each theory takes as *fundamental* in explaining right action. For the utilitarian, as we know, the explanation is in terms of maximizing aggregate utility; for the Kantian the explanation is in terms of treating humanity with respect—structural differences that I'm highlighting in the text.

Appendix
Standards for Evaluating Moral Theories

The following standards are explained in chapter 1, section 7, except for Publicity, which is introduced in chapter 7, section 6.

Consistency. A moral theory should be consistent in the sense that its principles, together with relevant factual information, yield consistent moral verdicts about the morality of actions, persons, and other objects of moral evaluation.

Determinacy. A moral theory should feature principles which, together with relevant factual information, yield determinate moral verdicts about the morality of actions, persons, and other objects of evaluation in a wide range of cases.

Applicability. The principles of a moral theory should be applicable in the sense that they specify relevant information about actions and other items of evaluation that human beings can typically obtain and use to arrive at moral verdicts on the basis of those principles.

Intuitive Appeal. A moral theory should develop and make sense of various intuitively appealing beliefs and ideas about morality.

Internal Support. A moral theory whose principles, together with relevant factual information, logically imply our considered moral beliefs receives support—internal support—from those beliefs. On the other hand, if the principles of a theory have implications that conflict with our considered moral beliefs, this is evidence against the correctness of the theory.

Explanatory Power. A moral theory should feature principles that explain our more specific considered moral beliefs, thus helping us understand why actions, persons, and other objects of moral evaluation are right or wrong, good or bad, have or lack moral worth.

External Support. The fact that the principles of a moral theory are supported by nonmoral beliefs and assumptions, including well-established beliefs and assumptions from various areas of nonmoral inquiry, is some evidence in its favor. On the other hand, the fact that the principles conflict with established nonmoral beliefs and assumptions is evidence against the theory.

Publicity. The principles of a moral theory should be such that they do not rule out as impermissible making public (by, for example, teaching) the principles and associated moral theory. Moral theories whose principles rule out such teaching fail to satisfy this standard.

Glossary

Entries are followed by chapter and section numbers where these terms are introduced.

absolutism (moral). The view that there are certain types of actions (e.g., intentionally killing innocent humans) that are always wrong regardless of the consequences of such actions. (chap. 4, sec. 2) *See also* deontological constraints.

acceptance utility. The net aggregate value that would result were a given rule to be accepted by a significant proportion of the members of some group. (chap. 6, sec. 6)

act consequentialism (AC). A type of moral theory according to which the deontic status of actions is determined by the value of the consequences that would be produced by performing those actions. (chap. 5, sec. 1)

actual consequence utilitarianism. A version of consequentialism according to which the deontic status of action is explained entirely in terms of the actual values of the outcomes that an action does have or would have if performed. (chap. 5, sec. 5) *See also* expected consequence utilitarianism.

actual utility. The utility that would (actually) result from an action were it to be performed. (chap. 5, sec. 5) *See also* expected utility.

act utilitarianism (AU). A version of consequentialism according to which the utilities associated with concrete actions determine the deontic status of actions. (chap. 5, sec. 4)

agent neutral theory. Moral theories according to which an assignment of value to whatever items have value does not make essential reference to the agent. (chap. 5, sec. 2). *See also* agent relative theory.

339

agent relative theory. Moral theories according to which an assignment of value to at least some items having value does make essential reference to the agent. (chap. 5, sec. 2) *See also* agent neutral theory.

agent utility. An action's agent utility refers to the net balance of intrinsic value that would accrue to the agent as a result of performing that action. (chap. 7, sec. 1)

all-things-considered duty. An action that, once all of the morally relevant considerations are brought to bear, is one's actual duty. (chap. 8, sec. 3) *See also* prima facie duty.

applicability standard. A standard for evaluating moral theories that states that in providing a decision procedure, a moral theory ought to specify a procedure that human beings, with their limitations, can actually use in moral deliberation. (chap. 5, sec. 7)

applied ethics. That branch of normative ethics that is concerned with specific moral issues, particularly controversial ones such as abortion, capital punishment, and treatment of animals. (chap. 1, sec. 8)

atomism. *See* reasons atomism.

care ethics. A type of moral theory that makes considerations of caring about individuals central in developing an overall theory of right conduct and value. (chap. 9, sec. 4)

caring about. Caring about someone or something involves "being invested" in that person or thing. (chap. 9, sec. 4)

casuistry. The art of applying principles to specific cases to reach justified moral conclusions about those cases. (chap. 7, sec. 5)

Categorical Imperative. Kant's supreme principle of morality. In the Humanity as an End in Itself formulation, it requires that we treat humanity, in ourselves and in others, always as an end in itself, never as a mere means. In the Universal Law formulation, it requires that we act only on those maxims that we can will to be universal laws. (chap. 7, sec. 4) *See also* hypothetical imperative (formal principle of).

categorical imperatives. In Kant's ethics, categorical imperatives express obligations that are valid for an agent simply because she is a free and rational agent and are thus valid independently of her desires. In Kant's moral theory, moral obligations are properly expressed as categorical imperatives. (chap. 7, sec. 2)

commensurability (of values). The idea that different values can be balanced, weighed, and thus compared according to a common scale. In cases where no such balancing and weighing is possible, values are said to be incommensurable. (chap. 5, sec. 3)

consequentialism (theory of right conduct). A type of moral theory that makes the deontic status of actions depend entirely on the values of the consequences of individual actions, rules, or motives associated with individual actions. (chap. 5, sec. 1)

considered moral beliefs. Those beliefs that are deeply held and widely shared and which one would continue to hold were one to reflect carefully on their correctness. (chap. 1, sec. 6)

consistency standard. A standard for evaluating a moral theory that requires that its principles (or rules) yield consistent moral verdicts about the morality of actions, persons, and other objects of moral evaluation. (chap. 1, sec. 7)

context sensitivity thesis (CS). A thesis that claims that the rightness or wrongness of an action (performed in some particular context) depends in part on nonmoral facts that hold in the context in question—facts concerning agents and their circumstances. (chap. 3, sec. 2)

decision procedure. In ethics a method of discovering answers to moral questions and in general guide moral decision making and choice. (chap. 1, sec. 2)

deontic concepts (categories). Concepts such as obligation, duty, right, wrong, forbidden, permissible, impermissible, optional. In ethics, they are used primarily for the evaluation of actions. (chap. 1, sec. 4)

deontic status of actions. The rightness or wrongness of actions. (chap. 1, sec. 4)

deontological constraints. Moral constraints (duties) that either entirely prohibit performing certain actions such as killing innocent people even in cases where good consequences would result from doing so. Such constraints are "absolutist," in allowing no exceptions. Non-absolutist deontological constraints require that violations of such constraints can only be justified if the consequences of non violation are extremely bad. (chap. 4, sec. 8 and chap. 6, sec. 1)

deontology. A term often used to classify moral theories in contrast to versions of consequentialism and virtue ethics. (chap. 1, note 10)

descriptive relativism. *See* moral diversity thesis.

desire fulfillment utilitarianism (DFU). A version of utilitarianism that understands utility in terms of fulfillment of desires. (chap. 6, sec. 7) *See also* utility, utilitarianism.

determinacy standard. A standard for evaluating a moral theory that says that the principles (or rules) of a moral theory should yield determinate moral verdicts about the morality of actions, persons, and other objects of evaluation in a wide range of cases. (chap. 1, sec. 6)

direct act consequentialism. The view that the consequences that matter for deontic evaluation are those that are (or would be) produced by individual actions. (chap. 5, sec. 1) *See also* indirect consequentialism.

direct violation (D). A violation of a basic value by an action in which (1) the action will bring about the hindrance or destruction of a basic value, and (2) that action cannot be justified by the principle of double effect. Such violations are part of the theory of right conduct for the natural law theory. (chap. 4, sec. 9)

divine command theory. In its unrestricted version the nature of right and wrong, good and bad entirely depends on God's commands. An action is obligatory, for example, because God commands that we do it. In its restricted version, only matters of obligation are dependent on God's commands. (chap. 2, sec. 1)

double effect. *See* principle of double effect.

duty-based theories. Moral theories that take the concept of duty to be more basic than value concepts or at least not less basic than value concepts.

egoism. *See* ethical egoism, rational egoism, and psychological egoism.

ethical egoism (EE). A consequentialist theory of right conduct according to which right and wrong action for an agent are determined by what is in the overall best interests of that agent. (chap. 7, sec. 1)

ethical hedonism (EH). The view that experiences of pleasure are intrinsically good and experiences of pain are intrinsically bad, and they are the only items of nonmoral intrinsic value with which ethics is concerned. (chap. 5, sec. 2)

ethics. That branch of philosophy concerned with morality; it includes normative ethics and metaethics as its main branches. (chap. 1, sec. 8)

ethics of character. That branch of ethics that addresses such questions as: What makes a character trait a virtue or a vice? In virtue of what is a person an overall morally good person, a person of moral worth? (chap. 10, sec. 3)

Euthyphro dilemma. For a theist, a dilemma that involves the issue of how God's commands are related to morality. On one hand, if morality is dependent on God's commands (as claimed by the divine command theory), then one must reject certain basic claims about God's nature—for example, that God is perfectly morally good and fully rational. On the other hand, if morality is independent of God's commands, then one must reject the idea that God is creator of all things. (chap. 2, sec. 3)

expected consequence utilitarianism (ECU). A version of utilitarianism that states that an action A is right if and only if A has as high an expected utility as any alternative action that the agent could perform instead. (chap. 5, sec. 6) *See also* actual consequence utilitarianism.

expected utility. The utility of an action that will probably result (can be expected to result) if the action is performed. (chap. 5, sec. 6) *See also* actual utility.

explanatory power standard. A standard for evaluating a moral theory that requires that the theory (its basic principles or rules) explain our more specific considered moral beliefs, thus helping us understand why actions, persons, and other objects of moral evaluation are right or wrong, good or bad. (chap. 1, sec. 7)

external support standard. A standard for evaluating a moral theory that asserts that the fact that the principles of a moral theory are supported by various nonmoral beliefs and assumptions—beliefs and assumptions that are "external to" morality—is some evidence in favor of the theory. (chap. 1, sec. 7)

extrinsic goodness (badness). Goodness (or badness) possessed by something in virtue of that thing being appropriately related to something that has intrinsic goodness (or badness). For example, the goodness of knowledge is extrinsic if such knowledge is a means to some intrinsic good such as happiness. Note that something can be both intrinsically and extrinsically good. (chap. 1, sec. 4) *See also* intrinsic goodness (badness).

fundamental morally relevant nonmoral feature. A nonmoral feature of some action or other object of evaluation that is fundamental in explaining the morality of the action or object. (chap. 10, sec. 1)

generalism (moral). The view that moral principles are needed for purposes of explaining the deontic status of particular action and useful for action guidance. *See also* particularism. (chap. 11, intro)

generic generalism thesis. (a) There is a small fixed set of morally relevant features of actions that are fundamental in explaining the deontic status of any action. We may call them basic or primary "moral" reasons, if we keep in mind that we are referring to underlying right- and wrong-making features that figure in explaining the morality of actions. (b) Such reasons are featured in generalizations—moral principles or rules—which are essential in providing explanations of the deontic status of actions.

generic principle of utility (GPU). A principle that states that an action A is right if and only if (and because) A has as high a utility as any alternative action that the agent could perform instead. (chap. 5, sec. 2) *See also* utilitarianism.

hedonism. The view, with respect to value, according to which only experiences of pleasure are intrinsically good and only experiences of pain are intrinsically bad. According to one prominent version of hedonism, what makes such experiences intrinsically good or bad is the pleasantness or unpleasantness of such experiences. (chap. 5, sec. 3) *See also* ethical hedonism, hedonistic conception of utility.

hedonistic conception of utility (HU). A conception that claims that the utility of an action is equal to the overall balance of pleasure versus pain that would be produced were the action to be performed. (chap. 5, sec. 3) *See also* utility.

hedonistic utilitarianism (PHU). A principle that states that an action is right if and only if (and because) it produces at least as high an overall balance of pleasure versus pain as would any other alternative action. (chap. 5, sec. 3)

holism. *See* reasons holism.

humanity as an end itself (HEI). A formulation of the Categorical Imperative that states: so act that you use humanity, whether in your own person or in the person of any other, always as an end, never merely as a means. (chap. 7, sec. 4)

hypothetical imperative (formal principle of) (HI). As described in Kant's moral theory, a formal principle of rational choice and action that requires that we adopt the necessary means to our ends. (chap. 7, sec. 2)

impartialist theory. Theories that embrace some form of impartiality in the moral evaluation of action. Agent neutral theories represent one form, non-prioritarian theories represent another form. These forms may be combined in one theory. (chap. 5, sec. 2) *See also* agent neutral theory, prioritarian theories.

indirect consequentialism. Versions of consequentialism (e.g. rule consequentialism) according to which the consequences relevant to the deontic evaluation of particular actions are indirectly related to those actions. (chap. 5, sec. 1). *See also* direct act consequentialism.

internal support standard. A standard for evaluating a moral theory that requires that the theory (its basic principles or rules), together with relevant information, logically imply our considered moral beliefs. (chap. 1, sec. 7)

intrinsic goodness (badness). Goodness (or badness) possessed by something where the goodness (or badness) is located in that thing. (chap. 1, sec. 4) *See also* extrinsic goodness (badness).

intrinsic value-neutrality. Items which are neither intrinsically good nor intrinsically bad. (chap. 1, sec. 4)

intuitive appeal standard. A standard for evaluating a moral theory that requires that the theory make sense of various beliefs about morality that are intuitively appealing. (chap. 1, sec. 6)

maxim. In Kant's moral theory, a "subjective principle of volition"—presumably an intention—upon which an agent acts. (chap. 7, sec. 7)

maximizing act consequentialism. Consequentialist views (including versions of utilitarianism) according to which from among one's alternative actions, the right actions are those whose outcomes are greater in value than the outcomes of one's other alternative actions. (chap. 5, sec. 2) *See also* satisficing consequentialism.

metaethics. That branch of ethics that concerns semantic, metaphysical, and epistemological questions about moral thought and discourse. (chap. 1, sec. 8) *See also* moral semantics, moral metaphysics, and moral epistemology.

monism. In ethics, the view that there is some single basic feature of actions in virtue of which they are right or wrong. One can also be a monist about value. (chap. 8, sec. 1) *See also* pluralism.

moral criteria (standards). Features of actions that purport to explain their deontic status and are featured in explanatory moral principles. (chap. 1, sec. 2)

moral disagreement. A disagreement that occurs when two or more parties disagree about the morality of some action or other object of evaluation. Such disagreement is fundamental when it stems from a disagreement over basic moral norms; otherwise it is nonfundamental. (chap. 3, sec. 5)

moral diversity thesis (MD). (1) The moral codes of some cultures include basic moral norms that conflict with the basic moral norms that are part of the moral codes of other cultures. (2) Such fundamental conflicts are widespread. This thesis is often called descriptive relativism. (chap. 3, sec. 3)

moral epistemology. That branch of metaethics that is concerned with knowledge and justification of moral claims. (chap. 1, sec. 8)

moral intuitions. Moral convictions one comes to have typically as a result of responding to actual or hypothetical cases of moral significance. (chap. 6, note 1)

moral judgment (phronesis). A developed capacity to arrive at moral verdicts about specific cases that cannot be fully explained in terms of the application of principles, rules, or any other rigorous method that would determine a correct verdict. (chap. 8, sec. 7)

moral metaphysics. That branch of metaethics that is concerned with questions about, e.g., the existence and nature of moral properties and facts. (chap. 1, sec. 8)

moral nativism. A research program in moral psychology that is often presented as the idea that human beings have a moral faculty, understood (roughly) as a specialized innate system whose job it is to generate moral judgments. (chap. 4, sec. 12)

moral norms. General moral statements that specify some action as either required, prohibited, or permissible. (chap. 3, sec. 1)

moral principle. A general moral statement that purports to set forth conditions under which an action is right or wrong or something is good or bad. (chap. 1, sec. 3)

moral relativism (MR). In its unrestricted version, the rightness and wrongness of actions (for a person living in a culture at some time) depend on the basic moral norms of that person's culture. A similar account is given about the nature of goodness and badness. In its restricted version, the rightness and wrongness of actions depends on the basic moral norms of an adequate moral code. (chap. 3, secs. 1 and 8)

moral rule. A general moral statement that specifies some type of action (or other object of evaluation) as having a certain moral quality. For example, "killing is wrong." (chap. 1, sec. 3)

moral semantics. The branch of metaethics that is concerned with questions about the meaning and truth of moral claims. (chap. 1, sec. 8)

moral theory. A branch of ethics that is primarily concerned with investigating the nature of the right and the good. (chap. 1, sec. 2)

moral value (worth). Value (or worth) that has to do with the goodness and badness of persons (as responsible agents) and, in particular, with the goodness and badness of those character traits and associated motives in virtue of which persons are morally good or bad. (chap. 1, sec. 4)

natural law theory. A type of moral theory that (on most versions) attempts to ground morality in facts about human nature. Also characteristic of the theory are perfectionism, moral absolutism, and the principle of double effect. (chap. 4, sec. 2)

natural law theory, Aquinas's basic principle of (NLT). Principle that states that life, procreation, knowledge, and sociability are to be preserved and promoted, their hindrance and destruction are to be avoided. (chap. 4, sec. 4)

normative ethics. That branch of ethics that attempts to answer both general moral questions about what to do and how to be (the main concern of moral theory) and moral questions about specific moral issues such as abortion, euthanasia, capital punishment, and so forth (the main concern of applied ethics). (chap. 1, sec. 8)

objective list theory of value. Certain items (other than, but perhaps including) subjective mental states possess intrinsic value and the value of such items does not depend on being the objects of desire or some other attitude. (chap. 6, sec. 7) *See also* objectivist theories of intrinsic value.

objective rightness. A concept of moral rightness according to which the rightness of an action does not depend on the agent's beliefs about the action's rightness or her beliefs about morally relevant features of the act or on her evidence regarding such factors. For example, for a utilitarian, objective rightness depends on the value of the consequences that would as a matter of objective fact result from the performance of alternative actions. (chap. 5, sec. 6) *See also* subjective rightness.

objectivist theories of intrinsic value. What has intrinsic value is not restricted to psychological states and does not depend on being the object of a person's desires or attitudes generally. (chap. 6, sec. 7) *See also* subjectivist theories of intrinsic value.

obligatory action. In ethics, an action that is morally required; something one ought to do; an action that is one's duty. (chap. 1, sec. 4)

optional action. In ethics, an action that is neither morally obligatory nor morally wrong; it is merely permitted. (chap. 1, sec. 4)

particularism (moral). The view according to which moral principles cannot (or at least need not) play the sorts of explanatory and action guidance roles in order to understand morality. Because standard moral theories feature principles in one or both of these roles, particularism is sometimes referred to as anti-theory. (chap. 11, sec. 1) *See also* generalism.

perfectionism. With respect to value, the view that the good of some kind of thing is a matter of its achieving perfection for things of that kind. Moral perfectionism refers to those moral theories that accept perfectionism about value in relation to human beings and make considerations of human perfection the basis for understanding right and wrong action. (chap. 4, sec. 3)

personal value. Value having to do with the quality of lives of persons and perhaps sentient creatures generally. (chap. 5, sec. 1)

phronesis. From a Greek word meaning intelligence. In ethics phronesis refers to moral judgment. (chap. 9, sec. 2) *See also* moral judgment.

pluralism. In ethics, the view with respect to right conduct that (1) there is a plurality of basic moral rules each of which specifies a feature that serve to explain right and wrong action, and (2) there is no underlying moral principle from which these rules can be derived and which can thus serve to justify them. One can also be a pluralist about value. (chap. 9, sec. 1) *See also* monism.

polarity thesis (P). The thesis that (basic) moral reason must always possess the same polarity in any context in which it is present. (chap. 11, sec. 2)

prima facie duty. An action that (1) possesses some morally relevant feature that counts in favor of one's doing the act and (2) is such that if it were the only morally relevant feature of one's situation, then the act in question would be one's all-things-considered duty. (chap. 8, sec. 3) *See also* all-things-considered duty.

principle abstinence. The thesis that a morally committed agent who wants to come to correct verdicts about particular cases and act accordingly should not (or at least need not) rely on moral principles for guidance. (chap. 11, sec. 1)

principle (doctrine) of double effect (PDE). A principle that claims that one is permitted to perform an action that has at least one good and one bad effect if and only if the following conditions are met: (1) the action, apart from its consequences, must not be wrong; (2) the bad effect must not be intended by the agent; and (3) the bad effect must not be "out of proportion" to the good effect. (chap. 4, sec. 7)

principle eliminativism. The thesis that are no correct or true moral principles that represent moral criteria and which are needed to explain the deontic status of particular actions. (chap. 11, sec. 1)

prioritarian consequentialism. A version of consequentialism according to which in ranking outcomes in terms of their value, extra weight is to be given to members of disadvantaged groups. (chap. 5, sec. 2)

prioritarian theories. Moral theories that allow priority or special consideration be given to disadvantaged groups in determining the deontic status of actions. Non-prioritarian theories rule out such special consideration. (chap. 5, sec. 2)

psychological altruism (PA). The denial of psychological egoism, according to which it is possible (and sometimes the case) that individuals are fundamentally motivated by direct concern for others. (chap. 7, sec. 3)

psychological egoism (PE). A descriptive thesis about individual human motivation according to which necessarily an individual's actions are fundamentally motivated by self-interest. (chap. 7, sec. 3)

publicity standard. The principles of a moral theory should be such that they do not rule out as impermissible making public (by, for example, teaching) the principles and associated moral theory. Moral theories whose principles rule out such teaching fail to satisfy this standard. (chap. 7, sec. 6)

rational egoism (RE). A normative view about the rationality of action and choice according to which one's action is rational (not irrational) if and only if (and because) it would produce at least as much agent utility as would any alternative action or choice. (chap. 7, sec. 2) *See also* agent utility.

reasons atomism (RA). The thesis that if a feature counts as a (basic) moral reason (and thus represents a morally relevant right- or wrong-making consideration) with a certain positive or negative polarity in one case, then it *must* be relevant and have the same polarity in all contexts in which it is present. That is, the relevance and polarity of a (basic) moral reason in a context is unaffected by other features that may be present in that context. The denial of reasons holism. (chap. 10, sec. 4)

reasons holism (RH). The thesis that if a feature that counts as a moral reason with a particular positive or negative polarity in one context, may not count as a reason at all in another context, or it may have an opposite polarity in another context. The denial of reasons atomism. (chap. 10, sec. 4)

right action. Broadly, any action that is not wrong. More narrowly, an action that is morally required and hence obligatory. (chap. 1, sec. 4)

right-making feature. A feature of an action that counts in favor of the action's rightness. Similarly for the notion of a good-making feature. (chap. 8, sec. 5)

rule consequentialism (RU). A form of consequentialism that makes the deontic status of an individual, concrete action depend on the utilities associated with the rules that apply to some situation. An action, on this view, is right if and only if (and because) it is allowed by a rule with as high a utility as any other alternative rule applying to the situation. (chap. 6, sec. 6) *See also* rule ethical egoism.

rule ethical egoism (REE). A form of ethical egoism according to which the deontic status of an action performed by an individual in some situation depends on (and is explained by) the agent utilities associated with rules that apply to the situation in question. (chap. 7, sec. 6) *See also* rule consequentialism.

satisficing consequentialism (SC). A version of consequentialism according to which right actions are those whose outcomes meet or exceed some threshold of value. (chap. 6, sec. 5) *See also* maximizing act consequentialism.

single true morality (STM). There is a single true morality for all human beings featuring moral norms that are universally valid and that specify for most if not all cases whether an action is right or wrong. (chap. 3, sec. 1)

situationism. A paradigm in social psychology that emphasizes the features of situations in explaining human behavior. (chap. 10, sec. 6)

subjective rightness. A concept of rightness that makes the rightness of action depend on the agent's beliefs about the deontic status of actions or on beliefs about morally relevant features of the act or on her evidence regarding such factors. (chap. 5, sec. 6) *See also* objective rightness.

subjectivist theories of intrinsic value. What has intrinsic value is either restricted to psychological states or depends on being the object of a person's desires or attitudes generally. (chap. 6, sec. 7) *See also* objectivist theories of intrinsic value.

theory of intrinsic value. The branch of moral theory concerned with the nature of goodness and badness. (chap. 1, sec. 4)

theory of moral worth. That branch of moral theory concerned with the evaluation of persons and their character. (chap. 1, sec. 5).

theory of right conduct. The branch of moral theory concerned with the nature of right and wrong action. (chap. 1, sec. 5)

unity thesis (U). A thesis that claims that there is a small fixed set of nonmoral features of actions (persons, institutions, and so forth) that are fundamental in explaining the deontic status of any action. Such features serve to unify moral phenomena. (chap. 10, sec. 1)

universalist moral theory. Theories according to which all individuals who will be affected by some decision or action count in matters of morality. (chap. 5, sec. 2)

universality thesis (UT). A thesis that states that there are moral norms whose correctness or validity is independent of the moral norms a culture does or might accept and thus express universally valid moral standards that apply to all cultures. (chap. 3, sec. 1)

universal law (UL). A formulation of the Categorical Imperative that states: act only in accordance with that maxim through which you can at the same time will that it become a universal law. (chap. 7, sec. 7)

universal relevance thesis (UR). A thesis according to which if a feature is a (basic) moral reason in one case, then it must be a moral reason in any context in which it is present. (chap. 11, sec. 2)

utilitarianism. A species of consequentialist moral theory according to which the deontic status of actions depends entirely on considerations of utility. (chap. 5, sec. 2) *See also* utility, generic principle of utility, act utilitarianism. **[AU7]**

utility. A technical term within the utilitarianism tradition that refers to net intrinsic value associated with actions, rules, or other items of moral evaluation, where value has to do with welfare. (chap. 5, sec. 2) *See also* agent utility.

value-based moral theory. A theory that takes considerations of value to be explanatorily prior to considerations of right conduct. Considerations of value are therefore used in such theories to explain the nature of right conduct. (chap. 1, sec. 5)

value concepts (categories). Categories, including good, bad, and evil, that are used in ethics primarily in evaluating the moral status of persons (including their character traits and associated motives) as well as things, experiences, and states of affairs. (chap. 1, sec. 4)

value pluralist consequentialism. A version of consequentialism that embraces a pluralist theory of value as a basis for explaining the deontic status of actions. (chap. 6, sec. 8)

vice. A trait of character or mind that typically involves dispositions to act, feel, and think in certain ways and is central in the negative evaluation of persons. The traits of dishonesty and disloyalty are examples. (chap. 10, sec. 1)

virtue. A trait of character or mind that typically involves dispositions to act, feel, and think in certain ways and is central in the positive evaluation of persons. The traits of honesty and loyalty are examples. (chap. 10, sec. 1)

virtue-based theory. Moral theories that take virtue to be more basic than right action and attempt to explain the right action (and the deontic evaluation of actions generally) in terms of virtue. (chap. 1, sec. 5).

virtue ethics. This term has come to be used for theories of right conduct that attempt to explain the deontic status of actions in terms of virtue. (chap. 10, sec. 3)

virtue theory. *See* ethics of character.

welfare. The well-being of individuals. (chap. 5, sec. 2)

welfarism. The view that the only kind of value that is of fundamental relevance for ethical evaluation is the welfare of individuals. (chap. 5, sec. 2)

wrong action. In ethics, an action that one ought not to do, an action that one is morally prohibited from doing, an action that one has a duty not to do. (chap. 1, sec. 4)

wrong-making feature. A feature of an action that counts toward an action's wrongness. Similarly for the notion of a bad-making feature. (chap. 9, sec. 5)

References

All articles from *The Stanford Encyclopedia of Philosophy* (*SEP*), ed. Edward N. Zalta, can be accessed by going to http://plato.stanford.edu and entering the entry's title in the search function.

Adams, Robert M. 1973. "A Modified Divine Command Theory of Ethical Wrongness." In *Religion and Morality: A Collection of Essays*, ed. Gene Outka and John P. Reeder. New York: Doubleday. Reprinted in *Divine Commands and Morality*, ed. Paul Helm. Oxford: Oxford University Press, 1981.

———. 1976. "Motive Utilitarianism." *Journal of Philosophy* 73: 467–81.

———. 1979. "Divine Command Ethics Modified Again." *Journal of Religious Ethics* 7: 71–79. Reprinted in *Divine Commands and Morality*, ed. Paul Helm. Oxford: Oxford University Press, 1981.

———. 1999. *Finite and Infinite Goods: A Framework for Ethics*. Oxford: Oxford University Press.

———. 2006. *A Theory of Virtue: Excellence in Being for the Good*. Oxford: Oxford University Press.

Alston, William P. 1990. "Some Suggestions for Divine Command Theorists." In *Christian Theism and the Problems of Philosophy*, ed. Michael D. Beaty. Notre Dame, IN: University of Notre Dame Press.

Annas, Julia. 1993. *The Morality of Happiness*. Oxford: Oxford University Press.

———. 2008. "Virtue Ethics and the Charge of Egoism." In *Morality and Self-Interest*, ed. Paul Bloomfield. Oxford: Oxford University Press.

Aquinas, Saint Thomas. 1988. *On Politics and Ethics*. Trans. Paul E. Sigmund. New York: Norton.

Aristotle. 1985. *Nicomachean Ethics*. Trans. Terence Irwin. Indianapolis, IN: Hackett.

Audi, Robert. 1997. *Moral Knowledge and Ethical Character*. Oxford: Oxford University Press.

———. 2004. *The Good in the Right: A Theory of Intuition and Intrinsic Value*. Princeton, NJ: Princeton University Press.

Baron, Marcia W. 1995. *Kantian Ethics Almost without Apology*. Ithaca, NY: Cornell University Press.

——, Philip Pettit, and Michael Slote. 1997. *Three Methods of Ethics*. Oxford: Blackwell.

Batson, C. Daniel. 1990. "How Social an Animal? The Human Capacity for Caring." *American Psychologist* 45: 336–46.

——. 1991. *The Altruism Question*. Hillsdale, NJ: Lawrence Erlbaum.

Benedict, Ruth. 1934. *Patterns of Culture*. New York: Houghton Mifflin.

Bentham, Jeremy. [1789] 1948. *An Introduction to the Principles of Morals and Legislation*. New York: Hafner.

Blustein, Jeffrey. 1991. *Care and Commitment*. Oxford: Oxford University Press.

Bradley, Ben. 2006. "Against Satisficing Consequentialism." *Utilitas* 18: 97–108.

Brandt, Richard B. 1959. *Ethical Theory*. Englewood Cliffs, NJ: Prentice-Hall.

——. 1963. "Toward a Credible Form of Utilitarianism." In *Morality and the Language of Conduct*, ed. H.-N. Castañeda and G. Nahknikian. Detroit, MI: Wayne State University Press.

——. 1979. *A Theory of the Good and the Right*. Oxford: Oxford University Press.

——. 1988. "Fairness to Indirect Optimific Theories in Ethics." *Ethics* 98: 341–60.

Brentano, Franz. [1889] 1969. *The Origin of Our Knowledge of Right and Wrong*. London: Routledge & Kegan Paul.

Brink, David O. 1989. *Moral Realism and the Foundations of Ethics*. Cambridge: Cambridge University Press.

——. 2006. "Some Forms and Limits of Consequentialism." In *The Oxford Handbook of Ethical Theory*, ed. David Copp. Oxford: Oxford University Press.

Brown, H. I. 1988. *Rationality*. London: Routledge.

Buchanan, Allen. 1996. "Intending Death: The Structure of the Problem and Proposed Solutions." In *Intending Death*, ed. Tom L. Beauchamp. Upper Saddle River, NJ: Prentice-Hall.

Burgess, E. W. 1928. "Factors Determining Success or Failure on Parole." In *The Workings of the Indeterminate Sentence Law and the Parole System in Illinois*, ed. A. A. Bruce. Springfield: Illinois Committee on Indeterminate-Sentence Law and Parole.

Cavanaugh, T. A. 2006. *Double Effect Reasoning*. Oxford: Oxford University Press.

Conly, Sarah. 1988. "Flourishing and the Failure of the Ethics of Virtue." *Midwest Studies in Philosophy* 13: 83–96.

Copp, David, and David Sobel. 2004. "Morality and Virtue: An Assessment of Some Recent Work in Virtue Ethics." *Ethics* 114: 514–54.

Crisp, Roger. 1997. *Mill on Utilitarianism*. London: Routledge.

——. 2000. "Particularizing Particularism." In *Moral Particularism*, ed. B. Hooker and M. Little. Oxford: Oxford University Press.

Cullity, Garrett, and Berys Gaut, eds. 1997. *Ethics and Practical Reason*. Oxford: Oxford University Press.

Dancy, Jonathan. 1993. *Moral Reasons*. Oxford: Blackwell.

——. 2004. *Ethics without Principles*. Oxford: Oxford University Press.

——. 2009. "Moral Particularism." *SEP.*

Darwall, Stephen. 1998. "Empathy, Sympathy, Care." *Philosophical Studies* 89: 261–82.

——. 2006. *The Second-Person Standpoint*. Cambridge, MA: Harvard University Press.

Das, Ramon. 2003. "Virtue Ethics and Right Action." *Australasian Journal of Philosophy* 81: 324–39.

Davis, Nancy. 1984. "The Doctrine of Double Effect: Problems of Interpretation." *Pacific Philosophical Quarterly* 65: 107–23.

de Lazari-Radek, Katarzyna, and Peter Singer. 2010. "Secrecy in Consequentialism: A Defense of Esoteric Morality." *Ratio* 23: 34–58.

Donner, Wendy. 1998. "Mill's Utilitarianism." In *The Cambridge Companion to Mill*, ed. John Skorupski. Cambridge: Cambridge University Press.

Doris, John M. 1998. "Persons, Situations, and Virtue Ethics." *Nous* 32: 504–30.

———. 2002. *Lack of Character: Personality and Moral Behavior*. Cambridge: Cambridge University Press.

———, and Alexandra Plakias. 2008. "How to Argue about Disagreement: Evaluator Diversity and Moral Realism." In *Moral Psychology*, vol. 2, ed. W. Sinnott-Armstrong. Cambridge, MA: MIT Press.

Dorsey, Dale. Forthcoming. "Consequentialism, Cognitive Limitations, and Moral Theory." In *Oxford Studies in Normative Ethics,* vol. 3, ed. M. Timmons. Oxford: Oxford University Press.

Dreier, James. 1993. "Structures of Normative Theories." *Monist* 76: 22–40.

Driver, Julia. 2012. *Consequentialism*. London: Routledge.

———. 2013. "What the Objective Standard Is Good For." In *Oxford Studies in Normative Ethics*, vol. 2, ed. M. Timmons. Oxford: Oxford University Press.

Eggleston, Ben. 2007. "Conflicts of Rules in Hooker's Rule-Consequentialism." *Canadian Journal of Philosophy* 37: 329–50.

Engstrom, Stephen. 2002. "The Inner Freedom of Virtue." In *Kant's Metaphysics of Morals: Interpretative Essays*, ed. M. Timmons. Oxford: Oxford University Press.

Fantino, E., B. A. Jaworski, D. A. Case, and S. Stolarz-Fantino. 2003. "Rules and Problem Solving: Another Look." *American Journal of Psychology* 116: 613–32.

Feinberg, J. [1968] 2008. "Psychological Egoism." In *Reason and Responsibility*, 14th ed., ed. J. Feinberg and R. Shafer-Landau. Belmont, CA: Thomson Wadsworth.

Feldman, Fred. 1978. *Introductory Ethics*. Englewood Cliffs, NJ: Prentice-Hall.

Finnis, John. 1980. *Natural Law and Natural Rights*. Oxford: Oxford University Press.

FitzPatrick, William J. 2013. "Intention, Permissibility, and Double Effect." In *Oxford Studies in Normative Ethics*, vol. 2, ed. M. Timmons. Oxford: Oxford University Press.

Flescher, Andrew M., and Daniel L. Worthen. 2007. *The Altruistic Species*. West Conshohocken, PA: Templeton Foundation Press.

Foot, Philippa. 1972. "Morality as a System of Hypothetical Imperatives." *Philosophical Review* 81: 305–16. Reprinted in Philippa Foot, *Virtues and Vices*. Berkeley and Los Angeles: University of California Press, 1978.

Frankena, William. 1973. *Ethics*. 2nd ed. Englewood Cliffs, NJ: Prentice-Hall.

Frankfurt, Harry G. 1999. "On Caring." In *Necessity, Volition, and Love*. Cambridge: Cambridge University Press.

Friedman, Marilyn. 1987. "Beyond Caring: The De-Moralization of Gender." In *Justice and Care*, ed. Virginia Held. Boulder, CO: Westview Press.

Gill, Michael, and Shaun Nichols. 2008. "Sentimentalist Pluralism: Moral Psychological and Philosophical Ethics." *Philosophical Issues* 18: 143–63.

Gilligan, Carol. 1982. *In a Different Voice*. Cambridge, MA: Harvard University Press.

———. 1987. "Moral Orientation and Moral Development." In *Women and Moral Theory*, ed. Eva Feder Kittay and Diana T. Meyers. Totowa, NJ: Rowman & Littlefield.

Greene, Joshua. 2008. "The Secret Joke of Kant's Soul." In *Moral Psychology*, vol. 3, ed. W. Sinnott-Armstrong. Cambridge, MA: MIT Press.

Griffin, James. 1986. *Well-Being*. Oxford: Oxford University Press.

Grove, William M., and Paul E. Meehl. 1996. "Comparative Efficiency of Informal (Subjective, Impressionistic) and Formal (Mechanical, Algorithmic) Prediction Procedures: The Clinical-Statistical Controversy." *Psychology, Public Policy, and Law* 2: 293–323.

Haidt, Jonathan. 2001. "The Emotional Dog and Its Rational Tail: A Social Intuitionist Approach to Moral Judgment." *Psychological Review* 108: 814–34.

Hare, R. M. 1981. *Moral Thinking*. Oxford: Oxford University Press.

Harman, Gilbert. 1983. "Human Flourishing, Ethics, and Liberty." *Philosophy & Public Affairs* 12: 307–22.

———. 1999a. "Moral Philosophy and Linguistics." In *Proceedings of the Twentieth World Congress*, vol. 1, *Ethics*, ed. K. Brinkmann. Bowling Green, OH: Philosophy Documentation Center.

———. 1999b. "Moral Philosophy Meets Moral Psychology." *Proceedings of the Aristotelian Society* 99: 315–31.

———. 2000. "The Nonexistence of Character Traits." *Proceedings of the Aristotelian Society* 100: 223–26.

Hauser, Marc D. 2006. *Moral Minds*. New York: HarperCollins.

———, Liane Young, and Fiery Cushman. 2008. "Reviving Rawls' Linguistic Analogy." In *Moral Psychology*, vol. 2, ed. W. Sinnott-Armstrong. Cambridge, MA: MIT Press.

Hernandez, Jill Graper. 2011. *The New Intuitionism*. New York and London: Continuum Press.

Himmelfarb, Gertrude. 1995. *The De-Moralization of Society*. New York: Knopf.

Hooker, Brad. 1990. "Rule-Consequentialism." *Mind* 99: 67–77.

———. 2000a. *Ideal Code, Real World*. Oxford: Oxford University Press.

———. 2000b. "Moral Particularism—Wrong and Bad." In *Moral Particularism*, ed. Brad Hooker and Margaret Little. Oxford: Oxford University Press.

———. 2008a. "Rule Consequentialism." *SEP*.

———. 2008b. "Moral Particularism and the Real World." In *Challenging Moral Particularism*, ed. M. Lance, M. Potrc, and V. Strahovnik. New York: Routledge.

Horgan, Terry, and Mark Timmons. 2007. "Morphological Rationalism and the Psychology of Moral Judgment." *Ethical Theory and Moral Practice* 10: 279–95.

Huemer, Michael. 2005. *Ethical Intuitionism*. New York: Palgrave Macmillan.

Hume, David. [1739] 1978. *A Treatise of Human Nature*, 2nd ed., ed. P. H. Nidditch. Oxford: Oxford University Press.

Hunt, Lester. 1999. "Flourishing Egoism." *Social Philosophy & Policy* 16: 72–95.

Hurka, Thomas. 1993. *Perfectionism*. Oxford: Oxford University Press.

Hurley, Paul. Forthcoming. "Consequentializing and Deontologizing: Clogging the Consequentialist Vacuum." In *Oxford Studies in Normative Ethics*, vol. 3, ed. M. Timmons. Oxford: Oxford University Press.

Hursthouse, Rosalind. 1999. *On Virtue Ethics*. Oxford: Oxford University Press.

Jackson, Frank, Philip Pettit, and Michael Smith. 2000. "Ethical Particularism and Patterns." In *Moral Particularism*, ed. Brad Hooker and Margaret Little. Oxford: Oxford University Press.

Johnson, Robert N. 1997. "Kant's Conception of Virtue." *Jahrbuch für Recht und Ethik (Annual Review of Law and Ethics)* 5: 365–87.

———. 2003. "Virtue and Right." *Ethics* 113: 810–34.

Kagan, Shelly. 1989. *The Limits of Morality*. Oxford: Oxford University Press.

Kant, Immanuel. [1797] 1997. *Practical Philosophy*. Trans. and ed. Mary Gregor. Cambridge: Cambridge University Press.

Kavka, Gregory. 1986. *Hobbesian Moral and Political Philosophy*. Princeton, NJ: Princeton University Press.

Kerstein, Samuel J. 2007. "Treating Oneself Merely as a Means." In *Kant's Ethics of Virtue*, ed. M. Betzler. Berlin: de Gruyter.

———. 2009. "Treating Others Merely as Means." *Utilitas* 21: 163–80.

———. 2011. "Treating Consenting Adults Merely as Means." In *Oxford Studies in Normative Ethics*, vol. 1, ed. M. Timmons. Oxford: Oxford University Press.

Kitcher, Philip. 1999. "Essence and Perfection." *Ethics* 110: 59–83.

Kluckhohn, Clyde. 1955. "Ethical Relativity: Sic et Non." *Journal of Philosophy* 52: 663–77.

Lance, Mark, and Margaret Little. 2006. "Particularism and Antitheory." In *The Oxford Handbook of Ethical Theory*, ed. D. Copp. Oxford: Oxford University Press.

Larmore, Charles E. 1987. *Patterns of Moral Complexity*. Cambridge: Cambridge University Press.

Larrick, R. P., J. N. Morgan, and R. E. Nisbett. 1990. "Teaching the Use of Cost-Benefit Reasoning in Everyday Life." *Psychological Science* 1: 362–70.

———, R. E. Nisbett, and J. N. Morgan. 1993. "Who Uses the Cost-Benefit Rules of Choice?" *Organizational Behavior and Human Decision Processes* 56: 331–47.

Lisska, Anthony J. 1996. *Aquinas's Theory of Natural Law*. New York: Oxford University Press.

Little, Margaret Olivia. 2001. "On Knowing the 'Why': Particularism and Moral Theory." *Hastings Center Report* 31: 32–40.

MacIntyre, Alasdair. 1981. *After Virtue*. Notre Dame, IN: University of Notre Dame Press.

Mackie, J. L. 1977. *Ethics: Inventing Right and Wrong*. Harmondsworth, England: Penguin Books.

Marquis, Donald B. 1991. "Four Versions of Double Effect." *Journal of Medicine and Philosophy* 16: 515–44.

Mason, Elinor. 2011. "Value Pluralism." *SEP*.

———. Forthcoming. "Objective and Subjective Utilitarianism." In *Cambridge Companion to Utilitarianism*, ed. B. Eggleston and D. E. Miller. Cambridge: Cambridge University Press.

McKeever, Sean, and Michael Ridge. 2006. *Principled Ethics: Generalism as a Regulative Ideal*. Oxford: Oxford University Press.

McNaughton, David. 1988. *Moral Vision*. Oxford: Blackwell.

———, and Piers Rawling. 2000. "Unprincipled Ethics." In *Moral Particularism*, ed. Brad Hooker and Margaret Little. Oxford: Oxford University Press.

Mill, John Stuart. [1863] 1979. *Utilitarianism*. Indianapolis, IN: Hackett.

Monroe, Kristin R. 1996. *The Heart of Altruism*. Princeton, NJ: Princeton University Press.

Moody-Adams, Michele M. 1997. *Fieldwork in Familiar Places Morality, Culture, and Philosophy*. Cambridge, MA: Harvard University Press.

Moore, G. E. 1903. *Principia Ethica*. Cambridge: Cambridge University Press.

Mortimer, Robert C. 1950. *Christian Ethics*. New York: Hutchinson's University Library.

Mulgan, Tim. 2001. *The Demands of Consequentialism*. Oxford: Oxford University Press.

Murphy, Mark. 2008. "Theological Voluntarism." *SEP*.

Nagel, Thomas. 1986. *The View from Nowhere*. Oxford: Oxford University Press.

Nichols, Shaun. 2005. "Innateness and Moral Psychology." In *The Innate Mind: Structure and Content*, ed. P. Carruthers, S. Laurence, and S. Stich. New York: Oxford University Press.

Nisbett, Richard E., and Dov Cohen. 1996. *Culture of Honor: The Psychology of Violence in the South*. Boulder, CO: Westview Press.

Nozick, Robert. 1974. *Anarchy, State, and Utopia*. New York: Basic Books.

Nucci, Larry. 1986. "Children's Conceptions of Morality, Social Convention, and Religious Prescription." In *Moral Dilemmas: Philosophical and Psychological Reconsiderations of the Development of Moral Reasoning*, ed. C. Harding. Chicago: Precedent Press.

O'Connor, John. 1967. *Aquinas and Natural Law*. London: Macmillan.

Parfit, Derek. 1997. "Equality and Priority." *Ratio* 10: 202–21.

———. 2011. *On What Matters*. Oxford: Oxford University Press.

Pincoffs, Edmund. 1986. *Quandaries and Virtues: Against Reductivism in Ethics*. Lawrence: University of Kansas Press.

Plato. 1976. *Euthyphro, Apology, Crito*. Trans. F. J. Church. Indianapolis, IN: Bobbs-Merrill.

Portmore, Douglas W. 2001. "Can an Act-Consequentialist Theory Be Agent-Relative?" *American Philosophical Quarterly* 38: 363–77.

———. 2007. "Consequentializing Moral Theories." *Pacific Philosophical Quarterly* 88: 39–73.

———. 2009. "Consequentializing." *Philosophy Compass* 4: 329–47. Online Library, doi: 10.IIII/j.1747-9991.2009.00198.x.

Prinz, Jesse J. 2008a. "Revisiting the Linguistic Analogy: A Commentary on Hauser, Young, and Cushman." In *Moral Psychology*, vol. 2, ed. W. Sinnott-Armstrong. Cambridge, MA: MIT Press.

———. 2008b. "Is Morality Innate?" In *Moral Psychology*, vol. 1, ed. W. Sinnott-Armstrong. Cambridge, MA: MIT Press.

———. 2009. "Against Moral Nativism." In *Stich and His Critics*, ed. D. Murphy and M. Bishop. Malden, MA, and Oxford: Blackwell.

Putnam, Hilary. 1981. *Reason, Truth, and History*. Cambridge: Cambridge University Press.

Quinn, Philip. 2006. "Theological Voluntarism." *Oxford Handbook of Ethical Theory*, ed. David Copp. Oxford: Oxford University Press.

Quinn, Warren. 1989. "Actions, Intentions, and Consequences: The Doctrine of Double Effect." *Philosophy & Public Affairs* 18: 334–51.

Rand, Ayn. 1964. *The Virtue of Selfishness*. New York: Signet.

Rawls, John. 1971. *A Theory of Justice*. Cambridge, MA: Harvard University Press.

———. 1975. "The Independence of Moral Theory." *Proceedings and Addresses of the American Philosophical Association* 48: 5–22. Reprinted in *John Rawls: Collected Papers*, ed. S. Freeman. Cambridge, MA: Harvard University Press, 1999.

Richardson, Henry S. 1990. "Specifying Norms as a Way to Resolve Concrete Ethical Problems." *Philosophy & Public Affairs* 19: 27–310.

Ridge, Michael. 2010. "Reasons for Action: Agent-Neutral vs. Agent-Relative." *SEP*.

Ross, W. D. 1930. *The Right and the Good*. Oxford: Oxford University Press.

———. 1939. *Foundations of Ethics*. Oxford: Oxford University Press.

Russell, Daniel C. 2009. *Practical Intelligence and the Virtues*. Oxford: Oxford University Press.

Sartre, Jean-Paul. 1965. *Essays in Existentialism*. New York: Philosophical Library.

Sayre-McCord, Geoff. 2001. "Mill's 'Proof' of the Principle of Utility: A More than Half-Hearted Defense." *Social Philosophy & Policy* 18: 330–60.

Scanlon, T. M. 2008. *Moral Dimensions*. Cambridge, MA: Harvard University Press.

Scheffler, Samuel. 1982. *The Rejection of Consequentialism*. Oxford: Oxford University Press.

Schroeder, Mark. 2008. "Value Theory." *SEP*.

Sen, Amartya. 1982. "Rights and Agency." *Philosophy & Public Affairs* 11: 3–39.

Shaver, Rob. 2002. "Egoism." *SEP*.

Shoemaker, David. 2012. "Egoisms." In *Conduct and Character: Readings in Moral Theory*, 6th ed., ed. M. Timmons. Belmont, CA: Thomson-Wadsworth.

Sidgwick, Henry. [1907] 1966. *The Methods of Ethics*. 7th ed. New York: Dover.

Singer, Peter. 1994. *Rethinking Life and Death*. New York: St. Martin's Press.

———. 2005. "Ethics and Intuitions." *Journal of Ethics* 9: 331–52.

Skelton, Anthony. 2010. "William David Ross." *SEP*.

Slote, Michael. 1985. *Common-Sense Morality and Consequentialism*. London: Routledge & Kegan Paul.

————. 2001. *Morals from Motives*. Oxford: Oxford University Press.

Smart, J. J. C., and Bernard Williams. 1973. *Utilitarianism: For and Against*. Cambridge: Cambridge University Press.

Smit, Houston, and Mark Timmons. 2013. "Kant's Grounding Project in *The Doctrine of Virtue*." In *Kant's Theory of Practical Justification: Interpretative Essays*, ed. M. Timmons and S. Baiasu. Oxford: Oxford University Press.

Smith, Holly. 2010. "Subjective Rightness." *Social Philosophy & Policy* 27: 64–110.

Snow, Nancy E. 2010. *Virtue as Social Intelligence: An Empirically Grounded Theory*. New York and Oxford: Routledge.

Sober, E., and D. S. Wilson. 1998. *Unto Others: The Evolution and Psychology of Unselfish Behavior*. Cambridge, MA: Harvard University Press.

Sripada, Chandra Sekhar. 2008. "Nativism and Moral Psychology." In *Moral Psychology*, vol. 1, ed. W. Sinnott-Armstrong. Cambridge, MA: MIT Press.

Stocker, Michael. 1976. "The Schizophrenia of Modern Moral Theories." *Journal of Philosophy* 73: 453–66.

Sumner, L. W. 1996. *Welfare, Happiness, and Ethics*. Oxford: Oxford University Press.

Sumner, William G. [1906] 1959. *Folkways*. New York: Dover.

Thomson, Judith Jarvis. 1999. "Physician-Assisted Suicide: Two Moral Arguments." *Ethics* 115: 497–518.

Timmons, Mark. 1997. "Decision Procedures, Moral Criteria, and the Problem of Relevant Descriptions in Kant's Ethics." *Jahrbuch für Recht und Ethik* (*Annual Review of Law and Ethics*) 5: 389–417.

————. 1999. *Morality without Foundations*. Oxford: Oxford University Press.

————. 2006. "The Categorical Imperative and Universalizability." In *Kant's Groundwork for the Metaphysics of Morals: New Interpretations*, ed. Christoph Horn and Dieter Schönecker. Berlin and New York: de Gruyter.

————. 2008. "Toward a Sentimentalist Deontology." In *Moral Psychology*, vol. 3, ed. W. Sinnott-Armstrong. Cambridge, MA: MIT Press.

Tronto, Joan C. 1989. "Women and Caring: What Can Feminists Learn about Morality from Caring?" In *Justice and Care*, ed. Virginia Held. Boulder, CO: Westview Press.

Väyrynen, Pekka. 2008. "Usable Moral Principles." In *Challenging Moral Particularism*, ed. M. Lance, M. Potrc, and V. Strahovnik. New York: Routledge.

Wedgwood, Ralph. 2011a. "Scanlon on Double Effect." *Philosophy and Phenomenological Research* 83: 464–72.

————. 2011b. "Defending Double Effect." *Ratio* 24: 384–401.

Williams, Bernard. 1995. "What Does Intuitionism Imply?" In *Making Sense of Humanity*. Cambridge: Cambridge University Press.

Wong, David. 2008. *Natural Moralities: A Defense of Pluralistic Relativism*. Oxford: Oxford University Press.

Zamzow, Jennifer. "Rules and Principles in Moral Decision-Making: A Practical Objection to Moral Particularism." Unpublished manuscript.

Zangwill, Nick. 2011a. "Codelia's Bond and Indirect Consequentialism." In *Oxford Studies in Normative Ethics*, vol. 1, ed. M. Timmons. Oxford: Oxford University Press.

————. 2011b. "A Way Out of the Euthyphro Dilemma." *Religious Studies* 48: 1–7.

Zimmerman, Michael. 2008. *Living with Uncertainty*. Cambridge: Cambridge University Press.

————. 2010. "Intrinsic vs. Extrinsic Value." *SEP*.

Index

About the Author

Mark Timmons is professor of philosophy at the University of Arizona. He has published extensively on topics in moral theory, metaethics, and Kant's ethics. He is author of *Morality without Foundations: A Defense of Ethical Contextualism* (1999) and editor of *Oxford Studies in Normative Ethics*. He and his colleague Terry Horgan are currently working on a book titled *Illuminating Reasons: An Essay in Moral Phenomenology*.